PERSONS OF INTEREST
AN INTIMATE ACCOUNT OF CECILY AND JOHN BURTON

PERSONS OF INTEREST

AN INTIMATE ACCOUNT OF CECILY AND JOHN BURTON

**PAMELA BURTON
WITH MEREDITH EDWARDS**

ANU PRESS

ANU PRESS

Published by ANU Press
The Australian National University
Canberra ACT 2600, Australia
Email: anupress@anu.edu.au

Available to download for free at press.anu.edu.au

ISBN (print): 9781760465087
ISBN (online): 9781760465094

WorldCat (print): 1306244562
WorldCat (online): 1306244581

DOI: 10.22459/PI.2022

This title is published under a Creative Commons Attribution-NonCommercial-NoDerivatives 4.0 International (CC BY-NC-ND 4.0).

The full licence terms are available at
creativecommons.org/licenses/by-nc-nd/4.0/legalcode

The ANU.Lives Series in Biography is an initiative of the National Centre of Biography at The Australian National University, ncb.anu.edu.au.

Cover design and layout by ANU Press. Cover photographs: Cecily Burton, 1951, Family collection; John Burton, 1951, Family collection.

This book is published under the aegis of the ANU.Lives Editorial Board of ANU Press.

This edition © 2022 ANU Press

Contents

Acknowledgements		vii
Prologue		xi
1.	Courting controversy	1
2.	Cecily's travels with Judith Wright	9
3.	A shared heritage	15
4.	John's father: A radical, mission-driven Methodist	23
5.	Embracing opportunities	33
6.	Paradise lost	41
7.	Honeymoon in dangerous times	49
8.	The sinking of the *Arandora Star*	59
9.	A remarkable rise in the public service	65
10.	The Burton plot: Reconstruction and Nugget Coombs	75
11.	Domesticity and babies	83
12.	Australia on the world stage	89
13.	Farming with an 'accommodating wife'	101
14.	A controversial head of department	113
15.	Reshaping Australia's foreign policy	121
16.	The Gnomes of Melbourne	131
17.	Political suicide	143
18.	John's short stint as high commissioner in Ceylon	153
19.	The beginning of the end of a marriage	165
20.	Cecily's life-changing encounter	171
21.	China: Neither 'dead nor red'	179
22.	Paying the price for a mission of peace	189
23.	An interlude: Farming the Burton way	195
24.	Holding it together	203
25.	The Petrov inquiry	213

26.	Indonesia with ASIO in tow	225
27.	A shift to the city: Enterprises and infidelity	235
28.	The Snowy Mountains bus, bubble cars and other ventures	249
29.	A family in crisis	257
30.	A love triangle	265
31.	Staging musicals: 'The Girl' and 'The Bloke'	275
32.	Turmoil	287
33.	The breakup	297
34.	Tugs of war of love and divorce	307
35.	Looking to Jung	319
36.	Coming into her own: Counselling Cecily style	325
37.	Revisiting relationship difficulties	333
38.	John's 'real career'	345
39.	Coming full circle: Cecily, Robert, John and all	355
40.	A family shattered: Loss of Clare	367
41.	Blue autumn: Cecily passes	375
	Select bibliography	385

Acknowledgements

Over the many years we have been thinking about how to tell what is essentially a family story, we have received input from family members and special friends. Our brother Mark, my daughters Amanda and Cassandra, step-family members, particularly Betty Nathan and Andrea Eisler, our nieces, nephews and cousins have between them contributed memories, anecdotes, family photos, letters, news clippings, family trees and snippets of information. We thank them for their help in bringing our story to life. Susie and Ian Hendry dug around in their basement boxes to make some extraordinary finds, Ruth Toop provided well-researched family histories and Ian Newman transcribed extracts from our grandfather's handwritten journals.

There are a lot of other people to thank. Some of those who knew about our work and volunteered relevant information, which they discovered in the course of research for their own subjects, are acknowledged in the narrative, but many others who have assisted us enormously – there are too many to name – have not. Penny Lockwood, Diane Bell, Marian Sawer, Kim Rubenstein, Alison Broinowski and Brett Yeats deserve special mention for their ongoing support and encouragement. Two special confidantes, Doug Cocks and Ann Moyal, are, sadly, no longer with us. George Martin, Leanne Akers, Kanti Jinna, Stephen Holt, John Myrtle, Greg Pemberton and Adam Hughes Henry accessed photos and historic information on our family about which we would otherwise have been unaware. We thank also, those who generously consented to be interviewed on personal matters to assist our understanding of Cecily; and Ernst Willheim, Adam Hughes Henry, Jack Waterford, Val Wake, Clive Edwards and Greg Pemberton for acknowledging and publicly repudiating peddled misinformation about our father.

Special thanks are due to the dedicated staff of several organisations who assisted us in our research and invited us to share the story with others: The National Library of Australia's Petherick Reading Room and its readers, Manning Clark House, Independent Scholars Association of Australia, the National Archives of Australia, the Copyright Agency, Flinders University, George Mason University's Institute for Conflict Analysis and Resolution (now the Jimmy and Rosalynn Carter School for Peace and Conflict Resolution) and its John Burton Library, The Australian National University's National Centre for Biography, and the University of Kent's Conflict Analysis Research Centre.

There are also the magnificent people who volunteered their time to read rough drafts of the whole or parts of the manuscript and who gave valuable editorial help, commented on structure, target audience and contributed historical knowledge: Robin Gibson, David Stephens, David Dunn, Melanie Nolan, Stuart Macintyre (sadly since deceased), Gaby Naher, Matthew Richardson and John Nethercote. David Stephens, together with Ward O'Neill, Geoff Pryor, Guy Hansen, Phillip Deery, Linsday Foyle and Bridget Griffen-Foley made special efforts to identify and textualise the political cartoons we found in our father's papers. We are grateful to the Firth family and Katie Molnar for permission to use their fathers' material, and to Ronald Fisher for providing a personal cassette tape of part of an interview he had with our father in the United States.

Turning a manuscript into published form requires special professional skills. Particular gratitude is due to Melanie Nolan at The Australian National University (ANU) for her enthusiasm and belief in the worth of the story, and for her work and that of her ANU.Lives committee members as well as the peer reviewers of the work in guiding progress. We thank the National Centre of Biography for its generous funding of the copyediting process. Heartfelt thanks go to Geoff Hunt for his thorough and dedicated copyediting, the hours he spent checking references, fixing the dreaded footnotes and, above all, his patience. Instant Colour Press used its magic to turn old photos and torn newspaper cuttings into clear images for reproduction. Last, but not least, in the publishing process is the extraordinary work of ANU Press. Thank you Emily Tinker and your team for bringing the book into the world.

Writing can be a lonely experience. I had the joyous bonus of having my sister Meredith travel with me, not just as an interested big sister, but as a best friend who put her research and interviewing skills to work and who read and reread my writing, provided comments and critique. We enjoyed working together and spending more time together than we had done in our previous busy lives. Finally, large thanks to my partner in life, Ken, my sounding board, a patient support person, whose time to do his own writing has been compromised by the intensity of mine.

Prologue

This is a story about our parents that we did not intend to write. One morning in October 2006, our father John Burton woke to read a newspaper report of a speech by former prime minister John Howard in which he referred to John as a 'philo-communist'.[1] Our father was then 91. What on earth motivated Howard to bring his name up? Our father's short, but controversial time as a young head of the Department of External Affairs was in the 1940s and 1950s. Howard's attack prompted our father to warn me and my sister Meredith to 'expect more trouble when I am gone'.

Trouble came. In 2010 John died and in 2011 Professor Desmond Ball decided to play havoc with our father's reputation by his mischief-making. The *Australian* published an article in which Ball said that John 'probably' had been a Russian agent. He attempted to back up his assertion by misconstruing some evidence John gave at the Royal Commission into Espionage (the Petrov inquiry) in 1954.[2] I had the transcript of evidence stored in my top cupboard and it was easy to check; Ball had got it wrong. I detailed his errors and rebutted other of his assertions in an article that the *Australian* published.[3] But in 2012, the paper published another article in which Ball made further assertions but failed to explain away his earlier errors.[4] I responded with an angry letter to the editor.[5] That did not stop

---

1   Andrew Fraser, 'Reagan, Thatcher, are PM's Heroes', *Canberra Times*, 4 October 2006, a report of Howard's speech in Sydney on the occasion of *Quadrant* magazine's 50th anniversary dinner.
2   Desmond Ball, 'The Moles at the Very Heart of Government', *Weekend Australian*, 16–17 April 2011.
3   Pamela Burton, 'Burton was a Patriotic Public Servant, Not a Traitor', *Weekend Australian*, 30 April – 1 May 2011.
4   Desmond Ball, 'Soviet Spies had Protection in Very High Places', *Weekend Australian,* 14–15 January 2012; and see revised version: Desmond Ball, 'From External Affairs to Academia: Coral's Encounter with the KGB's Spy Ring', in *Power and International Relations: Essays in Honour of Coral Bell*, ed. Desmond Ball and Sheryn Lee (Canberra: ANU Press, 2014), 12–16, doi.org/10.22459/PIR.11.2014.02.
5   'Bell Recollections on Espionage Ring Hollow', *Australian*, 17 January 2012.

commentators without Ball's academic credentials from running with the sensational spy story and elaborating on it. John soon was the subject of headlines: 'Australia's Kim Philby?' and 'Burton: Australia's Alger Hiss'.[6]

In 2013 I had a chance to vent my anger when, at a party with Meredith, journalist Jack Waterford gave me a warm wry grin and said: 'Ball's here – in the kitchen!' Jack knew what I would want to do. We three had known Ball well for some decades. I hunted him out and unashamedly baled him up in my host's kitchen and let loose. Our host slid out quietly but I was not quiet. 'I really want to know, after my article pointing out that you misinterpreted the transcript of my father's evidence at the Petrov Commission, why you didn't acknowledge you got it wrong, or apologise for it?' 'Because I believe in what I wrote,' was his answer. My interrogation continued for quite a time because I would not let him escape. He said: 'I have never said that your father was a spy, or even a member of the Communist Party', and that while Burton 'might have been regarded as a left-wing rat bag by the conservatives, they didn't suggest he was a Communist or a spy'. He added, 'I shared your father's views. I share his values'. He later told Waterford that he had not believed that John had spied for the Soviets – he was just 'having a stir'. The following day, upset and angry, I transcribed my questions and Ball's replies to the best of my recollection. I drew on it for an article I wrote in 2014 for *Honest History*.[7]

In a backhanded compliment to my provocateur, Ball, I must thank him. It was then that I resolved to write a book about my father to put the record straight about who he was and how he thought. It was a chance to demonstrate that John's public service career was only part of his story. He was a multifaceted, mission-driven man of extraordinary diversity: an innovative farmer, entrepreneur, patron of the arts, policy influencer, author and academic. He presented as an enigma to many, but, throughout his life, he remained intent on a quest to change lives in pursuit of world peace. This manifested in his 'real career' as he put it, as an internationally acclaimed leader in the field of conflict analysis and dispute resolution.

---

6   Angus Chapple, 'Australia's Cold War: Australia's Kim Philby? The Case of Dr John Burton', *News Weekly* (Melbourne), 30 April 2011; Rob Foot, 'Was John Burton Australia's Alger Hiss?' *Quadrant*, June 2016. This was the third in a trilogy of articles Foot wrote in *Quadrant* on John, the previous articles being, 'The Curious Case of Dr John Burton', November 2013, 44–53, and 'Dr Burton at the Royal Commission on Espionage', October 2015, 53–60.

7   Pamela Burton, 'John Burton: Undermined by Dishonest History', *Honest History*, 1 September 2014, being the illustrated text of talk delivered at Manning Clark House, Canberra, 18 August 2014 in the Honest History lecture series,honesthistory.net.au/wp/wp-content/uploads/385A-John-Burton-Undermined-by-dishonest-history.pdf.

I put my smug proposal to my sister, Meredith. She said, 'I'll help, but it can't be just about dad. Look at our mum. Her life is remarkable in quite different ways.' 'True, but no one knows her, and it would be two very different stories,' I replied. My persuasive big sister prevailed upon me. So, the imperatives for writing this story became twofold: to defend my father's reputation from recent malicious attacks and, driven by Meredith, to bring to light the intimate story of our introspective mother, Cecily, and the quiet work she achieved to help others find fulfilment in their lives, which, we learned, she felt she had failed to achieve for herself.

It did not take us long to find Australian Security Intelligence Organisation (ASIO) and other archival evidence to rebut Ball's sensational spy claims. That John was at university in Sydney in the same lecture halls as Cecily in 1934 is important to us. It is evidence that he was not in the Soviet Union in 1934 being recruited by the Soviet secret police agency, a forerunner of the KGB (NKVD), as one of Ball's lackeys would have it.[8] Public records show that John worked intensively on his university studies that year, earning himself a high distinction in psychology and his lecturer's documented praise. In any event, John's first passport was not issued until 1938.[9]

In delving into our parents' lives, we discovered private papers and letters of others who knew John and Cecily that revealed much more about our parents than we bargained for; stories of loyalty and friendships and of love triangles, infidelity and deceit. Indeed, we found two interrelated stories; one of a deeply introverted person who eventually came out of the shadow of the other who attracted controversy in both his public and private lives. In meshing the stories of our two enigmatic parents, we discovered they had very different perspectives on their lives, which they lived mostly together. We faced a dilemma: the separate stories of John's public and political life and Cecily's private psychological journey have different readership appeal. Students of politics, history and international relations who might be interested in a behind-the-scenes story of John's controversial life might shy away from the intimate revelations contained in Cecily's soul-searching story. Similarly, those attracted to Cecily's

---

8   Chapple, 'Australia's Kim Philby?'
9   Conversations with our mother. ASIO's archived records reveal that John applied for a passport on 24 August 1938 in order to travel to the United Kingdom (UK). All passports with which he was issued were subsequent to this date. National Archives of Australia (NAA): A6980, S200565, 101.

personal story may not have the same interest in politics, policy wrangles, spies and duplicity. We tried to separate them out; however, lives so entwined are beyond separating.

Our thanks go to Dr David Stephens who helped us here. After reading our draft manuscript his comments in a nutshell were: 'This is about relationships; your parents' with each other and theirs with other people.' He advised us to merge and reframe their life stories so that our father's public career was a context for their interesting, interweaving relationships. He was right. I was still angry with Ball, but the articles I had written to correct the public record are available for anyone to read and others more qualified than I had also published articles in my father's defence.[10] I learned, too, that Ball had earned a reputation by this time for damaging the reputation of others who were no longer around to defend themselves.[11] I now put hurt and anger behind me and redirected my focus.

Meredith and I then concentrated on our parents' full and fascinating life stories, the complexity of their personalities, their thinking and their intriguing relationships. Our curiosity about our father, as it transpired, was overtaken by curiosity surrounding our mother: what really lay under her warm and calming demeanour to cause her – as we discovered in her voluminous introspective writing – to soul-search the whole of her life? On the surface, our parents' relationship was fairly conventional for mid-twentieth-century times – in so far as Cecily was the dutiful wife at home and John's attitudes to women fitted those times – but in other aspects of their lives they questioned conventional thinking. Colour is added to their stories by the backdrop of post-war and Cold War politics in the young city of Canberra. It placed them in the inner circles of politicians, public servants, academics and their families who formed the bulk of the growing general community. It promised to be a long, winding path of discovery.

---

10 For example, Paul Barratt, a former secretary of the Department of Defence, 'Pamela Burton's Defence of Her Father', *Australian Observer* [web blog], 1 May 2011, aussieobserver.blogspot.com/2011/05/pamela-burtons-defence-of-her-father.html; Gregory Pemberton, 'Old Gossip, but No Evidence John Burton Was a Spy', *Australian*, 18 January 2012; Ernst Willheim, 'Sex, Spies and Lies? The Spurious Case against John Burton', *Canberra Times*, 4 November 2014, Public Sector Informant 9.

11 Ball included H. V. (Doc) Evatt as a possible spy and he reportedly told Professor Pat Troy at ANU that he believed that Katherine Susannah Pritchard, her son Ric Throssell and (by implication) Ric's father, all deceased, were Soviet spies. See Karen Throssell, *The Crime of Not Knowing Your Crime: Ric Throssell against ASIO* (Melbourne: Interventions Inc., 2021). He made similar allegations about journalist Rupert Lockwood after he died. Ball, 'I Believe Lockwood Lied to Petrov Commission to Save His Family's Honour', *Weekend Australian*, 23–24 April 2011.

Our research confirmed that our parents were deep thinkers who shared sound social values and who wanted to make the world a better place. There, perhaps, the similarities end. It supported what we knew about them personally: that they were emotionally complex and that our family life sometimes bordered on dysfunctional. However, posthumously we re-met our parents; we see them in a different light as unique individuals. We have gained a deeper understanding of them and particularly of our remarkable, non-judgemental and much-loved mother, who emerged to become the strong thread of the family and undisputed matriarch.

The book became something very different from the one I had envisaged. It morphed into a family memoir of a sort in which my sister's and my voices could be heard as we reacted to revelations our research uncovered and interpreted how our parents felt and thought. We knew that there were other accounts of parents' marriages by their children, but our decision to write about our own was made independently of that literature.[12] None of those other memoirs were about relationships like those of our parents; none of the authors approached the task in the way that we did as siblings. Cecily and John had very different psyches and their brilliance and complexities manifested in different ways and made them an unusual couple. I felt more able to answer the question so many people asked us: 'Why write about your parents? What is it about them that is so special that people would want to know?' I could answer: 'It's a unique, intimate and candid account of our parents' complexities and interweaving relationships. We tell it as their children with the benefit of a "retrospectoscope".'

We did not have any planned process for telling our parents' story. Meredith offered to help in the research, reading and interviewing of people, but delegated, as only a big sister can, the writing to me. Transforming a narrative into a memoir freed us up to draw on our own memories and journals as well as our parents' letters, writings and oral histories. We researched archives and public records to check theirs and our flawed memories. We compared memories. Meredith is five years older than me and I deferred to her recall of events when she was 10 and I was five. However, when it came to events from the time that she turned 20 and I was 15, my 'page to a day' teenage diaries were invaluable. They not only

---

12 Nigel Nicolson, *Portrait of a Marriage: Vita Sackville-West and Harold Nicolson* (London: Weidenfeld and Nicolson, 1973); John Rickard, *An Imperial Affair: Portrait of an Australian Marriage* (Clayton, Vic.: Monash University Publishing, 2013); Sheila Fitzpatrick, *My Father's Daughter: Memories of an Australian Childhood* (Clayton, Vic.: Melbourne University Publishing, 2019).

record my and the family's emotional ups and downs and moves from one home to another, but events, such as 'Nehru died' or 'Dad returned from Moscow', to which we gave credence.

Once, when Meredith and I were on a plane travelling together to Italy, I pulled out a sheet of paper and asked her to 'draw a floor plan' of our shack-like house at our farm situated in what was then the Weetangera district of outer Canberra. My picture of it was indelible in my memory. So was hers. We drew very different floor plans! When in Italy, I used every spare moment I could to tap her brain. It was difficult to 'trap' my busy sister at home to interview her. My travel log book is interspersed with 'Talking to Meredith' and scrawls of notes of her childhood recollections. Our journey back in time triggered facts and matters previously long-forgotten. When we were in Sri Lanka together, we had a driver take us around to the former Australian high commissioner's house where we had resided for a short time. It jogged both our memories of living there and, by exchanging our memories, we mostly reached a consensus.

Our recollections differed because of the way our different experiences informed them. For example, ASIO had shadowed our family for the whole of my sisters' and my home life. Growing up in turbulent McCarthyism times had a more painful impact on Meredith than me. By the 1990s, she had risen to deputy secretary in the Department of the Prime Minister and Cabinet. Max Moore Wilton was its secretary. At a performance review (in which he ranked her highly) he said she would never go anywhere under the then Howard Government, because of her 'antecedents'. He clarified this by referring to her 'genes', apparently referring to our father. Fortunately, at this time she was lured into academia. She suffered at school in the 1950s from being a Burton too, which explains why, to this day, she maintained her married name of Edwards. As a child, I was less affected by being the daughter of a controversial public figure. At school once in the late 1950s, when two of my friends and I were mucking up in a library class, the librarian chastised my friends and said: 'I expected better of both of you. Not of Pam Burton, though, being the daughter of a Communist.' I thought it funny, because I thought her ignorant. So far as I was concerned, everyone knew that my father, then running a bookshop, was industrious and clever.

The voice of our sister Clare (1942–1998) is sadly absent. Her memories and perspective would have been different still. But from her eternal resting place she had influence. I remember once, when I was 17 and she 20, she said to me over the dining table in an accusatory tone: 'You see mum and dad through rose-coloured glasses.' I have tried to write this work through untinted lenses. She surprised us with her request that her memorial service be held at our local church. We were all atheists, weren't we? Her reason was, she told us before she died, that the biggest influence of our parents on all of us was their Methodist work ethic. That gave Meredith and me cause to consider the effect on both parents of their Methodist heritages. We have another sibling, young Mark, born in 1968. He had a different mother from us and, like our father, is liable to stir the pot with his provocative comments. 'Hope you find that old dad was a spy, sis,' he said. 'It would be fun for my kids to have a spy for a grandfather!' Sorry, Mark. We found strong evidence that he was not a Soviet agent.

Finding sufficient source material never posed a problem. There is more in various public archives than we could sift through. ASIO's extensive records of the times, places and dates of our family events and activities and names of our family's friends, colleagues and associates proved helpful, sometimes amusing, if not always reliable. We found a far more valuable source in the extensive collection of political scientist Professor Robert Parker's papers in the manuscript room at the National Library of Australia (NLA). Cecily and he married in 1966. There we discovered correspondence that detailed John and Robert's lifelong friendship, stories about their and Cecily's lives and loves. We found missing pieces of the jigsaw and some intimate and not-so-pleasant truths. Cecily also gave a recorded oral history for the NLA of which Meredith was the appointed interviewer. John had recorded many oral histories: two for the NLA collection, one for Murdoch University library, and several for George Mason University in the United States.

Importantly, we have a mass of private family papers. In response to questions I asked Cecily in 1990 about her childhood and early life, she responded by writing me a moving account that she permitted me to reproduce in a book for the family, *Cecily*, in 1994.[13] Before she died, Cecily was more forthcoming about her life and how she felt she had lived it. She handed us her voluminous writings, journals, letters and poetry. Her papers chronicle her ongoing lifelong journey in search of a better understanding of life and our place in the universe. Cecily wanted us to know her as a whole person. This gave rise to a moral and ethical issue: how much of this intimate material on Cecily's inner feelings should we

---

13 Cecily Burton, *Cecily* (Canberra: self-printed, 1994), held on Cecily family file [henceforth *Cecily*].

release into the public arena? We did not want to sully her reputation when, after all, my original motivation was to write about my father to protect his reputation. The deeper we dug into her mind through her writings, the more convinced we became that she would have encouraged us to publish her story; she wanted to be understood, even after her death. Cecily had often told us that she loved John but found him difficult to live with: not just because of his unpredictability, his political rashness and his expectation that she would embrace his risk-taking ventures, but also because of his failure, in her view, to understand her. Feeling misunderstood can be a painful experience and Cecily found that so from the time she was a child. We concluded that she did not want to be remembered as only part of the person she was. We therefore drew on Cecily's private papers to assist us to interpret her psyche, feelings and influences on her life. We reveal that the extent of her introspection was almost unhealthy, but that does not demean her. On the contrary, it takes courage for one to bare themselves to others. Cecily's story might resonate with many others and, without doubt, it would be her wish for us to share her story to help others find themselves and become whole.

We are, of course, defensive of our parents, whom we loved and of whom we are very proud. With this in mind, we have done our best to portray a complete picture of both our parents. However, in the case of John, we hope to contribute to, and correct where needed, the historical record. He was a head of the Department of External Affairs during a contentious political period of nation-building activity and changes in Cold War allegiances between powerful nations. We hope that our perspectives of John will help readers and scholars judge for themselves just who he was and what he stood for. We do not purport to have written a biography of John and, instead, point to some public records and opinions of others that interested readers might pursue. We would welcome a balanced biographical account of John and perhaps our 'insider' story will encourage an appropriate scholar to do this.

To sum up our parents, Cecily embraced the motto 'While I live, I grow' in her search to find her place in the world. Our father's response to this was to say, 'While I grow, I live', indicative of his habit of challenging accepted positions and turning assumptions on their head if needed to solve a problem. Yet, in turn, John also grew while he lived and Cecily lived well while she grew.

Pamela Burton and Meredith Edwards, March 2022

1

Courting controversy

Cecily Nixon knew John Burton by sight when they were both at school in Sydney in the interwar period. She was attracted to his trim physique, his smooth black hair and his blue eyes framed by round tortoiseshell glasses. She sometimes saw him step off a train at Ashfield station when she climbed onto one. Something about him and his demeanour intrigued her, so she observed him when she could. She sat and watched him at football matches at Newington College, in Sydney's inner west. She noticed that he played only sometimes and more often appeared to be wandering around near the oval, on his own. She sensed he was a loner, a kindred spirit she thought in hindsight, as they must have been unconscious intimations at the time.[1]

Then, to her joy, he turned up in her Psychology 1 class at the University of Sydney in 1934. John was 19 at the time and she was just 17. He had repeated a year at school and spent one year sick in bed with thyroid troubles, allowing his and Cecily's paths to cross again. He had a sureness about him and a quiet, unhurried presence that drew her in. 'I used to try to sit behind him in lectures, because he was so beautiful to look at, especially the back of his neck,' Cecily told us.[2] In retrospect, Cecily considered that rather than it being John's good looks that attracted her to him, although important, she recognised something in his face that echoed something in her – a 'kind of unhappiness, a sulky look', she thought. Cecily, we discovered, had a self-image so very different from what her appearance portrayed. Photographs of her in her late teens

---

1 Where not otherwise referenced, information in this chapter has been drawn from Cecily's letters to me in August 1990, reproduced in *Cecily*, 1994.
2 *Cecily*, 23–24.

depict her lolling on the beach with a gregarious bunch of friends, clad in a flattering swimsuit or short shorts for yachting, with boyfriends looking at her adoringly. Yet, she felt self-conscious and unsure of herself on commencing university; terrified, she claimed, that she might not be asked to the next ball. Self-doubt was something that we learned persisted throughout her life. Despite having had a childhood rich in activities and learning, she perceived herself as being unhappy as a child.

At university, Cecily met and made new friends; she became close friends with Gwen Wilkins and Peggy King as well as Judith Wright, who became one of Australia's national treasures and celebrated poets. They played tennis, went to the cinema at Bondi by tram and regarded themselves as modern women.[3] The four could not have been more different. Gwen was tall, lovely in looks and personality and shy. King, a science student, was full of vitality and, from Cecily's perspective, attracted every man she met. Wright was a thinker and a romantic. She was short, had thick hair and thick glasses because she was short-sighted. Wright recollected:

> soon I was part of a group of undeniably beautiful women and my glasses and thick ankles seemed to cease to matter. Men, unlucky with the others, fell back on me, so to speak, and there were plenty of them.[4]

Wright stated frankly that she used to pick out popular and beautiful women to befriend and hang around in order to meet popular men.[5] In her memoir she described this as a reason for her befriending Cecily:

> Fairly astute over how to get where I wanted to be, I made friends with beautiful girls. Cecily Nixon, with extraordinary depths in her green eyes and her wide white smile in a tanned face, was one of the students in Philosophy 1. The classroom under the Fisher Library was sparsely occupied when I slunk into a seat alone. Cecily was in the seat beside me, for once without a male nearby. I inveigled her into my seat and clung to her thereafter, since she was taking the same subjects. In spite of the fact that she had been to Fort Street High [sic] and had many friends, she put up with me from then on and I tagged near her picking up male crumbs from her table.[6]

---

3   Georgina Arnett, *The Unknown Judith Wright* (Crawley, WA: UWA Publishing, 2016), 110.
4   Patricia Clarke, ed., *Judith Wright: Half a Life-time* (Melbourne: Text Publishing, 1999), 124.
5   Arnett, *The Unknown Judith Wright*, 109–10.
6   Clarke, *Judith Wright*, 124.

Cecily seemed unaware of the strong impression she initially made on Wright. Wright worked in a voluntary capacity for the university student magazine *Honi Soit*, and started the magazine's social comment column. She recalled that she 'so often reported on the beautiful Cecily Nixon's latest doings', and even mentioned 'Nixon's weekend tennis parties'.[7] Leafing through the magazine tells that Cecily, at least in Wright's eyes, was one of the 'belles' at university balls. She was one of the fashionable young women who 'stood out in their bright colours and floral materials', and was noted for her 'on-stage performances and ball attire'; the tone of Cecily's dress was 'sometimes cheeky and sometimes subtle' and, on one occasion, she wore 'a chiffon with broad stripes arranged in an intriguing fashion'.[8]

The detailed attention Wright gave Cecily at university is not something Cecily mentioned to us and we are grateful to have this perspective of her. Cecily did, however, talk to us about her ambivalence towards Wright in the years after they left university, the reasons for which we have tried to uncover in better understanding Cecily, our mother. Cecily did recall that eventually she felt in her element at university. She had fun in her social life and she had a love of learning. She chose her courses to coincide with her interests but with no direction in mind: English, philosophy, psychology and anthropology. Wright tackled similar subjects, allowing them to foster their friendship. Both were privileged to have one of Australia's most influential philosophers, libertarian Challis Professor of Philosophy John Anderson, as their lecturer. Yet, Cecily claimed that she did not enjoy her first year of philosophy, because it seemed to her, 'when it came to exercises in logic, to be worse, no, about the same, as mathematics, and likely to reduce me to tears at exam times'.[9] Otherwise, she did well, completing an honours course concurrently with her pass courses, and she graduated in 1937 gaining second-class honours.

Cecily flirted with her many admirers, but John was not part of her university social circle. Sharing lecture halls with him was not enough. She wanted to meet him. Her challenge was how to make that happen. At the end of 1934 she took a bold step and asked a past boyfriend, who was also a friend of John's at school and university, to introduce them. Roscoe Fay did just that. Cecily said that she had not been so forward before, nor was she again, but something drove her to bring their meeting about. It worked. John was taken with her. He shed his current girlfriend in favour of this beautiful young woman, Cecily.

---

7   Arnett, *The Unknown Judith Wright*, 110, fn. 279; *Honi Soit*, no. 8 (1935): 2, no. 24 (1935): 2.
8   *Honi Soit*, nos 17 and 20 (1935); noted in Arnett, *The Unknown Judith Wright*, 136.
9   *Cecily*, 22.

PERSONS OF INTEREST

Cecily, 1935.
Source: Family collection.

1. COURTING CONTROVERSY

John, 1935.
Source: Family collection.

John and Cecily's infatuation with each other deepened, but Cecily underestimated the impact that her individualism, beauty and intelligence had on him. He wanted her to himself. As an indication of things to come, he insisted she give up her circle of admiring friends, particularly those who were former boyfriends. She did, and she missed them. She later recalled that, even while they were courting, she bowed to him, chased him to the bus-stop and apologised to him when he rejected something she said or did, hoping to pacify him and get him to accept her again. But she loved him deeply. Not that love reliably brings happiness, she knew. Once Cecily became accustomed to John's unpredictability, nothing about him was likely to surprise her. However, she could not have imagined then how controversial he would become, nor how adaptable she would need to be to live with this multifaceted man. It would be a big job for Cecily to take John on as her life partner. Intellectually and philosophically, Cecily and John were compatible. Emotional compatibility became more problematic as time wore on. But she trusted him and stood by him for 30 years, even while, over time, others tried to besmirch his reputation and attempted to associate his social philosophies with the evils of communism.

***

When John commenced his university studies, influenced by his father, he had a theological vocation in mind. He chose subjects he was interested in and appropriate for that calling. His father initially doubted that his son was capable of attaining a university degree. John felt he suffered from being the only boy in the family. His older sisters were scholars and his parents seemed to think that as John was a practical type who could service the family car and mow the lawns he would probably have a vocation in a mechanical trade or become a carpenter. John was quietly determined, however, to prove his parents wrong. He enjoyed debating at school – his strength was to question assumptions upon which argument was based. He held strong views about social and political issues from a young age and was confident about the worth of his viewpoints and the influence he might have on broad social issues. He attended a coaching college and passed his university entrance examinations. From there, nothing seemed to hold him back.

At university, John did some lay preaching and became secretary of both the university's Student Christian Movement and the League of Nations Union, which canvassed students on relevant social and political issues.

However, 'after reading a few books at the library' as he often told us, he soon questioned the value of the church and other religious institutions in promoting world peace. He then changed his mind about going into the church. Religion had been at the source of conflict and wars for centuries, and John decided that the church was not a tool he could use in the pursuit of improving humanity. He believed that more effective changes to society could be made from inside the public service rather than from the pulpit. In 1936, during his final year at university, John ran a peace campaign on campus and arranged and participated in debates on peace and economic issues. Students were concerned that war was likely to break out so there was heightened interest in politics and world affairs. Memories were fresh of World War One and it was the year in which economist John Maynard Keynes published his revolutionary work, *The General Theory of Employment, Interest and Money*. Germany and Italy were ravaged early by the Great Depression and Keynes turned accepted economic theory on its head.

John graduated with a bachelor of arts in 1937, majoring in English, economics and psychology, with first-class honours in the last having submitted his thesis 'Psychological Factors in Juvenile Unemployment and Delinquency', which he would draw on in later years. His close friend Robert Parker graduated with first-class honours in economics at the University of Sydney in the same year.[10] John followed suit and gained another first-class honour in economics after completing a part-time evening course while working in what he saw as an easy, if demeaning, job as a graduate clerk in the Postmaster-General's Office. This bottom-of-the-rung position, at a pay range of £96 to £306 a year, was a common point of entry for graduates commencing a career in the Commonwealth Public Service.

Economics, he said later, was the best possible peace weapon.[11] By the time he graduated, he had become interested in new thinking on global economics and its potential to have an impact on global peace and stability. He believed that international trade and economic policies were important aspects of foreign policy – and it was influencing Australia's economic and foreign policy that he was intent on doing.

---

10   Papers of R. S. Parker, National Library of Australia (NLA), MS 8200, box 46, file 189, 'General Correspondence Burton John W, 1938–88'. In 1941, Parker completed a master's in economics also with first-class honours.
11   George Blaikie, 'Who Is This Dr. Burton?', *Courier-Mail* (Brisbane), 19 June 1952.

John's and Robert's life passages took different directions, but they remained best friends and continued to share academic interests. He and Robert, or 'Big Boy' as John affectionately called him, would exchange views on economic policy over the ensuing decades. John confided in Robert about Cecily, in good times and bad. In time, Cecily would confide in Robert about John, in good times and sad. The threads of our parents' relationships with Robert Parker, his wife Nancy, Wright and her late and secret love Nugget Coombs – another of Australia's 'national treasures' – would weave in and out of our parents' life stories. Robert became a pivotal player in Cecily and John's relationship saga, changing the lives of each of them forever. Remarkably, all three remained in touch with and retained respect for each other throughout and beyond their marriages.

2
Cecily's travels with Judith Wright

Cecily had difficulty concentrating on her last honours exam in February 1937. She was about to set off overseas on a trip arranged by her mother as a graduation reward. John tried to persuade her not to go. He would be travelling overseas soon, he told her, and he wanted to marry her and take her with him. Cecily loved John and accepted that inevitably she would marry him, although intuitively she felt that the relationship was not good for her. She was unsure of her own future and was influenced by her mother's view that John would not make a good husband and family man. As for deferring her travels to go with him, 'When would that be?' she asked. In two years, he hoped.[1] It turned out to be the case, but Cecily could not have known or relied on that, and was never good at 'blind faith', she said. Anyway, John had neither money nor particular plans at the time, and Cecily felt the tug-of-war between John and her mother for her soul. She ignored John's pleadings. Her mother had given her the opportunity to travel and she took it. Within a month, missing her graduation ceremony and leaving her boyfriend behind, she boarded the Orient Line's *Orama:* in first-class luxury she was on her way to the United Kingdom with her university girlfriend's family, the Wilkins.

Wright was on a one-class steamer, the *Moreton Bay*, ahead of Cecily's ship. Wright's father funded a trip for her to attend the coronation of George VI in London and to see some of Europe. She wanted to go 'even though Europe was withdrawing itself under clouds of war, fascism and

---

1   Cecily's story about her trip with Judith is drawn from *Cecily* (1994).

Nazism as the Spanish Civil War went on'.² Cecily and Wright planned to meet up after the coronation. When they did meet up, in early May 1937, Wright had a young New Zealander, Tony, in tow, whom she had met on the boat. The three young people hired 'a very unreliable car', which both Tony and Cecily could drive, and set off on a trip to see England.³ They enjoyed what Wright described as 'the leafy lanes and spring flowers' of Devon and Cornwall, then they turned north to head for Wales where Tony left them. Cecily was the only driver 'and neither of us a mechanic', Wright said in her memoir.⁴

Wright's father had requested her to take notes at a cattle show in Hereford of studs and bulls and they went to Aberystwth in Wales to inquire into research on pastures and cattle diseases. Having read Judith's account of their travels in Wales, it is possible that it was there they came across the pretty name, Meredith, for both of them would give this name to one of their daughters. The pair next headed for Scotland because Wright felt that, for Cecily's sake, they should break free from her father's instructions. The car, however, finally 'gave a gasp and stopped'.⁵ After costly repairs to get it going, Cecily, presumably nervous it might breakdown again, decided to drive it back to London. Determined, Wright took to the road as a hitch-hiker – a brave act, but she wanted to see the country from where her ancestors came.

The friendship survived, as did Wright, and back in London the two women joined up again for a trip to Europe. A travel agent friend of Cecily's mother had provided a rich itinerary for them that included contacts in various countries with families willing to host them or guide them on what to see and do. However, Italy was not accessible because of its invasion of Abyssinia; nor Spain because its civil war was not yet at an end. Ignoring warnings and rumours of war elsewhere, they went to Europe anyway, starting with Paris and on to Holland before travelling further east. In Germany, according to Wright, they stayed with a 'somewhat run-down baronial family, at Unkel-am-Rhein, where we were introduced to the Nazi faiths, and the worst of German sausage'.⁶ In Austria they felt apprehension seeing Germans marching at the borders. In Budapest, Hungary, their awareness of the Nazi threat was heightened. There, they

---

2   Clarke, *Judith Wright*, 131.
3   Clarke, *Judith Wright*, 132.
4   Clarke, *Judith Wright*, 132.
5   Clarke, *Judith Wright*, 133.
6   Clarke, *Judith Wright*, 134.

befriended two young male students who wanted to escape to America, or anywhere, 'beyond the immediate reach of the European threat'.[7] One, Andrei, a chemistry student, had Jewish blood and displayed a deal of anxiety about his future. The other had qualified as a doctor. The doctor, according to Wright, was tall and handsome, 'Cecily's choice', whereas Andrei, 'stouter and unhandsome was allocated to me'.[8] In the three days they had, the two men entertained them and they visited museums and galleries, boated on the Danube, and 'drank curious drinks on terraces above the river' at café tables shaded by umbrellas. Andrei wanted to keep in touch and yet, although Wright said she would, she resisted his passionate and persistent wooing of her. He wanted her to help him out of the country and she could sponsor his passage to Australia to do this. His grandmother was Jewish and, he told Wright, he feared the 'threatened purge that would eliminate all Jewish people to the tenth generation'.[9] He understood that 'only those of "pure Aryan strain" would be spared when Hitler's legions took over Hungary'.[10] Cecily and Judith boarded the Vienna express back to England, Judith knowing that Andrei regarded her as his 'last hope of escape'.[11] Cecily's doctor friend eventually reached New York and, after Wright returned home, pleading letters from Andrei asking her to marry him, and gifts he sent her, caught up with her. Once Hungary fell, Andrei's letters ceased abruptly and Andrei's fate remained unknown to Judith. 'I fear it is only too predictable,' she wrote Cecily decades on. That she did not try to raise money for surety to bring Andrei to Australia remained on Wright's conscience forever.[12] But, she said, 'I could not see myself as fiancee or wife to Andrei, and I failed the test of self-sacrifice'.[13]

Cecily noticed that Wright knew how to get a lot more out of her travels, putting countries into their historical and political perspectives and, for example, taking notes about life in Germany under rationing. The trip opened Wright's eyes to 'the weighty realities of the wider world, with the growing threat of war'.[14] Cecily, it seems, held no particular views

---

7   Clarke, *Judith Wright*, 134.
8   Clarke, *Judith Wright*, 135.
9   Clarke, *Judith Wright*, 134–35.
10 Clarke, *Judith Wright*, 135.
11 Clarke, *Judith Wright*, 137.
12 Letter, Judith to Cecily, undated, written from her Braidwood home in the 1990s, Cecily family file.
13 Clarke, *Judith Wright*, 138.
14 Patricia Clarke and Meredith McKinney, eds, *With Love and Fury: Selected Letters of Judith Wright* (Canberra: National Library of Australia, 2006), 3.

of the world at the time of her travels and had no focus. Wright and Cecily also seemed to have had different perceptions of their relationship with each other. Cecily believed that they turned out to be incompatible when travelling together, despite their close three-year friendship. They were very different personalities with very different interests. She felt timid with Wright and probably secretly envied her sense of freedom and adventure, not appreciating the high regard Wright had for her until she read Wright's published memoir.[15] Impacting on their relationship, too, was Wright's friendship with Cecily's mother, Muriel – a relationship that Cecily envied. Wright later explained to Cecily, 'Your mother was a real friend to me when I needed one'.[16]

Wright and Cecily had more in common, however, than Cecily appeared to realise. They both suffered emotional scarring in their childhood. We explore later Cecily's suffering as a child from her perceived loss of her mother's doting attention after her sister was born. When looking back on her life, she imagined how she must have felt as a child:

> Overnight I was thrust aside, expected to abandon my birthright to a usurper. Where did she come from? What right had she to be there? None! Everything I believed in vanished. I was outraged, thrown into disaster, my faith and trust destroyed. I was no longer supreme in a world which devoted itself to me. The unimaginable had happened. There was another claimant to my parents, to this world, to my world![17]

Wright, who displayed a tougher exterior and a matter-of-fact approach to life, also experienced grief when, at two-and-a-half years old, her brother was born. In fact, Wright expressed the same strong feeling as Cecily did. 'He supplanted me,' Wright later wrote.[18]

Cecily became unhappy during her travels, not just when she was with Wright but at times when she was on her own back in London. Her misery was compounded by John pestering her, wanting her with him in Sydney. At one stage, while travelling with Wright in Switzerland, Cecily was so miserable she sent a cable home, asking if she could return. This, she thought in hindsight, was a terrible thing to do to her mother who

---

15   Letter Cecily to Judith, undated [1991], Cecily family file.
16   Letter Judith to Cecily, 29 October 1996, Cecily family file.
17   *Cecily*, 6.
18   Arnett, *The Unknown Judith Wright*, 75.

had given her this great gift – a blessing that she had been unable to value enough. Despite her periodic misery, she kept to her schedule and returned to Sydney the following November, 1937.

On arriving home, Cecily found her mother was ill. She had been unwell when Cecily was at university and never really regained good health. Now, having had appendicitis, she developed complications and was hospitalised. In March 1938, when her mother was aged 52, Cecily's father Robert came home from the hospital one evening and announced to the children that their mother had died. She had suffered cardiac failure while being operated upon. Cecily remembers that she and her father sat on the front porch and Robert put his head on her shoulder briefly, and that was that. At age 21, Cecily was numb. Being the eldest child, Cecily received many visitors and their condolences. She did not know how to respond to them. Her sister Eleanor took over their mother's role in the house, while Cecily perceived herself as doing nothing much, having no real feeling of belonging. Looking back, Cecily often wondered whether she had contributed to her mother's illness and death by her lack of consideration. She could not remember how she reacted to her mother's suffering, and with self-analysis believed that she must have repressed most of her feeling about her mother. In her senior years she expressed gratitude towards her mother and some admiration and compassion, noting that she gave her mother a very hard time as an adolescent; she hated her, attacked her ideas, criticised her and never grew to like her.

None of Cecily's uncertainty seemed apparent to Wright when they were young friends and, despite the complexities in their relationship, their friendship was enduring. In her 80s, Wright wrote to Cecily stating, 'You always seemed thoroughly at home in the world to me, while I had been knocked off my feet by my mother's death and a stepmother I didn't like … and losing touch with my home and family'.[19]

It seems that both Wright and Cecily had had unresolved issues about their mothers. Wright's mother had suffered serious illness from influenza and poorly understood complications thereafter. Wright watched her weaken and become worse with pain. Only 11 when she died, Wright later recalled, 'Apart from grief, I had guilt to contend with. I knew I had not been able to comfort her or help her through those dreadful days at

---

19   Letter, Judith to Cecily, undated, written from her Braidwood home in the 1990s, Cecily family file.

all …'.²⁰ Her story, as told through her published selected letters, reveals that she suffered 'a deepening sense of alienation that fed and was fed by poetry'. By way of contrast, Cecily's childhood emotions fed her passion as an adult for psychology.

Cecily resumed her relationship with John when she returned from her travels. Her mother was no longer around to discourage her from marrying him but Cecily continued to worry about whether he was the right person for her to spend her life with. Yet, they had much in common: a high intellect, similar political and moral philosophies and the influences of having shared a Methodist upbringing.

---

20   Clarke, *Judith Wright*, 103.

3
A shared heritage

Cecily and John had a Methodist heritage in common, one that strongly shaped the values of them both. John's father's strong Methodism came through the influence of his mother and her sister-in-law's family the Wears; Cecily's Methodist heritage also came from the maternal side of the family, the Fletchers. The forebears of both hailed from England.

Cecily's mother's direct ascertainable Methodist family history starts with Joseph Fletcher, Yeoman of Oxford. According to an uncle of Cecily's, a diligent man traced every family of Fletchers in Britain in the early 1900s, looking for a schoolmaster named Fletcher who had done him a good turn in his youth in London. His research revealed that every branch of the family in England, but one, was Methodist. The Yeoman's first son, Joseph, wrote in 1867 that in 1809, when he was 18, he was introduced to the Methodist Society and 'Like Bunyan's Pilgrim I now entered the wicket gate'.[1] He became the Reverend Joseph Fletcher of Taunton, Somerset, the county where both John Wesley, the eighteenth-century English founder of Methodism, and his protégé John Fletcher (not related to Cecily's Fletcher forebears) lived. Joseph married Mary Horner in 1822, before sailing to the West Indies on his first appointment. In 1823, while in the West Indies, Joseph and Mary's first son was born, Joseph Horner Fletcher, the eldest of seven children. Joseph and his brothers John and George followed their father into the church. John Fletcher was Cecily's great-grandfather. He and his brother Joseph emigrated to New Zealand in the mid-1800s where John married Eliza Bale. His brother Joseph founded

---

1 'Sketch of the life of Rev Joseph Fletcher', dated 27 February 1867, 2, attachment to letter Lionel Fletcher [Cecily's uncle] to Muriel [Cecily's mother], 21 August 1925, held in Cecily family file.

the Wesleyan College and Seminary at Auckland in 1858 and, in 1865, was invited to become president of Newington College, Sydney, which John Burton would later attend. John and Eliza Fletcher also migrated to Australia and settled in Sydney in around 1880. Three of their sons became ordained Methodist ministers and all seven sons were preachers. One of those sons, Ernest, married Thirza Bowden, and they became the parents of Cecily's mother, Muriel. In 1884, Joseph Horner Fletcher went on to be elected president of the General Conference of the Australasian Wesleyan Methodist Church. John Burton's father held this position from 1945. By this time, though, it was titled the General Conference of the Methodist Church of Australasia, the Methodist Church having brought together four Methodist bodies on 1 January 1902.

Methodists appear on Cecily's father's side of the family too. Cecily's forebears, Robert James and Sarah Nixon, emigrated to New South Wales in the early 1830s with their son James Robert, born in 1831. James Robert married Sarah Buttsworth in 1854, and they moved from the Colo River area in 1860 and settled on the Wallamba River at Willow Point in 1863. Initially Anglican, James established the first church services on the Wallamba. The family, however, converted to the Wesleyan faith, James having become so disgusted with the behaviour of a visiting Anglican parson, very much the worse for liquor. The drunken Anglican is said to have caused great commotion flogging and cursing a horse he was riding, galloping to and fro about the town. As Wesleyans, James's family later had a strong association with the temperance movement. The couple's second son was James Henry Nixon, Cecily's grandfather. Cecily's father Robert was James Nixon's eldest child, born 13 December 1885. His family moved to the Manning area in 1893 and purchased a farm at Glenthorne across from Taree. The family and Cecily's father remained Methodists.

Our father's heritage is even more entrenched in Methodism. John Wear Burton senior was born on 7 March 1875 in Yorkshire. There is a little-known story that should not be lost in time. It explains both the origin of John's father's Methodist heritage and the passing down of the name Wear (pronounced 'Weer') in the Burton family. Grandfather Jack (the name he was called by his family and which I will use in this story to avoid confusion with our father, John) was named after a nephew of Jack's mother, the Reverend John Wear Bell who, a few months before Jack was born, died as a missionary on the Gold Coast of Africa.[2] Bell was named

---

2 Jack was the second-born child, his brother George having died when Jack was about 18 months old. He had four younger siblings.

after his maternal grandfather, John Wear, a strong Methodist and friend of John Wesley, who led the controversial Methodist revival movement within the Church of England. The Wears had been closely associated with the introduction of Methodism into Kettlewell, Yorkshire.

The families of the Wears, Bells and Burtons all hailed from what was then the North Riding of Yorkshire and from where the River Wear started its winding journey to the North Sea. The family relationship connection was that Jack Burton's mother, Maria, and John Bell's father, Robert, were siblings. John Bell's mother, Elizabeth Wear, was the daughter of John Wear – and hence the inclusion of Wear in her eldest son's name. Elizabeth and Robert Bell had three children: John was followed by Joseph and then Eleanor. The two missionary brothers both lost their lives at a young age in the course of their work, one in Africa and the other in China. Their sister Eleanor wrote and published a little-known work on the brothers' story of their missionary zeal in Yorkshire and abroad in times when hatred was expressed by some towards the new Methodism.[3]

Jack's father, Robert Burton, was a carpenter by trade. We have in our family collection of papers the original indenture certificate dated 9 May 1862 witnessing that Robert was apprenticed to George Carter 'in the Art of a Carpenter and Wheelwright'. He then became a blacksmith and a skilful engineer employed at an ironworks in Middlesbrough, then north Yorkshire. He came from a small-farm family and had an intermittent education; whereas his wife, Maria, the youngest of 13 children, was a well-educated daughter of a mine manager in Cumberland. Her father had seen to it that his youngest daughter was given a good 'dame-school' education.[4] Robert and Maria had sat together in the 'singing pew' in the little Wesleyan chapel in Lazenby, 'a small drab village' as their son described it, in the North Riding of Yorkshire. Robert's strong baritone voice and Maria's soprano combined well, as did they as a couple in time. They married in the chapel and lived in a small house next door to it. Robert Burton left his position in the ironworks and went into partnership with a farmer who had some training as a mechanical engineer. They bought a piece of land on which there was a blacksmith's shop. To the smithy they

---

3   J. E. Hellier, *The Missionary Brothers: Memoirs of the Rev. John Wear Bell and the Rev. Joseph Bell* (Leeds: Walker and Laycock, 1889).
4   Information for this chapter is also drawn from J. W. Burton, 'The Weaver's Shuttle: Memories and Reflections of an Octogenarian', Jack's unpublished autobiography, c. 1956. A copy of the work is held at the Mitchell Library, Sydney: J. W. Burton 1875–1970; John Wear Burton further papers, 1900–1970, MLMSS 2899 Add On 990 Textual Records.

added a machine shop with lathes, drilling machine and tools, and then a carpenter's and wheelwright's shop was built. As a little boy, Jack played with blocks, chips and shavings in the smithy workshop among the huge planks stacked for seasoning – oak, ash, hickory and pine. Robert had an 'inventive mind with a genius for improvisation' and derived sheer joy from making things. Here began Jack's love of carpentry, which, in turn, would be passed on to our father, John.

The family's blissful life in England came to an end when Maria, failing in health, required a warmer climate. They heard about New Zealand's long hours of sunshine from a brother of Maria's and the family emigrated in 1884 with an assisted passage to Wellington. New Zealand was in the throes of a great depression when the Yorkshire Burtons arrived, and Robert Burton found that work was scarce. Jack left school at age 12 to help his family. He first worked as a fleece-picker and later as an apprentice wheelwright to his father at Masterton. Then, reflecting his mother's strong Methodism, he became a local lay preacher at age 17 and went on to study theology. He was accepted as a candidate for the Ministry at the Napier Synod in 1894, and in 1897 he was sent to Upper Thames Goldfields to begin his ministry.[5] He was ordained in 1901.

John and Cecily, then, each had two parents committed to the Methodist faith. However, both Cecily's and John's education, curiosity and intellect saw them develop into rationalists. They moved away from a commitment to any formal religion, but not from its core social values nor, in fact, from the social and spiritual offerings of their local church society. Both had family influences of a strong work ethic, driven by a desire to improve the world around them. Cecily, although never sure how she might do this, initially believed her role was to support John in his mission-driven idealism.

From an early age, John had a strong belief in himself. Before he thought of joining the church, he told his family that he wanted to be in charge of Australia's foreign policy; foreign policy making, he believed, could foster world peace. He was no less humble in 1985 when he looked back on this and said: 'At the age of 14 I said to a friend that I wanted to head the Foreign Office ... At age 32, I was head of the Foreign Office'.[6] John's vision for an

---

5 'Rev. J. W. Burton: New Methodist President', *Sydney Morning Herald*, 26 February 1931, 10.
6 Burton interview, *Resolution* (Center for Conflict Analysis and Resolution, George Mason University) magazine, 1, no. 5 (November 1985), 4–5; and see Peter Clack, 'Theories amidst Cows and Hills', *Canberra Times*, 8 September 1991, 24. In a recorded interview, John explained that he was told that he wrote this in a letter to a friend when he was 14: John Burton, interview by John Clements, London, 25 February 1981, John Clements Oral History Collection, Murdoch University.

egalitarian society and his secular missionary zeal to explore peaceful ways for nations to avoid wars made him vulnerable to attacks by those who wanted to discredit his work. As a young adult, he was dubbed 'a socialist' for adhering to principles of social democracy and advocating policies that promoted social progress and economic justice. John saw economic hardship as a major cause of war and propounded the view that oppressive colonial rule combined with economic hardship caused social and civil unrest and made conditions ripe for the spread of communism. Some political conservatives viewed John's stance as anti-colonial and evidence that he was a communist sympathiser. John argued that the opposite was the case. Our belief is that his ideology came, not from any admiration of communism as some would have it – as children we knew that he loathed authoritarian regimes of both left and right political extremes – but from a combination of his intellect and the egalitarian values his Methodist forebears preached. That is, his 'democratic socialism' was informed by Jack's adherence to 'Christian socialism'.[7]

A strong Methodist heritage that guided John's commitment to its social principles is probably the single most important factor in the origin of our father's political and social values. The influence of his missionary father is seen particularly in John's 'human needs' theory, which he expounded later when developing principles of conflict analysis and resolution. Jack had advocated conflict resolution in the course of his missionary work. He recognised the importance of addressing not just the spiritual but also the material needs of oppressed communities. In *Papua for Christ*, for example, Jack wrote of Australia's special responsibility towards those in the territories it governed and he said that:

> As Australian Methodists the responsibility is still more immediate, for these people are our own peculiar charge, and none other is working amongst them. If we do not help them they will not be helped. We must make their needs known, for experience has proved that when Christian people know of need they respond to it with eagerness and delight.[8]

---

7   Jack declared his dislike of labels of every sort; however, if forced to choose one that came nearest to his thought and conviction, it would be 'Christian Socialism'. Burton, 'The Weaver's Shuttle', 200.
8   The Rev. J. W. Burton, *Papua for Christ*, also entitled *Our Task in Papua* (London: Epworth Press, 1926), 124.

These words are echoed in our father's written work. John wrote, for example:

> Implied in conflict resolution ... is the proposition that aggressions and conflicts are the direct result of some institutions and social norms being incompatible with inherent human needs.[9]

Adjusting for style and the religiosity of Jack as against the pragmatic social policy approach of his son John, a reader of the father's and son's published works might be forgiven for confusing the writings of the two. Their humanitarian concerns, geopolitical interest and radical thinking coincided. Interestingly, their life courses and activities of preaching, writing and pursuing lost causes occurred during a substantial overlapping period of time.

While both Jack and John spoke of the importance of satisfying human needs if communities were to live together peacefully, they took entirely different paths to pursue similar missions. 'Burton was very much his father's son', wrote author and academic David Dunn, in 2013. He explained:

> The father ... was a reformer and religion was about doing good, about social improvement. He was, by all accounts, a forceful character who did, in fact, effect significant reforms. He set an example for John junior to follow. The younger Burton ... joined the Australian Civil Service, where he hoped and assumed he would be of service.[10]

Similarly, historian Professor Peter Edwards, in describing John's influence later in the Department of External Affairs, noted that 'to many, Burton appeared to have inherited the father's missionary zeal in a secular form and to have become a crusader for his ideals in this world'.[11]

---

9   John W. Burton, 'Conflict Resolution: The Human Dimension', *International Journal of Peace Studies* 3, no. 1 (January 1998), accessed 2 April 2021, www3.gmu.edu/programs/icar/ijps/vol3_1/burton.htm?gmuw-rd=sm&gmuw-rdm=ht.
10 David Dunn, 'Engaging Provention: A Pressing Question of Need', Occasional Paper no. 28 (George Mason University School of Conflict Analysis and Resolution, 2013), 1, accessed 2 April 2021, activity.scar.gmu.edu/sites/default/files/Dunn%20Working%20Paper.pdf.
11 P. G. Edwards, *Prime Ministers and Diplomats: The Making of Australian Foreign Policy 1901–1949* (Oxford: Oxford University Press: 1983), 145.

In his autobiography, 'The Weaver's Shuttle', Jack indicated that the major focus of his work with Christian Missions was the welfare of native races, about which he wrote in many published works.[12] His message over the decades was that 'Christians should support political and secular attempts to improve human social conditions'. John had a more grandiose vision of how to achieve improvement in social conditions: his mission was to develop a definitive theory for achieving world peace and to persuade others to put it into practice. In 1985, when talking about his work in the area of analysis of conflict and its resolution, he unashamedly said, 'I'm looking for disciples'.[13] Both father and son were mission driven. There is no better way, I suggest, of understanding John Wear Burton, his world view and core values, than by taking a look at the rebellious, if religious, path his father Jack trod.

---

12 Burton, 'The Weaver's Shuttle', Apologia, 2.
13 Burton interview, *Resolution* magazine, 5. This accords with the view of a critic of Burton, Susan Strange, who stated in 1989 that Burton 'was more interested in recruiting disciples than teaching students to think for themselves', cited by David J. Dunn, *From Power Politics to Conflict Resolution: The Work of John W. Burton* (New York: Palgrave Macmillan, 2004), 4–5.

4

John's father: A radical, mission-driven Methodist

Glimpses of the fascinating life of our grandfather, Jack, grabbed my attention in some cameo stories included in his autobiography, 'The Weaver's Shuttle'. The manuscript focuses on his missionary career devoid of much personal detail about his adult life. However, he passed on a story of the mistake he made in becoming engaged to a 'good Methodist woman' in New Zealand.[1] He gave her a ring that John Wesley had given Jack's Yorkshire grandparents, but then Jack broke the engagement because he met Florence Mildred Hadfield, a 'rosy-cheeked, vivacious girl of singular charm', of about 21.[2] The family never saw the Wesley ring again. We can only assume that the Wesley ring that Jack lost to his forsaken fiancée had been gifted to the Burtons from John Wesley through the family connection they had to this now famous religious leader.

Florence had a beautiful contralto voice and sang in the church choir. She was born in Christchurch, New Zealand, in 1883, the niece of Methodist Reverend Joseph Oram. The couple married on 24 April 1902 at Richmond Church and enjoyed a 51-year-long marriage. They had a reception held under a large old elm tree at the side of the church, having no time to linger. After it, they rushed off to catch the Lyttleton boat to Wellington from where they set off that night for Fiji. Jack was to take up an appointment as the founder and first superintendent of the Indian Mission in Fiji. Between 1902 and 1911, Jack made his mark in Fiji with

---

1 Jack's daughter, Rewa, retold the story in an unpublished memoir, undated, p. 3, Burton Snr family file.
2 Burton, 'The Weaver's Shuttle', 46–47.

a radical approach to his work that broke with the missionary tradition of the church. He announced that he did not see his task so much as to save the heathen from hell but, rather, to save them from unhappy social conditions.³ Jack listened to the people and tried to understand causes of unrest.

The Rev. J. W. Burton with an unidentified colleague, New Zealand, early 1900s.
Source: Family collection, Leanne Akers.

In pursuit of this, when he was posted to Davuilevu, Fiji, Jack made it his business to trace the path of Thomas Baker, a previous missionary and resident of Davuilevu, who was killed by natives in Nandrau in 1867. Jack tells the story in his autobiography – one not for the faint hearted.⁴ Baker paid the ultimate price for his attempts to 'tame the natives'. He was ambushed, slain and eaten – Fiji's only missionary martyr according to Jack.⁵ It was the last known act of cannibalism in Fiji. After making the arduous journey to Nandrau with a guide, Jack was shown to the Chief's

---

3   Gregory Pemberton, 'John Burton: The Heretic', *Evatt Papers* 3, no. 2 (1995), 97.
4   A full account of the death and Jack's journey can be read in Burton, 'The Weaver's Shuttle', 73–76; for an earlier account, see J.W.B., 'A Missionary Martyr: Rev. Thomas Baker, of Fiji', *Sydney Morning Herald*, 3 September 1927.
5   J.W.B., 'A Missionary Martyr'.

4. JOHN'S FATHER

house, which was filled with people who welcomed him. He met and ate with several old men who had taken part in the eating of Baker. They gaily described that feast to Jack, telling him with merriment how they had dismembered Baker's body, parts of which were sent to other villages. One man presented Jack with a cannibal fork that he avowed he had used to eat the flesh of the missionary. Another told that flesh of man was better than flesh of pig, but the flesh of a white man was inferior to that of a Fijian.

The difference between Baker and Burton was not just that one was eaten by people he was trying to convert to Christianity and the other dined with them on regular native Fijian food, but the very different ways Baker and Burton approached their work. Baker believed it was his mission to civilise the natives, whereas it was Jack's goal to guide his charges – Fijian Indians – to Christianity by understanding them and their needs. Importantly, between 1902 and 1911, while Jack was working in Fiji, he identified the indenture system under which the Indians worked the sugar cane fields as a primary cause of misery. He saw it simply as slavery. At first, the very workers he wanted to help threw rotten eggs at him as he preached. By the time he left Fiji, the Indians worshipped him as the hero who freed them from oppression. In 2017 in Canberra, I sat down at a boardroom table and a Fijian Indian proudly announced to the board members that he was sitting beside 'the Reverend John Wear Burton's grand-daughter'.[6]

Initially based in Suva, Jack took up work at Nausori, in the Rewa River sugar-growing area, one of the largest Indian settlements some 22 miles by river launch from Suva. He and Florence lived in a small cottage on ground leased from the Colonial Sugar Refinery (CSR), which had a large mill on the bank of the wide Rewa River. Later a house was built for them on the other side of the river at nearby Davuilevu where Jack pioneered an orphanage and girls' home, Dilkusha, and initiated technical and industrial training.

Jack was appalled by the conditions provided for Indian indentured labourers who had been shipped to the islands by Fiji's British colonial rulers between 1879 and 1916 to work on Fiji's sugar cane plantations. Sugar planters, who had secured large tracts of the richest land in the

---

6   Kanti Jinna, OAM, Vice President of Hindu Council of Australia. He is a Fijian-born Gujarati who, prior to migrating to Australia and arriving in Canberra 36 years ago, had been chief national librarian of Fiji and whom we thank for providing material to assist us with this book.

colony, had looked to India, from where workers had migrated to the West Indies and to South Africa, for labourers willing and able to toil on steamy plantations for a pittance. They were promised a shilling for each completed 'task' that a European overseer might reasonably expect them to complete within an eight-hour day. If a man were strong he might finish it by mid-afternoon; many were not strong and failed to compete the amount of work set. The sugar companies provided the labourers with miserable living accommodation and few amenities. Until the missionaries came, there had been no provision for education; the children 'ran wild' while their fathers and mothers were at work in the cane fields, until they were old enough to work too.[7] The labourers were indentured to a plantation for five years, after which they were 'free' to take up land for themselves or engage in other occupations for a further period of five years. They could then, if they so chose, accept a passage-paid return to India. Few did. Jack turned his energy into a long-running campaign to end the exploitative migration from India. The opposition of wealthy plantation owners to Jack's mission made his wife's life difficult. Florence was ostracised from the European community whose livelihoods were tied up with the sugar industry and enjoyed access to cheap and regular labour. Florence, nevertheless, supported and encouraged her husband's work. She assisted in alleviating the sickness of the Indian people and mothering orphaned children.

Towards the end of their stay in Fiji, Jack travelled to India to recruit Christian teachers and, while there, spoke to influential people to alert their formative leaders to the evils of indenture in Fiji. By this time, he spoke Hindustani, and went about learning as much as he could of Indian life and custom and philosophy. His direct exposure to India made him even more confrontational and less pro-British Empire than before.[8]

When Jack returned to New Zealand, he wrote a long illustrated pamphlet, *Our Indian Work in Fiji*, the first of many works in which he drew attention to the poor working conditions of the indentured labourers in Fiji. It was followed by a more substantial book, *The Fiji of Today*, which exposed the abuses of the indenture system.[9] His book shocked the governor of the colony, who criticised it in a Legislative Council paper. Historian Gregory

---

7   Burton, 'The Weaver's Shuttle', 55.
8   Burton, 'The Weaver's Shuttle', 162.
9   John W. Burton, *Our Indian Work in Fiji* (Suva: Fiji, 1909) reprinted in almost identical form in John W. Burton, *The Fiji of Today* (London: Charles H. Kelly, 1910).

Pemberton found that the Colonial Office wanted to ban the book, but recognised that Jack's assertions were supported by evidence.[10] Pemberton thought it a 'nice irony' that another 'colonial administration', notably the Menzies Government in Australia, would later consider banning the young John Burton's first book, *The Alternative*.[11] It 'seems like stirring the possum runs in the family', Pemberton noted in a letter to the family.

Jack's book, though controversial, was influential and sold well in Britain, Australia and India. War broke out in 1914 and printing of a new edition was deferred, but the disclosures in it had already caused widespread indignation, in India in particular. One of India's most distinguished men of letters, Banarsidas Chaturvedi, read the book and, impressed, wrote to Jack who had by this time moved to Australia. Chaturvedi made contact with Mahatma Gandhi, who had already opposed indenture in South Africa and Mauritius. Author John Garrett suggests that, in response, Gandhi 'conspired' with Chaturvedi to send Anglican clergyman Charles Freer Andrews and the Reverend 'Willie' Pearson from India to Fiji in 1915 to investigate Jack's claims about the condition of Indian indentured labour in Fiji.[12] On their return, they wrote a joint report strongly condemning the indenture system as leading inevitably to moral degradation.[13]

On their outward and inward journeys, Andrews and Pearson were guests of the Burtons at their home in East Malvern in Victoria where the family then lived. On one visit they joined the family in their Christmas festivities. Andrews, a bachelor, carried baby John around and played with the older children.[14] Jack's oldest, Rewa, recalled that on one of their visits Andrews entertained the children by reading *Alice in Wonderland* while they were supposed to sit quietly on a rug on the lawn. As a young child she struggled to control John and their baby sister Ruth who, unaware of the historic moment, were restless and bored with 'the rather tedious academic Oxford voice'.[15]

---

10 Pemberton, 'John Burton: The Heretic', 101.
11 Pemberton, 'John Burton: The Heretic', 102. The book Pemberton referred to was: J. W. Burton, *The Alternative: A Dynamic Approach to Our Relations with Asia* (Sydney: Morgans Publications, 1954).
12 John Garrett, *Footsteps in the Sea: Christianity in Oceania to World War II* (Suva and Geneva: WCC Publications, Institute of the South Pacific in association with World Council of Churches, 1992), 161.
13 C. F. Andrews and W. W. Pearson, *Report on Indentured Labour in Fiji: An Independent Enquiry* (Calcutta: Star Printing Works, 1916).
14 Burton, 'The Weaver's Shuttle', 72.
15 Rewa Newman's unpublished memoir, 4, Burton Snr family collection.

Jack tells in his autobiography that Andrews spoke out against CSR and its general manager, Edward Knox. The clash of Andrews and Burton with CSR, which was not willing to let go of its reliance on indentured labour, inevitably led to divided opinions within the Methodist Mission in both Australia and Fiji. In meetings of the mission board in Sydney, some Methodists protested about help given to Andrews by missionaries in Fiji.[16] CSR was influential in the Fijian economy and the government. Methodist missionaries looked to the government for support and subsidy for their work, especially their schools, causing a co-dependence on CSR's activity in Fiji. Nevertheless, demonstrations led by Gandhi in the streets of India finally compelled the British to end indentured labour in Fiji in 1916. Andrews and Pearson's intervention and Andrews's continued agitation helped to terminate the indenture system entirely in 1920.[17] Jack acknowledged that their report resulted in every Fijian Indian becoming free to live his own life in his own way.[18] In turn, Andrews acknowledged that Jack's book was a precipitating force. He wrote:

> I do feel very strongly that your book (the 'Fiji of Today') was the pioneer and did the pioneer work, and it is due to that book perhaps more than to any other single cause that the whole indenture system was shown up in its proper light.[19]

Indian communities in Fiji felt the same way. Jack was presented with a letter of gratitude on 14 August 1924 signed on parchment on behalf of the Indian community of Lautoka and another, on 24 August 1924, signed for and on behalf of the Indian community of Levuka.[20] As recently as 2019, an eminent Fijian lawyer acknowledged Jack's role in ending the indenture system.[21]

In 1911, after nine years in Fiji, the family returned to the New Plymouth Circuit in New Zealand because of the ill-health of Florence and one of their daughters. There, the growing family was happy. Jack's horse and carriage was replaced with a motorcycle on which he did his parish visits. His two daughters, Florence, who became known as Rewa to avoid

---

16 Garrett, *Footsteps in the Sea*, 162.
17 Garrett, *Footsteps in the Sea*, 163.
18 Burton, 'The Weaver's Shuttle', 72.
19 Letter Andrews to the Conference Secretary for Foreign Missions for Victoria, quoted by the Rev. J. W. Burton, 'India in Fiji', *Missionary Review* (Sydney), 4 September 1916, 10.
20 Originals held in Burton Snr family collection.
21 Nazhat Shameem, 2 October 2019, former judge and current Ambassador for Fiji at Geneva on the finale of the 150th birth anniversary of Mahatma Gandhi.

confusion with her mother, and Clare, later rode in a red-painted sidecar, woolly caps pulled down over their ears. Clare and third-born Nancy were given the middle names of Rewa Wear, named after the River Wear in Yorkshire and the Rewa River in Fiji (also, strangely, anagrams of each other). The middle name Rewa was dropped when John was born and he and his baby sister Ruth were each given the one middle name of Wear.

In 1914, Jack was appointed secretary of the Overseas Missions Department in Victoria and transferred to Melbourne, where he became the conference foreign mission secretary for Victoria and Tasmania, a position he held for a decade. During this time, he completed his degree and gained his master of arts degree with honours in the School of Philosophy – and bought his first car, a Bianci. Inheriting mechanical abilities from his father, he used to take the engine of his much-loved car apart and do most of his own repair work.

The Burton family, Melbourne, c. 1918.
Left to right: Clare, John, Jack, Rewa, Florence with Ruth on her knee and Nancy.
Source: Family collection, courtesy Leanne Akers.

Jack wrote about the church's work in the Pacific and proclaimed 'there is something in the genius of Methodism which fits peculiarly well into the life of simple peoples such as those we have in the Pacific'.[22] He went on to say that everyone has one talent or another they could contribute to bettering society and that there was something for all to do: 'We thus teach the native people to minister to one another, and thus they are led to feel that the Church belongs to them, and they have responsibility for its welfare.'

John, our father, was born in Kerford Street, Caulfield, Melbourne, on 2 March 1915, Jack and Florence's only son. Ruth, the youngest, followed in 1917. In 1918, Jack went to London to help with the demobilisation of the Australian armed forces. On his return, the family moved to Auburn in Melbourne where young John attended Scotch College at six years of age. In 1923 the family moved to Burwood in Sydney for Jack to take up an organising position at the headquarters of the Methodist Missionary. John transferred to Newington College, Sydney, in 1924. He twice repeated a year, having suffered from changing schools and finding it difficult to follow what went on in class; school was 'quite boring', he told us, admitting he had an 'aversion to facts and details'.[23]

In 1926, Jack was appointed general secretary of the Foreign Mission Society of Australasia. The following year he visited the mission over which Thomas Webb was in charge in Arnhem Land, Northern Territory. Jack gained a positive regard for Aboriginal people and their culture from this experience and influenced Webb in initiating changes in the mission.[24] In February 1931, Jack was elected president of the Methodist Conference. His jurisdiction stretched from north India along the north Australian coast from Darwin to the Gulf of Carpentaria, down through Papua and New Guinea to Fiji, Samoa and the little Kingdom of Tonga. His wife, Florence, was actively interested in world affairs, travelled extensively with Jack and made a contribution to the life of the church in her own right. She inaugurated the Methodist Women's Federation and was its first president. Florence had a strong personality, a high intellect and exerted considerable influence over her children. She died in 1953, in Sydney.

---

22 Burton, *Papua for Christ*, 75.
23 John Wear Burton, 'Oral History Project notes', 2, undated [c. 1995] in preparation for interview by Michael J. Wilson, 23 August 1995, Australian Diplomacy 1950–1990 Oral History Project, NLA, TRC 2981/23, held on Burton family file.
24 Burton's work in the Northern Territory is well documented by John Kadiba, 'The Methodist Mission and the Emerging Aboriginal Church in Arnhem Land 1916–1977' (PhD diss., Northern Territory University, 1998).

4. JOHN'S FATHER

John with his mother Florence and unidentified visitors to their Melbourne home, c. 1916.
Source: Family collection, courtesy Leanne Akers.

As a child, John was used to Pacific Islanders, Asians and Aborigines often visiting their home. He became aware of the importance of his missionary father's work. He listened to his father's conversations about past activities and current concerns. He was impressed by stories, for example, that missionary activity was to teach 'natives' how to build houses, boats and furniture, and generally to improve their quality of life. It was primarily this, not religious indoctrination, that caused John initially to want to pursue such work himself through the church. Religion was practised in the family, 'but in a matter-of-fact way that did not lead to discussion of it', he said. 'I guess this practical atmosphere was an important influence and probably accounts for [my] later interests.'[25] From research of my grandfather's life, it is clear to me that Jack's missionary story is one of what we might describe today as a social 'disrupter'. John talked of his father being a 'welfare socialist'. Jack's concern for the human needs of people and communities, I surmise, is perhaps the major influence that John absorbed.

---

25   Burton, 'Oral History Project notes', 2, Burton family file.

5
Embracing opportunities

John found his work in the post office in 1937 uninspiring: 'changing cards from one box to another', as he described it. He said that when he objected to the menial task he was smartly put in his place. Colleague and later diplomat Colin Moodie, who in the same year was fortunate enough to obtain a position as a graduate clerk in the Department of External Affairs, heard otherwise. John 'was said to have promoted a reform in the mail system', he recalled.[1] That fits with the father we came to know; there was nothing much he came across in and out of the public service that he did not try to change.

Opportunities came his way. Towards the end of 1937, aided by his impressive first-class honours degree in economics, John received an offer of a position in the Department of Commerce in Canberra. From there he progressed in the public service by being 'head hunted', though not without causing controversy at an early stage of his working life, partly by reason of his young age. He would boast later that his first job was the only one he had to apply for, thereafter 'accidents' determined his whole future career.[2] People he happened to know and chance events directed his course.

---

1   Colin Moodie, Memoir of Colin Moodie, between approximately 1990 and 2000, NLA, MS Acc13.173, 26.
2   Burton, 'Oral History Project notes', 2, Burton family file.

PERSONS OF INTEREST

From Hotel Kurrajong, Barton, where John first lived in Canberra, he walked to West Block where he worked, 'shooing sheep away in front of me as I walked'.[3] These were days when some public servants rode their horses to work, including a former head of External Affairs, Roy Hodgson. Some brought in their dogs and seated them under their desks while they worked. In March 1938, John was promoted and in his new position he was asked to report on Australian economic events to the Australian trade commissioners overseas who needed to be informed about what was going on at home. There was then very limited radio news, and all but the local newspaper took days to arrive. The *Canberra Times*, reliant on telegram and cable communications for news, was the main source of reliable domestic and foreign news. It sometimes comprised as many as four pages, he recalled. He returned to his Sydney home some weekends and on others, particularly from June 1938 when John and his university friend Parker moved into a flat together, Cecily visited him in Canberra.

John and Parker's flat was in Elimatta Street, Braddon, close enough to walk to Civic, the town centre, where they could buy groceries. Parker had moved to Canberra in 1938 on being appointed an administrative officer at the Canberra University College. The two bachelors, so very different in personality, bonded. Parker was more open with his feelings, softly spoken, always polite and so much more predictable than John, as Cecily would come to learn. The men shared the weekly rent of 1 pound and 15 shillings (£1 15s) and other expenses. Parker was a meticulous record keeper and kept a small black leather-bound booklet in which he noted every item of expenditure they incurred. At the end of each week he calculated to the penny what one owed the other. John, on the occasion he assumed this task, did it with minimal detail and not so neatly. They had an item for 'capital equipment' in their first week of purchases, which included a rubbish tin that cost 8 shillings and 11 pence (8s 11d) and a table cloth for 2 shillings. Food items such as potatoes were 6 pence (6d) a week, and butter was 1s 7d. One of the bachelors, at least, embraced cooking – the notebook records the purchase of a pie dish. John also bought a bicycle so that he could cycle across the Molongo River to work.[4]

---

3   Canberra, 11 August 1997, the occasion being the launch by Jack Waterford of his book *Violence Explained: The Sources of Conflict, Violence and Crime and Their Provention* (Manchester: Manchester University Press, 1997) in the office of the *Canberra Times*.
4   R. S. Parker papers, NLA, MS 8200, box 46, file 189, booklet 1938.

John's work went well for a time. Then, in August that year, someone decided that his reports to the trade commissioners were too 'left-wing' in thinking, or so he was told when his superior carpeted him. He was upset and travelled back to Sydney that weekend to see Cecily. He wept on the way, fearing for his job. A letter was waiting for him, however, when he arrived at his parents' home in the suburb of Roseville where his family then lived. It was an invitation to him to join the Statistician's Branch of the department. It informed him that he had won a cadetship and had been selected to go to London for a two-year course of postgraduate training in business administration at the London School of Economics – all paid for by the Australian Public Service. He was the first 'cadet' to be granted the newly established scholarship. It offered the opportunity of a lifetime, and an escape from any action over his job performance. His tears dried. It was an easy decision to make, but for one matter – Cecily. John asked her to join him and marry him in London. She did not decline and nor did she accept; her response was not the enthusiastic one he had hoped for.

John returned to Canberra to pack up. 'Dear Big Boy,' he scrawled in a pencilled letter he left for Robert, 'You won't forget the bike at Williams. £3 I asked. Seem to be a few collars missing – may be at laundry.' After warning Parker that 'Etty is expecting you to go to the Forestry Ball – watch her!' he wrote, almost as an aside, 'I am studying International Trade – Empire Trade – Australian markets … Fancy me doing International Trade – oh well!' Then back to the matter of the rubbish tin outside the flat, which he directed Parker to deal with: 'It belongs to the firm. Don't leave it!' He also apologised to the flatmate he was abandoning: 'Has been a bloody awful rush this week. Sorry I have left flat in such a mess. Love JWB'. From his parents' home in Sydney he wrote again to 'Big Boy' on a new portable typewriter. He sent his love 'to the harem', adding, 'but more to Helen than Ethel! She made me feel that she is a bit repressed when I was there – or not repressed enough. But don't tell her that …'.[5]

---

5   R. S. Parker papers, NLA, MS 8200, box 46, folder 190, undated.

PERSONS OF INTEREST

Cecily working in market research, Sydney, 1938.
Source: Family collection.

Cecily could not bring herself to accept John's proposal to marry him and accompany him to London. He had continually pressed her to marry him over five years of courtship while she worried whether he was the right man for her. Now she wanted to join him but knew that, in her own interest, she should not. Instead, she aimlessly spent the whole of 1938 in a variety of work. She did IQ testing at the Children's Court, some market research and tutored English to schoolgirls, with no clear plans for a career. At an earlier stage she had considered being a doctor like her father but was put off the idea by taking a look at the images of surgery in her father's medical books. In her spare time she played the piano, did some dressmaking and learned typing and shorthand. In June 1938, her grandfather, Ernest Fletcher, was killed when a car knocked him down on Parramatta Road. Another family loss.

On 8 September 1938, then, John departed without Cecily for London by the P&O liner RMS *Strathaird*. On board 'Friday, near Equator', he posted a letter to his friend Robert: 'I hope you have the women under control, especially Ethel who I found was apt to lead young men astray.'[6] He missed Cecily terribly and kept urging her to join him but she was reluctant to go to England if she was unemployed, because his income was insufficient to support them both. There had been 'no heart-thrills on board', John told Parker, and so he had had a good rest, but it was 'Bloody Hell' without Cecily, he admitted. He perceived she was overly influenced by her family's middle-class attitudes. 'But what can I do?' he wrote. 'Poor dear is so oppressed by public opinion she cannot decide. Give her some support!'[7]

John arrived in London in early October. War was looming, and Chamberlain had already returned from his two 'appeasement' mission meetings with Hitler. The Australian high commissioner, Stanley (later Lord) Bruce, supported Chamberlain's peace efforts to find a compromise with Hitler.[8] John had a lot to think about. He was given a room in Australia House, now a heritage-listed building and a prominent landmark on the Strand – an indication of the strength of Australia's relationship with Britain. It was within walking distance of the London School of Economics (LSE) where he would commence a two-year master's degree

---

6   R. S. Parker papers, NLA, MS 8200, box 46, file 190.
7   R. S. Parker papers, NLA, MS 8200, box 46, file 190, in a postscript to an undated letter written around November 1938.
8   David Lee, *Stanley Melbourne Bruce: Australian Internationalist* (London: Continuum International Publishing Group, 2010), 126.

under the supervision of economist Lionel Robbins, later Lord Robbins. John was also expected to work on some Australian diplomatic activities. John's job and studies kept him busy. He worked for a time for the high commissioner's office on problems relating to food supplies. Robbins was impressed with John's academic work and suggested that he convert his master's thesis into a PhD. John agreed and worked on his thesis for his doctorate on trade policy.[9] Despite LSE's left-leaning origins, Robbins was 'a conservative laissez-faire economist', certainly more conservative than outspoken LSE socialist professor of economics Harold Laski.[10] John was impressed when he heard Laski speak, but in correspondence with Parker, John spoke mainly about Robbins's influence on his work, not that of Laski. Despite their different political philosophies, Robbins strongly supported John's research to define what government interventions were required to promote economic development and those that were dysfunctional and restrictive.

John rowed for recreation and, in the style of a true Englishman, wore a black coat and hat (black because he found London so filthy that he had to 'change three collars in one day which were not merely dirty, but black'), let his hair grow long and brushed it right back, wore gloves but stopped short of having a stick.[11] He and Cecily corresponded. She sent John pieces she wrote on psychology, a subject she was interested in – perhaps the beginning of committing her introspective thoughts to paper. There were early signs that John appreciated Cecily's intelligence and fine gift for language but that his ego compromised his ability to praise her. We glean from a letter John wrote to Parker that he had shared one of Cecily's written pieces with him. Parker liked it and John agreed, saying: 'I thought it was good – after I revised it! See the combination? I will turn out some ideas for a thesis but she will have to write it.'[12]

Parker was John's closest mate. John sought his comments on his thesis and the two exchanged ideas on political and economic theories and debated assumptions behind the current trade policies that drove them. 'You are

---

9   Its working title became 'A study of the origins of restricted intervention, its significance as a case of mal-adjustment in protective structure, unemployment and international disharmonies of economic interest'.
10 John's description of Robbins, 'Oral History Project notes', 4, Burton family file. For a history of the LSE, see Joan Abse, ed., *My LSE* (London: Robson, 1977).
11 R. S. Parker papers, NLA, MS 8200, box 46, file 190, 17 November 1938, 3. This file contains many letters about John's observations on London, English life, the looming war, economic and trade policies, and socialism.
12 R. S. Parker papers, NLA, MS 8200, box 46, file 190, 21 October 1938.

the one person (besides the wife!) who catches on to my all too vague concepts,' John told Parker. Their correspondence, however, suggests that John was more interested in Parker's response to his work, than John was in responding to the latter's detailed intellectual ruminations.

Cecily's indecision about joining John frustrated him. She told him she wanted to come – 'a whole lot' – and she decided she would, but she was prevented by parental affection, as John expressed it to Parker, 'for the fear that I shall not be able to make the most of £350' (his salary). She did not want to come until she had a return fare and enough cash to last while she was unemployed. 'Of course all very damned reasonable but a bloody bother,' he wrote to his friend. 'I have been wanting a woman a good deal – it gives you a nasty feeling to be seeing things and going places and not sharing it with the wife.'[13] Indeed, amid the intellectual exchanges of John and Parker, the two young men always returned to matters of the heart. Poor Etty was the subject of much discussion. John wrote:

> Glad Etty is looking after you – I was not in the least concerned and don't think for one moment that a man with *reasonable* tastes could fall for such a woman – but that is just as well. I have been most terribly faithful though out quite a lot. What fools we men are.[14]

Parker escaped Ethel. He married Nancy Bolton the following year on 30 August. John eventually won over Cecily. Bored and restless and finding that there was not much for her at home, Cecily felt the tug to join John. On 8 January 1939, she cabled him to say she was coming. John wrote to Parker the same day '– these women. I received a letter yesterday asking what I thought about the idea!'[15]

First her mother then it was her father who did not want Cecily to follow John to London to marry him. Her father wanted her to stay home and look after him. Cecily resisted. He had the assistance of a housekeeper as well as his other daughters, and she and John had made wedding plans for March 1939. Then, before Cecily left for London, her father announced he was to marry again, the widow of a colleague. Cecily was shocked but felt vindicated. What if she had put off her own marriage?[16] Of course,

---

13   R. S. Parker papers, NLA, MS 8200, box 46, file 190, undated.
14   R. S. Parker papers, NLA, MS 8200, box 46, undated.
15   R. S. Parker papers, NLA, MS 8200, box 46, file 190, 8 January 1939.
16   *Cecily*, 29.

her decision to leave her father might have hastened his decision to remarry. He was a man who, throughout his medical career, had domestic services provided by his wife or daughters and they had been there for him emotionally. His other two daughters would soon be approaching marrying age – a good reason for him to marry again. Cecily's father moved into the Double Bay home of his new wife, Alison Harris, and returned to Petersham each day to his practice. Cecily was relieved that he could not tug at her soul as her mother had, and she set off for England optimistic about her new life.

Looking back, Cecily reflected on her mother's opposition to her marrying John. 'He won't make you happy,' she urged. 'She was quite right,' Cecily later conceded, knowing even at the time that she would be unhappy with him, but she also knew that she couldn't 'not get married' to John.[17] She wanted to be with him, around him and loved by him, and, she later explained, she already was unhappy and 'didn't have any conception of life being otherwise'.[18] This expression of such sadness warranted us exploring Cecily's younger life. It helped us understand why she spent so much time trying to get John to understand her.

---

17 *Cecily*, 27.
18 *Cecily*, 27.

6

Paradise lost

Cecily was the firstborn of Muriel Bowden Nixon (née Fletcher) and Robert James Nixon. Born on 4 December 1916, she later told us: 'I like those numbers – eight fours. It was a Monday. I looked at my perpetual calendar.'[1] She arrived in what she thought must have been the joyous early years of her parents' marriage when they were living in Abermain, a small town on the New South Wales coalfields, about 3 miles west of Kurri Kurri. Her father worked there as a newly fledged doctor. She was a further joy to them – wanted and welcomed. They felt proud and fulfilled. She was warm and comfortable, loved, played with, responded to.

Her father, Robert, had decided at the age of 20 to train as a doctor, but he had first to obtain his 'Junior' and 'Senior' school certificates (equivalent to the Intermediate and Leaving). To do so, he enrolled in the Woodford Academy in the Blue Mountains and obtained both in little over one year. He commenced medical studies at the age of 21 and graduated in 1910. He completed his residency at Prince Alfred Hospital in Sydney where he met Muriel. She was a well-regarded nurse, having been head nurse at Grenfell Hospital in 1913 where a considerable amount of surgical work was done. In 1915, he married Muriel and commenced practice at Abermain. When Cecily was three months old, the family moved to Petersham, a western suburb of Sydney, and eventually into a large 1870s two-storey brick and cedar home from where her father ran his general practice. His medical career was interrupted when he served in the armed forces, returning in 1918 to his medical practice. He became honorary surgeon at Lewisham Hospital in 1927, and he practised from his home

---

1   *Cecily*, 13. Where not otherwise referenced, information in this chapter has been drawn from Cecily's letters to me in August 1990 reproduced in *Cecily* (1994).

for the rest of his life as a general practitioner and general surgeon. A great deal of Robert's surgery work was in skin grafting, then experimental, and for which innovative work he earned a wide reputation.

Cecily and her mother, Sydney, 1917.
Source: Family collection.

6. PARADISE LOST

Cecily wrote in 1990: 'For nearly two years I lived in something like paradise.'[2] Her perception that she was adored by her parents as a baby was 'reflected back to me from my parents' faces'.[3] Her feeling of being special, however, was short-lived. Cecily claimed to have had a strong recall of a deep feeling of rejection by her mother and of feeling inadequate by the time she was two. She attributed the source of these feelings to the sudden appearance of her sister Eleanor: 'And where was paradise then? Gone! I no longer had my mother, my parents to myself.'[4] She recalled this so strongly that she later told us that ever since she was a small child she had felt that she was an orphan and did not really have any parents.

By no means was Cecily's childhood traumatic and she did recall things that made her happy. Nevertheless, she never left her past behind and her perception that her poor and unsatisfactory relationship with her mother had commenced when she was a tiny child never faded. She came to believe that her mother found Cecily to be a troublesome young child who tried to reclaim her former position and have her baby sister banished. She knew her parents did not understand how she felt, because otherwise they would have sent her sister, this foreigner, back to where she came from.

Eventually Cecily had to accept disapproval, anger and punishment – new experiences for her, and a living nightmare. Her doting parents were monsters, especially her mother who lost patience with her. Angels had turned into devils, heaven had turned into hell, overnight. She expressed this in her poem entitled 'The Witch Mother' in 1988:

> The witch mother
> scratches my skin,
> enters,
> takes up residence,
> skates around my innards,
> and screams from inside me.
> Helpless I suffer,
> restless I stagger,
> from one place to another.[5]

---

2   *Cecily*, 5.
3   *Cecily*, 5.
4   *Cecily*, 13–14.
5   All of Cecily's poetry quoted in this book have been extracted from a poetry collection of her work, held on Cecily family file.

From left to right, Pam, Cecily and Eleanor Nixon, Sydney, c. 1920.
Source: Family collection.

In turn, Cecily believed that her parents' angelic baby became a monster making their life hell. A governess arrived to help keep peace at home, which somewhat mollified her. Cecily could neither trust nor forgive her mother.

At two and a half Cecily was taken 'out of the way' by her governess each day to nursery school. Her enlightened mother chose a Montessori school – probably the only one to take such a young child in those days. She loved it: paradise again, where there were no babies, no rivals, only other children – all old enough to talk to her and play with her – and grown-up guardian angels. No one was angry and Cecily was never chided. Cecily enjoyed playing and working with shapes, colours, textures and music at school. She loved to draw and paint, to dance and sing, being busy and at rest. She could choose what she wanted to play with or learn about, and felt proud putting things away tidily when she had finished with them. She loved being a bit late for the train because she and her governess had to jump into the first available carriage, obliged to sit second class where the seats were of woven cane. She loved their colour and texture and the pattern of weaving.

The Montessori school was a place of peace, harmony, gentleness, colour and order that stimulated the children's mind and senses. It became a great influence on Cecily's life. She stayed until she was about six, during which time she fell in love with a little boy called Bob. Her plan to capture him as her dance partner was ingenious. The children were all to pick a coloured cap from a basket, and they were to dance with the child who held the same coloured cap. Cecily picked a red cap, and kept her fingers on its twin, until Bob came to choose his, when she let it go. She had a clear memory of him, unaffected by photographs or stories told to her later. When, 50 years later, she learned that he was working in Papua New Guinea, she wrote to him and he replied, but she did not find out more about how he had reacted to her feminine wiles at school.

When Eleanor turned two and a half or three she joined Cecily at school. By then their younger sister Pamela was born and brother, Peter, was yet to come. Cecily was learning that while paradise did not belong to her alone, it could be shared. This shared contentment she accepted naturally, as though she had always known that it existed somewhere. Her behaviour improved and, remarkably, her mother's did too. But a scarring rift between them remained. Cecily adored her father, but it was her mother's strong personality that had lasting impact on Cecily's emotional development. Robert was busy and relied on Muriel to manage the household. However, Muriel was a strong and independent woman with modern ideas – so much so that when the children were young and her husband was fully occupied with his career, she took herself abroad for six months, leaving the household in the care of a housekeeper. A smiling photograph of her on the ship's deck, about to leave her young family, suggests that she had a strong view of her own entitlement. Sturdy shoes, skirt and striped top, her black hair neatly groomed, she looked ready for adventure, free of responsibility. Her youngest, Peter, was just old enough to recall her return – the abandonment, at barely three years old, never forgotten. At age 93, free of guilt, he told us, 'I didn't like her'.

Cecily attended Normanhurst, a private school with a regular curriculum and strong leadership, for most of her primary education. It began in a cottage in Bland Street in Ashfield, expanding into a two-storey house next door. Cecily knew it as 'The Cottage'. It was among the oldest private schools for girls in New South Wales, founded in 1882, and proud of the many brilliant students it produced. Here, her emotional responses were tested. On her first day, Cecily made a new class friend, Betty, who Cecily recalled as an 'angel figure' who had 'golden skin, golden-brown or brown-gold hair which hung straight …'. Sadly, Betty died before they entered upper school. At the end of first year in upper school Cecily won a volume of the complete works of Shakespeare, as a prize in English, given in memory of Betty, a treasure she kept for life. Then, another girl, Beryl, a small dark-haired child, died from tuberculosis. Next, when Cecily was in her teens, her Latin teacher, Miss Gallagher, died. Cecily did not know how to react. When she came home from school she told her mother that 'Giss' had died. Not knowing how to talk about death and feeling embarrassed, she delivered the news half laughing and half crying (without producing tears) because she knew it was sad. She had liked Miss Gallagher for her unusual ideas and sense of humour. She later reflected how confused she was and how little she knew about her emotions.

Benefiting from an excellent primary school education, Cecily learned about Greek myths and illustrated them. She was no artist and recalled crude drawings she created to accompany Pygmalion and Galatea. The myths stayed with her, perhaps symbolic to her in some way of coming truly alive, she suggested, or of idealism, of wishes coming true? Hans Christian Andersen's fairy story of Kai and Gerda and the Snow Queen also stayed with her. She remembered it as 'The Ice Queen', probably because Gerda saved her friend Kai when he was almost immobile on a frozen lake by the power of her love – kissing him and weeping warm tears on him, melting his heart. It was not dissimilar to the myths about people coming alive, she thought. Reflecting on her intrigue with the Snow Queen, Cecily felt that it said something about her, too. She remembered and dwelt on this fairy tale even in adulthood, in her search of understanding of herself. Literature and words entranced her. Once, when she referred to a 'galosher', someone corrected her, saying 'galosh'. It was an enlightening moment, making her think about words, and like them. There were subjects she did not like or excel at, like needlework. Her sewing teacher told her that her hemming was like cats' teeth.

The joys of learning and making friends and engaging in social life, however, did not improve Cecily's self-confidence. At primary school she 'felt foolish'. She did not know how to take teasing and always felt different. People expected her to behave in certain ways that she knew nothing about; she felt ignorant and innocent, in comparison with some of the girls. She later considered that she probably asked unexpected questions and thought in unusual ways – so that she felt that she did not fit in. Although nothing troubling happened at school, she perceived that she was not quite of their world, 'or of anyone else's, except perhaps my own'. Feeling 'different', which possibly many introverted people feel, became something she believed for the rest of her life. In 1988 when asked to pen a quick response after 'clustering' associations to the phrase 'Birds of a feather flock together' as a writing exercise, this emerged:

> Aloneness or comfort?
> Comfort from crowds?
> But I am an eagle
> and choose to be alone.
> Crowds are no comfort to me.
> How out of place I'd feel
> Even in a flock of eagles!

Cecily was an enigma. She expressed feelings of being a misfit at home and misunderstood by her mother in particular, yet she talked about so many happy times with her family. Her childhood was full. Two playful dogs, Mr Woozle and Kipper, formed a part of it, as did her father's A-model Ford and the many visitors they had with children who Cecily and her siblings played with. One of them, Humphrey, who she did not really like, asked eight-year-old Cecily if she would marry him. She replied, 'I suppose so'. Then, as an adult she wondered what this said about her and her expectations of happiness in life.

Cecily had been in the upper school at Normanhurst for one year when the school amalgamated in 1929 with another girls' school close by, 'Elmswood', and the school was run by the 'horrid Miss Miles and her sister Miss Elsie'.[6] They did away with the gymnasium, which Cecily saw as one of the disasters in her life. She played tennis at school but otherwise did not excel at sport, probably because she was young for her classes, and behind her cohort in height and strength as well as confidence. But she had loved the gym ropes and bars, the rings and the vaulting box. The school deteriorated and many of Cecily's friends left to go elsewhere. Her leaving pass was abysmal in her view, apart from an 'A' in English because she enjoyed it and learning Latin and Greek roots. She tried to squeeze out a few tears to show remorse, but felt nothing much. With some coaching she managed to matriculate – just – and went on to university the next year.

---

6   *Cecily*, 20.

The rift between Cecily and Muriel never closed. Cecily found her father by contrast gentle, less assertive than her mother, and more loveable. Muriel seemed not to understand how to deal with sensitive and introverted Cecily, so differently constructed emotionally than she. Mother and child suffered all their lives from each never understanding the rejection by the other. The depth of Cecily's feelings about her mother are revealed in another poem, 'Forgiveness', which she wrote in 1988, the first stanza from which reads:

> But I forgive you, mother,
> I forgive you
> because now I need you,
> and I need you to be
> just as you were, because –
> because of you, I am myself.

In the same year, she also wrote 'Paradox':

> Your face means death – and life.
> You gave me life, and yet
> you killed me.
> You loved me,
> and you took away from me
> all that I had.
> You haunt me,
> because I love you.
> I was wounded.

Had Cecily not experienced paradise at such an early stage, its comparison with her happiness in other stages of her life would not have been so stark – like one who is born colour-blind and does not know the brilliance of colours never seen. Cecily wanted to retain the early bliss of being loved and understood. It might be around the next corner, but finding it eluded her and her later childhood feelings of being misunderstood perpetuated well into adulthood. For the whole of her life Cecily seemed to feel that others tried to capture her soul. After her mother died and her father had embarked on a new life with a new wife, Cecily might have then gained control of her life had she not lost her emotional tug-of-war with John. Two complex people drawn to each other, neither ever fully understanding the other's vulnerabilities, embarked on a most unusual life together.

7

Honeymoon in dangerous times

The Dutch cargo boat, the *Grootekerk*, on which Cecily travelled to join John, fell behind schedule. Fearing she would not get to London in time for her marriage to John and their planned honeymoon, she left the boat at Bordeaux and travelled overland to England. How she arranged this and by what means she travelled we did not learn. Anyway, she was too late. John had taken a fortnight's leave for their honeymoon, and as Cecily did not make it, he used his leave to travel around England with a group of friends.

The couple had not planned an elaborate wedding and their scheduled registry office ceremony was deferred to coincide with John's one-day leave on Anzac Day. On 24 April 1939, coincidentally, the date of John's own parents' wedding, Cecily and John married in a registry office in South Kensington. Cecily's green eyes were radiant and her smile large under an upturned brim hat. Her jacket hung softly over a light woollen top. John's thick, dark hair was combed back and his full lips and soft blue-grey eyes behind tortoiseshell glasses gave him a boyish look. He smiled sometimes, not broadly, and rarely broke into a laugh. Cecily's aunt Gertrude and two male friends of John's made up the few present. As elderly as Gertrude was, her character could not be contained and John enjoyed her. They spent their honeyoon night in a village pub out of London. A few days later, Gertrude hosted a reception for them and a few friends at Gertrude's London club where they toasted with sherry and cut into a magnificent wedding cake.

'Just Married', Cecily and John, London, April 1939.
Source: Family collection.

'The wedding party', John and Cecily's aunt Gertrude and a friend, London, April 1939.
Source: Family collection.

John and Cecily had as good as eloped so far as John's family was concerned. They were less than impressed. His youngest sister Ruth, in a letter to her elder sister Rewa dated 11 May, reported:

> Well my dear I have just been writing to John and Cecily and it is a relief to turn to you! They were married at Kensington in a Registry Office and had a Sherry Party a few days later for their friends.
>
> Poor Mother and Daddy were laid low with shame about it. Mother was so distressed that she can't bear to write to them so muggins had to do it. They really are selfish and thoughtless little brats. We had no news at all until a day or two ago. The wedding was on the Monday and they did not write until the week-end.

John enjoyed being married. He wrote to his friend Parker saying that it was 'not bad is it?' and that he was getting spoiled – 'but the wife enjoys spoiling me so why worry'.[1]

In May and June 1939, part of John's duties was to advise the Australian representative to the International Wheat Conference in London. Despite this responsible work, he was in receipt only of a small scholarship allowance, about £7 a week. It did not allow for luxuries. Cecily took an office job conducting market research, and with her earnings they saved enough money to travel to Europe at last – the honeymoon they had not had.

The cloud on the horizon was the prospect of war. Looking back, it seems strange that the danger of war breaking out in Europe was not an apparent source of concern when Cecily discussed with John whether to join him in London at this time. Yet, as historian David Lee pointed out, while Chamberlain was pursing peace options, 'the British people quietly prepared for war; children were evacuated to the countryside and families queued for gas masks'.[2] Cecily became concerned war might break out while they were in Europe. John knew better. 'Don't worry,' he said, 'it will start a fortnight after we return!'[3] They arranged a trip to the Soviet Union and a return through Scandinavia, planning it to coincide with an international conference that John was to attend as an Australian delegate in Norway. Their desire to visit Russia became the source of quite some

---

1   R. S. Parker papers, NLA, MS 8200, box 46, file 190, undated.
2   Lee, *Stanley Melbourne Bruce*, 126.
3   *Cecily*, 32.

excitement to those mischief-makers of the twenty-first century who jumped at the chance to suggest that John's presence in Moscow was an opportunity for him to have been recruited by the Russians to spy for them. ASIO, too, found it an event worth recording, although nothing about it was found to be sinister.

So, why did our parents want to visit Russia? At the time, while not on the itinerary of general tourists, many Australian intellectuals made a point of visiting in the decades between the two World Wars. Also, at that time the Soviet Union promoted USSR in Britain as a place to visit for leisure and intellectual interest. The country became:

> an increasingly common destination for Western intellectuals drawn by the allure of a grandiose social experiment that seemed so much in contrast to the economic depression, social strife and political unrest overshadowing their lives at home. For most of those who travelled there – and certainly for Australians no less than others – the trip itself was an ideological gesture; for many it held the promise of a visit to the future.[4]

I cannot be sure whether it was John or Cecily who was most curious to visit the country. However, the visit would likely have been of interest to John in particular, being an economist whose work and studies concerned the impact of international trade restrictions. It is speculation on my part, but another influence on John is likely to have been the stories his own father brought back from his trip to Moscow in 1936. In 1937, his father gave an address to clergy on his experience in Russia that was published the following day in an article 'Some Impressions of Russia'.[5]

On 5 August 1939, Cecily and John departed by boat for Leningrad accompanied by other Australian tourists, including a nurse from Tasmania and a woman from Sydney, NSW. They arrived on 12 August and registered their tourist visa with the police. There was a lot to see in the city that was once, and is again, St Petersburg: the Hermitage collections, the Church of Spilled Blood, St Ivan's Tower and Cathedral, and grand palaces, although Cecily found the city to be dilapidated. They then travelled on to Moscow by train.

---

4   John McNair, 'Mary Poppins and the Soviet Pilgrimage: P. L. Travers's Moscow Excursion (1934)', *Portal: Journal of Multidisciplinary International Studies* 10, no. 1 (2013): 1–12.
5   The Rev. J. W. Burton, Sydney, 24 May 1937, delivered under the auspices of the Australian Society for the Promotion of Cultural Relations with the Peoples of the Soviet Union, published in *Australian Christian World* (Sydney), 25 June 1937, 7.

Cecily, now much better travelled and experienced, observed the communities she visited, as Wright had so impressively done when they travelled together two years earlier. Socially and culturally, Russia seemed to Cecily very advanced but, due to its policy of self-sufficiency, the people were short of many things – things that Cecily thought Australians would consider essential – although she thought the Russian people did not seem to mind. While the country was busy producing machinery and armaments and large buildings, it had a shortage of labour, such that there was no one to produce 'clothes, pins and saucepans', she noted in a letter to her family.[6] She was critical too, observing that while the architecture of some of the buildings was magnificent, little attention was paid to private housing and it seemed that even some of the Moscow population lived very poorly. She was impressed by the underground Metro railway, its efficiency and artistry and probably, then, one of the best in the world. The hotels were good but the factories were untidy and not the marvels they had been led to believe, displaying greater keenness on quantity than quality. In a letter Cecily wrote home from Moscow, she said that, despite the stories they had heard and believed before they arrived, they were not restrained from doing anything or going anywhere, other than taking photographs. The only other restriction that applied to tourists was a strict censorship of books and papers brought into the country. Theirs were examined but none were confiscated. In Moscow they visited a government shop where old clothes were bought and sold. Many tourists sold clothes for extra cash, although it was not possible to make large fortunes this way because roubles were not changeable back into foreign currency, and could only be used in Russia. John sold a worn out suit for 350 roubles (about £17 then, though not to the Russians because their exchange was controlled) and Cecily sold her 'swagger' top coat, which had cost her about £2 10s, for the equivalent of £25. With the sale of a couple of pairs of stockings and one or two other odds and ends, they made enough money to fly, rather than take a train, to Stockholm, buying themselves additional time to enjoy Sweden.[7]

---

6   Letter 27 August 1939, written from Hotel Norge, Bergen, Burton family file.
7   This first-hand contemporaneous account of Cecily's rebuts the allegations made by Rob Foot in 'The Curious Case of Dr John Burton', *Quadrant*, November 2013, that John was invited to Moscow while he was at the conference in Norway and, having no money to return to the UK, sold clothes to pay for his homebound fare. ASIO's records confirm Cecily's account that they were first in Russia and from there flew to Sweden; see NAA: A6119, 128, Dr John Wear Burton vol. 2, 39, in which it is also noted that, on John's return to Australia, he told a colleague that he sold his suit in Moscow to pay for the fares.

Having left Russia, Cecily wrote a full account to her family of her impressions of the country. She concluded that as long as the Soviet Government could do everything before its people got restless, the country would do alright. 'I don't think they will be able to,' she wrote, adding: 'It is a pity they should break down economically, when they are so highly developed in other ways. You know, all the social advantages, of course, a free medical service, proper holidays, good working conditions, rest homes, parts of culture, and so on.' She saw no evidence of the country becoming capitalised, but noted that there were large wage differences. 'They pay according to merit, and not yet according to needs as they hope to do eventually. Everyone has plenty of money, but there is not enough to buy with it.'[8]

In Sweden, they travelled to Gothenburg for a barge cruise on the Gota, leaving them time to travel to Norway to attend the international conference in Bergen on 27 August. In that time period, the Molotov-Ribbentrop German–Soviet Nonaggression Pact was agreed to. It was a dangerous time to be travelling to northern Europe.

Cecily found it strange going from Moscow to Stockholm, which then had just about the highest standard of living in the world and many of the social and cultural advantages of Russia. She concluded after two days in Sweden that it 'is an example of a well run capitalist system with a socially minded government'.[9] She decided that Sweden would be a delightful place to live with its efficiency and beautiful architecture. A widespread cooperative movement gave the people houses, food, clothing and other products at good prices and a return on the money they spent on cooperative produced goods. It was 'Swedish efficiency', she thought, that stood in the most direct contrast to Russia. In Stockholm, their comfort was enhanced by a variety of little gadgets and everything was perfectly arranged. In Russia, on the other hand, walls were cracked, lights were broken, baths were scratchy, floors squeaked, meals were slow, plugs were missing. They suffered a shortage of paper, including toilet paper, making things a bit difficult for them at times.

---

8   Letter, 27 August 1939.
9   Letter, 27 August 1939.

7. HONEYMOON IN DANGEROUS TIMES

The highlight of their trip, from Cecily's point of view, was the three glorious days in August they spent crossing Sweden to Gothenburg by the Gota canal. It was summer and the days were long. She and John alighted from the boat and walked along the canal beside it. She remembered it as a romantic time in their long-awaited honeymoon.

They then travelled across Norway by train to Bergen where the International Studies Conference that John was to attend was to be held. The conference was not due to end until 2 September. It commenced, but was aborted after two days because it became clear that war was about to break out. In that short time, John had, however, talked with two senior Japanese scholars who distributed prepared papers that outlined the consequence of British and other anti-depression policies that denied Japan access to raw materials and markets in South-East Asia. Meeting these scholars set John thinking and influenced the thesis he was developing. He had chosen the topic of restrictive trade and constructive intervention in anticipation of World War Two and adjusted its focus in anticipation of the Japanese joining the Axis Powers. Later, after decades of Australia's security agency, ASIO, shadowing him and recording his movements, he commented wryly that if ASIO officers had read his dissertation and been able to understand its implications, they would not have needed to develop such a large ASIO file on him! It was clear to John that the Japanese delegates were warning that the government of the small and heavily populated island of Japan would have no option but to join the enemy powers if British, French and other Colonial Powers were to pursue their 1930s depression policies of excluding Japan from access to raw materials and markets in the colonial territories of the Pacific and South-East Asia. John resolved to warn the Australian Government of this as soon as he could.

The delegates returned to London the following Wednesday, 30 August, on the first available ship. Germany invaded Poland on 1 September 1939. War was declared on 3 September. John had to return too, as he was recalled to Australia House to work on food supplies from Australia. He wanted Cecily to stay in Norway. She rejected the suggestion that they separate. With hindsight it was the right decision. Norway was later overrun by Germans. Instead, she went to stay with some of John's relatives in Yorkshire, near Bradford.

On his return to Australia House in London, John made a report to High Commissioner Bruce, foreshadowing that Japan would inevitably join Germany as a response to exclusion from markets. Bruce agreed with him about the importance of not provoking Japan. John later explained, 'We were negotiating long-term contracts with Britain for war-time supplies from Australia, and it seemed relevant to me to observe that trading patterns could change significantly if Japan were at war.'[10] Bruce cabled Prime Minister Robert Menzies who totally rejected the suggestion that 'Australia's close and loyal allies of the last war would join Hitler!' John said, 'As a junior official I was put in my place.'[11]

Cecily spent 10 days in Yorkshire. She did not like her hosts. The 'papa' of the family trapped her behind doors and tried to maul her. When she could, she retreated to enjoy solitude walking over the moors. War was anticipated and blackouts were ordered. Every night she walked in the dark to the local public telephone booth to ring John. Nothing happened; there was no war – only the 'phoney war' (as the period between Germany's invasion of Poland and then of France was described) – and she returned to London to join him. The threat of war meant that there were few joyous activities to do in London, so John and Cecily spent a lot of time together in a small rented room with a kitchen in a three-storey private house. John worked there and they both listened to the wireless – war news, war songs and British comedy shows. Cecily knew how to boil an egg but otherwise could not cook. It seems that Cecily's mother relied on the maid to cook, and the children were generally not allowed into the kitchen. John, with his boy scouts training and bachelor flatting experience, taught her how to grill lamb chops. London's winter of 1939 was bitter; their washed clothes froze stiff overnight. They both caught the flu and took turns to cook and look after each other, depending on who was feeling slightly better.

The 'phoney war' appeared to end in April 1940 when London moved to a higher alert.[12] The London School of Economics was evacuated to Cambridge and John and Cecily with it. There the school was provided with lecture theatres, a library, sports facilities, offices and lodgings. Cecily and John boarded with a woman who, Cecily was relieved to find, also provided their meals. There, despite their qualms, they enjoyed

---

10   Burton, 'Oral History Project notes', 3, Burton family file.
11   John W. Burton, 'Conflict Analysis: Its Past and Its Future (An Introspective Account)', 1994, Burton family file.
12   Abse, *My LSE*, 46.

several warm summer weeks in May. They explored the city and accepted invitations to afternoon teas. Cecily wandered around the town and by the river where she could lose herself under the blossoms and in the lushness of the green grass. It was light until 10 pm or so and sometimes she and John went punting on the river. Even John thought it fun, 'though I think all the young unmarrieds enjoy it more than we old things can tell', he told his friend Parker in a letter dated simply, 'The Day Belgium gave in' – 28 May 1940.[13]

John worked solely on his thesis while in Cambridge, supposedly to finish it, but he found work at this time almost impossible and he was not happy when Robbins, his supervisor, criticised aspects of his work. Cecily was nervous and wanted to keep busy. Rather than standing about and doing nothing to help in the event of an air raid, she volunteered as an ambulance driver. She learned to drive the heavy vehicle but she was only called on once or twice to drive it, in daylight and in the absence of any emergency.

Then came what they thought was the real thing. Sirens wailed at night accompanied by the thunder of bombers flying overhead. They woke, hearing the planes approach, closer and louder. Cecily started to shiver and shake and the closer they came the more she shook. Were they British planes going to bomb Europe, or German planes coming to bomb us, she would ask herself. Then, as they passed over, the noise faded, as did her shivering, and she would fall into a sound sleep. Sometimes, on the sound of sirens, they accompanied their landlady and others downstairs to shelter under the staircase. John appeared to Cecily not to be perturbed by the nightly events, although he helped her eat the chocolate she kept by her bedside to restore their energy that had drained away due to the frightening moments. It was a powerfully emotional experience, though no bombs were dropped while they were in Cambridge.

Back in London they went to another boarding house. They had their own room and shared a bathroom and toilet with others on their floor. John waited to hear whether he was to return to Canberra or stay in England. He had hoped he would be told to stay. Cecily hoped he would be called home. On the nights of real air-raid warnings, sirens would wail and all the residents would stumble to the cellar in the basement. Cecily's fear took a different form. Her teeth chattered uncontrollably

---

13   R. S. Parker papers, NLA, MS 8200, box 46, file 189.

as they descended the steps, while the English women simply chatted, carrying their cups of tea and their knitting as though nothing was out of the ordinary. Cecily sat, her teeth chattering loudly, until the noisy planes passed over and she felt safe again. She felt ashamed by her fear, even though it was hardly noticeable to others. She thought later that this physical reaction occurred, as with other emotions earlier in her life, because she could not acknowledge or express her fears, never felt them emotionally, and they were forced to show themselves through her body.

Cecily stood beside John at the telephone when the message they had been waiting for finally came. It was late June 1940. He was recalled home. They left London before bombs started to fall on the city; before the Blitz began.

8

The sinking of the *Arandora Star*

John decided they should journey home via the United States of America (USA). He wanted to visit his newly married sister Nancy on the West Coast. Cecily did not believe they had enough money to do this and, at the time, nobody was allowed to take more than 10 pounds out of England. John always seemed to live 'a halfpenny or sixpence beyond his income, believing that it would increase, or his financial needs would in some other way be provided for – which always seemed to happen', Cecily observed over the years.[1] They paid for everything in advance and counted on Nancy putting them up, for they had no spare money to stay anywhere else.

They obtained a passage on the British Cunard Line's *Samaria* that left from Liverpool on 29 June 1940, with 788 passengers bound for New York, escorted by a destroyer and a plane. Thirty miles behind them was Blue Star Line's *Arandora Star*. The two liners travelled in convoy. The fate of the two liners remained indelibly in Cecily's mind. The *Arandora Star* had been a luxury liner sailing from Southampton in the 1930s with a 400-passenger capacity. When war broke out, it was called up for trooping duties and refitted to carry 1,700 men. On board was a full complement of German and Italian prisoners of war, headed for Canadian internment camps. On the morning of day three, 2 July 1940, passengers on the *Samaria* noticed the absence of the *Arandora Star*. They were now off the north-west coast of Ireland, and the ship had last been seen across

---

1   *Cecily*, 39.

the clear flat waters behind them the evening before. No one on board the *Samaria* knew then quite what had happened, nor that their destroyer and escort plane had wheeled away to go to the missing ship's aid, but rumours circulated that submarines had been seen. The weather was now foggy and the *Samaria* went north for quite a way. Cecily found the trip frightening, as well as uncomfortable. Young children were riotous playing on the decks while their mothers sat in the deck chairs throughout the boat and chaos reigned. Cecily concluded that the women with children had left the children's nannies behind, and the mothers were not used to looking after them. What Cecily had not been made aware of, or forgot with time, was that among the nearly 800 passengers the *Samaria* was carrying were 350 British refugee children, ranging from babies to young adults, many of them the sons and daughters of British Army and Navy officers.[2] Not all were with their parents or guardians; one woman accompanied eight children, only three of whom were her own. In the circumstances, Cecily and John were lucky or privileged to have obtained a passage on that boat.

The crossing was dangerous. Everyone on board was aware of the risk of being attacked. Cecily realised how desperate it would have been in an emergency if they had had to leave by lifeboat. The lifebelts they were given were kapok-filled but full of holes. If their boat had been struck, it would have been difficult to get to the lifeboats, and the passengers wondered if there were enough of them, and if they were any more seaworthy than the lifebelts. The passengers had been instructed to count the hoots on the foghorn. Twelve was normal and would mean all was well, but 13 meant crisis and possible disaster. So, everyone sat there counting! Most people would not go to bed at night, and instead slept on the deck. For those in steerage any emergency would have been fatal. Cecily and John went to their cabins to sleep, but like many people did not get fully undressed in case they needed to access the deck quickly in an emergency. Their room was only a couple of decks down from the disembarkation point and it would have been pretty chilly and miserable sleeping on deck at night.

On board were two young Chinese women who had names that, when translated, were English flowers. John called them Hanging Orchid and Drooping Dandelion. One was from north China and one from south,

---

2   This acceptance of children from Great Britain was an initiative of the National Child Refugee Committee, formed under the leadership of Marshall Field and the honorary chairmanship of Mrs Franklin D. Roosevelt, as she was then addressed, as an extension of the US Committee for the Care of European Children.

and so they did not speak the same language and their English was poor. Cecily used to interpret their broken English from one to the other. Her feeling for words and natural empathy helped her to do this. She was pleased she could help them. John and Hanging Orchid got on like a house on fire. The young woman had a quick mind and they could parry with each other and perhaps share ideas too. Cecily felt mildly jealous, a new feeling for her. When John had been enchanted by a young woman in their London boarding house, Marcia, she had not felt jealous. Marcia was nothing less than malicious to Cecily's mind and, watching them, she was bemused that John would be captured by the admiring things she said to him and not hear Marcia's nastiness towards Cecily. Men don't seem to recognise bitches, she later decided. She and John also spent time talking to and playing with children on the deck, or going to the ship's cinema, but otherwise there was not much else to do.

The ship docked in New York on 8 July 1940. It was not until they read the newspapers that they discovered that the *Arandora Star* had met with disaster.[3] It had been torpedoed in mistake for the *Samaria*, which had been carrying a cargo of gold as well as children being evacuated from Britain. In fact, the Samaria carried 1,200 boxes of gold valued at about US$67,200,000. The wrong ship was sunk by a German U-boat with no warning early on the morning of 2 July. About half the passengers and crew lost their lives. Many were picked up and were taken back to Liverpool. Many of the prisoners of war were transported to prison camps in Australia the following week. It was a near miss for John and Cecily and the many refugee children and others on board. On 24 February 1941, the *Grootekerk*, the Dutch steam merchant vessel that Cecily had sailed on to Europe two years earlier, would also be sunk by a German U-boat – 66 dead, no survivors – from a misidentification that it was *Nestor* or *Ulysses* of the Blue Funnel Line. On 8 June 1940, the *Orama* on which Cecily first travelled to Europe had been sunk, 300 miles west of Narvik, Norway, by the German High Seas Fleet. It had been converted to a troop ship only months before. These were grim times for passenger cruise ships.

---

3   See Des Hickey and Gus Smith, *The Star of Shame: The Secret Voyage of the Arandora Star* (Kenthurst, NSW: Rosenberg Publishing, 2006), for a factual account. See also *Life,* 9, no. 4, 22 July 1940; *Oswego Palladium-Times,* 8 July 1940.

Ten days after the arrival of the *Samaria*, as a result of the fate of the *Arandora Star*, the British Government announced that it was unable to take responsibility for sending shiploads of children away from the country without convoy. The war at sea had left no fighting ships available for passenger convoy.

Cecily and John spent less than a day in New York by reason of their lack of cash, and Cecily recalled only its buildings and having to be careful of the traffic on the wrong side of the road. They went on to Washington where they stayed overnight with Peter Heydon, who was then second secretary at the Australian Embassy. Cecily recalls eating what she described as the best steak she had ever had in her life. They then journeyed for three days by rail to the West Coast, via Chicago, with prepaid seats in sleeper cars. After two days, Cecily began to feel ill, 'train sick'. In hindsight, she might in fact have been pregnant. The two spent about a week in Stanford, California, with John's sister Nancy and her new husband Robert Bush.[4] Their hosts were warm and welcoming and Cecily was intrigued by American food, the restaurants, the modern architecture and the Bush's friends. She still felt inadequate, however, and daunted by Nancy's proficiencies. Cecily tried to make a white sharkskin dress while she was there, 'In my hopeless, muddle-headed way', sewing it by hand. 'Quite absurd, and absolutely no good,' she remembered and wondered what Nancy would have thought about this.[5] In those days, hem lengths were a dictate of fashion. Over the years, Cecily seemed to be forever taking dresses up or letting them down an inch.

On 20 July, they departed for Australia, third class, on the *Mariposa*, a boat that seemed only to have first and third class, the latter having about 10 times the number of people and one-tenth of the space. The passengers sat around the very narrow deck in a single row with their backs to the wall, their feet nearly reaching the railings; every now and then an adult jumped up to prevent a young child from slipping between the railings overboard. Quite often, Cecily used to leave John sitting on deck, go away and be sick, and come back again. Blackouts were imposed at night, but there was no real danger in the Pacific at that time. It was a tedious trip with nothing to do but entertain each other during the day. At night, they were separated. Cecily shared a cabin with several women

---

4   They married 29 March 1940 at Stanford University Memorial Chapel, California; see Family Notices, 'Bush—Burton. —9 March 1940', *Sydney Morning Herald*, 2 April 1940, 8.
5   *Cecily*, 42.

and John with several men. They somehow managed some intimacies once or twice along the way, she remembered. Their friends, Jack (later Sir John) and Jessie Crawford were on board, travelling first class. Despite it being against the rules Cecily and John managed to sneak in sometimes to visit them.

The boat called in at Hawaii and Fiji, its scheduled stops, but making matters worse for Cecily, the trip took a week longer than usual because, on this occasion, the ship sailed south to Tahiti. The American Matson Line had arranged for its cruise ships, the *Mariposa* and the *Monterey*, to time their departures from California and Australia respectively, so as to arrive and birth in Tahiti majestically together. Passengers travelling on one were transferred to the other for the rest of their journey.[6] Poor Cecily. She saw practically nothing of Papeete. As soon as she got to shore, she began to suffer agonising pains in her stomach and had to return to her cabin, but not before being horrified by the sick children with yaws and other diseases and other signs of dismalness and decay. Back on board, her pain was so severe she fainted – mercifully, she later said. The ship's doctor suggested she might have had a miscarriage and gave her something to ease her nausea. Whether it helped or not, she recovered.

Cecily must have forgotten as time went by that she and her fellow cruise passengers were transferred from one liner to the other. Shipping records confirm that on 5 August the two ships commenced their return voyages home, the *Monterey* stopping at Fiji and Auckland, New Zealand, arriving in Sydney 18 August 1940.

---

6   Peter Plowman, *The Chandris Liners and Celebrity Cruises* (Kenthurst, NSW: Rosenberg Publishing, 2006), tells the story of the two cruise ships. On the outbreak of war there had been an increase in passenger numbers on these liners, as most of the British liners serving Australia were taken up for military duty. Into the 1940s, war prevented many people from travelling and passenger numbers began to drop. In order to boost numbers, the Matson Line organised the unusual two-ship cruise.

9

A remarkable rise in the public service

Cecily and John returned to Canberra in August 1940 and John resumed his position of research officer in the statistician's branch of the Department of Commerce. On his modest income of around £300 he and Cecily set about turning their rented house in McCaughey Street, Turner, into a home. They furnished it simply, planted prunus trees outside the back western windows to help cool the house in summer, and made friends with their neighbours and beyond.

Everyone knew everyone in the small but growing community of Canberra. Haig Park, the pine break north of Canberra's city centre, marked the city's northern boundary. Cecily learned to ride a bicycle as a means of getting around town. Everyone did. People would rug up in Canberra's freezing winter temperatures and cycle to work. In the hot dry summers they would throw their bathers and towels in their bicycle baskets and cool off in the Molonglo River or at the Manuka swimming pool. The Blue Moon in Civic Centre was the only café in town and the modest but grandly named Albert Hall was hired for eisteddfods, live shows and school socials. Performances of the newly formed repertory company staged at Radio 2CA's theatrette were well-attended, as were the 'flicks' or pictures, as movies were then referred to, at the Capitol Theatre in Manuka on the other side of the Molonglo River that divided the north from the south side of the town. These, Cecily recalled, were good days. Canberra was the nation's capital city in the making. The Commonwealth governed the territory in which it sat. Public servants transferred to Canberra from Sydney and Melbourne as government departments shifted to be close to the Commonwealth Parliament. In 1941, wartime Canberra had a population of about 15,000. There was a large manpower shortage as a result of the war and there was only a handful of men in the public service with postgraduate degrees. As a result, opportunities opened in the public service for the young and talented, and John's career began an inevitable rise.

In February 1941, Dr Ronald Wilson recruited some impressive economists and bright young university graduates to a small Post-War Reconstruction Division he had established in the Department of Labour and National Service, which he headed. Wilson, as Commonwealth statistician, had headed John's statistician's branch in the Department of Commerce. Wilson recruited both John and Mick (later Sir Keith) Shann to his new division to deal with Australia's postwar reconstruction initiatives.[1] John completed his doctoral thesis, 'Restrictive and Constructive Intervention', while working under Wilson (although wartime paper shortages delayed him being formally awarded his doctorate until later in 1942). Other of Wilson's recruits were Arthur (later Sir Arthur) Tange, from the foreign exchange operations of the Bank of New South Wales in Fiji; Leslie Finlay (Fin) Crisp on his return from Oxford; Pierce Curtin, a political scientist recently returned from the London School of Economics; Percy Judd, an agricultural economist from the Rural Bank; Phil Dorrian from the state public service of NSW; and Gerald Firth, an economist from the University of Melbourne. The work provided John with an opportunity to devise new policy directions. Still in touch with his friend Parker, who by then was a New Zealand academic at Victoria University of Wellington, John sought ideas from him as to how Commonwealth and State relationship problems could be managed to facilitate the implementation of postwar reconstruction policies when the war ceased.[2] John worked in the reconstruction division for four months from February 1941.

---

1   Wilson was appointed secretary of the Department of Labour and National Service in Melbourne as a wartime secondment in 1940. In February 1941, he was appointed to head an interdepartmental committee to coordinate planning for postwar reconstruction. See H. C. Coombs, *Trial Balance: Issues of My Working Life* (Melbourne: Sun Books, 1981), 22–23, for his inside account of the work of the Reconstruction Division under the Menzies Government. For a full account of the planning for Australia's reconstruction see Stuart Macintyre, *Australia's Boldest Experiment: War and Reconstruction in the 1940s* (Sydney: NewSouth Publishing, 2015).
2   R. S. Parker papers, NLA, MS 8200, box 46, file 189, letter dated 13 February 1941 on Department of Labour and National Services letterhead.

9. A REMARKABLE RISE IN THE PUBLIC SERVICE

Cecily and John with baby Meredith, Canberra, 1942.
Source: Family collection.

At this time, Meredith was on her way. If Cecily had had a miscarriage at sea, this meant that she must have conceived again almost immediately. However, close to full term and during a busy period for John, Cecily suffered a threatened miscarriage from possible placenta previa. The baby's condition was cause for alarm and needed to be monitored. Cecily went to Sydney where she could be confined to bed and looked after by her family in Petersham until the birth. Her sister Eleanor was studying medicine and helping to run the household for their father and the family. John arrived in Sydney six weeks later to be there for Meredith's arrival. As was usual for fathers, he was not present for the birth but walked up and down the hospital corridor smoking during Cecily's labour. After a 24-hour period of labour and aided by forceps, baby Meredith was delivered safely by Cecily's father on 10 May 1941 in Braeside Hospital, Stanmore. It was a terrifying time for Cecily, as for any new mum with no experience about birthing. Nevertheless, in her euphoria of delight with Meredith, a healthy nearly seven-pound baby who 'looked beautiful; she wasn't red and crinkled, as most babies are', Cecily expressed gratitude to everyone around.[3] John drove them back to Canberra with Meredith tucked in a small wicker clothes basket on the back seat of the car.

Cecily described herself, again, as muddling through. In later years, she considered she had been inept as a mother, because she had felt compelled to do things 'by the book' despite a niggling feeling that the standard practices did not always feel natural. She let her little baby cry and cry when, in hindsight, she thought she should have picked her up. 'I knew nothing, nothing!'[4] But then, how many mothers dared challenge the advice of experts on child care at the time?

By contrast, John was not feeling inept. He was still ambitious to use his economics degree to influence Australian foreign policy and he seized another career opportunity that came his way. He was one of the new breed of young public servants who networked regularly over drinks at Hotel Canberra, a short walk from Parliament House and West Block where many worked. Here, John learned of the need for an economist in the small Department of External Affairs.[5] The USA and UK were pursuing postwar reconstruction initiatives, partly to persuade wavering states to join the Allies. Australia was invited to a Food and Agriculture conference and other conferences on economic matters. External Affairs, whose responsibility these were, did not have an economist. The department also lacked funds, skilled administrators and prestige. On 30 June 1941, John Hood, then acting secretary of the Department of External Affairs, invited John to transfer temporarily to the political section of the department. Life for both Cecily and John would become complex from here on in, but never boring. In his new position, not temporary for long, John pushed for more effective postwar reconstruction policies. He continued to liaise with the division he had just left. Herbert Cole (Nugget) Coombs, at the time a senior economist in the Department of Treasury but who later became a significant figure in postwar reconstruction, described the reconstruction group as having 'close, if frequently difficult, links' with John. Coombs saw John as 'fighting to carve out for External Affairs an independent role in the international aspects of economic policies'.[6]

---

3   *Cecily*, 47.
4   *Cecily*, 47.
5   In 1937, when Colin Moodie joined the department, it had a staff of nine, working to its secretary, Colonel Roy Hodgson; see Memoir of Colin Moodie, NLA, MS Acc13.173, 9.
6   Coombs, *Trial Balance*, 23.

On 4 September 1941, John was promoted to acting third secretary of External Affairs. In the same month, following the announcement of the Atlantic Charter by United States President Franklin D. Roosevelt and British Prime Minister Winston Churchill, John and Paul Hasluck, who headed the political section, attempted to reinvigorate the stalled activities of the subcommittee that dealt with international aspects of reconstruction. John was appointed to represent External Affairs on that committee, Fin Crisp was selected to represent the Post-War Reconstruction Division and Nugget Coombs represented Treasury. On 3 October 1941, the short-term Fadden Government that had succeeded the minority government of Prime Minister Menzies was defeated when two independents voted with the Labor Party.[7] On 7 October 1941, Prime Minister John Curtin was sworn in leading a minority Labor Government. Dr H. V. (Bert) Evatt, or 'the Doc' as he was called, became attorney-general and minister for External Affairs. John was confirmed as third secretary of External Affairs on 20 November. Under Menzies, Evatt, as a newly elected Labor member of parliament, had served on the multi-party Advisory War Council in 1940–41, in which position John perceived that Evatt seemed to have taken charge of the postwar reconstruction agenda. John now saw that he was in a strong position to demonstrate the critical importance of international trade and economic policies in Australia's foreign policy.

Arthur Tange, seconded to the Department of External Affairs in 1945, noted in his memoirs that, under John's urging, the department had sought a role in policy in the economic fields vital to postwar reconstruction, 'particularly with the prospect of the United Nations and the other institutions being set up with various regulatory powers'. He said that, apart from John, 'the Department was devoid of experience in economic matters'.[8]

One of the first things John discussed with his new minister, Evatt, was his concerns about Japan's reaction to restricted markets. Evatt sent a message to US Secretary of State Cordell Hull, asking him to approach the Japanese Ambassador and assure him that the USA would put pressure on the colonial powers to make possible free entry into colonial markets.

---

7   Prime Minister Menzies, leader of the United Australia Party and a minority government, had depended on the support of two independents at the time. On 28 August 1941, Menzies resigned the prime ministership and Arthur Fadden, the only member of the Country Party to become prime minister other than in a 'caretaker' capacity, had succeeded him, but for only 40 days.

8   Sir Arthur Tange, *Defence Policy-Making: A Close-Up View, 1950–1980 – A Personal Memoir*, ed. Peter Edwards (Canberra: ANU E Press, 2008), ch. 1, doi.org/10.22459/DPM.07.2008.

According to Asian historian Robert Cribb, the Japanese decision to go to war was largely a response to the economic blockade.[9] But the Japanese fleet was already on its way to Pearl Harbor, and John's fear was realised. John's early interest in problems of intervention and the example of Japan drove his later theorising on the futility of power being employed to coerce behaviours that are beyond the capabilities of those being coerced. The problems of coercive intervention, he said, remained with him after he left his public service career and became the theme of a 'peace theory' he developed later in his written works.

With Japan on the doorstep, Evatt as minister for foreign affairs was busy. On a Friday afternoon in November 1941 John's telephone rang. 'Come over and see me,' Bert Evatt demanded. 'What about?' John asked. 'Just do it, don't ask me questions.'[10] John walked across from his West Block office to Parliament House to see Evatt. He then drove to Sydney for the weekend with Evatt and, as John tells it:

> I was sitting in this damned office in Martin Place during the whole weekend, receiving telegrams and one thing and another; and I guess I was there for two or three years as a result.[11]

Evatt trusted John had the ability to provide the advice he needed in a changing political environment.[12] The Curtin and Chifley Labor governments leaned towards a more independent foreign policy relationship with both Great Britain and the USA than Australia's traditional subservience to the UK Foreign Office. Evatt supported that, as did John. As Paul Hasluck put it, 'Burton instantly commended himself to Evatt'.[13]

---

9 Robert Cribb, 'The Problem of Justice: Prosecuting Japanese for War Crimes after the Second World War', speech delivered at Manning Clark House, Canberra, 22 August 2018.
10 John Wear Burton, interview by Michael J. Wilson, 23 August 1995, Oral History Collection, NLA, ORAL TRC 2981/23, 4.
11 Burton, interview by Michael J. Wilson, 1995, 4.
12 See Bonita Maywald, 'Is It Possible to Re-imagine an Australian IR through John W. Burton's Experience and Seeing Other-wise to Develop Alternative Approaches in Our International Relations?' (Master's diss., The Australian National University, 1999), 126; Burton, interview by Michael J. Wilson, 1995, 6; Edwards, *Prime Ministers and Diplomats*, 145.
13 Paul Hasluck, *Diplomatic Witness: Australian Foreign Affairs, 1941–1947* (Carlton, Vic.: Melbourne University Press, 1980), 15.

Evatt arranged to have John work directly with him in his offices, in Canberra, Sydney or Melbourne, as required.[14] They developed a close personal and professional relationship, but it was a 'complex dynamic and not without significant tensions'.[15] On one occasion, the story goes, Evatt strode through parliament to make a fiery speech, stripping off his coat and flinging it dramatically to the floor as he went. John is reported to have hurried after him, gathering up the coat from the floor, neatly folding it and placing it over the back of Evatt's chair. Calming Evatt was something few others could do.

Hasluck, who later served as minister for External Affairs in the second Menzies Government, thought that Wilson, who had initially handpicked John to join his postwar reconstruction group, 'did not mind losing Burton', and that Roy Hodgson, secretary of the Department of External Affairs, 'did not wish to keep him'.[16] Hasluck and Evatt did not like each other and Hasluck's attitude was to 'let the Minister have him'.[17] However, Hasluck recognised John's shift to External Affairs as 'a fateful move'. He said, 'Evatt ran a substitute for the Department from his own ministerial office with Burton doing more of the fixing and arranging than any departmental officer did and having much more influence on shaping the minister's opinions than anyone in the department had.'[18] John confirmed this assessment. He wrote to Hasluck and said of Evatt, 'he will accept a draft quite easily. I have not had so many ideas put over for a long time!'[19] John described his 'very curious position' as a kind of liaison between Evatt and the department. 'He was very suspicious, I guess of the department and I don't think he saw much of Hodgson at all,' John said, and that, 'it all came to me, piles of telegrams'.[20]

---

14   29 December 1941, Evatt wrote to the Public Service Board requesting John's services and opined that the work warranted a salary at least equivalent to that granted to private secretaries.
15   Adam Hughes Henry, 'Reflections on Dr John Wear Burton: The Forgotten Mandarin?' *ISAA Review* 12, no. 1 (2013), 68.
16   Hasluck, *Diplomatic Witness*, 15.
17   Dunn, *From Power Politics to Conflict Resolution*, 20. Hodgson headed the department from 1935 until 21 June 1945.
18   Hasluck, *Diplomatic Witness*, 15.
19   Geoffrey Bolton, 'Paul Hasluck with Dr Evatt at the United Nations', in *The Seven Dwarfs and the Age of the Mandarins: Australian Government Administration in the Post-War Reconstruction Era*, ed. Samuel Furphy (Canberra: ANU Press, 2015), 210, doi.org/10.22459/SDAM.07.2015.11.
20   Burton, interview by Michael J. Wilson, 1995, 5.

PERSONS OF INTEREST

Our family home life was disrupted by a demanding Evatt. Frequent travel, late nights, early mornings and little sleep for John became the norm for the next several years. Minister Arthur Calwell recalled telling Evatt on one occasion that he was very unfair in keeping John in his office until 3 am, 'just to wait on him and make him a cup of tea or coffee and be around if he wanted anything'.[21] He said to Evatt, 'This young man has a wife and two babies. He ought to be home with them, and not here.' The next day, John thanked Calwell but asked him not to intercede on his behalf again: 'I got hell after you left,' he said.[22]

Foreign policy was implemented by telegrams and cables in response to wartime emergencies. Piles of both came to Evatt's office. Decisions had to be made quickly and were made with little contact with the department. Cables would come in at night and Evatt expected John to draft responses. Not knowing Evatt well at the early stage of working with him, John had to decide whether a cable warranted waking Evatt at night or not. Then he learned to place those he wanted Evatt to read in the morning on top of the pile, and the things he did not need him to read on the bottom. He soon learned how quickly Evatt absorbed material, and where his special interests lay, and John kept the files updated on changing circumstances so that he could quickly provide Evatt with background briefings. Hodgson, as departmental head, was annoyed at cables being answered overnight without his knowledge and at not being sufficiently consulted. On 15 February 1942, Singapore having fallen to the Japanese, Hodgson stayed up playing cards in case any cables came in. It was the night that Lieutenant General Gordon Bennett handed command of the 8th Division in Singapore to a brigadier and, along with some of his staff officers, commandeered a small boat and left the island, leaving others to become prisoners of the Japanese. John slept all night and no one woke him to consult Evatt about the event. He found a cable in the morning stating that the commandeered boat was heading for Indonesia and that the men would be arrested and dealt with on arrival. Evatt was furious, demanding to know what John had done about the cable. Walking along a corridor in Parliament House the next morning Evatt boomed at him, 'These soldiers are going to be shot on arrival in Indonesia!'[23] John knew that it was not his fault he had not been woken and shouted back, 'Don't talk to me like that! You'd better get into Cabinet and get a decision and

---

21   A. A. Calwell, *Calwell: Be Just and Fear Not* (Hawthorn, Vic.: Lloyd O'Neil, 1972), 199.
22   Calwell, *Be Just and Fear Not*, 199.
23   Burton, interview by Michael J. Wilson, 1995, 5.

9. A REMARKABLE RISE IN THE PUBLIC SERVICE

I'll get a telegram off.' John's story is that Evatt quietly walked off, later returned from Cabinet and handed a piece of paper to John, saying, 'Send this.' John never had to suffer Evatt's rudeness again.

Only days later, a series of cables went back and forth concerning the control of two divisions of Australian troops returning from the Middle East with the original intent of returning to the Dutch East Indies. Curtin, 'unable to sleep for days at a time' while the troops were crossing the Indian Ocean, was urging Churchill to send the troops back to Australia, to defend its shores from Japanese attack.[24] Nevertheless, Churchill ordered the diversion of one division, the Australian 7th, to Burma. An urgent response was required. Evatt was not well, Frank Forde, minister for army, was not available and, according to John, 'There wasn't a Minister around. No one wanted to be responsible for making this decision.'[25] Curtin could not be found. He went 'missing' about an hour before midnight – the deadline for sending the crucial cable – 'the one telling Churchill we wanted our troops back', John recalled.[26] When Curtin suffered sleepless nights, he would customarily pace the grounds of the Lodge, but he was nowhere to be found. 'We sent messages … there were only two cinemas in Canberra then … we sent messages and put it on the screen: "Is the Prime Minister there?" No responses.'[27] Curtin walked in just before midnight. He had been walking around Mount Ainslie contemplating, drafting words in his head. He asked for a stenographer, and rapidly dictated a short cable to Churchill demanding that the troops be sent straight back.[28] It was a step in the direction of Australia developing an independent foreign policy, one which John would continue to urge was in Australia's best interest.

---

24   David Day, 'John Joseph Curtin', in *Australian Prime Ministers*, ed. Michelle Grattan (Sydney: New Holland Publishers, 2000), 218, 233–34.
25   Burton, interview by Michael J. Wilson, 1995, 8.
26   Interview with Phillip Adams for *Weekend Australian Magazine,* 17–18 July 2004, 46.
27   Burton interview by Michael J. Wilson, 1995, 8.
28   Curtin to Churchill, 23 February 1942, cited in David Black, ed., *In His Own Words: John Curtin's Speeches and Writings* (Bentley, WA: Paradigm Books, Curtin University of Technology, 1995), 200.

10

The Burton plot: Reconstruction and Nugget Coombs

In 1942, while John was still working in Evatt's office, he led an unofficial group of young economists to develop a plan aimed at giving new leadership to Australia's postwar reconstruction activities. Historian Stuart Macintyre observed that 'the planning of post-war reconstruction was neglected and ineffective'.[1] The reconstituted reconstruction subcommittee had met only once, on 4 December 1941, because three days later Japan launched its attack on Pearl Harbor and the meeting the following week was abandoned. The unofficial group believed that Herbert Cole 'Nugget' Coombs, one of the so-named 'seven dwarfs' (university-educated, powerful postwar permanent heads of departments who were all relatively short), was the most capable person to develop relevant economic and trade policies and to influence allied nations with ideas. John's plan was to have Coombs put in charge of postwar reconstruction.

First, Roland Wilson as head of Post-War Reconstruction had to be convinced that its status should be lifted and to have Coombs head it. The background story is detailed through journal entries of one of the plotters, Gerald Firth, who records his and John's activities and those of another main player, Wilson's economic adviser Dick Heyward. On 6 April 1942, the trio discussed 'Burton's bold plan'. Firth wrote:

---

1   Stuart Macintyre, 'The Post-War Reconstruction Project', in Furphy, *The Seven Dwarfs and the Age of the Mandarins*, 40, doi.org/10.22459/SDAM.07.2015.02.

> John is definitely thinking in a Big Way, and spent a lot of time persuading us to 'go and stick pins into Wilson'. This we apparently agreed to do, though the more I think of it the less I like it; but yet – to get Coombs made de facto head of a reconstructed Reconstruction Division is probably worth a little strife.[2]

The 'Burton Plan' filled his mind, he wrote, noting that Heyward had arranged for the three to take Wilson to the 'Ritz' the following Thursday (or presumably somewhere 'Ritz-like' as I don't believe there was a Ritz in Canberra then). 'An enterprising scheme,' wrote Firth, 'which would never have occurred to me.'[3] The four men enjoyed the dinner and engaged in some lively discussions, but the 'fate of Reconstruction' was not entirely resolved. Wilson agreed that Coombs was the man suitable to take on the role but he doubted that Coombs's boss, Stuart Macfarlane, who headed Treasury, would agree to take on the work of the Reconstruction Division, or that Coombs would leave Treasury to go to the Department of Labour, where the group hoped the division might be placed. Coombs had to be tackled directly; Firth and Heyward decided they would 'see what could be done about the Macfarlane bogey'.[4] Coombs was receptive and suggested it might be possible to contrive a 'loose connection' with Treasury 'by getting Chifley [the Treasurer] to take over Reconstruction more or less as a separate portfolio'. In this way, Coombs would be responsible directly to Chifley in regard to reconstruction and Macfarlane would keep the major percentage of Coombs's services, with little chance to 'hamstring the [Reconstruction] Division'.[5]

Firth got to know John better as the game was being played. He engaged him in discussions over economic planning and borrowed a copy of John's doctoral thesis to read. That proved to be the high point of their relationship. Firth soon learned that John was a difficult person to relate to. He was no more communicative or consultative with his colleagues than he was at home with Cecily, it would seem. In early May 1942, Firth met up with John at the Burton family flat. There, according to Firth, John 'went out of his way to warn me to keep off too much economics in the interests of the wretched diplomats', before proceeding then to preach to him along the lines of his doctoral thesis.[6] The relationship developed

---

2   Papers of Gerald Firth, NLA, MS Acc01.273, box 3.
3   Papers of Gerald Firth, NLA, MS Acc01.273, box 3, 7 April 1942.
4   Papers of Gerald Firth, NLA, MS Acc01.273, box 3, 9 April 1942.
5   Papers of Gerald Firth, NLA, MS Acc01.273, box 3, 10 April 1942.
6   Papers of Gerald Firth, NLA, MS Acc01.273, box 3, 4 May 1942.

tensions, John appearing to Firth to be hostile and somewhat supercilious. Two months later, at dinner with the Burtons, Firth lectured John on the need to appease Fred Wheeler who worked in Treasury, not that John was likely to have listened, Firth noted in his journal. Later, he wrote: 'I <u>do</u> wish Burton would occasionally condescend to stop and think.'[7]

Meantime, John had been thinking. As the political and wider community urged stronger action on postwar planning activities, he joined the developing push for postwar reconstruction to have a ministry of its own. He persuaded Calwell to call on the prime minister to create a more powerful body capable of faster progress on reconstruction initiatives. On 6 May 1942, in parliamentary question time, Calwell obliged. Firth perceived that 'Burton wanted Reconstruction to be placed under his control within the Department of External Affairs'.[8] The plotters put their suggestion to Curtin that Coombs (highly regarded by Curtin) should lead Reconstruction. By the end of 1942 Curtin was persuaded – partly at Wilson's urging and thanks to the group of plotters – that postwar reconstruction required a department of its own. On 22 December 1942, Curtin appointed Ben Chifley its minister and Coombs its director-general.[9] The new department was charged with planning and coordinating the work of other departments, state governments and various agencies with a goal of transitioning Australia from a war economy to a peacetime economy that could achieve and maintain full employment.[10] John, then still working with Evatt, remained a key player in the work of the department alongside Allen Brown, John Crawford and Wilson, three of the other 'Dwarfs', and Arthur Tange, Firth and Fin Crisp. But its work was set back by Chifley's requirement for Coombs to be absent from Canberra for the most part of six months following its establishment.

Chifley wanted Coombs – under his rather than Evatt's direction – to guide talks and raise Australia's concerns in Washington as one of Australia's representatives in a group invited by the US Government in April 1943 to discuss a proposal for an International Stabilisation

---

7   Papers of Gerald Firth, NLA, MS Acc01.273, box 3, 28 June 1942, original emphasis.
8   Papers of Gerald Firth, NLA, MS Acc01.273, box 3, 5 May 1942.
9   Tim Rowse, *Nugget Coombs: A Reforming Life* (Port Melbourne, Vic.: Cambridge University Press, 2002), 99.
10 Rowse, *Nugget Coombs*, 99.

Fund to regulate exchange rates.[11] Evatt headed the mission and John accompanied him. Since one of the objects of the mission was to persuade US President Roosevelt to allocate greater military resources to the Pacific, the delegation included military and supply experts as well as influential businessman and industrialist William Sydney Robinson.[12] Coombs was bemused by his own inclusion in the group, having not yet fully taken up his new role of head of the new department in charge of reconstruction.

The trip was memorable for all, according to both John's and Coombs's accounts. The intimacy of the travel arrangements and the diverse personalities of the group tested their relationships. To add colour and humour to the trip was the inclusion of artist Sam Atyeo and war correspondent and later novelist George Johnston. Evatt had a pathological fear of flying and made a point of never flying without his wife Mary Alice. No doubt Mary Alice, having close connections with the art world, saw that only someone like Atyeo, a close confidante of Evatt, could lift the Doc out of his surliness and the spirits of those around him. It was true. Coombs commented, 'when the rest of us were doing our best to stay out of range of the Doc's temper, he would bowl blithely in, smack the Doc on the back and say, "Come on you bad-tempered old bastard, stop scowling"'.[13]

Coombs started out weary and anxious, having nearly missed the plane, which contributed to him becoming airsick. As the plane taxied down the runway in Brisbane, Coombs, too sick to care he said, saw a great flame of burning gases stream past his window. Evatt, convinced they were on fire, 'staggered pale-faced up the aisle, to warn the crew of our impending doom', Coombs records, only to be looked at with 'the contemptuous pity of the professionals' and Evatt was led back to his seat where Mary Alice wiped his brow with a cologne-soaked handkerchief.[14] They arrived in one piece in San Francisco on 7 April 1943.

---

11   Coombs, *Trial Balance*, 36; Macintyre, *Australia's Boldest Experiment*, 151. The proposal had been outlined at the first British Commonwealth conference on the international economy in London the previous October 1942 by economist Keynes.
12   Robinson, a mining magnate and world authority on base metals, was also an adviser during the war to Curtin on the distribution of Australian metals and concentrates. He undertook dealings on behalf of Curtin, Chifley and Evatt, and accompanied Evatt on several missions to America to acquire aircraft for Australia's defence.
13   Coombs, *Trial Balance*, 46.
14   Coombs, *Trial Balance*, 37.

10. THE BURTON PLOT

Both Coombs and John shared a commitment to Chifley's ideals and consolidated their relationship and mutual respect, helped particularly by each bringing out a degree of larrikinism in the other when they had time to relax. John recalls an occasion when the two young men had over-imbibed and chased some women up the steps of an international hotel. What happened next, neither reported. Back home, and receiving a cable from Coombs, Firth had concerns about John's influence – even over Coombs. Firth wrote in his journal:

> My own theory is that Evatt and bloody Burton are putting the hard word on [Coombs] for 'political' reasons – but anyway [Lyndhurst Falkiner] Giblin, [Leslie Galfreid] Melville and Wheeler put their heads together and concocted a cable which should bring Nugget back to the straight and narrow with something of a jerk. It is good to see everyone agreeing with me(!) for once in a way.[15]

Firth's diary note is a reminder of the times; it was a small community of notable bureaucrats and politicians living in each other's pockets who could act as they saw fit without excessive hierarchical bureaucratic restrictions.

The group's trip was extended to allow five of the delegation, including John in his own right, to represent Australia at the Food and Agriculture conference in Virginia in May 1943.[16] It was to consider how united action could enhance global nutrition and help alleviate rural poverty with the object of laying the foundations for conditions for high employment and economic stability that, it was thought, would help to prevent war in the future. Its agenda was one that John was keen on and qualified to contribute to.[17]

The venue was at Hot Spring's Homestead Hotel, a luxurious, rambling colonial-style building that accommodated the participating representatives of around 50 nations. There, John met up again with his doctorate supervisor at the London School of Economics, Robbins,

---

15   Papers of Gerald Firth, NLA, MS Acc01.273, box 3, 13 May 1943.
16   The conference had been convened by President Roosevelt to establish the United Nations Food and Agricultural Organization; however, its origins were Australian. Before the war, Stanley Bruce, Australia's high commissioner in London and a member of the Imperial War Cabinet, had urged that improvement in nutritional standards of all peoples was the solution to the poverty and depression that faced farmers around the world.
17   Evatt outlined guiding principles for Coombs to follow in a document dated 28 May 1943: Evatt Collection, Flinders University Library, Evatt Album 29.

who was one of the UK's representatives. This was the first international conference on postwar issues and the last in which, apart from the United Nations itself, the USSR participated as an ally.[18]

The Australian party returned to Baltimore where Evatt was joined by Mary Alice, who had been ill and hospitalised for an operation. On 15 June, the party travelled to London. There, Coombs dined out several times with Maynard Keynes, noting that the famous economist was 'at his most persuasive and charming best', and that, 'He was not always so'.[19] As a result of these discussions and Keynes's influence, according to Coombs, it came to be accepted that the UK's best chance of restoring its international role lay in the achievement of an expanding world trade in which real incomes would increase in all countries.

The London talks continued into July. Coombs, like John, found Evatt difficult in a number of ways when working closely with him, but he enjoyed his companionship when he was in a more relaxed state. Often late at night when John and Coombs were having a night cap, Evatt would join them to talk about people he had met during the day, books he was reading, the baseball scores, and about the major social issues that underlay the backbiting and treacheries of politics. Coombs observed that Evatt was a different man in this mood. However, Evatt's fear of flying was a recurring feature of the trip. The contingent had a short stay in Limerick, Ireland, and, despite bad weather, the group at Robinson's urging boarded a plane at Limerick to fly across the Atlantic back to Washington. Evatt whispered to Coombs, 'You see how much these big business men hate us – they would risk dying themselves to get rid of me'.[20] The party arrived safely in Washington and went on to Ottawa for more consultations about the Stabilisation Fund before returning home.[21]

The Curtin Government was returned on 21 August 1943. A week later, perhaps by way of celebration, Coombs joined John in putting on 'Burton's cinema show' at the Hotel Canberra. They turned on sherry and ran some films and agreed between them that it was 'definitely a good party'.[22] Coombs had returned to his department to work on postwar

---

18 Coombs, *Trial Balance*, 41.
19 Coombs, *Trial Balance* 45.
20 Coombs, *Trial Balance*, 38.
21 News clipping from *Birmingham Gazette*, Evatt Collection, Flinders University Library, Evatt Album 8.
22 Papers of Gerald Firth, NLA, MS Acc01/273, box 3, 28–29 August 1943.

10. THE BURTON PLOT

reconstruction and, at the end of September 1943, John left Evatt's office to return to the Department of External Affairs, also to work on aspects of reconstruction. By November, John occupied the position of second secretary, which was confirmed in September the following year.

Tensions continued in the Firth–Burton relationship and Firth learned to keep some distance from John. They continued to hold different views on the Stabilisation Fund. In January 1944, Firth had a chat about it with Fred (later Sir Frederick) Wheeler 'over 5 bottles of beer', according to Firth's journal, in which he happily noted that 'John Burton was not present'.[23] He also noted that Wheeler and John had had 'a first-rate bust-up' over an issue that was beyond his powers of comprehension, but which was 'all John's fault', according to a comment later made by Tange. The scene took place in the room of former prime minister Scullin, who was then an unofficial adviser to Curtin. While Burton and Wheeler were going at it 'hammer and tongs' and Firth was screaming into a phone, Coombs walked in and remarked that it sounded like a Caucus meeting.[24] In February 1944, Firth wrote in his journal:

> John Burton arrived with Cecily this evening – and was exceedingly offensive about 'subsidies'. I didn't bite very hard, but the episode more or less convinced me that I have done well to keep away from John these past few months. Why go out of your way to be infuriated?[25]

Firth, by then, was also critical of John for his apparent lack of concern for Cecily. The difficulty Cecily had at home coping with John's busy life and lengthy travel absences had not gone unnoticed by him and his wife, Maggie.[26]

---

23   Papers of Gerald Firth, NLA, MS Acc01/273, box 3, 16 January 1944, original emphasis.
24   Papers of Gerald Firth, NLA, MS Acc01.273, box 3, 18 January 1944.
25   Papers of Gerald Firth, NLA, MS Acc01.273, box 3, 14 February 1944.
26   Papers of Gerald Firth, NLA, MS Acc01.273, box 3, 24 May 1943.

11

Domesticity and babies

At home, Cecily felt challenged by child-rearing virtually on her own. Clare had arrived into the world on 30 October 1942 at the (then) Canberra Community Hospital, having been surgically induced. She was a healthy, heavy baby, but Cecily suffered a severe haemorrhage afterwards and within a couple of days her yellow skin demonstrated she lacked iron. The family's flat was in Barton Court on the south side of the city. John was in Canberra for Clare's birth, but from Cecily's perspective, he was not as interested in Clare as he had been with Meredith. Perhaps he was disappointed by not getting a son, Cecily suggested. Equally likely is that his mind was focused on his work and meeting Evatt's demands.

Clare cried a great deal and no one could discover why. Eventually, Cecily decided something more imaginative needed to be done about Clare's misery and her own. She took both babies to Sydney and consulted her father and his medical colleagues. She was referred to a paediatrician who turned out to be 'more scientific than human' and put Cecily and Clare through what Cecily could only describe as agony.[1] He experimented with various alternatives to mother's milk, alternating between them. This meant that every time Clare did not feed from her mother, she had to be fed something else. Finally, a diagnosis: Clare could not tolerate fats. A no-fat, no-mother's milk formula worked, and Clare slept happily.

Although Cecily's life was difficult and she never felt at ease caring for her babies, it never lacked interest. While living at Barton Court in the early 1940s, Cecily and John had the company of some senior, though young,

---

1   *Cecily*, 51.

bureaucrats and their families. They included Mick Shann, who later worked with John in External Affairs; Professor Douglas Copland (later Sir Douglas), who had been seconded from the University of Melbourne to Canberra as Commonwealth prices commissioner and became economic consultant to the prime minister in the years 1941 to 1945 before being appointed as Australian minister to China in 1946; and Richard (Dick) Downing, an economist, who came to Canberra to assist Copland in his consulting role to the prime minister. Downing took a shine to Cecily. He had an extravagant personality, striking features and an expressive face, and Cecily enjoyed his wit and interest in music and theatre. However, his interest in her became haunting; he watched her hang out clothes one day and told her she was like a 'French gamine'.[2] She began to feel he was stalking her, so she had to ask him to stop; then she was concerned that she had been hurtful.

John and Cecily saw a lot of Coombs during this time and Cecily became very fond of him. John admired Coombs's values and intellect, diverse interests and sense of humour. Cecily enjoyed his company because he was sensitive, understanding, a romantic and he made time for her. She joined him on outings and on one occasion, on a beautiful moonlit night, she accompanied him on a walk. In a letter to Coombs more than half a century later, Cecily wrote:

> I have fond memories of the early years of our friendship, of the rewarding times we had together – about fifty years ago – and of the occasional things you said to me when I expressed my rather confused ideas and feelings about life. You seemed to have a clearer view of life than I had, to be more sure of yourself, and to have your own answers to life's dilemmas … You were kind, respectful and affectionate towards me, and I hope I was the same to you. My friendship with you has contributed much of lasting value to my life.[3]

At times when John was overseas for extended periods, Cecily felt depressed at home, finding it a struggle looking after two babies on her own in a small flat. In April 1943, when John was abroad, Cecily suffered from exhaustion. She had difficulty in simply dressing Meredith and Clare, putting them in a pram and walking from Barton to Kingston, a nearby suburb, to shop. Meredith was 'helpful' in that she had taken to

---

2   Cecily Parker, interview by Meredith Edwards, 2004, transcript, 33, NLA, ORAL TRC 5094.
3   Copy held in Cecily family file.

wheeling Clare around – in those days, Clare could be left safely in her pram outside the flats – and one day, Cecily found Meredith headed for Telopea Park with Clare. The stretch of green parkland, quite a way away, contained an attractive but dangerous culvert of flowing water. Cecily decided to move to a house more suitable for her and the children. Too gutless to put the proposition to John, she said later, she sought the help of Tange who found her a house in Geerilong Gardens in Reid that had a garden for Meredith and Clare to play in, a safer street environment and many other children nearby for them to play with. Cecily happily oversaw the children roaming safely up and down and across the community parkland, leaving a trail of playthings and belongings to be collected at the end of the day.

On his homecoming in July 1943, John found that Cecily had made some domestic decisions without consulting him – generally a habit of his, not hers – and he did not like the house. It was one of the original quality Canberra homes built early in the century on generous blocks that circled the grassy park. John saw only that it was dark. He told Cecily that the old and badly furnished house was the most depressing he had lived in. Much of the woodwork, the floors and the skirtings were varnished in dark brown or black, and the house and its rooms were small. There was an Indian drugget carpet in the living room that fell to pieces when it was dry-cleaned, and awful curtains – half of the window was covered with dark red chenille and the other half was covered with a coarse fawn net. Cecily later tore down the red chenille from which she made an attractive dress.

The Firths lived close by and, according to Firth's journal, John had arrived home from the USA with 'a swag of Booty' that needed a test tasting. In August 1943, the Firths were invited to join Burtons 'for a spot of Dinkum Oil on the States'.[4] It was, no doubt, a house-warming party of sorts, of the house John did not like living in. John suggested they look for a house to buy. However, it was wartime; prices were pegged and there were few properties available. The family made the best of their situation for the time, as they always did. They acquired a cat and John started a vegetable garden. They had a fuel stove that had to be blackened, a lino floor in the kitchen that had to be polished and an ice-chest before refrigerators were available. Cecily used to ride her bicycle to Civic to

---

4 Papers of Gerald Firth, NLA, MS Acc01.273, box 3, 16 August 1943.

shop and to buy eggs and vegetables from the now historic Blundell's Farmhouse nearby. Sometimes she cycled to cocktail parties. John's father gave them their first car. By 1945, Jack was 70, deaf and dangerous on the road and, reluctantly, gave up driving.

Cecily's health had not improved. One evening in March 1944, Firth noted in his journal that having met up with him outside a neighbour's gate, John was 'unusually affable' and gave him marrows from his garden. Then, as he might have guessed, he discovered there was a purpose to John's offering. His wife, Maggie, told him that Cecily had rung her because she was sick and Maggie had offered to mind Clare from time to time. Gerald and Maggie confided that 'John could well do more to help'.[5] Cecily's ill-health and exhaustion continued and at some time in 1944 and into 1945 she became chronically ill; she was tired, headachy, had a stiff neck and swollen glands. Her doctor found nothing wrong and gave her phenobarbitone to help her relax and sleep. Feeling wretched, she cried into the sink when she was washing up, too tired to continue, but forced herself to cope. Cecily knew she was ill and not in need of barbiturates. She turned again to her father for help. Tests were done and it transpired that a haemorrhage Cecily had suffered after Clare's birth, tonsillitis and other ailments had left her weak, causing the onset of chronic glandular fever syndrome. Her sister Eleanor, now a doctor, prescribed sulpha drugs, probably inappropriately, for Cecily then suffered more agony and returned to Canberra still unwell. It transpired that she was anaemic, sometimes a consequence of glandular fever, but in her case, possibly contributed to by the sulpha drugs. Iron tablets did not help her and for nearly three years Cecily had to have iron and liver injections. Neighbours and friends helped during John's absences overseas.

Clare still did not sleep or feed well. In 1945, she fell ill with scarlet fever and spent a month or more in hospital in an isolation ward. She had the company of other children but her parents could only wave through a window from the footpath. It was traumatic for such a young child. Then Cecily sent Clare to nursery school. Clare hated it and cried each time she was put on the bus in the morning with other children to travel to Acton (now the grounds of The Australian National University). It was against Cecily's instincts to let Clare suffer in this way, but she had been told that sending her there was the right thing to do. Despite this, Clare

---

5   Papers of Gerald Firth, NLA, MS Acc01.273, box 3, 9 March 1944.

surprised Cecily by displaying 'a misplaced trust' in her. On one occasion when Cecily was pushing Clare, then a preschooler, on the swing in the park opposite their house, Cecily asked Clare if she had had enough and wanted to get off. Clare replied 'Yes', and promptly let go of the ropes expecting Cecily to catch her. She fell – fortunately without injury.

Clare was amusing as a child and acted the clown, although she developed later into a more serious child and not always a happy one. Unlike Meredith, she spoke well at a young age, her first word being 'hair brush' at 11 months. Meredith had chatted away in a language of her own but not one that anyone could understand. Tange said is sounded like Gaelic. Just as Cecily was beginning to get the hang of it, Meredith at age three, broke into English.

Both Clare and Meredith had a church christening, despite John and Cecily not being believers or churchgoers. Again, it seemed the expected thing to do, although they had a battle with the local parson to have him accept their formulation of words. Cecily's lack of confidence in child-raising persisted. She felt that visitors were critical of her casual permissiveness with the children. Meredith was allowed to stay up late and used to come to the table when the adults were eating. John would hand her a chicken bone to chew. In time, John and Cecily would teach us children dinner protocols for occasions, such as when we visited John's older sister's family in north shore Sydney. We were grateful that we did not have to follow the rules at home; we could sprinkle salt on our food rather than take a spoonful from a salt dish and put it on the side or our plate, pick corn up in our fingers without using special little forks, wipe our hands on serviettes, rather than have to dunk them in finger bowls, and smash our boiled eggs any which way, rather than cracking them neatly on top with a teaspoon – and so on.

Apart from Cecily's poor health and what John thought of the house, our parents lived a full and active life while they were in Reid. Both enjoyed socialising in an emerging public service town. Cecily became close friends with Marjorie Tange and Peg Wheeler, the wives of Arthur Tange and Fred Wheeler. She also befriended neighbours, including the Buttsworths who were distant relatives of hers, and she became the first president of the parents and citizens association of the nearby Reid preschool in Dirrawan Gardens when it opened in 1945.

John was in his element. He was gaining a sense that he could influence government policy. He utilised his belief in himself, the power of his personality and his innovative thinking to do so. His head was abuzz with ideas and big-picture perspectives on how to bring trade and economic issues to the forefront in the government's approach to foreign policy and postwar reconstruction. This was necessary, in his view, to promote peaceful coexistence in the Asia-Pacific region. It could not have been easy for Cecily to live with John with his head space constantly distracted by matters outside the home. She felt he paid little attention to how she was feeling or coping. It is unlikely that she understood the momentous effect John was having on the course of Australia's foreign policy at the time, or that John, himself, saw the enormity of it. At home, his communication about anything was minimalist; at work, he was outspoken.

12

Australia on the world stage

In April 1944 John attended the International Labour Organization Conference in Philadelphia. His role was to brief Australia's chief delegate, Jack Beasley, minister for supply and shipping, who was to deliver a speech on Australia's foreign economic policy. John had asked Evatt if he could accompany Beasley because, as John told us, he believed the minister was 'hopeless'. On arriving in Philadelphia, John arranged for an American official to show Beasley around to get him away from the conference. In Beasley's absence, John attempted to push through a resolution obliging countries to pursue full employment policies. The US secretary of labor went along with it, but the State Department did not. The Australian Embassy argued that John had overstepped the mark. John sent a telegram to Evatt explaining the 'messy situation' and sought instructions. Evatt's telegraphic reply was not the reprimand John expected: 'You have to break eggs before you scramble them. Regards'.[1] At the conclusion of the conference, John flew home to report on outcomes and Beasley returned sedately by ship.[2]

For a time John served in the Post-Hostilities Division of External Affairs headed by Paul Hasluck where he worked closely with Coombs on postwar reconstruction. However, he lost enthusiasm for the work, believing that policy implementation had to be carried out across departments rather

---

1 John Burton, 'Herbert Vere Evatt: A Man Out of His Time', chapter 1 in *Brave New World: Dr H. V. Evatt and Australian Foreign Policy 1941–1949*, ed. David Day (St Lucia, Qld: University of Queensland Press, 1966), 9.
2 Betty Nathan, notes taken from personal communication with John, 20 December 2009, Burton family file.

than from a separate one and he severed his connection with the division at the end of 1944. Approval was given for the establishment of an Economic Relations Division, which John headed and which took over some of the work done by the Post-Hostilities Division.

The following year, John travelled with Evatt to San Francisco to attend the United Nations Conference on International Organization (the Charter conference) on 25 April 1945, where Australia played a significant role.[3] David Horner, in his *Official History of ASIO*, credited Evatt for putting Australia on the world stage at this time.[4] He concluded that Evatt gained international prominence at the Charter conference and was seen as 'the hero of the small nations'.[5] At the time, John placed faith in the newly formed United Nations organisation, but he became disillusioned about its work decades later. He said:

> We thought we'd made a great achievement. Twenty years later when I started teaching international relations, I realised that the whole philosophical base was false. The UN was modelled on the nation with its central authority, but this whole idea of a central world government in control is false.[6]

The Australians put forward an amendment to include the Domestic Jurisdiction Clause, which became Article 2(7) of the United Nations Charter – that is, a clause to limit the authority of the organisation in respect of disputes that are essentially within the domestic jurisdiction of the member state – which John later regretted. In 1985 he said that, at the time, 'Australia wanted it put in because we had our own domestic problems with migration,' but that, 'I am ashamed of that now'.[7] The Domestic Jurisdiction Clause meant that the United Nations cannot act in regard to conflict within a country and, he noted, that 'this is where

---

3   The team included Bailey, Forsyth, Hasluck and Watt. John, in an interview for *Resolution* magazine (November 1985), said that the Dumbarton Oaks draft leading to the creation of the United Nations was immature and needed many amendments, which were made in establishing the United Nations Charter in San Francisco.
4   David Horner, *The Spy Catchers: The Official History of ASIO, 1949–1963*, vol. 1 (Crows Nest, NSW: Allen & Unwin, 2015).
5   In a speech to parliament on 30 August 1945 in support of a bill to approve the Charter of the United Nations, Evatt paid special tribute to the work of his team, see *Current Notes on International Affairs* 16, no. 6 (August–September 1945), 26. He made no mention there, however, of Jessie Street who was the only woman in the Australian contingent, and who played an important role in ensuring equal rights of men and women were recognised in the Charter's Preamble.
6   Burton, interview for *Resolution* magazine (November 1985), 1.
7   Burton, interview for *Resolution* magazine (November 1985), 4. There were eight committees of the United Nations and the small delegation of Australians meant that each was given a committee responsibility; John's was the Economic and Social Council.

most of the conflict in the world right now is located'.[8] In his view, the provision for the Great Powers to have a veto on issues that affected them also contributed to the ineffectiveness of the United Nations. More fundamental in John's view, developed from the insight he later gained working in the international arena of conflict resolution, was that when the United Nations did get the chance to act constructively, it adopted traditional mediating processes with little chance of effecting a sustainable peace settlement; a problem-solving framework was required.

Evatt and John, the United Nations Conference on International Organization, San Francisco, April 1945.
Source: Family collection.

---

8   Burton, interview for *Resolution* magazine (November 1985), 4.

In the meantime, John's father, Jack Burton, was also politically active. On 20 April 1945, in his capacity as general secretary to the Methodist Overseas Mission, he wrote to Curtin about his concern for 40 to 60 natives in Australia's New Guinea Territories under sentence of death by the military for treason. He commenced his letter with 'I scarcely know to whom I should write on this very important matter, but I address myself to you as the Head of the Commonwealth Government'.[9] Twenty-eight natives had previously been executed at Buna for 'treason and murder' and, despite recommendations for mercy by a Judge 'who had considerable knowledge of native life', the Army hanged the men.[10] He urged that a competent anthropologist investigate before any sentence of death was passed. He argued that the death sentences of the large number of natives who were not directly responsible for the murders should be commuted to imprisonment. John Vincent Barry KC wrote to the Minister for Territories Eddie Ward informing Ward that the military were about to execute around 50 natives in Aitape.[11] Ward had appointed Barry to head several official inquiries relating to postwar affairs in Papua and New Guinea. Whether Jack Burton acted independently or sought his son's or Barry's advice as to how and to whom to address the issue is not clear. Curtin replied to Jack on 23 April 1945 informing him that he was making enquiries into the matter. Chifley, as acting prime minister, followed up with a letter to Jack on 15 June 1945, confirming the government's condemnation of the use of the death penalty as punishment of natives in Papua and New Guinea.[12] Ward wrote to Jack on 3 July 1945 stating: 'As promised, I took this matter up with my colleagues in the Government, and it was decided by the Cabinet that the death sentences would be commuted to terms of imprisonment.'[13] Some of

---

9   This and other quoted extracts from Jack's letter where not otherwise indicated were sourced by John Myrtle whose research uncovered Jack Burton's letter to Curtin. I am grateful to Myrtle for sharing his research and information with me.
10   Jack Burton, letter 20 April 1945.
11   20 April 1945 and 23 April 1945: Mark Finnane, *J V Barry: A Life* (Sydney: University of New South Wales Press, 2007), 129. At p. 130, mention is made of Barry's recall that Lieutenant-General Herring (commander of Kokoda forces) had authorised, in 1942, the execution of 'about 28 natives'.
12   Curtin died in office on 5 July 1945, only weeks before Japan surrendered. Evatt and John were in London at the Empire Conference when Frank Forde became prime minister temporarily, his eight days in office beating the shortness of Fadden (39 days). Chifley defeated him in the leadership ballot and became prime minister.
13   Letter 3 July 1945, Burton Snr family file.

the executions proceeded, however, before Ward intervened.[14] Despite its commission of those executions, Australia would play a major role in the war crimes trials.[15]

Evatt urged that Japan's Emperor Hirohito should be included in the list of those Australia recommended to the United Nations War Crimes Commission (UNWCC) to be tried. On 26 May 1945, while at the San Francisco conference, Evatt had cabled the acting minister in Canberra warning that 'nothing should be said in Australia to indicate any weakening of our policy of bringing Japanese criminals to justice irrespective of their office or eminence of their position'.[16] Accordingly, in September 1945, External Affairs compiled a list of 64 names, including that of the Emperor, for further investigation for potential prosecution. In October 1945, John, then acting head of the department, sent the list for the endorsement of Justice William Webb who had been appointed to investigate Japanese war crimes and report to the UNWCC. Webb resisted including the Emperor on the list. John was insistent and the list was dispatched on 26 October with the Emperor's name on it for the UNWCC for its consideration. Cables between the two tell the story.[17] However, in December 1945, Webb was appointed Australia's representative on the International Military Tribunal for the Far East and declined to approve the Emperor being included on the list. In any event, General Douglas MacArthur had decided that the Emperor himself was not to be prosecuted.

---

14 Finnane, *J V Barry: A Life*, 130. The *War Crimes Act 1945* ended capital and corporate punishment for Australian citizens or residents. It was permitted again, however, on Australia becoming a participant in the war crimes trials.
15 Australia conducted some 300 trials, of mostly Japanese, in Darwin and off-shore countries and islands in the Asia-Pacific.
16 NAC A1838/T184, 3103/10/13/1 Part 1 cited in D. C. Sissons, 'The Australian War Crimes Trials and Investigations (1942–51)', text taken from *Bridging Australia and Japan: The Writings of David Sissons, Historian and Political Scientist*, vol. 2, ed. Keiko Tamura and Arthur Stockwin (Canberra: ANU Press, 2020), 69, doi.org/10.22459/BAJ.2020.04.
17 By cable 22 October 1945 Webb replied: 'Out of deference to the British view-point, as indicated to me, but by no means pressed … I respectfully suggest that we omit the Emperor from this tentative list.' He nevertheless indicated by cable 24 October 1945, that the case of Hirohito should be pursued, by having it decided 'at the highest political and diplomatic levels': Sissons, 'The Australian War Crimes Trials and Investigations (1942–51)', 71; Papers of David Sissons, NLA, MS 3092, MS Acc09.106, subseries 1–3, Australian War Crimes Trials, file 24. John rejected this in his cabled reply of 25 October 1945, distinguishing between having Hirohito's name listed for investigation and having a decision taken at the highest level before taking action to bring a person on the list to trial.

PERSONS OF INTEREST

Evatt and John walking near 10 Downing Street, London, 1945.
Source: Family collection.

12. AUSTRALIA ON THE WORLD STAGE

Towards the end of 1945, Cecily, still struggling with and adjusting to what was akin to single motherhood with John absent so much, became pregnant again. It is difficult to understand why she considered having me, a third child, when she was having so much difficulty coping with two. However, the joy of another baby is often felt to be a remedy for domestic discontent and, further, she hoped to produce the son that John wanted. In 1946, Cecily was left at home alone for many months, heavily pregnant, and then with a newborn as well as my two older sisters to care for, while John was abroad.

In April and May 1946, John was part of the Australian contingent attending the second Commonwealth Prime Ministers' Conference in London. He and Coombs later told stories about their adventurous trip with Prime Minister Chifley, Sir Frederick Shedden, Murray Tyrrell, Chifley's private secretary, Sam Landau from the Department of Defence, and defence advisers L. D. Tilbury and D. K. Rogers.[18] The journey was made in a special British Sunderland flying boat patrol bomber that the British manufacturers were urging on the government for Australian postwar international aviation. It offered space enough for them to confer and to sleep comfortably – or so it was thought. Tyrrell's photo collection includes pictures of the group alighting from the plane, a G-AGJL Short S25 Sunderland that, based in Poole, joined the BOAC fleet on New Year's Eve of 1945. 'It was not an auspicious demonstration,' Coombs said.[19] Caught in unpleasant pre-monsoonal weather between Calcutta and Karachi it lacked the speed and power to get around or above the unpleasantness. He described its progression as a series of 'prolonged upward sweeps followed by a sickening drop for which one waited in agonising suspense'.[20] The plane landed in Rangoon (Burma), Colombo (Ceylon) and Calcuta (India) in order to refuel, and its passengers were forced to alight each time.

---

18   Coombs, *Trial Balance,* 77.
19   Coombs, *Trial Balance,* 77.
20   Coombs, *Trial Balance,* 77 and see 77–84 for his story.

PERSONS OF INTEREST

British Sunderland flying boat, en route to the UK, 1946.

Source: Murray Tyrrell family collection, courtesy George Martin.

British Sunderland flying boat (John second from right), UK, 1946.

Source: Murray Tyrrell family collection; courtesy George Martin.

Once in London for the Prime Ministers' Conference, the party was presented to the King and Queen and Princesses Elizabeth and Margaret. According to Coombs, Tyrrell was greatly impressed with Princess Elizabeth: 'She is the only girl I have seen in England that I would like to take to Bondi Beach.'[21] Coombs speculated that this accounts for why Tyrrell accepted his subsequent position of Governor-General's private secretary – to give him more opportunities to meet the young Princess. The group had afternoon tea with the Royal Family, John told Meredith when he came home.

They travelled on to the USA for various trade and defence meetings. The flight across the Atlantic is one that John retold to us as children. In his memoir, Coombs recalled its detail vividly. When the plane approached Newfoundland, the island was fogbound and they had to continue to the mainland. As they approached the coast it appeared that they were unlikely to be able to land even in New York. The passengers became anxious. They had all gone through the 'ditching drill' in 'perfunctory style' when they boarded and now the crew made them go through it all again with meticulous attention to detail – not an encouraging sign. The plane had a narrow fuselage and the emergency exit was through a kind of porthole in the roof of the cabin. While going through the ditching drill, Chifley, large in stature in contrast to Coombs, began to laugh. 'Doc,' he said to Coombs, 'I'm just imagining you and me struggling to see who would get first through that porthole.'[22] They landed safely at Washington after a 23.5-hour flight. Chifley was calm 'without the solace of his pipe'.[23]

In Washington they stayed in Blair House, an official guest house of the White House. The main objectives of the Washington visit were to discuss Australia's concerns about political and military issues in the Pacific, the extent of the American presence, the future of American bases there and regional security arrangements. Coombs and John were also to open discussions to find a resolution to Australia's obligations under the Lend

---

21 Coombs, *Trial Balance*, 81.
22 Coombs, *Trial Balance*, 84.
23 Coombs, *Trial Balance*, 84.

Lease agreement it had made with the USA.[24] The issue was resolved simply by Chifley, as it transpired. In a hurry to leave for Japan, Chifley impressively negotiated a purely financial settlement over the telephone with the secretary of state.

John returned home just as I was ready to come into the world. Cecily had been to a concert or a play at the Albert Hall and returned home around 11 pm on 29 June, only to be admitted to the Canberra Community Hospital. I was born about two hours later on 30 June 1946 – not the boy they had hoped for. John had lived in a household of females as a child, and he would adjust to living in another. Less than a month later, John left to join Evatt as a delegate to the Paris Peace Conference, which ran from the end of July to the end of August.

Before he left, however, a house and acreage for sale, 'Melrose Valley', had turned up that caught John's eye. The property was around 240 hectares with a large double-storey house well situated to benefit from landscape views from every window. It was 9 miles out of Canberra on a school bus route, near Tuggeranong railway siding off the Monaro Highway. Despite its pegged wartime deflated price, it was unaffordable in Cecily's view. John's rationale for pursing the opportunity was that the house Cecily chose in Reid depressed him. He sought bank finance on the strength of his public servant income and commenced negotiations for its purchase amid his overseas travels in July 1946. The timing explains how I came by my middle name 'Melrose', five months before we purchased the property and moved into it in December 1946. At Melrose Valley, John indulged in weekend farming, which was the beginning of what he described as his 'second and accidental' career as a farmer. For John, it was perfect: 'A school bus. An accommodating wife. What more could one want.'[25]

---

24 The American Lend Lease program involved the distribution of military and other aid to the allies during the war to help the war effort against Germany, Japan and Italy. In return, the Allied nations were to provide goods or services and, on the cessation of the war, all weaponry and military materials were to be destroyed or returned. Australia had received quantities of military supplies from the USA during the early stages of the Pacific War. Its reciprocation of provisions for US forces of food, clothing and other military resources left a credit balance in favour of the USA. An issue arose over the value of the substantial amount of goods delivered and not consumed. Chifley was concerned as he wanted to avoid Australia entering into any longer-term arrangements that would tie it to the USA at a time it was trying to break free of imperial ties with the UK.
25 Burton, 'Oral History Project notes', 5, Burton family file.

12. AUSTRALIA ON THE WORLD STAGE

Evatt and Burton at the Paris Peace Conference, July 1946.
Source: Family collection.

Cecily nursing Pamela with Meredith and Clare, Canberra, 1946.
Source: Family collection.

13

Farming with an 'accommodating wife'

John went heavily into debt to buy Melrose Valley. He ran up accounts at petrol stations and produce stores, but somehow made ends meet. In a rare display of humour, he wrote to his sister:

> I have borrowed more money than I am ever likely to be able to pay back, but that is the problem of the Mutual Life with whom I have taken out a life assurance which might be mistaken for a national debt.[1]

He arranged with the seller of the property to defer payment for some plant and stock for a year or so and he purchased sheep on credit from stock and station agents. 'It is a lot of fun,' he said. 'Inflation will pay about 50% back and I might manage the rest.'[2]

The drive entrance on the Old Tuggeranong Road looks down into the valley to the gracious two-storey New England–style homestead and a separate cottage. Based on the design of a Connecticut farmhouse, the home was built in 1938 with dark brown, oiled jarrah weatherboard. In addition to its five bedrooms, it had three living rooms, a 'maid's room' – although we never had a maid – and a double garage. There were

---

1   Letter to Rewa, 7 November 1946, Burton family file. John had not been in touch with his sister since the birth of Meredith, and included the information that he now had two more children. He mentioned that he had been told 'by Mother that I am a disgrace etc.'. He offered to write again when he 'had two more kids'.
2   Letter to Rewa, 7 November 1946.

large open fireplaces in all main rooms including the bedrooms.[3] They were needed in winter. Snow lay thick on the ground on the outskirts of Canberra at times, as it did to my delight on my second birthday in June 1948. The house with its interesting angles and features was a magic haven for children; there were small places for us to hide under dark stairwells, where I would go to wind up my small mechanical toy to watch it flash coloured sparks; attic rooms with pitched roofs; and many other hide-and-seek possies and places to play. There was a large garden surrounding the house with two orchards and a tennis court and John built a swimming pool. The views were outstanding, although the paddocks were too rugged, steep and stony to produce a livelihood from farming. However, we had three creeks and dozens of springs and John was able to run about 500 sheep and four milking cows that came with the property. He and Cecily developed a vegetable patch and we enjoyed eggs from our chickens – and, sadly, we probably ate the turkeys he raised at some stage.

John busied himself on the farm and indoors. He finished making our dining room table and chairs and a cot for me that was practical in design but flawed in concept: I howled, apparently, when I caught my fingers in the sliding wire door. In addition, he set about writing a book on 'international government' because 'it is a race between me and the bomb' and running the Department of External Affairs as its acting head, he told his sister, Rewa.[4] Cecily adjusted, as John expected she would, to her role as the farmer's wife. However, the demands on her were enormous. As John commuted to the department every day, she was left to cope with daily happenings and farm emergencies. We had no electricity. We used hurricane lamps at night and relied on an Esse hot water system and a wood fuel stove for cooking in the big kitchen. John sometimes brought newly hatched chickens into the study to keep them warm beside a gas flame heater. As young children, we had sleeping difficulties. Cecily and John spent time walking the floor at nights, both becoming too tired to function at their best. They even resorted to giving me sedatives so that I would sleep – and that they might too. As John's work became all-consuming, Cecily soon learned that he 'trusted' people, including her, to learn skills and do things that he wanted done. In time Cecily learned

---

3   Dr F. A. Ormiston completed the house and lived there from 1938 until he sold it to the Burtons in December 1946.
4   Letter to Rewa, 7 November 1946, Burton family file.

13. FARMING WITH AN 'ACCOMMODATING WIFE'

to love the country, as hard a struggle as it was for her to raise young children and survive the physical demands of farm life. The experience made Cecily stronger and richer in spirit.

Parker and his family visited us shortly after we settled in. A photograph taken in 1947 of Cecily, Meredith, Clare and me, his wife Nancy and their son Rod on the veranda of our new home depicts Cecily feeding me with a bottle and Rod 'fraternising self-consciously with the two elder Burton daughters'.[5] Nancy was and looked pregnant. Parker probably took the picture as Nancy believed that John 'would have been treading heavily about in gum boots at the bottom of the paddock playing farmer'.[6] And playing at farming was all John soon had time to do. Three months after our move to Melrose Valley, Evatt telephoned him to ask him to fill the permanent position of secretary of the department. On 27 March 1947, having just turned 32, John took over the position from Sir William Dunk.

We needed but could not afford a second car. John used the family car to go to and from Canberra for work. How was Cecily to deliver and collect Meredith and Clare the mile or so along the hilly dirt road to the Monaro Highway where the school van stopped? Meredith had a little red scooter on which she sometimes scooted downhill to meet the panel van. John found a solution when he discovered a man living nearby in a tent beside the railway line. The man and his wife had a car, but no home. We had a vacant cottage. John explained to his sister, Rewa:

> He is a fettler who was a farmer before the war and escaped war by turning railway. He has a wife who will not live in a tent with him. He has a car which could take the children down to the school car a mile away. So I invited him and wife to live in a nice house – to which he said he would pay board to which I said no, I will pay you. He knocks off work at four each day. There must be a catch somewhere.[7]

---

5   Nancy Sawer, *Telling It to Abi* (Broulee, NSW: Nancy Sawer, 2000), 157.
6   Sawer, *Telling It to Abi*, 157.
7   Letter to Rewa, 7 November 1946, Burton family file.

Making life easier for John and Cecily too, was the help of some migrant workers 'allocated by' the government. Calwell, an Irish Catholic and Labor's first federal minister for migration, introduced an immigration program that John embraced. John and Cecily referred to their helpers, politically incorrectly Cecily later believed, as 'the Balts'. In fact, the term 'Balts' was coined by Calwell himself: 'The beautiful Balts,' he called them in the course of a campaign to sell the virtues of the Displaced Person's Scheme in 1947. Ella Kagra was placed with our family as a private 'domestic' in April 1948.[8] As children, we do not remember her carrying out any domestic work, and we would not be surprised if John and Cecily simply provided her with accommodation and were grateful for any support she gave Cecily. I do remember Otto, one of the migrant farm workers who lived with his wife Tekla in a room at the end of our large house with their young baby. Otto amused me playing his trumpet. 'Otto chews the boom boom,' my mother said I told her.

Another helper was Trixie, our obedient blue heeler, who efficiently brought in sheep on John's or Cecily's command. The farm came with four cows and four horses and, much to Cecily's dismay, John presented us with three ponies one Christmas without consulting her. Meredith climbed onto hers, Prince, and fell straight off the other side. Clare's was the family's favourite, Sambo, a solid speckled black pony that she shared with Cecily, and I, then barely two, was given a grey mare. We accumulated other dogs and pets. There was a pet snake too, or so I thought when I saw my father place a saucer of milk under a shed near the house for it – or to lure it out, I later learned. I didn't associate the dried skins hanging over the fence with my snake that no longer appeared for a saucer of milk. I also had, what I believed to be, a pet rabbit. John had brought it in for us to stroke before doing what a farmer must. It escaped from the clutches of my arms in the living room and ran under a couch. I thought it slept there and I talked to it for several days, wondering why it did not come out from under the couch. As an adult, I reminded my mother of this pet rabbit. Cecily, puzzled, said, 'A rabbit as a pet, dear? On a farm, I don't think so.' In retrospect I accepted that the fate of our rabbit must have been similar to that of the snake.

---

8   NAA: B550/1, 1948/23/2428.

Meredith on her pony Prince with John, Melrose Valley, 1949.
Source: Family collection.

On one occasion in 1948, Cecily contracted chicken pox. With a fever and feeling ill, she tried to cope alone with three children. One night when John was either away or working late, she was carrying me to my cot under one arm and a hurricane lamp in the other and thought she would collapse. Which to drop? Risk hurting the baby, or cause a fire? She made it – without dropping either – and was then hospitalised for a week. John arranged for us to be cared for, avoiding friends with children who had not had chicken pox. Librarian Harold White and his wife Elizabeth took Meredith. They had looked after her before when floods prevented her returning from school to the farm. Tom and Joyce Critchley, who had no children, offered to take both Clare and me. Tom was a departmental colleague and friend of John's. Cecily lay in hospital worried about the couple's lack of experience in caring for such young children. They must have looked after us well because Clare, at the tender age of four, fell in love with Tom, she told our mother.

Fortunately, John was around one weekend to help Cecily when fire broke out in the homestead. Our immigrant farm helpers, Otto and Tekla, relied on a gas heater for warmth. It was situated against a wooden wall and it caught alight when they were out. There were high winds on the farm and when John saw smoke rise from the room, he called the fire brigade and then rushed to the garage to fetch a fire extinguisher. He pulled the ring to unlock the operating handle, threw the extinguisher into the room (as John described it), and shut the door. Cecily tried to direct Meredith, then about seven or eight to put on her gumboots and run across to the house of the manager of the local railway siding. Meredith looked at Cecily and asked: 'Do I have to?' 'Yes,' she was told, but before she set off a fire truck arrived. However, John's action had worked and the fire was already out. He offered the firefighters a beer, which they accepted.

John liked to experiment and be the first to embrace new ideas. In 1949, he decided we could afford a vehicle that could cope with rough land. He ordered a Land Rover from England, one of the first off the production line. It was dispatched to Sydney in January on the *Stratheden*, the passenger liner of which our family would have first-hand experience just two years later. He opted for 'extras' such as a power take-off device to allow him to transfer mechanical power from the vehicle's engine to a loader or winch and to operate other machinery in the paddocks.[9] It was his first serious farm toy.

On one occasion, a calf of a calving cow got stuck. It was going to die and the cow was at risk too. John was in a conference in town and could not get home. Cecily called the vet who drove to the farm immediately. He was practical: 'Let's do it the quick and easy way,' he said. Cecily piled the three of us children into the back of the Land Rover and drove the vet and one of our migrant farm workers across the paddocks to the cow. The vet attached a chain to the cow and the fence, and a rope to the calf and the Land Rover. Cecily had to drive forward slowly to pull the calf out. We all goggled at the scene from the Land Rover. She commanded as she drove, 'Don't look, don't look', and of course we turned around to see what it was we should not look at. Cecily saw her 'Balt' helper turn green, noting later that this was the only time in her life she had actually seen someone turn green from watching a nauseating sight. The cow and calf survived.

John's colleague, Colin Moodie, recalls driving back to the farm with John one evening in the Land Rover, having first gone around the alleyways of Manuka shopping centre to collect scraps discarded by grocery shops to feed the farm animals. 'As if his own job wasn't enough', Moodie, in his memoir, commented on John running a farm as well as a department.[10] John cajoled Moodie and other colleagues into helping with some farm

---

9   Land Rovers came into production in the UK in 1948. Rob Sprason, a Land Rover enthusiast, unearthed records of the early Burton purchase of one of the first 2,000 Land Rovers produced. Other 'extras' he chose included larger tyres to handle rocky surfaces, and a numbered key, in case it had to be replaced.
10   Memoir of Colin Moodie, NLA, MS Acc13.173, 26.

work. He would hand them a shovel when they arrived and lead the way to the chicken or pig pens. 'You can shovel some shit while we talk,' he'd say, and then started to throw out his ideas. He insisted that he did his best thinking 'shovelling shit'.

John sometimes invited his small department to Melrose Valley for barbecues. One notable occasion was two days after Chifley called troops in that saw the end to the 1949 coal strike. John had his department to the farm and formed them into cricket teams for entertainment.

The farm was an ideal escape for John on weekends. He claimed that wandering among sheep and milking cows helped him think clearly. 'It was my salvation,' he said.[11] The farm gave him security and independence. It was 'a bargaining asset', he wrote, because 'Dr Evatt was quite convinced that I could withdraw to it if I did not get my way!'[12] He said, 'When you worked with Evatt you needed an escape … I didn't want to become a yes-man'.[13] However, he was a 'Yes, Prime Minister' man in true Sir Humphrey style in that he managed to influence government policy when he worked for Chifley.

External Affairs staff cricket teams, Melrose Valley, 1949.
Source: Family collection.

---

11   Clack, 'Theories amidst Cows and Hills', *Canberra Times*, 8 September 1991, 24.
12   Burton, 'Oral History Project notes', 5, Burton family file.
13   Clack, *Canberra Times*, 8 September 1991, 24.

Taking a break, from left to right, Alex Borthwick, Keith Brennan, John, Trevor Pyman, David and Alison Hay, Melrose Valley, 1949.
Source: Family collection.

One thing John did that endeared him to Chifley was akin to the presentation of 'an apple for the teacher', but, in John's case, it was farm-produced cream that Chifley received. John rose at dawn each day to milk his cows, separate out the milk fats and deliver cream to the Hotel Kurrajong in time for Chifley's breakfast.[14] This he did even after broken sleep from a phone call at night or the need to deal with an overseas cable on behalf of Evatt. Cream was rationed during the war and Chifley loved thick cream with his breakfast, notwithstanding its ill-effect on his health. And, indeed, Chifley died of a heart attack while in office in June 1951. Having delivered Chifley's cream, John arrived at work around 8 am with the night's cables already answered to the annoyance of others who arrived to find sent responses on their desk.

Sometimes, John's afternoon was interrupted by an urgent call to say the school van had left without picking me up. I was just four when I started preschool in 1950. There were times when Cecily, having driven to the highway to collect us, was shaken to see Meredith and Clare alight from the panel van without me. The arrangement was that I would be put on

---

14 Dr John Burton, 'Looking to the Future: An International Relations for the New Millennium', *Evatt Papers* 3, no. 2 (1995), 115.

a bus by my preschool teacher at the Girls' Grammar School in Deakin. I was instructed to get off the bus at Manuka shops and wait for the panel van that collected Meredith and Clare and other children from Telopea Park School in Barton. My bus was often late and the girls' panel van left Manuka without me. I would stand and cry and wait for someone to find me. Someone always did, but often had trouble finding out who I belonged to. I was taught to recite my address but once, muddled, I recited instead, 'Pamela Melrose Valley Tuggeranong', which, as it turned out, was sufficient to link me with John Burton, by now well-known as the controversial head of External Affairs who lived at Melrose Valley. He left work to collect me and drove me home. After that, I was given a bracelet on which my name and address were engraved.

As well as caring for three children, coping with fires, snow and floods that made the dirt road to the farm impassable, Cecily had to live with John's unpredictability and the controversy that he often stirred in the community. We know that Cecily understood and supported the rationale for John's controversial foreign policy stand. She believed that her role in life – and she always believed one must have one to improve the world – was to support John. Years later, she found that she could play a role in her own right. At the time, though, sharing his ethical and intellectual convictions, she devoted herself to John's cause. She learned that no amount of controversy or criticism would deter him from persisting with a particular crusade – on the contrary, it would encourage him to work harder to have his critics better understand his mission. Cecily, from childhood, understood the pain of being misunderstood. She would sympathise with his need, but not necessarily his methods, to try to have people see things his way.

What Cecily found difficult was John's lack of consultation about anything, particularly matters that affected her and the family. John made decisions about large family purchases, holidays, place of living and career changes. He expressed hurt if she questioned his choices or asked why he had not consulted her, and accused her of being unappreciative when he shocked her by producing what he thought was a generous offering, or a happy surprise. Every Christmas and birthday we children came to expect that John would give Cecily the latest electrical gadget for the kitchen and we noticed she was less than fully satisfied with these gifts as expressions of love. She would have been more convinced of his love for her if he listened harder to understand and appreciate her as a person.

Cecily was a carer and listener by nature and tried to be there for John. Then again, John was not very communicative at home; he did not seem to share with her his own inner insecurities, which we now understand he had. Our strong impression is that when he came home from work, he had shut his mind off from his work and got involved in some physical farming or other activity. Did either of them fully comprehend what the other was going through? In their senior years, Cecily talked to us about her unsatisfactory relationship with John, not about any turmoil he suffered from the political circumstances of the time, and John talked a lot about his controversial political past, not about the toll it took on Cecily. It would seem that both suffered emotionally somewhat alone.

Cecily's feelings of inadequacy persisted despite how strong she appeared on the outside. John never learned, or never saw the need, to help her over this. Her feeling of being an inadequate mum went a little far on one occasion. She phoned the headmistress of Meredith's infant school because she had forgotten to check that morning if Meredith was wearing underpants. The no-fuss headmistress called Meredith out of the assembly to ask her. Meredith pulled up her skirt to show her pants.

Despite the challenges, Melrose Valley was a memorable social time for Cecily. She felt inept and often was unhappy, but she was not lonely. There were plenty of visitors, particularly at weekends: politicians, trade unionists, diplomats, public servants, neighbours and other friends. Once in 1948 when John was away, Calwell arrived at the farm at around teatime. Cecily was tired and feeling helpless so she boiled some eggs for us all to eat. She handed me to Calwell who sat me on his knee and spoon fed me an egg. I now know that Calwell and his wife Elizabeth lost their 11-year-old son that same year from leukaemia, and it is sad to think that, at the time I was being nursed by Calwell, his own son was either very ill or had recently died. Despite, or because of her own deep feelings of inadequacy, Cecily engaged deeply with people and felt their own suffering and Calwell was deeply affected by his son's death. He wore a black tie in token of his mourning to the end of his days.[15]

While Cecily would not have agreed with all of Calwell's views, she saw his humanity and liked him. Politically, Calwell was an enigma. He was 'old guard' Labor and came to be best remembered for the major contribution he made to Australia's successful postwar immigration policy, but he was

---

15   *Sun-Herald* (Sydney), 15 September 1973.

disliked by many for his 'white Australia' policy. His attitude to Asian refugees was in stark contrast to the compassion he showed for Australia's Indigenous population. He was a strong advocate for Aboriginal rights, their land rights and for their recognition as Australian peoples in the Constitution. Cecily enjoyed the company of Paul Hasluck too, despite his conservative politics, because, like her, he expressed his feelings through poetry. We found a poem of his, 'Recognition', in her personal papers. Cecily enjoyed reading, film, music and dance – and solitude. However, she was always interested in people, their thoughts and why they thought the way they did. She often said to us, 'if you have a choice between people or things – choose people'. No matter how low or tired she felt, she would always put down her book, or sewing, or leave the kitchen, to warmly greet people who visited. By every account, Cecily was a beautiful, intelligent woman, graceful, dignified, diligent and well-loved; she was not dominating or egocentric.

As for John, we assess that those who got to know him, liked him. He was a man of few words, self-assured about the rightness of his views, and he did not suffer fools. An ASIO source, who had John under surveillance some years later, described him as 'a quiet speaker who uses forceful language'.[16] However, he was egalitarian in approach and encouraged people he met from all walks of life to realise his or her potential. He was respected by his colleagues for his ideas and his work ethic, liked for this by some and disliked for both by others.

---

16   NAA: A6119, 130, Burton vol. 4, 30.

14

A controversial head of department

John's elevation in 1947, having just turned 32, to head the Department of External Affairs was controversial. It displeased older senior diplomats such as Alan (later Sir Alan) Watt who, as assistant secretary, had previously been overlooked by the Labor Government for the position of head in favour of Sir William Dunk. He was given a diplomatic posting to Moscow instead.[1] John Hood, who had joined External Affairs in 1939 and who had filled in as acting secretary of the department, believed that of the potential candidates only John could work well enough with Evatt. He saw John's appointment as necessary. Colin Moodie had sympathy for John:

> Poor Burton; like most idealists, he was born for disappointment and soon found we were no different in essence from the men we replaced. He relied on emotion and instinct, which are dangerous guides without knowledge, especially when working for a Minister like Evatt, who wanted to bestride the world …[2]

Evatt was difficult to work with, but so was John. After a few major clashes during which John stood his ground, they got on well. John told us that Evatt rushed out of a cabinet meeting on an occasion, and ran down the hall of Parliament House to ask him, 'Do you want a knighthood?' John did not want to be 'Sir John Burton', and allegedly answered, 'No. I have a title, I have a PhD.' According to John, 'the kingdom was awash with

---
1 'Mr A. S. Watt Minister to Moscow', *Sydney Morning Herald*, 6 February 1947, 1.
2 Memoir of Colin Moodie, NLA, MS Acc13.173, 25.

knights – but not with Doctors of Philosophy'. From then on, John said, the Doc insisted that the staff call him 'Dr Burton'. The title 'Dr Burton' in newspaper headlines stuck. I now understand that the handing out of knighthoods to departmental heads was not common under Labor; nevertheless, whether the story is true or not, it reflects John's recall that Evatt valued his head of department having a doctorate.

Evatt's influence on shaping Australia's foreign policy and John's influence on Evatt have been the subject of debate over the last 70 years. According to John, his and Evatt's shared philosophical outlook explains what many historians later found puzzling: namely, the little documented evidence that Evatt had provided John with any precise policy directives. Instead, the archived telegrams and cables available to historians appear, on their face, to reflect that decisions were made by John rather than Evatt – particularly on matters concerning South-East Asia. John states that he did seek instructions but that Evatt responded with a general philosophical discussion. John was left to deduce from the general. Evatt might say, for example, 'You were at San Francisco. You know what the Charter says. You know what my policies are.'[3]

One Friday after a busy postwar Cabinet week during which John saw little of Evatt, John travelled with Evatt to Goulburn in order to get Evatt's decision on several matters. Another car followed, to bring John back to Canberra. John tried to get direct answers but failed to steer Evatt's conversation to the matters of concern. Instead, they had one of their not unusual conversations that covered all kinds of topics that John enjoyed. John wrote, 'The driver, had he not known otherwise, could have thought we were a couple of political philosophers from the Australian National University'.[4] On his drive home, passing Lake George, he wondered how he could deal with the issues that needed a decision. It was then that he realised that with Evatt, 'provided the philosophical framework was understood, decision making was no problem'.[5] John had a lot of freedom and, on reflection, he said:

> As a consequence I am associated with initiatives far beyond those of a public servant, for example, to establish links with the people of this region, to assist in their struggles for independence and to move away from pre-war reliance on strategic alliances. But these were no more than the day-to-day, event-following-event

---

3   Burton, 'Oral History Project notes', 4, Burton family file.
4   Burton, 'Herbert Vere Evatt: A Man Out of His Time', in Day, *Brave New World*, 2.
5   Burton, 'Herbert Vere Evatt', in Day, *Brave New World*, 3.

applications of a well-discussed policy approach. The directive was that Australian security and welfare in the future must rest on Australia's independent decision-making, and in particular the promotion of stability in the region based on independent and secure autonomies which would, because of their self-esteem and security, have no reason to seek assistance from any power outside the region.⁶

During the war and postwar, Australia's defence and foreign policy was primarily run from the Defence Department under Sir Frederick Shedden. Distrust and antagonism had already developed between Shedden's department in Melbourne and the much smaller Department of External Affairs in Canberra before John became its head. When John arrived, he had easy access to Evatt his minister and Chifley as prime minister, and he was able to respond quickly overnight or early in the morning to cables, some of which had policy implications, without consulting others. Shedden complained that he was not always being informed of cables External Affairs received concerning Defence's areas of interest. In a lengthy personal cable to John, Shedden spoke of 'the difficulty with which we are confronted when called upon for our comments at the last minute on a matter on which there has been an extensive exchange of views over a lengthy period, of which we have no knowledge'.⁷ He urged the fullest cooperation and exchange of information between the two departments. Tensions mounted. The relationship between the two men did not improve with time. Arthur Tange, who had been seconded into the Department of External Affairs in 1945, later offered his perspective on this in his memoir:

> Knowing Burton well, and observing Shedden, I came to believe in later years that the differences were the product of many things: age, education, respect for conventional Public Service practices; but particularly fundamental differences on the issues in East-West relations, on the policy of non-alignment by emerging ex-colonies, and related questions. There was also the competition between a well rooted, if conservative and somewhat complacent, Department and a small group of untried newcomers in Canberra elevated into influence by a radical Labor leadership.⁸

---

6   Burton, 'Looking to the Future', 116.
7   Department of Foreign Affairs and Trade (DFAT) Historical Documents, vol. 12, *1947, (other than Indonesia)*, Document (Doc.) 164, Shedden to Burton, 28 April 1947, 'Secret Personal' [AA: A1838, TS669/3, i].
8   Tange, *Defence Policy-Making*, 2.

When the Council of Defence directed External Affairs to furnish a review of the international situation in 1948, an interdepartmental dispute between the departments of Defence and External Affairs erupted.[9] The different perspectives of the two departments on how hostility towards other nations should be handled is seen in some discussions on whether Australia's support of the UK in the Middle East would best protect it from Soviet aggression – 'the enemy likely to jeopardise Australian security'. In a Minute to Evatt on 15 April 1948, John referred to a conversation he had with Shedden about Defence's view on the approach to be taken with respect to regional relations. He said that Shedden argued that:

> it is necessary, in making a strategic appreciation, to make certain assumptions regarding possible enemies without implying that in fact a country singled out is regarded politically as an enemy.[10]

John conveyed his own view to Evatt:

> I have always argued that strategic appreciations can and should be made without reference to a political appreciation pointing to likely enemies, and that, in any case, no foreign policy directed at securing peace could be based on possible enemies.[11]

Instead, John argued that what was required was direction on the basis of Australian Government policy on the use of Australian manpower and resources in the event of any conflict, however brought about and by whatever country. He concluded:

> It would seem to me that it is this direction which the Chiefs of Staff do not wish to get, as it would completely change their planning and would prevent them making appreciations designating a particular country – Russia – as an enemy.[12]

An External Affairs strategic report, an 'Appreciation', of September 1948 challenged the opinion of the Chiefs of Staff and argued that a combination of Chinese and communist influence in South-East Asia and the Pacific was a more direct threat to Australian security than its possible threat to

---

9 See extracts from cables: Pamela Andre and Sue Langford, eds, *Australia and the Postwar World: The Commonwealth, Asia and the Pacific: Documents 1948–49* (Canberra: Department of Foreign Affairs and Trade, 1998), Introduction, x–xi.
10 DFAT Historical Documents, vol. 14, *1948–49, The Commonwealth, Asia and the Pacific*, Doc. 120, Burton to Evatt, Minute 15 April 1948, 'Top Secret Defence Council', accessed 24 May 2021, dfat.gov.au/about-us/publications/historical-documents/Pages/volume-14/120-burton-to-evatt.
11 DFAT, Doc. 120, Burton to Evatt, Minute 15 April 1948.
12 DFAT, Doc. 120, Burton to Evatt, Minute 15 April 1948.

14. A CONTROVERSIAL HEAD OF DEPARTMENT

UK interests in the Middle East. It recommended that Australia should plan to counteract a threat to its own region by non-military means rather than by readying itself to support the UK's military in the Middle East. The Defence response was delayed for six months and then mislaid in John's department for a further two months, exacerbating the policy direction differences between the two departments. The department's official summary of the direction taken under John's influence as indicated in its Appreciation suggests that:

> In many ways the External Affairs appreciation also expressed Burton's desire for a more active Australian presence in the region. It outlined a plan of 'early and determined action' through a programme of economic and technological assistance and the extension of consular posts to Borneo, Sumatra, French Indo-China and Burma. In this way Australia would help improve social conditions, thereby combating the attraction of communism, and achieve some degree of influence with governments in the region.[13]

Moodie had been privy to the preparation of the Appreciation and recalled:

> He prepared an appreciation of our strategic position (which was supposed to be a joint External Affairs/Defence product), slanted against China and away from Russia with the help of a junior officer, gave me a copy and sent the other copy to the Secretary of Defence Dept. His words to me were: 'If there's a leakage, we'll know it's either you or that bastard Shedden'.[14]

In October 1948, John accompanied Evatt to London for the Imperial Prime Ministers' Conference when Evatt represented Australia as minister for External Affairs. John advised Evatt following Chifley's direction. All the while, the Joint Intelligence Committee continued to produce appreciations that took no account of those prepared by External Affairs.

Chifley, Evatt and John were of like minds in emphasising the importance of strengthening relations with neighbouring countries. Defence, on the other hand, continued to focus on securing the country against potential enemies. The threat of the spread of communism in the region posed an agreed risk, but the two departments charged with implementing defence and foreign policy were at war with the way to combat it. Defence continued to support the traditional military-based approach of

---

13 Andre and Langford, *Australia and the Postwar World*, Introduction, xi.
14 Memoir of Colin Moodie, NLA, MS Acc13.173, 25.

the colonial powers; External Affairs saw the need to address grievances that arose from colonial rule in order to strengthen the region's resistance to communist infiltration. John favoured open diplomacy that would introduce circuit-breaking dialogues and relationships into Australia's foreign policy thinking. He thought it important to understand what was driving the thinking of Australia's close neighbours. Shedden, on the other hand, accepted in 1948 the British assessments that Moscow was directing communist subversion in South-East Asia. Hasluck expressed cynicism, holding the view that 'Burton was essentially a crusader. He had to advance a cause and was as ardent as any crusader because of his conviction that whatever cause he favoured was the only cause worth service'.[15] John had fallen out with Hasluck after denying him a permanent posting to the United Nations. With hindsight, John realised his mistake, but was nevertheless surprised that Hasluck joined the Liberal Party and decided to enter federal politics when John thought he was a Labor man.[16]

A footnote to Evatt's and John's push for engagement with Australia's Pacific neighbours is the involvement of John's father, Jack, in the region. Evatt, John and some other senior officers of External Affairs initiated the formation of a consultative regional forum for the Pacific. Australia, France, the Netherlands, New Zealand, the UK and the USA officially launched the South Pacific Commission on 6 February 1947 to promote development in Pacific Island territories under their administration.[17] Evatt appointed John's father as one of two Australian commissioners to the commission. Jack attended its inaugural meeting in 1948 with Evatt.[18]

---

15 Hasluck, *Diplomatic Witness*, 35.
16 See Burton, interview by Michael J. Wilson, 1995, 9–11, for John's description of his relationship with Hasluck; and see Henry, 'Reflections on Dr. John Wear Burton', 71.
17 Daniel Oakman, *Facing Asia: A History of the Colombo Plan* (Canberra: ANU E Press, 2010), 15, doi.org/10.22459/FA.10.2010.
18 Andre and Langford, *Australia and the Postwar World*, 241.

14. A CONTROVERSIAL HEAD OF DEPARTMENT

Father and son, John and Jack Burton, Evatt appointees, late 1940s.
Source: Family collection.

15
Reshaping Australia's foreign policy

John's work from 1945 to 1950 in support of Indonesia's independence from the Dutch was a major legacy he left as an Australian public servant. Indonesia, one of Australia's closest neighbours, had declared its independence on 17 August 1945. Sukarno became its first president (1949–66), but Dutch resistance started a diplomatic struggle that erupted into sporadic armed conflict. Indonesia needed its neighbours' support. Historian David Fettling said:

> Burton became the foremost champion in Australian government of a national reorientation to Asia … [His] fundamental objective was to attain security and stability in Australia's immediate region, including from communist insurrections: in this way he was an exemplar of, not an exception to, the long Australian 'search for security'.[1]

Brian Toohey, journalist and author, concluded of John that 'he was a significant strategic thinker who opposed communism and supported independence for Indonesia and other colonies as being in Australia's long-term interest'.[2] Academic and former diplomat Garry Woodard

---

1   David Fettling, *Encounters with Asian Decolonisation* (North Melbourne, Vic.: Australian Scholarly Publishing, 2017), 189–90.
2   Brian Toohey, *Secret: The Making of Australia's Security State* (Carlton, Vic.: Melbourne University Press, 2019), 259.

concluded that John's work on Indonesia 'has received the accolades of history'.[3] British officials described Burton as 'the power behind the Evatt Throne' and 'Evatt's ideas man'.[4]

At the time, however, not everyone applauded John's work in implementing the Chifley Government's foreign policy towards Asia and its approach to postwar Australian diplomacy. According to Gregory Pemberton, when John left the service, the Dutch foreign minister 'scrawled joyously across the report: "Good news, one lunatic less in politics"'.[5] Pemberton's research was thorough. He said:

> I have now researched in the archives of twelve countries' foreign ministries and I can say without fear of contradiction that no Australian public official and very few ministers have been as much talked about internationally as has John Burton. No Australian, except Dr Evatt himself, has provoked such controversy or interest or made such a widely felt impact, both positive and negative.[6]

He found some colourful descriptions of John in his archival searches: 'A strong man from Moscow' is how Naval intelligence described John in the 1940s; a 'wild man', according to New Zealand officials in 1947; and 'As usual when Dr Burton enters the scene the skies darken', came from the British in 1949.[7]

Within months of John heading the department, in late March and early April 1947, Indian Prime Minister Jawaharlal Nehru initiated an Asian Relations Conference in New Delhi. John decided to sponsor Australian observers at that conference from the Australian Institute of International Affairs and the Australian Institute of Political Science. The government's support reflected the hope that Nehru and India would play a vital role in ensuring the economic and political security of the region.[8] At the same time, by having no official government presence, Australia avoided

---

3   Garry Woodard, 'Cold War Downunder: Foreign policy and defence in Australia 1945–50', paper produced for the Australasian Political Studies Association 1997 conference, reproduced in *Australasian Political Studies 1997: Proceedings of the 1997 Australasian Political Studies Association Conference 29 September–1 October 1997*, vol. 3, ed. George Crowder (Adelaide: Dept of Politics, Flinders University of South Australia, 1997).
4   Pemberton, 'John Burton: The Heretic', 93 at 98; Gregory Pemberton, 'A Matter of Independence', *Canberra Times*, 17 August 1991, Saturday Magazine C1.
5   Pemberton, 'John Burton: The Heretic', 96.
6   Pemberton, 'John Burton: The Heretic', 96.
7   Pemberton, 'John Burton: The Heretic', 96.
8   Julie Suares, 'Engaging with Asia: The Chifley Government and the New Delhi Conferences of 1947 and 1949', *Australian Journal of Politics and History* 57, no. 4 (2011), 503.

the risk of its 'white Australia' policy being the subject of attack.[9] John strongly supported Nehru's view, with which Chifley agreed, that the best way to counter the spread of communism in Asia was to allow, not repress, independence movements. Political reform and improved living standards would provide a better defence to unrest and communist agitation against colonial rule than would a military response.[10] Moodie, then official secretary to Australia's first high commissioner for Australia in India, sent many cables, reports and newspaper articles about the conference proceedings back to the Department of External Affairs. The presence of Australia, according to scholar Julie Suares, was of historic significance, and a 'manifestation of a growing awareness of appreciation of a distinctive Australian geographic identity'.[11]

In mid-1947, however, the Dutch conflict in Indonesia worsened and, on 20 July, the first Dutch police action against the republic began after the Dutch terminated their diplomatic agreement with the Indonesian Republic.[12] There was growing sympathy towards Indonesia's wish for independence, and Chifley and Evatt became concerned about Dutch colonialism and its propensity for violence.[13] In July 1947, Australia joined India to urge that the dispute go to the United Nations, but the British and US governments resisted, stating that they could manage the conflict themselves. John took issue with this 'great power management' approach and its traditional imperial implications.[14] Pemberton studied cables that tell the story:

> Over several days cables kept pouring into London from Canberra urging the British to act. Finally, they agreed to allow Australia to take the dispute to the Security Council. British officials were confounded as to who was the author of these cables, as their usual irritant, Evatt, was overseas. Then an explanatory message came in from the British High Commissioner in New Zealand: Burton was responsible, he is regarded as a 'wild man' here.[15]

---

9   Eric Meadows, '"He No Doubt Felt Insulted": The White Australia Policy and Australia's Relations with India, 1944–1964', chapter 5 in *Australia and the World: A Festschrift for Neville Meaney*, ed. Joan Beaumont and Matthew Jordan (Sydney: Sydney University Press, 2013), 86.
10   Suares, 'Engaging with Asia', 497; L. F. Crisp, *Ben Chifley: A Biography* (London: Longmans, 1961), 292.
11   Suares, 'Engaging with Asia', 503.
12   See David Lee, ed., *Australia & Indonesia's Independence: The Transfer of Sovereignty: Documents 1949* (Canberra: Department of Foreign Affairs and Trade, 1998), ix, and see xiii.
13   Henry, 'Reflections on Dr. John Wear Burton', 73.
14   Dunn, *From Power Politics to Conflict Resolution*, 22–23.
15   Pemberton, 'A Matter of Independence'; and see David Fettling, 'J. B. Chifley and the Indonesian Revolution, 1945–1949', *Australian Journal of Politics and History* 59, no. 4 (December 2013): 517–31.

Ric Throssell, a member of the United Nations Division of John's department, sent a cable to the Australian Mission to the UN and instructed them to put a strong resolution to the UN Security Council, of which Australia was a non-permanent member. He believed that India's resolution at the UN was inadequate.[16] Under UN procedural rules the resolution would take precedence over other draft resolutions before the council. Australia's resolution was adopted and, a week later, the UN issued a cease-fire order to both parties. It saw the termination of the first Dutch attack on the emerging Indonesia Republic. Soon after, Sukarno said that Australia's action had 'probably saved the Republic'.[17] John later explained that he had constant communication with Sukarno by late evening radio broadcasts, short wave being the only means of messaging. He arranged for the Royal Australian Air Force to fly back to Sukarno the leading seaman of those who were off-loaded from Dutch ships who were in camps in Queensland and who could help Sukarno in forming an interim government. John conceded that:

> All of this had to be done without publicity. For reasons of race we should have been helping the Dutch ship arms to Indonesia and to help them to regain control. Furthermore, treating people, especially Asians, as humans, was considered 'communism' (despite reports of the way in which the person was being treated in the Soviet Union).[18]

Fettling noted the British High Commission's view of John that, 'in [Burton's] mind the Indonesians loomed large, and the Dutch small'.[19] Fettling concluded, however, that the Chifley Government's actions were driven by the grievances of the Indonesians and not by a prejudicial anti-Dutch stance. John's concern was that violence might result from the grievances that in turn would threaten the stability of the region and, hence, Australia's security. John attributed Dutch economic exploitation of Indonesia to causing mass inequality, which led to the violent unrest. Profits from what he regarded as exploitation of the rich natural resources of the East Indies flowed to Holland with an insufficient proportion retained to raise the standards of living of the local population. He opposed the Dutch blockade that deprived some 35 million people

---

16 Pemberton, 'A Matter of Independence', C1.
17 Pemberton, 'A Matter of Independence', C1.
18 Letter from John to journalist Peter Freeman, 2 November 2001, Burton family file.
19 Fettling, *Encounters with Asian Decolonisation*, 189.

of goods essential to life. John believed in the legitimacy of Indonesia's desire for independence and thought Sukarno's regime should be given the opportunity to create a more egalitarian society than was possible under the Dutch.[20]

In 1996, John suggested that Australia's motivation for intervening in Dutch–Indonesian affairs by referring the matter to the Security Council was not understood. He explained that:

> It was primarily to help to promote harmonious relationships in the geographical region in which Australia existed. Japan had to have its sources of raw materials and markets, indigenous peoples in the region had to have the self-government for which they had been struggling for years before the war, and which they had experienced to a limited degree during Japanese temporary military occupation. There could be no going back.[21]

However, Australia's work on the issue was not done. Dutch offensives continued despite the Security Council ordering another ceasefire in December 1948. In early January 1949, Nehru called a conference of Afro-Asian nations at ministerial level to be held in New Delhi to consider the Indonesian situation.[22] Australia was invited. As a consequence, John embarked on an adventure that led him to work closely with Nehru to discuss the Indonesia problem and end the conflict.

***

The story of John meeting Nehru in India begins in January 1949 when Evatt, because of his fear of flying, was at sea on his way home from London. Prime Minister Chifley was acting minister for External Affairs in Evatt's absence and looked to John for advice on Indonesia and its developing conflict. Chifley was on holiday in Tasmania when the invitation to the conference in India arrived. Cables went to and fro. Chifley was in support of Australia attending the conference, concerned about the impact on Australia of instability in the region. At the same time, he appreciated the risk of Australia being identified with any extreme

---

20 See Fettling's account in *Encounters with Asian Decolonisation*.
21 Burton, 'Indonesia: Unfinished Diplomacy', a paper presented to the New Directions in Australian Foreign Policy: Australia and Indonesia 1945–50 conference, Monash University, Melbourne, 31 May–1 June 1996, 4. The John W. Burton Papers, George Mason University, accessed 21 August 2021, wizwah.gmu.edu/johnwburton/items/show/1048878.
22 See Suares, *Engaging with Asia*, 503.

Asian nationalist sentiments that might emerge from the conference, or that Australia might be seen to support any moves made at the conference to override the Security Council whose actions had failed to control the Dutch. John felt strongly that there should be an Australian presence. Chifley resolved the problem with diplomacy. He decided that in order to preserve Australia's relations with colonial powers, Australia should not be represented at a ministerial level, but that lower-level representation was appropriate.[23] John cabled Evatt on 3 January 1949 to get his support for Chifley's thinking:

> Prime Minister's reaction at the moment favourable but awaiting your comment. Invitation now received and made public and the United Kingdom already suggesting we should not accept without consultation with them. This is a regional matter of vital importance to us and the United Kingdom has failed to appreciate our primary concern and to give support. It seems to me we must attend looked at from any point of view.[24]

Chifley considered John to be senior enough 'to offset any concern that the Minister was not in attendance' and, on 4 January, announced his decision that two senior officers from the Department of External Affairs, Burton and Moodie, who had just completed his post in New Delhi, would attend as observers.[25] Evatt was not happy. He cabled John from the SS *Dominion Monarch*, saying that:

> Suggestion you should go to India at present is impracticable: clearly you should stick to your post, meeting me Perth as arranged. Gollan or Critchley or McIntyre could attend on official level if conference met in meantime. Obviously you must be close at hand from time of my arrival in Australia. Please inform the Prime Minister.[26]

---

23   See Lee, *Australia & Indonesia's Independence*, xiii. This volume contains cables referred to here or they can be found online at DFAT Historical Documents: vol. 15, *1949, Indonesia*, www.dfat.gov.au/about-us/publications/historical-documents/Pages/volume-15/1949-indonesia-volume-15; and see Suares, *Engaging with Asia*, 504, for a perspective.
24   DFAT, vol. 15, Doc. 4, Burton to Evatt, Cablegram E1, 3 January 1949 [AA: A9420, 7].
25   Lee, *Australia & Indonesia's Independence*, vol. XV, 16; and DFAT, vol. 15, Doc. 21, Burton to Evatt, Cablegram E3, 5 January 1949 [AA: A9420, 7].
26   DFAT, vol. 15, Doc. 38, Evatt to Burton, Cablegram unnumbered, 7 January 1949 [AA: A9420, 7].

15. RESHAPING AUSTRALIA'S FOREIGN POLICY

John replied:

> Have spoken to Prime Minister who sends message he was aware of difficulties and inconvenience to you and to me, but considered this the only compromise which would overcome the local political difficulties of sending a Minister and avoid a rebuff to India and other countries.[27]

And inconvenient to John it was. He had applied for leave in order to stand for and campaign for preselection for the federal seat of Canberra with both Chifley's and Evatt's support. He was scheduled to give a preselection speech to party members at the time he would be in India. Chifley had forgotten this and John did not remind him. His public service obligations came first. In addition, John probably judged that this was an opportunity for him to exert influence over Australia's foreign policy in the Asia-Pacific region – which after all was a prime reason for his desire to stand for parliament. With an object of strong engagement with Australia's Asian neighbours, John saw the most important issue on the conference agenda for Australia was how to end foreign domination of Asia, politically and economically. He wanted to be there, to contribute.

Both Moodie and John looked forward to the conference, although Moodie was apprehensive about 'the hard work inevitably arising from any association with that human dynamo we have for a Secretary'.[28] He also thought John was 'blithely confident'. 'We'll run the Conference for them,' John said to Moodie.[29] They arrived in New Delhi on 12 January and the two were welcomed at an informal meeting at the home of Prime Minister Nehru to discuss conference procedures. They were the only 'Europeans' there for the conference, the others being from Asia and the Middle East.

Despite the honour, John was disappointed at the lukewarm welcome they initially received from Nehru. In a cable to Evatt, John attributed this to adverse press comments in Australia about Australia's presence

---

27 Burton argued back. DFAT, vol. 15, Doc. 39, Burton to Evatt, Cablegram E5, 7 January 1949 [AA: A9420, 7]; and see Lee, *Australia & Indonesia's Independence*, 39, Doc. 54, Burton to Evatt, 9 January 1949.
28 DFAT, vol. 15, Doc. 227, Letter Moodie to McIntyre, 17 February 1949 [AA: A1838,383/1/2/5].
29 Memoir of Colin Moodie, NLA, MS Acc13.173, 26.

at the conference.³⁰ It is more likely that Nehru was put out by John's paternalistic attitude. Before he arrived in Delhi, John had sent through detailed suggested programs for the conference, and at Nehru's home John repeated his proposals. According to Moodie, he and Burton had 'anticipated arriving in Delhi well equipped with ... ideas and finding all sorts of gaps in Indian information and not a very clear idea in [Indian] minds on what the Conference should do'. The Indians had 'politely but firmly made clear to us that [they] were well able to run their own Conference without [our] help ...'.³¹

Fettling suggests that Nehru's commanding presence on the opening day of the conference on 20 January had momentarily shaken John's confidence. Nehru stood in traditional dress in front of Hyderabad House, New Delhi, to greet the delegates and as John reached Nehru:

> a spectacular moment of awkwardness ensured. As Burton remembered it: 'I walked right past without shaking hands. He didn't put out his hand to me at all.'³²

Realising that Nehru and the Indian officials needed no help from him, John remained silent at the opening session of the conference. Nehru unexpectedly asked each delegation to make opening remarks and John declined, which did not endear him to Nehru. 'I didn't quite know how to handle it,' John admitted in hindsight to Fettling.³³ Fettling thought that John had been anxious that the Asian delegates would make statements condemning the white powers.

Once John was reassured by the positive tone of other speakers, he decided to address the conference after all. He said that Nehru's comments 'were so much in accord with those of Australia that ... there was little he need say in addition'.³⁴ But he did say more. He called for the conference to resist reprisals against the Netherlands and to assist the UN to remedy

---

30   DFAT, vol. 15, Doc. 111, Burton to Evatt, cablegram 50, New Delhi, 19 January 1949 [AA: A1838, 854/10/4/5].
31   Memoir of Colin Moodie, NLA, MS Acc13.173, 26.
32   Fettling, *Encounters with Asian Decolonisation*, ch. 6, 'John Burton and the Rise of Asia, 1945–1950', 188.
33   John Burton, interview by David Fettling, Canberra, 2010.
34   NAA: A1838, Doc. 383, '"Grave Mistakes" in Indonesia', 20 January 1949; and see DFAT, Doc. 117, 'Speech by Burton at New Delhi Conference', 20 January 1949 in Lee, *Australia & Indonesia's Independence*, 112.

the 'grave mistakes' caused by the second Dutch police action. 'Wisdom does not rest only in countries having great economic and military power,' he said.[35]

John's speech was warmly received by the conference. John then reported to Evatt on how amazing he was finding the conference and that Nehru was coming to accept them.[36] Moodie's reaction was that he had never worked with 'anyone like Burton before or since'. He understood that Nehru, thereafter, always spoke of Burton with 'warm approval'.[37] In turn, John was impressed with Nehru and the other Asian attendees. He said in a dispatch to Evatt:

> This conference is so far most amazing for good common sense and honest purpose amongst the middle and small powers. I have never known an international committee to be so subject to reasoned argument and so little influenced by political or emotional irrelevancies.[38]

Nehru was talked about as a hero in our household as we children grew up. It is clear that John's experience in India helped inform his advocacy of non-alignment in Australia's foreign policy.

On the strength of his speech and John's detailed knowledge of the Indonesian dispute, and notwithstanding his observer status, he was appointed to the drafting committee of four tasked to draft the resolutions of the conference to be put forward as recommendations to the UN Security Council for the early settlement of the Indonesian dispute.[39] After this, Nehru chaired a series of sessions in which three resolutions were drafted to be sent to the Security Council relating to and including timelines for the withdrawal of Dutch troops and Indonesia's transition to a sovereign state.

---

35 'Plenary Session of Indonesia Conference' under subheading 'Mistake Affecting World Peace', *Statesman* (New Delhi), 21 January 1949, 7.
36 DFAT, vol. 15, Doc. 136, Burton to Evatt, Cablegram 68, New Delhi, 21 January 1949 [AA: A1838, 854/10/4/5]; Lee, *Australia & Indonesia's Independence*, Doc. 136, 131–32.
37 Memoir of Colin Moodie, NLA, MS Acc13.173, 26.
38 DFAT, Doc. 136, Burton to Evatt, 21 January 1949; and Lee, *Australia & Indonesia's Independence*, Doc. 136, 131–32.
39 Along with India, Pakistan and Ceylon; and see *Sydney Morning Herald*, 22 January 1949; and Lee, *Australia & Indonesia's Independence*, xiv.

John's work and influence at the conference are well documented.[40] On the one hand, Australia's participation at the conference when the delegation of two were supposed to be observers gave rise to hostile opposition by non-Labor critics. Robert Menzies, as leader of the Liberal Party Opposition in 1949, argued that it was a great blunder for Australia to be seen taking sides against the European colonial powers. John was particularly unpopular with the Dutch Government for his active role in supporting Indonesian independence at the conference. On the other hand, Pemberton's reading of the records suggests that, 'after Nehru, the 33-year-old Burton was the dominating figure' at the conference. 'Many of the key speeches made, and resolutions initiated, were Burton's ... the New Delhi Conference was a triumph for Burton's foreign policy.'[41] Woodard observed, 'The success of Australia's Indonesia policy provides its own justification and it is doubtful that it could have been carried through had it been handled in any less personalised way than by Burton working directly and informally to Evatt and, increasingly, Chifley.'[42] Commentator Norman Abjorensen saw Chifley's Labor Government playing a critical, but never fully appreciated, role in Indonesia's break from Dutch rule. He went further:

> Indeed, without Australia's championing of the nationalist cause in the struggle against the Dutch attempt to restore their pre-war overseas empire, it is doubtful whether the Indonesian nation would have been born. Australia was the midwife.[43]

---

40   DFAT, vol. 15, Doc. 116, Notes by Burton, 'Australia an Asian Country?' New Delhi, 20 January 1949; NAA: A1838, Doc. 278, 401/3/1/1 Pt. 6; DFAT, vol. 15, Doc. 117, Speech by Burton at New Delhi Conference, '"Grave Mistakes" in Indonesia', New Delhi, 20 January 1949, a summary of Burton's speech by the office of the Australian High Commission in India, [NAA: A1838, 383/1/25]. See also Suares, *Engaging with Asia*, 507; Christine Weir, 'An Accidental Biographer? On Encountering, Yet Again, the Ideas and Actions of J. W. Burton', chapter 16 in *Telling Pacific Lives: Prisms of Process*, ed. Brij V. Lal and Vicki Luker (Canberra: ANU E Press, 2008), 215–25, doi.org/10.22459/TPL.06.2008.16. In a personal communication, 15 January 2016, Weir suggested that the respect John was given by Nehru and Indian officials was due more to him being 'The Reverend Dr John Burton's son' than being an Australian public servant, in that Jack Burton was held in very high regard as a result of his work for Indian plantation labourers in Fiji.
41   Pemberton, 'A Matter of Independence', C1.
42   Woodard, 'Cold War Downunder', 15.
43   Norman Abjorensen, 'Australia's Finest Diplomatic Hour', *Canberra Times*, 12 September 1998, Panorama 5.

16

The Gnomes of Melbourne

In the late 1940s, a back story concerning alleged espionage and counter-espionage was in play. It saw the emergence of an Australian intelligence organisation with strong ties to and reliance upon British and US intelligence, the establishment of which John strongly opposed. The perceived need for a stronger and more secretive organisation can be traced back to wartime when a McCarthyist fear of the spread of communism took hold. When John became departmental head in March 1947, he was obliged as a public servant to swear an official oath of secrecy relating to security classified matters. However, he bristled when Colonel Charles Spry, director of Military Intelligence, asked him to swear another oath that would require him not to convey to anyone, even Evatt as his minister, any information John might receive from intelligence services in the course of participating in the Joint Intelligence Committee (JIC).[1] Until 1949, Evatt was also the attorney-general under the Curtin and Chifley governments and had responsibility for the Security Service. John refused to sign or to participate in the JIC. He did not want to be privy to any information that he could not pass on to his minister or the prime minister.[2] How could he brief Evatt on matters of security without keeping him informed of current perceived threats? Moreover, in any event, John did not trust Spry's agenda.

---

1 *National Times* (Broadway, NSW), 28 September – 4 October 1984, 11; *Herald* (Melbourne), 23 February 1972, 4.
2 Burton, *National Times*, 28 September–4 October 1984, 11.

Spry was a complex character and a military traditionalist with a hatred of communism. He gave public lectures on its evils and argued that, while World War Two was over, Australia was facing an equally dangerous threat. Historian David Horner, in an obituary on Spry, described him as courteous and charming, that he wore a military, Hitler-style moustache and a homburg hat, and had a gift of the gab and sharp wit. He told of the time when Spry, serving in Greece in April 1941 and having just avoided being captured by the Germans by evacuating to Crete, sent a telegram to his wife from Palestine saying: 'successfully degreeced and excreted'.[3] Journalist Alan Ramsey wrote that Spry's lifelong army career, which included him serving under the Raj in the mid-1930s on India's north-western frontier in the Duke of Wellington's regiment, shaped his life and attitudes. He described Spry as 'a man of the empire', such that serving the interests of Britain and the Empire had priority over Australia's regional interests and security.[4]

John believed Spry was intent on influencing policy and political outcomes and feared that Spry's intense focus on security concerns could damage Australia's relations with perceived hostile nations. He arranged for Moodie to represent the department on the JIC and told him that, whatever oath he took, he had to pass on relevant information to the department and to the government. However, on one occasion in late 1949, when Moodie was on leave, John attended a meeting himself, giving no warning and arriving late. According to Moodie, no one knew him except Spry who passed a note to the chairman, saying: 'This is Burton'. The chairman was wondering 'who the boy was' that Moodie had sent to attend the subordinate committee meeting, but did not read the note until after Burton started to speak. John began with, 'When I was talking to the Prime Minister the other day, I told him about this "bloody nonsense".'[5] The chair, having by this time read the note, moved swiftly to the next item. According to Moodie, John was proud of himself and, on Moodie's return from leave, John simply said: 'You can't justify attending that show', so Moodie did not attend again.

---

3   Obituary by David Horner, 'Spy Chief Led Fight against Communism', *Australian,* 7 June 1994. Brigadier, Sir Charles Spry CBE, DSO, Director of ASIO 1950 to 1969; born Brisbane 1910, died Melbourne 1994, age 83, NLA, Biographical cuttings on Charles Spry, Sir, Brigadier, Director-general of ASIO, 1950–1969, containing one or more cuttings from newspapers or journals.
4   Alan Ramsey, 'The Spry Who Came in from the Cold War', *National Times,* 28 September–4 October 1994, 13.
5   Memoir of Colin Moodie, NLA, MS Acc13.173, 26.

16. THE GNOMES OF MELBOURNE

John objected to the JIC's group of intelligence officers wielding power over defence and foreign policy. He understood that it was a matter of interest to them if a possible change of government was likely to change defence policies. He explained in 1972, 'I would not be a party to any attempt to take policy responsibility in practice if not in form, out of the hands of the elected government'.[6] He believed that such 'a secret group' had been responsible for the downfall of Menzies in 1941 'for getting too friendly with the Japanese' (before Japan entered the war).[7] Moodie thought that John was 'paranoid on defence matters', exampling it in his memoir with reference to John calling JIC a 'little fascist group in Melbourne'.[8] This group John later dubbed 'The Gnomes of Melbourne'.[9] According to John, the members of 'the Gnomes' were a fluctuating elitist reserve group of 10 to 15 military intelligence officers that Spry controlled – heads of Naval, Army and Air Force intelligence and nominees of the departments of Defence and External Affairs – who saw themselves as the true preservers of the Australian heritage and democracy.[10] They liaised with senior intelligence officers of the USA and Britain who were then resident in Australia.

Behind the scenes, a counter-intelligence program that had been initiated in 1943 by American intelligence agencies and code-named 'Venona' was ongoing. The Venona project later led to another project, 'the Lapstone Experiment' initiated by John with then prime minister Chifley's permission. Together, they form a backdrop for the 'Petrov affair' that led to the 1954 Royal Commission into Espionage in Australia. That inquiry and ASIO's extensive surveillance of civilians would affect the lives of many ordinary Australians including John, Cecily and our family and friends.

In November 1947, the Americans told Britain's MI5 that a Venona intercepted Soviet telegram revealed the existence of Soviet espionage in Australia. In January 1948, MI5 informed British Prime Minister Clement Attlee that evidence of leaks from Australia's Department of External Affairs relating back to the years 1944–46 had been revealed. The possible

---

6   It explained his reasons for refusing to sign the oath in a press interview. *Herald*, 23 February 1972, 4.
7   *Herald*, 23 February 1972, 4.
8   Memoir of Colin Moodie, NLA, MS Acc13.173, 25.
9   After Colonel Spry became director of military intelligence and when he headed ASIO, John used the 'Gnomes of Melbourne' for Spry and the group who surrounded him, some of whom were short like Spry, but who John said, 'crept around in the background like gnomes'.
10 John Stubbs, 'Petrov', *National Times*, 28 September–4 October 1984, 11; Malcolm Elder, '"Gnomes of Melbourne" Blamed', *Sun* (Sydney), 2 April 1973.

source of the leaks had to be investigated and Spry was brought in to assist the MI5 team. In April 1948, Shedden, as head of Defence, sent a letter to John, as head of External Affairs, raising MI5's concerns about the leakage of a particular document in 1945 and informed him that investigations pointed to Ian Milner from John's department being suspected. John was perplexed. He had not been told in what form the leakage took place, or what had occurred recently to warrant a leak that had taken place some years ago being raised now.[11]

Attlee sent the director general of MI5, Sir Percy Sillitoe, and Roger Hollis, a future head of the service, to Australia in February 1948 to brief Chifley about the leaks and to discuss ways to improve Australian security. They planned not to tell Chifley about the Soviet decryptions that had revealed the leaks. However, according to Christopher Andrew, a Cambridge professor of history and recognised leading expert on British intelligence, the men did not count on somebody like Evatt, 'who questioned them forensically and just tore their cover story to shreds'.[12] Andrew said, 'I did not come across any other example in the history of MI5 when its representatives were so clearly out-argued by somebody'. He noted that, while they did not like Evatt, 'they admitted to their own superiors that he had been too smart for them'.[13] That Evatt managed to force Britain's top spies to come clean about Soviet intelligence was not revealed until 2009 when secret archives of MI5 were released of the 1948 meeting with Evatt. The irony was that Attlee, Evatt and Chifley were told about this material but not US President Harry Truman. Because the FBI believed that the CIA had been penetrated by Soviet agents, US officials withheld information about Venona from Truman who FBI Chief Edgar Hoover thought would tell the CIA.

Hollis returned to Australia in August 1948 and together with a junior member of MI5, Robert Hemblys-Scales, on 4 August drove from Canberra to visit John at our farm at Melrose Valley, Tuggeranong. John, in his overalls, welcomed them as he did other visitors, but, on this occasion, he was unlikely to have asked them to pick up a shovel and help him in the cowshed while they talked. More likely, Cecily made them tea and made herself scarce while the men had an amenable discussion in the living room. MI5's interest in John was to hear about his period of service in the

---

11   DFAT Historical Documents, vol. 16, *1948–49, Australia and the Postwar World – Beyond the Region*, Doc. 360, Shedden to Burton, 7 April 1948 [AA: A6691, AS3/1, section 6]; John's reply: DFAT, Doc. 361, Burton to Shedden, 22 April 1948 [AA: A6691, AS3/1, section 6].
12   Peter Wilson, 'How Herbert "Doc" Evatt Outwitted MI5', *Australian*, 8 October 2009.
13   Wilson, *Australian*, 8 October 2009.

Post-Hostilities Division of External Affairs in 1944 and 1945 because the place and time was the focus of much of the Venona material. John was sceptical that there might have been any security leaks from External Affairs, and stated frankly that he believed Shedden wanted to blame the department John now headed in order to destroy John. Hollis appreciated John's honesty in revealing his hostility towards Shedden and the fact that, when John was presented with evidence that implicated Milner, he took it seriously. John asked for time to consider the material and requested another meeting with Hollis and Hemblys-Scales at his office.

On 9 August 1948, Hollis and Hemblys-Scales visited John at his departmental office in West Block. Hollis told Sillitoe in a letter dated 11 August 1948 that Burton was 'most friendly and pleasant' and that he 'very quickly saw that there was a great deal more information, much of it inescapably connected with his Department'. According to Horner's research, they were 'favourably impressed with Burton'.[14] He said that Hollis described John as 'a tough, practical, self-reliant type who is not afraid to take on big commitments'. Hemblys-Scales, while knowing others had doubts about John, is reported as saying that the important thing about John is that he 'gets things done, which is unusual around here'.[15] John was alarmed that there might have been security leaks from the department he now headed, but doubted that any of the material described to have been leaked was of any consequence. Hollis reported that John agreed with MI5's suspicion that, if the information was accurate, the culprit must be Milner. John had objected to Milner being recruited to the department when he saw the selection of officers to fill advertised appointments. A later ASIO note recorded that John had said: 'We can't have Milner, he's a Communist.'[16] However, John was never convinced that Milner was a Soviet spy.[17]

---

14 Horner, *The Spy Catchers*, 72–33.
15 Peter Wilson, 'British Lessons in the Spying Game', *Weekend Australian,* 16 April 2011.
16 NAA: A6119, 127, Burton vol. 1, 135. Another ASIO note concedes that it erred in suggesting that John knew Milner before he came to work for External Affairs. It arose from a reference to Milner meeting 'John Burton' in New Zealand, and ASIO later noted: 'It is now considered that the Burton in New Zealand at that time was almost certainly Dr John Wear Burton's father the Rev. Dr John Wear Burton …'. It transpires that Milner's father was, like John's father, a New Zealand cleric. Through his father, young Milner apparently met Jack Burton in 1940, but not John. NAA: A6119, 128, Burton vol. 2, 42. However, the same document described Jack as being described as 'an active pacifist who had possibly become mentally deranged owing to injuries received in the first world war'. As Jack did not fight in the war and had a leading role in the Methodist Church between 1914 and 1918, it has to be considered that he was not the 'John Burton' referred to at all.
17 Gregory Pemberton agrees, see 'Spy Mystery That Will Not Die', *Canberra Times*, 19 June 1991, 21.

Jim Hill was the other officer of the Department of External Affairs suspected of leaking information. John had been aware that Hill, a lawyer, had joined the department in 1945 and worked on war crimes but did not know him particularly well until John returned to the department from Evatt's office. At the time of MI5's visit, Hill was working in the United Nations Division drafting a resolution, according to John, to counter proposals being put forward by the Soviets. John undertook to Hollis that as well as keeping an eye on Milner, he would 'keep closely in touch' with Hill and take 'full personal responsibility for him as a member of the Department'.[18]

Consequently, John got to know Hill quite well after Hollis's visit, as he later told a royal commission, 'quite deliberately' in order to cooperate with MI5. He and Cecily came to like Hill and his family. John told the commission that Hill was 'one of the most capable officers in the Department' and for whose ability John had high respect.[19] After Hollis left, Hemblys-Scales handed John a list of spy suspects, not all identified by name; some had descriptions like 'someone in Evatt's office'.[20] John found the list curious. People named were the sort of 'very Australian' types who did not want policies to be dictated from overseas. 'Few of them', he said, 'could possibly have any secret information.'[21] Nevertheless, John agreed to cooperate with MI5 in its investigations into the allegation of an Australian espionage network. He saw it as an opportunity to demonstrate that Australia was capable of handling its own security matters. He was fearful that, otherwise, pressure would be on for an 'intelligence' organisation run by people like the Gnomes of Melbourne, whose agendas John did not trust, and likely to be under the control of MI5.

In September 1948, John devised a surveillance plan. A large Russian delegation was scheduled to attend an international conference at the Lapstone Hotel in the Blue Mountains in New South Wales the following November. The Lapstone Conference was convened by the United Nations' Economic Commission for Asia and the Far East (ECAFE). After consulting Hemblys-Scales, John approached Chifley and put the

---

18   Burton, *In camera* official transcript of proceedings, Royal Commission on Espionage, 2 November 1954, 7.
19   Burton, Royal Commission on Espionage, 2 November 1954, 6–7.
20   Stubbs, 'Petrov', 11.
21   Stubbs, 'Petrov', 11. Stubbs interviewed then retired Sir Roger Hollis in Somerset, UK, and John in Canberra for his article.

case for employing the existing Commonwealth Investigation Service (CIS) to carry out surveillance of the delegation. He asked permission to arrange the bugging of all of the hotel rooms that were to be occupied by the Russians in Sydney and at Lapstone. The object was to ascertain if they had any contacts in Australia. Special drivers and selected cadets were to help monitor the recordings. John recalled:

> I argued further to the Prime Minister, that even though there was no outcome of such investigation, it would be useful to demonstrate to the British authorities that the Australian Government was able to safeguard the security of the organisation [sic] with wide executive powers.[22]

Chifley approved the project that came to be known as 'the Lapstone Experiment'.

Spry, in his military intelligence capacity, helped John keep track of the project. John thought that they had got to know each other very well. They spent long hours each day and night in John's office waiting to receive and review surveillance reports as they came in. While waiting, they had the opportunity of talking in depth about their divergent views on the role of intelligence in democracies. According to John, Spry, having always worked in the military and intelligence, was looking forward to holding a new role in Australian intelligence. Spry told John that it was the role of security services 'to protect democracies against themselves' and that he believed that 'no political party should attain office on one programme, and in office pursue another'.[23] He made it clear to John that his particular worry was that a future Labor Government would recognise China, while Defence, following its overseas counterparts, was against this. John was alarmed at Spry's expressed view that a secret service – a group of people communicating together who undertook not to communicate to their own government – was essential for democracy. John quoted Spry as saying: 'Indeed, you couldn't have a democracy, with its changes of policy and its changes of parties, working efficiently unless there was this kind of reserve power – this reserve group – that would try to control things in certain circumstances.'[24]

---

22   John Burton's submission to the royal commission was released in 1972 and reproduced in part by Peter Smark and Bruce Stannard, 'The Birth of ASIO', *Australian*, 19 February 1972, Saturday Review 13. For a full account, see also Laurence W. Maher, 'The Lapstone Experiment and the Beginnings of ASIO', *Labour History*, no. 64 (May 1993): 103–8.
23   Burton, 'The Petrov Affair in Perspective', drafted in the 1990s, Burton family file.
24   Stubbs, 'Petrov', 12.

Spry had a different recollection. In a series of public exchanges in 1973 between Spry and Max Suich, editor of the *National Times*, headed 'Dear Sir Charles', Spry confirmed that John consulted him regarding this special investigation. However, he said:

> It appeared to me that he was reporting directly to Mr Chifley on this matter. He asked that I run the operation. I declined, emphasising the view that it was a civil and not a military matter. This was accepted and another person was appointed to direct.[25]

He went on to say that, in his capacity as director of Military Intelligence, he was a member of the JIC and that:

> Mostly my meetings in Canberra with Dr Burton were of a courtesy nature. I found him to be an intelligent person who possessed very firm political views. However, I considered that his assessment of contemporaneous international affairs was not always correct. I cannot support what you quote him as saying – 'It was his (Spry's) view that a secret service – a group of people communicating together who undertook not to communicate to their own Government – was essential.' This would ignore political realities. Any person who controls a security intelligence organisation knows that this cannot be done nor would it be, in the interests of democracy.[26]

The Lapstone Experiment revealed nothing untoward in respect of document handovers or leaks of secret material. John later recalled that, when assembled in the minister's room to hear the tapes that had been flown from Sydney with an interpreter Noel Deschamps, excitement heightened at hearing the name 'Dalziel' mentioned in a telephone conversation between one Russian delegate and another. Allan Dalziel, a former journalist, was Evatt's electoral secretary in Sydney. There was no mention of any other Australian. Deschamps laughed as he listened to the conversation and then translated the speaker's words into English: 'If you have any trouble over transport, ring Dalziel who is the transport official for the conference.'[27] John told a television interviewer:

> That was as near as communication of any information we got during that whole episode which cost a very large sum of money. But what it did show was the Soviet people had not contacted

---

25 'Dear Sir Charles …', *National Times*, 3–8 September 1973, 34.
26 *National Times*, 3–8 September 1973, 34.
27 Burton, notes for NLA oral interview with Edgar Waters, 1 January 2000, 3, Burton family file.

anyone and secondly it showed that if it had we could have picked it up. And my recommendation to the Prime Minister was that we did not have an ASIO or any organisation of that nature.[28]

Unfortunately for John, the success of the project led to the very outcome he sought to avoid; the establishment of a new intelligence organisation in Australia. From MI5's point of view, little progress was being made to find the source of the leak of material to the Russians ('The Case' as it became known).[29] MI5 officials took advantage of Australian cooperation and, as Spry had no confidence in the CIS, Chifley was persuaded to establish a new intelligence organisation. In 1949, the Australian Security Intelligence Organization (ASIO) was established. This was despite Chifley and Evatt not being in favour of a separate security organisation. Evatt, in particular, was concerned about civil liberties implications in surveillance activities. Chifley was reluctant to agree to the demand, but apparently thought that a small organisation would placate MI5 and reduce tensions. In his official history of ASIO, Horner wrongly attributed John with persuading Chifley that ASIO should be established. He stated, 'unexpectedly the most persuasive voice was that of Burton'.[30] Horner concluded that John talked to Chifley about cooperating with MI5 because of the mounting evidence against Milner and another suspect, Frances Bernie. Horner drew support for his account from Hollis who is reported to have said: 'I think it not unlikely that the Prime Minister will have listened more attentively to Burton than to us, if only because he must have been so surprised to hear Burton speaking on the subject.'[31] John's urging of Chifley to cooperate with MI5 in the Lapstone Experiment might have misled Horner in that regard. John had the opposite purpose in mind, namely to prove that the CIS could handle security and that a separate intelligence organisation run by Defence was not warranted. John asserted that he wrote a report to Evatt, then the attorney-general, arguing the case against the setting up of ASIO. He said that, five years later, he discovered that the report had been intercepted and suppressed by Spry's elitist military group – by these 'Gnomes of Melbourne'.[32]

---

28 Transcript of ABC TV interview, 9 November 1989, family collection.
29 Desmond Ball and David Horner, *Breaking the Codes: Australia's KGB Network, 1944–1950* (St Leonards, NSW: Allen & Unwin, 1998), 295.
30 Horner, *The Spy Catchers*, 76.
31 Horner, *The Spy Catchers*, 76.
32 'File against ASIO Vetoed – Expert', *Sun*, 2 April 1973; 'Report Opposing ASIO "Stopped"', *Canberra Times*, 2 April 1973.

The British Government sent Hollis, by this time director of MI5, to help set up ASIO. John was sure that Chifley never dreamed that he was creating an uncontrollable organisation staffed by persons selected for their political ideologies rather than any defined professionalism. Chifley and Evatt, aware of the dangers of a spy agency, placed it under the judiciary. Established administratively with a one-page memorandum from government, Justice Geoffrey Sandford Reed, a South Australian judge, was appointed its director-general in March 1949. Its key task was related to espionage but its role was extended to surveillance of any person or organisation who might be judged to be subversive of the security of the Commonwealth. Its original charter provided that the security service be kept free of any political bias or influence and it was not given any executive or police powers.

When the Menzies Government came into office in December 1949, control was handed to Spry as a professional intelligence officer seconded from the army to become director-general of ASIO. Reed had not intended to have the role for more than a year but, had Labor remained in power, Spry would not have been appointed to take over his role. According to John, under Spry, ASIO developed away from the British model on which it was based towards the American model of military intelligence that lacked judicial oversight. Chifley's fears about establishing such an organisation were realised when Spry took over civilian security as part of Defence services. John concluded:

> By placing a military intelligence officer in charge of civilian security, the government gave the intelligence service unlimited opportunity, not merely to control policy decisions, but to interfere with the political life of the community.[33]

ASIO was not given a legislative base until 1956.

Horner's historic account confirms that there was extensive surveillance by ASIO under Spry of ordinary Australians who held progressive views. He notes too, the failure of ASIO to watch extremists on the right.[34] Lawyer and writer Ernst Willheim detailed the extent of the resources that were devoted by ASIO to surveillance; surveillance not simply of suspected spies, but of thousands of ordinary Australians with 'leftist'

---

33 *Herald*, 23 February 1972, 4.
34 Horner, *The Spy Catchers*, 63.

views.[35] Spry, set on targeting communists, completely revamped ASIO. The Cold War was at its height: Stalin's Soviet Union had gained control over eastern Europe, North Korea had just invaded South Korea and the Australian Communist party dominated many trade unions. Spry moved ASIO's Sydney headquarters to Melbourne and engaged new staff to set up new sections to penetrate the Communist Party. In 1954, Spry had his greatest 'success'. Vladimir Petrov and his wife, Evdokia Petrova, both KGB officers, defected from the Soviet Embassy. The inquiry surrounding it and the information they purported to give the authorities would have a major impact on our family. But before that occurred, John managed to orchestrate more havoc for himself and our family.

---

35   Ernst Willheim, 'Is David Horner's Official History of ASIO "Honest History"? Was Colonel Spry a Traitor?' *Honest History*, 14 April 2015, accessed 9 April 2021, honesthistory.net.au/wp/is-david-horners-official-history-of-asio-honest-history/. The article was originally a lecture delivered at Manning Clark House, 26 March 2015, in the *Honest History* series, accessed 9 April 2021, malpaya.files.wordpress.com/2015/04/honest-history-asio-paper.pdf.

17

Political suicide

In December 1948, John sought Labor preselection for the new federal seat of Canberra following a recent move by the Chifley Government to give Canberrans representation in the federal parliament. John's move caused commentators to speculate that John, as Evatt's protégé, did not simply wanted a seat in federal parliament but wanted to become foreign minister. Why else would he relinquish his £2,500 salary per year as secretary of a department for a federal member of parliament's salary of £1,500?[1] If John did have his sights on Evatt's portfolio, his ambition was not likely to have been driven by monetary considerations, as Cecily knew well. Nevertheless, it fuelled a rumour that Evatt intended to retire from politics, leaving a ministerial vacancy.

The preselection ballot took place on 10 April 1949. Despite Chifley's and Evatt's backing, John's bid for preselection went disastrously wrong. Canberra was a public service town and there was a known cell of public servants who were linked to the Catholic Social Studies Movement (the Movement), which adopted a pro-American foreign policy stance. It was driven by B. A. Santamaria from Melbourne and established to combat communist influence in the Australian labour movement. Santamaria's Movement was disturbed when John entered the preselection contest. He distrusted John as he distrusted Coombs and other public servants with advanced tertiary education – a new breed of left-leaning bureaucrats who seemed to be doing well in the Chifley era. Alarming the Movement further, John brought in Jim Hill, who some suspected was a communist,

---

1   John W. Burton papers, NLA, MS 8405, box 4, file 18, Newspaper clippings 1947–91, various clippings, December 1948.

to help his campaign.² The Movement was in no position to present a rival candidate from its own ranks, but, intent on stopping Burton from obtaining preselection, it threw its weight behind the secretary of the Australian Capital Territory Trades and Labour Council, Sid Rhodes, a 58-year-old public servant. Jim Fraser, younger brother of veteran politician Allan Fraser, also entered the race.

John had already been disadvantaged by not being able to participate in preselection speeches in the run up to the ballot in early 1949 because he was at Nehru's conference in New Delhi. In any event, John did not command the numbers. The anti-Burton group disputed his eligibility for nomination because his continuity of party membership had lapsed. The Burton camp sought to defer the ballot because some members of the local Australian Labor Party (ALP) branch also lacked valid party tickets. They put the matter to the NSW Labor Party Executive that had jurisdiction over the Australian Capital Territory (ACT) at the time. There, Chifley could and did direct the state executive to appoint John as the nominee without a ballot. Then, on 28 February 1949, the anti-Burton team attended the annual election of local ALP branch officials and gained election to sufficient key positions to take control of the ACT branch. The state executive backed off and authorised the ACT branch to go ahead with its preselection ballot.

The Movement's activity was effective. John lost to Rhodes after the distribution of preferences of the third-placed Jim Fraser. On 17 April 1949, one week after his preselection loss, John flew to London with Chifley for the Commonwealth Prime Ministers' Conference.³ The *Sydney Morning Herald* under a heading 'Missed Out', sneered:

> Dr Burton will not need to share ideas on how to win elections after their return. He missed out badly, despite Chif's and Evatt's strong backing, to a 'stalwart' from the old school … It is the first bad break in clever, shrewd, John Burton's meteoric career … If Department heads decide to go into politics, they should at least make sure of their pre-selection; if not of election.⁴

---

2   For an analysis of Labor's ideology war, see Stephen Holt, 'The Ideological War over Our First MP', *Canberra Times*, February 2013, Public Sector Informant 20.
3   Chifley broke with tradition, and took John, as secretary of External Affairs, instead of Shedden, secretary of Defence.
4   *Sydney Morning Herald*, 17 April 1949.

17. POLITICAL SUICIDE

Outside 10 Downing Street, London, occasion of the Commonwealth Prime Ministers' Conference, 1949.
Source: Family collection.

To stand for a seat in parliament with no certainty of success was seen as a suicidal career move for a supposedly apolitical departmental head. It was a high stakes gamble. Had John succeeded and had Labor been successful at the general election, he would likely have been on his way to becoming foreign minister.

Labor lost power in the general election when, on 10 December 1949, the Opposition formed government under Prime Minister Menzies. Menzies had made it clear that should he become prime minister he would have no confidence in Burton's advice as head of External Affairs.[5] Yet, he took no action to remove John as head of department. For a time, it was 'business as usual', surprising commentators.

Through the years ahead, the Movement continued to criticise every attempt John made to influence local party affairs. In hindsight, and after further failed attempts to enter parliament, John declared that he did not regret failing to enter politics. He formed a view that little could be achieved in an adversarial parliamentary environment where palpable party lines had to be followed. Academia would give him more scope for pushing independent views. Knowing him as we did, John would have been frustrated as a politician where implementation of ideas requires effective team-playing and compromise; neither being notable attributes of John's. He was too much his own person and insufficiently self-aware to be an effective politician. For instance, the advent of Communist China in 1949 changed the views of Labor's right wing on the strategy that Australia should follow, but it did not change John's. Given its geographic presence in the Asia-Pacific region, he remained strongly of the view that it was in Australia's interests to engage with China. The emergence of a new attitude towards China pitted John politically and professionally against many of his ALP colleagues.

On Friday 3 February 1950, according to one headline, John gave 'Canberra's most intriguing cocktail party'.[6] It was for his new minister for foreign affairs, Percy Spender. 'Intriguing', because it was believed that John would not retain his position of department head having declared himself an ALP political candidate. However, Spender asked John to stay on. The new parliament met in March 1950. John, to the amazement of most, worked closely with Spender. The *Sunday Sun* headlined a story, 'Little break in foreign policy', observing that Labor would have difficulty finding anything to object to in Spender's clear statement of foreign policy:

---

5   'Has Menzies Forgotten?', *Century* (Sydney), 17 March 1950.
6   *Sydney Morning Herald,* 5 February 1950.

> On all vital points, the Evatt policy, often derided as a one-man policy, is carried on.
>
> If the British Foreign Office is entitled to credit for continuity of British policy, then no one can deny credit to External Affairs Secretary John Burton.
>
> The vigorous mind of Spender stamped itself unmistakably on the speech but the skilled mind of Burton was also evident.[7]

The Century posed the question in its news heading on 17 March 1950, 'Has Menzies Forgotten?' After referring to John's defeat in the ALP preselection ballot, it went on to observe: 'Now he seems closer to Percy Spender than he ever was to Dr Evatt … While Spender made his speech on foreign affairs, Burton "sat on the official bench looking very pleased with himself"'.[8] 'Spender asked me to stay. I got on very well with Spender. Indeed, I used to get on fairly well with Menzies,' John said.[9] Subsequently, Professor H. S. Albinski, a policy expert, supported this, noting:

> until Burton's departure from his post as Secretary, there is every reason to believe that Burton and Spender coexisted happily and even had mutual respect for one another.[10]

For a time, John felt comfortable in his role. In May 1950, Spender appointed John to lead the Australian delegation to a conference in Baguio, in the Philippines. It was the first combined conference of representatives of Asian and Western Pacific countries and was presided over by the president of the Philippines, Elpidio Quirino.[11]

---

7   *Sunday Sun* (Sydney), 12 March 1950.
8   'Has Menzies Forgotten?', *Century*, 17 March 1950.
9   Burton, interview by Michael J. Wilson, 1995, 22.
10 Henry S. Albinski, *Australian Policies and Attitudes toward China* (Princeton, NJ: Princeton University Press, 1965), 67.
11 'Ready for Baguio Talks', *Canberra Times*, 24 May 1950, 1, with John pictured in an accompanying photograph.

John, second from left, walking beside President Elpidio Quirino, third from left, Baguio, the Philippines, 1950.
Source: Family collection.

Understanding Menzies's and Spender's attitude to Australia's relationships with its regional neighbours explains why the Liberals retained faith in John's foreign policy advice. In April 1939, when Menzies had previously been prime minister, he had indicated the need for Australia to have its own diplomatic representation in China, observing: 'What Great Britain calls the Far East is to us the near north.'[12] Menzies and his government had recognised the importance of Australia strengthening its relationship with China both before war broke out in the Pacific region in 1941 and postwar until 1949 when Mao Zedong came to power.[13]

---

12 *Sydney Morning Herald*, 27 April 1939, 9, accessible in DFAT Historical Documents, vol. 2, *1939*, Doc. 73, 'Broadcast Speech by Mr R.G. Menzies, Prime Minister', 26 April 1939.
13 In 1941 Richard Casey had sent a minister to China, as an insurance premium in case war broke out. Frederick Eggleston, Australia's first ambassador to China, arrived in 1941, three months before the Pacific War began. Eggleston believed that Australia and the region stood to benefit from the emerging rise of China. Douglas Copland was economic adviser to three wartime prime ministers: Menzies, Fadden and Curtin. Copland, when in China (January 1946 – June 1948) became convinced the communists would take political control of China and he advocated Australia's recognition of China.

17. POLITICAL SUICIDE

Prime Minister Robert Menzies and Cecily (in sari) with guests at the Indian High Commission, Canberra, 1950.
Source: Family collection.

While Menzies's attitude changed with Mao's China, Spender continued to stress the importance of Australia's geography. He warned: 'No nation can escape its geography … that is an axiom which should be written deep in the mind of every Australian.'[14] Daniel Oakman, in his history of the Colombo Plan, gave credit to Spender:

> Threats that seemed to emanate from Asia compelled Australia to take action and reassess its place in the region: Britain's 'Far East' became Australia's 'Near North'. And so, in the early 1950s, Australia embarked on its most ambitious attempt – outside of war – to engage with Asia: the Colombo Plan.[15]

Thus, in 1950, Spender as foreign minister was prepared to go to the Colombo conference and pursue regional relations in the same way. There is little wonder that Spender was happy at that time to have John by his side as foreign policy adviser. In 2011, Pemberton opined:

---

14 Australian House of Representatives, *Parliamentary Debates*, vol. 6, 9 March 1950, 628, quoted by Daniel Oakman in *Facing Asia: A History of the Colombo Plan*, 1.
15 Oakman, *Facing Asia*, 'Introduction', 1.

> Burton steered a largely uninterested Evatt and Australia towards support for Indonesian and even Vietnamese independence from the Europeans, engagement with India and communist China and an Asian aid program implemented by Robert Menzies' government as the Colombo Plan.
>
> Liberal external affairs minister Percy Spender … embraced Burton's idea and disagreed with Menzies by urging the need for an Asian-Pacific focus.[16]

However, the controversy that surrounded John mounted with the advent of the Korean War. John pushed policy ideas that threatened the political philosophies of conservatives, some of whom attributed sinister motives to John's thoughts and actions. In 1950, instability worsened in the Asia-Pacific region and in the Korean Peninsula in particular. Incoming messages from Australia's representative serving on a United Nations observer mission told of provocative moves made from the South to induce Northern soldiers to cross the border. John and his department responded by sending cables to the US State Department in Washington warning against patrols trying to provoke the North Koreans. 'It was clear US patrols were going too far north hoping the Koreans would follow them back,' he told a journalist years later.[17] 'It was a foolish tactic,' according to John. 'It was not a war that could be won.'[18] On 25 June 1950, fighting in Korea broke out. John recalled that the reply from the US State Department was to the effect of, 'Don't worry, the war will be over in a few days'.

Searches of the archives by historians have failed to unearth the series of cables that John insisted were exchanged. Over time he was consistent in his insistence that he remembered sending a cable with Menzies's approval, and receiving a response.[19] 'I wouldn't make something like that up,' he often said. It was far too important a matter for him to do so. He feared that war would break out, and it did. It was, in his view, avoidable. Cables came and went as a common means of quick communication. However, all were not necessarily filed. John concluded that the lost paperwork was eliminated from the files to save US embarrassment.[20] Ron Leave, writing

---

16 Greg Pemberton, 'First Envoys Beat an Early Path to Asia', *Weekend Australian*, 16–17 April 2011.
17 Clack, 'Theories amidst Cows and Hills', *Canberra Times*, 8 September 1991, 24.
18 Clack, *Canberra Times*, 8 September 1991, 24.
19 Burton, interview by Michael J. Wilson, 1995, 20–21.
20 'Should We Recognise Communist China?', *Nation's Forum of the Air*, ABC program, 9 September 1959.

for *The Guardian*, noted that provocation from forces in the south had been pointed out on many occasions in the past, but that John's view gave the claim weight as he had access to information as departmental head that was not available to the public at large.[21] Missing cable issue aside, the evidence is strong that aggression from the south was pursued with intent to justify southern forces crossing the 38th parallel to invade North Korea. Stone's *The Hidden History of Korea*, published soon after the war, raised the issue of whether the north was provoked into the offensive by forces in the south.[22] Michael Pembroke's well-researched book, *Korea: Where the American Century Began*, tells the story of the USA's unconscionable role in extending the war by two years longer than it should have been.[23]

In the meantime, Spender, who had grave doubts about the United Nations' ability to protect Australia's interest, pursued Australia's military alliance with the USA as a more effective means of protecting Australia, alongside a policy of economic diplomacy with Australia's neighbours. His approach meant that:

> the era of the Evatt/Burton analysis of world affairs was over and the United States, not the UN, was to be the mainstay of Australia's future survival in South-East Asia and the Pacific.[24]

Against John's advice, Menzies gave support to Australia's involvement in the Korean War. Unhappy about the direction the government was moving in Cold War foreign policy, John said so. He saw Menzies as being intent on Australia remaining a 'colony' of the UK and of supporting the USA's aggressive stand against 'non-aligned' countries in the region. He decided that he had no option but to resign or at least to take an extended break.[25]

Spender asked John to stay on during this difficult time for Australia. However, John was tired and disillusioned. He explained later that a major factor was that he had suffered from absolute fatigue: 'I'd been seven years up day and night.'[26] There had been no relaxation when working with

---

21 'Dr Burton Tells Truth about Korea', *Guardian*, 17 September 1959.
22 I. F. Stone, *The Hidden History of the Korean War: 1950–1951: A Nonconformist History of our Times*, 2nd ed. (UK: Little Brown, 1988).
23 Michael Pembroke, *Korea: Where the American Century Began* (Richmond, Vic.: Hardie Grant Books, 2018), see particularly, ch. 6, 'American Hubris', 73.
24 Oakman, *Facing Asia*, 45.
25 Burton, interview by John Clements, 1981.
26 Burton, interview by Michael J. Wilson, 1995, 22.

Evatt. Cecily could attest to that – she witnessed how long and hard John worked. Spender acknowledged publicly that John was taking the leave that he had been unable to take under the previous Labor Government because of the pressure of work. He elaborated to the press that 'during and since the war [Dr Burton] had worked at high pressure and had made eleven short visits overseas'.[27]

John had planned for all events. He had already negotiated the purchase of a larger and more fertile acreage that, if necessary, he could farm for a living and he talked about writing a book on foreign policy. On 17 June 1950, John took paid recreation leave – then undecided as to whether he would return to his position as head of the department. Then, as we prepared to move to our new farm, John requested an additional six months leave without pay. 'I am going to farm,' he declared.[28] His extended absence necessitated his resignation of his position as departmental secretary. He retained his public service rights but gave up his £2,500 a year salary and left open the question of whether or not he would return to the department in some other capacity. Menzies recalled Alan Watt from his posting to Moscow and appointed him permanent head, the position that might have been his in 1947 but for Labor gaining office. John was not sacked or asked to leave as some commentators would later assert. Albinski suggested that John's resignation was one of 'mutual consent', but confirmed that he was not 'eased out over a quarrel on China policy or any other substantive matter'.[29] Spender spoke respectfully of John. He said that John had given him 'objective advice during their association as well as could be expected from a Permanent Head'. Chifley, as leader of the Opposition, paid tribute to 'the magnificent work' he had done. If the department was to lose Burton, he said, 'It was losing one of the most splendid public servants Australia had ever produced. He was young, able, and enthusiastic'.[30] Indeed, John's time in the public sphere was not yet over. In a short time, his impetuous actions would end his public service career, but not his influence on foreign policy.

---

27   John W. Burton papers, NLA, MS 8405, box 4, file 18, Newspaper clippings 1947–91.
28   'Dr Burton Replaced as Departmental Head', *Sun*, 15 June 1950.
29   Albinski, *Australian Policies and Attitudes toward China*, 67.
30   John W. Burton papers, NLA, MS 8405, box 4, file 18, News clippings, 1947–91.

18

John's short stint as high commissioner in Ceylon

In July 1950, we three children headed by car to what became our next loved home, with Meredith insisting that she wanted to kiss goodbye to all the windows of our gracious homestead at Melrose Valley. Situated in the Weetangera district on the western outskirts of Canberra, as coincidence would have it, the property's name was 'Melrose'. John paid £16,100 for a cottage and its surrounding 806 acres (326 ha), later to be developed into parts of the Canberra city suburbs of Holt and Higgins. It was snowing when we arrived. The gum trees looked like cauliflowers, or so Cecily recalls my description of them as a four-year-old. The house was not much more than a large shack made from corrugated iron with internal dividing fibro walls. The kitchen, with its worn linoleum floor, was a mere galley throughway from the living areas to the back veranda and laundry. Making the best of everything, Cecily came to enjoy the compact kitchen; everything was within arms' reach. Cecily had not been keen to leave Melrose Valley but went along with the enormous upheaval that moving the family involved. The larger and more fertile acreage was financially viable to farm should John have to rely on it for a living. Cecily might not have agreed so readily had she known that we would barely be settled into our new environment before we had to pack up and leave it.

When John's six-months leave from the public service drew to a close at the end of 1950, Spender had to decide what to do with him. The press speculated that he would give John a 'special assignment' of some kind, because it was thought unlikely that John would agree to return to the department he had previously controlled as a subordinate officer to the new head, Alan Watt.[1] In early January 1951, before John took a seat at a desk, Spender offered him the post of high commissioner to Ceylon, a decision the minister would regret. On 19 January 1951, John's appointment as Australia's high commissioner to Ceylon was announced. Publicly, it appeared to be a political 'kick upstairs' – the action of an incoming government happy to replace an influential department head with one more amenable to its views. In fact, Spender needed him in Ceylon and expected him to commit himself to the work. The previous October, the Liberal Government had terminated the Labor Government's appointee to the post, Charles Frost. He had been criticised for neglecting Australia's new trade interest with Ceylon, and John was known to be committed to Australia engaging in trade relations with its Asian neighbours. In addition, one of his responsibilities in Ceylon would be to report on the progress made with Spender's Colombo Plan, intended to provide financial aid for South-East Asian countries. John and Arthur Tange had overseen its implementation, and the role they played in it has been acknowledged in more recent times.[2] Oakman tells of its importance in his account of the Colombo Plan:

> The Colombo Plan reached into almost every aspect of Australian foreign policy, from strategic planning and diplomatic initiatives, to economic and cultural engagement. More generally, it encouraged officials and politicians to define an Australian approach to the Cold War and the challenges of decolonisation.[3]

At age 35 John was a young senior representative abroad. By some accounts, he was initially happy to take the appointment. With the benefit of hindsight, some commentators suggested that the appointment suited him because he had his eye on another attempt to enter politics, the next federal election being three years down the track. John denied that he had any such agenda at the time. He later stated that he had viewed the post as being 'a very junior position' – that is, an insult given his capabilities – and that he accepted it because, given the publicity about him at the time, he believed the public would not understand if he turned it down. Not that he had shown any concern about what the public thought about him at this or any other time, to our observation. In the event, his diplomatic career was to be short-lived. Six weeks after taking up the appointment, circumstances occurred to change his mind about a possible political career.

---

1   'Dr Burton Back in Canberra', *Sydney Morning Herald*, 3 January 1951, 4.
2   Alexander Downer, former Liberal minister for foreign affairs, paid tribute publicly to their work in a speech on 23 May 2005.
3   Oakman, *Facing Asia*, 3.

18. JOHN'S SHORT STINT AS HIGH COMMISSIONER IN CEYLON

Australian Envoy Arrives

DR. J. W. BURTON, the new High Commissioner for Australia in Ceylon, and Mrs. Burton, who arrived here yesterday.

Dr. Burton gives a message

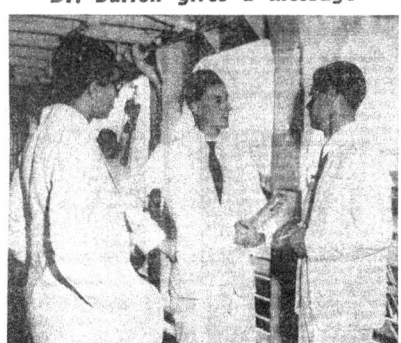

Dr. John Burton (right) the new Australian High Commissioner, who arrived in Colombo yesterday in the Stratheden, was met on board by Mr. A. H. Borthwick (centre) of the Australian High Commissioner's Office and Mr. S. K. D. Jayamanne, of the Ministry of External Affairs and Defence.

In a press statement, he said his wife and himself were looking forward to their stay in Ceylon, and to making good friends amongst the people of Ceylon. "Australia and Ceylon as members of the British Commonwealth and as neighbours, have always worked together and endeavoured to help each other. It is my duty and it will be a very pleasant one, to see that this continues to be the case."

MRS. J. W. BURTON, wife of the new High Commissioner for Australia in Ceylon says that since they were only told of this appointment in January, it was rather a rush to pack everything and be ready to sail for

Ceylon early in February—especially with three children in the family.

The children, girls of nine, eight and four are named Meredith (what a pretty and unusual name, I thought)

by CHATTERBOX

Clare, and Pamela, respectively. They have already started school here, and seem to like it.

In Australia, the Burtons lived on a small farm—800 acres is small by Australian standards—a few miles out of Canberra. Mrs. Burton says that looking after three children and doing the main part of the domestic work (domestic help is practically unobtainable) leaves her little time for any hobby. But one thing she does get down to whenever possible is dressmaking. She is very interested in making her own clothes.

Mrs. Burton has already visited the shops and says that there are some very lovely silks and sarees to be had in the shops here which are not available in Australia. She also hopes to have time to play tennis here, as she used to before her marriage. Another thing she is keen on is swimming, and she especially wants the children to learn it. I'm sure she will find some of our beaches ideal for the purpose.

Press reports of John and Cecily's arrival in Colombo, Ceylon, February 1954.
Source: Family collection.

We left for Ceylon on 2 February 1951, leaving the farm in the capable hands of our friends and farm helpers Puss and Don Kelly. Cecily decided to treat the ordeal as an adventure. Having felt at home in her corduroy overalls and gumboots as the farmer's wife, she bought and made new clothes befitting of a diplomat's wife. We travelled by steamer, the *Stratheden*, from Sydney to Colombo. My strongest memory of the trip were the celebrations when we crossed the equator. The younger passengers dressed up as King Neptune's pirates. I was four and a half and someone painted a skull and cross bones in black crayon on my chest. I was embarrassed at having a bare chest. My older sisters had their chests covered and laughed and danced unselfconsciously. The liner docked in Colombo in late February 1951. Alex Borthwick, official secretary at the Australian High Commission, boarded with an official from the Ceylonese Ministry of External Affairs and Defence and others to welcome us, and we travelled to the port by police launch. News reporters and photographers greeted us. Cecily, in a wide-brimmed black straw hat and wearing a simple but elegant cotton dress, and John, in a tropical white suit, looked ready to take on their new roles as they were photographed and interviewed.

We were driven to the high commissioner's residence on the corner of Albert Avenue and Cambridge Place in Colombo's District 7. It was a far cry from our Weetangera farmhouse. Our new home was a white-painted, two-storey colonial mansion with red-tiled roof.[4] The gracious house was situated across the road from the National Museum, and within a block or so from the Ladies College that we children would attend. Cecily was presented with a staff of 14 servants, one of whom, Elsie, was to be our nanny or 'nurse'. This was Cecily's first challenge, never before having to manage a household of this kind. The formality and extravagance of our new lifestyle meant more adjustment for her. Daily menus had to be created and directions given. It was part of her culture shock. We did not help. Meredith remembers meals being brought upstairs for us, and her naughtiness on one occasion; she sent one of the servants up and down the stairs to fetch just one item at a time, like vegemite and honey. My sin was to ask Elsie to get the kitchen staff to keep making more jaggery (a fudge-like sweet made from cane or palm sugar). With the house came a black chauffeur-driven Humber limousine. We kids sat on the 'dickie seats' that popped out from behind the front seats. John felt uncomfortable with

---

4   It was sold by the Australian Government in 2007 to Dhammika Perara, who became Sri Lanka's richest businessman and who extensively renovated and enlarged it, and its external and internal grandeur is notable.

the lifestyle and tried to get rid of the limousine but was not allowed. He purchased a small green Morris sedan to drive himself and the rest of us on family outings.

Elsie did her best to look after us boisterous farm-raised children. She was not much taller than Meredith and she was more slightly built than we were. We were aged nine, eight and four, and so we had to go to school. I suffered more embarrassment when I found that I was not up to scratch in my own and only language, English. Sitting cross-legged on the floor with children from various parts of the world, I did not expect to have to learn to speak English. My teacher used a cane to point at a poster. It depicted a busy street scene and she asked her class to name in English the objects to which she pointed. 'Bike,' I shouted confidently. The teacher frowned and said, 'bicycle'. 'Footpath' was my second confident attempt. 'Pavement' was the correct word. When I called out 'car', she looked puzzled as if she had not heard of the word and told the class it was a 'motor vehicle' in the street scene.

While we were at school, Cecily took up dressmaking as one of her few hobbies. She browsed the markets and found silks and saris not available in Australia.[5] She played tennis and after school took the opportunity of teaching us to swim at the nearby Galle Face beach. At weekends or after work, John drove us to Mount Lavinia where we played on its long scenic beach and he helped Cecily with our swimming lessons. The Buddhist and Hindu religions awoke Cecily to the sweetness and gentleness of the people: the religious feeling, the reverence for flowers – symbols of life that they took to their place of worship. Cecily picked up a flower from a woman's basket once and smelled it. She was going to put it back in the basket and the woman said, 'No, you have to throw that away'. There was much yet to learn in this new cultural environment. She did not visit temples or read about Buddhism, but she hoped to absorb the impact of Buddhism on people's daily lives.

John, too, suffered culture shock, perhaps not as willing as Cecily to embrace new experiences. Borthwick observed John's 'visceral reaction to the heat, smells, filth and crowds'.[6] John went about his official duties, one of the first of which was to present the championship trophy made of

---

5 'By Chatterbox', [news clipping, newspaper unidentified], February 1954, family file.
6 David Fettling, 'An Australian Response to Asian Decolonisation: Jawaharlal Nehru, John Burton and New Delhi Conference of Non-Western Nations', *Australian Historical Studies* 45, no. 2 (2014), 203.

Australian oak at Colombo's beach carnival. He was not happy with the work he was expected to do. There were aspects of Australia's political and trade agenda with which he did not agree. He later told the media this, but he did not reveal what these were. He told a journalist simply that 'I objected to certain things I was ordered to do. I cannot disclose what they were, but they were against my conscience'.[7]

Then, on Easter Friday, 23 March 1951, John dropped a bombshell. Spender asked John to meet the New South Wales attorney-general, Major Clarence Edward Martin, on board the liner *Himalaya*, and to 'extend him every courtesy'. Martin had been visiting India and Pakistan while on vacation for his health and the boat stopped at Colombo on its return to Sydney. While on board, John and Martin discussed election prospects in Australia. On 19 March, Governor-General William McKell, a Labor appointee, had granted the government's request for a double dissolution over parliament's failure to pass the Commonwealth Bank Bill. John later stated that he told Martin, 'I would like to return to Australia for the election, to which Martin had replied "why not?"'[8] Martin later said that it had been his idea that John explore the possibility of standing for a seat. He said that they had had a long discussion and, both being critical of the government's policy in South-East Asia, John had asked if he should go home to help in the election, and that he, Martin, had replied, 'go for preselection'.[9] John said that Martin had urged him to 'get on a plane the following day, adding, "if you wait for the next one you will miss the political bus entirely"'.[10] John's reported response was that he did not think he would be able to get a plane home, nor a federal seat to fight.

John left the *Himalaya* for Colombo by launch and found some Qantas officials who told him the plane due to leave for Australia the following day was delayed until Easter Sunday. He managed to secure the last seat on the Qantas Constellation leaving at 5 am on Easter Sunday. In the meantime, Martin busied himself. He sent a cable from the liner to the federal president of the ALP, indicating that Burton was anxious to contest the election and that he was prepared to stand for a borderline seat and he urged that Burton should be given every consideration. That evening, John informed Cecily of his rash decision to return to Australia to seek

---

7   Blaikie, 'Who Is This Dr. Burton?' *Courier-Mail*, 19 June 1952, 2.
8   'New Light on Envoy's Departure: Burton "Talked with State Attorney"', *Sunday Herald* (Sydney), 1 April 1951.
9   'What Martin Told Burton, Inside Story', *Sydney Morning Herald*, 4 April 1951.
10 *Sunday Herald*, 1 April 1951.

18. JOHN'S SHORT STINT AS HIGH COMMISSIONER IN CEYLON

preselection, although he had made no approach to the Labor Party executive for a seat and had no assurance he would be selected for one. Cecily had a lot of questions to which John was not able to give answers. She was to stay behind with us, until a passage home was secured for us.

The next morning, John dictated cables from the office of the High Commission to Spender and to the Australian ambassador in Djakarta, John Hood, his friend. Because it was the Easter weekend only a typist was on duty. He left the cables and instructions with her. Borthwick was away from Colombo until the following Monday. Perhaps the typist felt uncomfortable sending them prior to her superior's return. As it transpired, the cables were not sent until Monday after Borthwick returned. John reported his actions to Cecily and verified that he had sent a cable to inform Spender of his actions and notifying that he intended to take leave without pay. He did not have to wait for a reply, he later explained, as the request was a mere formality.[11] There was protocol in place for people to take leave of their office to stand for election. He would later be challenged for leaving his post without permission. Cecily supported his claim as she recalled his conversation detailing the instructions he left at the office concerning his departure from Ceylon. He believed that he had complied with public service regulations for seeking leave without pay for the purpose of contesting a federal election.

In his rush, John left Ceylon without his passport. In fact, he had picked up Cecily's passport by mistake, leaving his own and his health documents behind in the safe. He cabled officials in a panic. To secure a seat for the flight home, he had paid his own fare, intending to claim it back. His privately arranged flight made it more difficult, however, for him to claim that he was an Australian official who needed temporary travel documents to return home. Nevertheless, somehow he persuaded the officials and managed to leave Ceylon and enter Australia without his official papers. They were sent on to him for collection in Darwin shortly after he landed there on 26 March. Borthwick again took charge of the High Commission as he had done for the months before John's arrival. (He would, some 25 years later, become Australia's high commissioner to Ceylon after it had become Sri Lanka.) He held the fort, coping with

---

11   'Dr John Burton Forsakes His Post', *Sun*, 28 March 1951.

cables coming and going between Colombo and Canberra in the wake of the controversy John caused. Initially, Cecily had nothing but a rare telegram to keep her informed of John's doings. And John was doing a lot.

From Darwin on Monday 26 March, John telephoned the opposition leader, Chifley, to canvass the prospect of selection for a seat.[12] He then flew to Sydney, tendered his official resignation as Australian high commissioner to Ceylon and formally offered himself to the ALP as a candidate for the federal election. Spender was furious. He asserted that he was first notified of John's resignation through press channels, after which he was delivered John's signed letter.[13] Dispute surrounded the telegram John believed had been sent three days earlier, which in fact only arrived at Spender's office at around 8:30 am that Tuesday morning.

On Tuesday 27 March, the Central Executive of the NSW ALP endorsed John's selection as Labor candidate for the seat of Lowe. The seat was securely held by a Liberal member, William McMahon. John Kerr had been frontrunner for Labor's preselection. Lowe was regarded as an unwinnable seat for Labor and it seems that Kerr was only too keen for John to take his place. There are two versions of how this came about. Kerr, who later became controversial as a governor-general, had one version. He told Cecily in the presence of Robert Parker some years later that John had rung him from Ceylon and suggested he withdraw to allow John to take the Labor candidacy. John denied this, insisting that having indicated to Chifley that he was looking for preselection, Kerr offered to withdraw from the preselection race so that John could stand for Lowe. Either way, John was endorsed as Labor's candidate for the seat, having burnt his bridges in Colombo to pursue what transpired to be a futile mission.

The press had a field day. In an interview on Wednesday 28 March, in the Commonwealth Bank Building, Martin Place, Sydney, John announced that he had resigned his post in Ceylon and from the public service, a prerequisite for standing for election.[14] Spender, as minister for External Affairs, and Alan Watt, the departmental secretary, were conferring in the same building discussing Burton's 'unauthorised' return. Spender stated that Burton's resignation as high commissioner was 'the only wise thing he

---

12 'Burton after Labor Selection', *Sun*, 27 March 1951.
13 'Burton Asked to Explain', *Mirror* (Sydney), 28 March 1951.
14 'Dr Burton's Resignation Goes to Minister', *Daily Telegraph* (Sydney), 29 March 1951; 'Dr Burton Resigns Post', *Mercury* (Hobart), 29 March 1951, 1.

had done in this sorry episode'.[15] Journalists speculated that John Burton had gone to Ceylon with a plan to resign his post in three years in order to return to enter politics, confident that the current 19th parliament would run its full course. Evatt and others were sure that Menzies was posturing and that the governor-general would not grant the government's request for a double dissolution. But the government was not bluffing and the governor-general, against Labor speculation, granted it. Martin publicly put paid to the suggestion. He told the press that he had seen Burton in Australia before he had left for Ceylon and John had made no suggestion then that he was interested in entering politics. He also said that when he next spoke to John on board the *Himalaya*, there was no assurance that John would be selected and John had no seat in mind. 'I'll stake my public name against that,' he told the press on 4 April 1951.[16]

John electioneered hard and was surprisingly effective. He and his supporters distributed a long, closely typed, hand-signed letter dated 23 April 1951 to households in the electorate. It set out his policies on national issues that, in his view, people had been waiting for, under headings of 'War or Peace', 'Communism' and 'Prices'.[17] He knew it was an unwinnable blue ribbon Liberal seat, but, he said, it gave him 'the satisfaction of being free to make a few statements' opposing government policy that he otherwise could not do.[18] He put a lot of work into the seat and did not win it, but surprised people by the gains he made; a swing to Labor of 1.3 per cent. It was a commendable effort on John's part given that, overall, Labor lost the election and its majority in the Senate.[19] In conceding defeat, John congratulated McMahon and noted that the campaign was fought without bitterness or resort to personalities. He warned, however, that democracy throughout the world was endangered and that Australians 'should be on their guard to preserve their democratic way of life'. In turn, McMahon conceded that 'Dr Burton came to an electorate which had been fully worked over by the Liberal Party, and he made a remarkable achievement'.[20]

---

15   'Dr Burton Resigns as Ceylon High Commissioner', *Sydney Morning Herald*, 29 March 1951.
16   *Sydney Morning Herald*, 4 April 1951.
17   To 'Dear Elector', signed John W. Burton, Burton family file.
18   Burton, interview by John Clements, 1981.
19   McMahon polled 22,200 votes and Burton 16,195.
20   'Dr Burton in Doubt on Future Work', *Sydney Morning Herald*, 5 May 1951.

PERSONS OF INTEREST

Polling Day, Saturday, 28th April

To

THE ELECTORS

Lowe Electorate

N.S.W.

VOTE—

[1] Dr. BURTON

Official Labor Candidate

DR. JOHN W. BURTON, B.A. (Syd.), Ph.D. (Lond.) (Econ.).

John's 'How to Vote' card (front), 1951.

LABOR IS PLEDGED TO:

- Arrest the run-away pound by preventing price increases, by increasing production through co-operation with the trades union movement.
- In the meantime to give immediate relief to pensioners of all kinds who are at present carrying the main burden of inflation.
- To assist financially home-builders and newly marrieds whose savings inflation has decreased.
- To increase child endowment for the first child.
- To oppose Japanese rearmament.
- To oppose conscription abroad.
- To struggle for international peace by co-operation with British Commonwealth countries.

DR. BURTON who, at the age of 36, voluntarily gave up his life-time career with Ambassadorial rank to contest this election, has drawn to him widespread support for his Australianism, his courage and his sincerity.

He is fighting these elections because he believes an attempt is being made to change Australian democratic political institutions by replacing co-operation in industrial life with coercion, by introducing the principle of prove-yourself-innocent for the Australian practise of innocent-until-proved guilty, and by pointing the bone at persons and organisations prepared to voice moral opposition to the government.

He is fighting these elections because he believes that it is only the Labor Party that now has the answer to the vital problems of willingness to work, of combating anti-Australian elements in industry, and of the promotion of peaceful international relations.

Authorised by

Ron Weatherlake, 7 Turner Ave., Concord

Vote [1] **BURTON, J. W.** for **LABOR**

John's 'How to Vote' card (back), 1951.
Source: Family collection.

Having dramatically ended his diplomatic career to pursue a political folly, John had to consider how he might now earn a living. He later admitted that he had been very rash, but in retrospect he was happy that he did not get involved in the longer term in diplomacy. He came to believe that diplomacy would be more effective if carried out by visits by relevant officials when required, and direct communication between governments. To be able to return to the public service, John had to apply for readmission within two months of his resignation. Publicly, John stated that he was undecided yet on his future and that he would take a break on his farm for a few weeks before making decisions. It is not clear to us what effect Chifley's sudden death on 13 June 1951 had on John or whether it affected his decision in any way. When he received the news, he might have gone to the woolshed and 'shovelled shit' and cried inside – this would be his style. Evatt became leader of the ALP and, on 3 July 1951, John declared that he would not return to the public service. His comparative success in his campaign in Lowe meant that he retained Labor endorsement in the seat for the next federal election and he wanted to be free to take part in political affairs and make whatever contribution he could to the 'defence of democracy in Australia', he said.[21]

John later cited various reasons for his resignation, high on the list being the government's support of the direction of US policy in Korea. He also had concerns about Australia and New Zealand entering into a new alliance with the USA in the form of the 1951 ANZUS Treaty. He feared that it would extend areas of possible conflict in that it 'antagonises all Asian neighbours who have been excluded from it, and draws Australia into any and every conflict in which America might become involved in the Pacific'.[22] In doing this, he believed, 'Australia has left itself no more freedom of action than if it were a state of the American Union'.[23] He wanted time to write a book that might get this across to Australian foreign policy makers; a book, he hoped, might have more influence than he could exert as a public servant under the direction of a conservative government. For the time being, he would earn a living on the farm, which would give him time to write while he waited for another opportunity to enter politics.

---

21 'Dr Burton Not Returning to Public Service', *Sydney Morning Herald*, 3 July 1951.
22 Burton, *The Alternative*, 74.
23 Burton, *The Alternative*, 75.

19

The beginning of the end of a marriage

Cecily's time in Ceylon was a defining moment in her life. She had to make constant adjustments at short notice on how to handle life around planet John, and this was one of those times. The world revolved around him but Cecily was on that planet, too. From her point of view, we had barely settled into our new farm life before the family had to pack up and leave. Then, after a month in Ceylon, John was gone again – home to contest a federal seat he was unlikely to win. She was left to cope in a strange country with three young children until the *Stratheden* returned from the UK some weeks later on its homeward voyage. After John departed, journalists found a way of contacting Cecily to try and question her, though how much news of John filtered through to her in Colombo is not clear. Borthwick would have kept her informed to a degree and John's and Cecily's Hindu friend, Raju, had access to press channels and information. Cecily's situation became intolerable. As soon as the High Commission arranged for Cecily's and our passage home, an outcry broke out in Australia about the family's travel costs; nearly £1,000.[1] Cecily was left in the public spotlight and at the mercy of gossip in the judgemental diplomatic Colombo community.

Meanwhile the British ambassador and his wife had already planned a welcome for John as the new Australian high commissioner. Cecily tried to excuse herself rather than go alone. The diplomat's wife, horridly in Cecily's opinion, insisted that she attend when Cecily thought it prudent that she should not. The hostess said, 'Oh, yes, you must come, you must

---

1 'Burton Family Fares Queried', *Sun*, 30 March 1951.

come.' Cecily went along, only to find that a seat for John at the table opposite her was left empty. Even if Cecily had understood that it was customary for a host to leave a vacant dinner chair for an important guest who failed for some reason to attend, she would not have forgiven her host for making her feel so uncomfortable. Cecily felt humiliated, insulted and miserable in the hands of this nastiness.

Meredith then fell ill from serious sunstroke; she was in some danger of liver infection, which, fortunately, did not eventuate. How much more could Cecily endure? Perhaps not much, had it not been for Raju, who Cecily liked and trusted. Before he left Ceylon, John entrusted Cecily's care to Raju. John had befriended him previously at an international conference. Raju had been nicknamed 'Fiji' because he was a black man attending an all-white conference. He was a wealthy, well-respected Brahman government official who lived with his family in Colombo. Raju turned out to be the friend Cecily needed in whom to confide. He recognised that Cecily would suffer in Colombo, being perceived as a deserted high commissioner's wife; the handsome young diplomat, John Burton, arrived only to abandon his beautiful young wife and family seemingly without explanation.

A few days after John's departure, Raju visited Cecily. He entered the large living room where Cecily was sitting alone and unable to disguise how unhappy she was feeling. He said in a gentle voice, 'You look browned off.' She looked up at him, taking in his concern, his sensitivity, and admitted that she was pretty miserable. Was it that moment, or later with hindsight, she knew that Raju's tenderness was something she had missed all her life? Here was a man showing her that he cared. He understood how she felt. Raju's gentle presence awoke something in her. His emotional intelligence, his warmth of spirit and enjoyment of her as a person struck through her heart. She not only relied on him to talk to and to console her, she became infatuated with him. She felt a sense of belonging when she was with him, removing her from a community of diplomats to which she felt she did not belong.

Cecily's excitement over Raju overwhelmed her. She could not eat and could hardly stand up on her shaking legs when she answered phone calls from him. Her infatuation with Raju was both a symptom of a deep dissatisfaction she had in her relationship with John and a distraction from the reality of the social situation John had left her to endure. Raju visited, took her on outings and kept her busy while we waited for our passage home. He also returned her affection. Perhaps his culture and

19. THE BEGINNING OF THE END OF A MARRIAGE

social status in the Ceylonese hierarchy played a part in allowing their affair to develop. He took her for drives at night. They made love in the confines of his car, for there was nowhere else they could go.

Cecily enjoyed Raju's affection in the month they had together, although her stay in Colombo with us children must have felt like an eternity. Raju came with his wife to see us off when the *Stratheden* finally docked in Colombo to take us home. Cecily had to bury her feelings. She was unhappy, confused about who she was and for what purpose she was put on this earth. For the next few weeks, she had three children to look after, emptiness in her heart and no John for support. Internally she was at the end of her tether, not recognising for some time that she was on the verge of a mental breakdown.

We kids jumped on the rails of the deck to wave to the crowd below, blissfully unaware of Cecily's breaking heart and how desperately hard it was for her to farewell Raju, knowing that she would miss his love, comfort and understanding. Why, she asked herself, did she feel so desperate? What was it that she wanted at that moment? An outward display of affection in the presence of his wife? She felt that Raju's wife had some idea of their affair because she stood close beside her husband. Almost certainly Cecily was unaware of the culture of Raju's class that imposed acceptance on the part of his wife of a husband's liaisons with other women. Standing beside her husband was important to preserving his and her public image. Boarding the liner gave Cecily an enhanced sense of loneliness in the midst of a crowd. She had to show a brave face to her children. There were nearly 1,000 passengers on the liner who consisted mainly of European migrants: 50 Dutch, 40 Swiss and 12 'stateless' people, including a Russian family who had been living in Persia for some years. Most spoke no English. Given her intense interest in people and their psyches, their plight offered Cecily a mild distraction from her grief in leaving Raju.

On 24 April 1951, Cecily and John's wedding anniversary, the *Stratheden* with Cecily and us aboard passed through Fremantle. John, having by then gained Labor preselection for the federal seat of Lowe, met us some days later when it docked in Melbourne and we were surrounded by media and more controversy. We sat on a cabin bed to pose for a photograph for a daily newspaper of John reading his three little girls a story, although we knew nothing at the time of the controversy surrounding him.

Left to right: Pam, Clare, John and Meredith, on return journey aboard the *Stratheden*, April 1951.
Source: Family collection.

John's father, Jack, was not happy about his leaving Ceylon and said so.[2] But John was steadfast and by now preoccupied with his political campaign. When we arrived home to our farm in Weetangera, John went straight back to Sydney and into his campaign. He drove the farm truck to Sydney, towing our caravan in which he would sleep while working in the electorate. Meredith, old enough to understand his political ambition, joined him for a few days of the campaign.

At this point, Cecily thought she was going mad. As she well knew, John seized opportunities as and when they arose. However, his unpredictability and propensity for controversy was more than she could comprehend. Here John was, off again leaving her to manage the farm. She was in a mental muddle, particularly feeling a terrible tension about her time in Ceylon and Raju. Now, she was home coping emotionally while John was consumed by another mission. She had no idea what John might do next should he fail in his bid to enter federal politics. Should he win the seat of Lowe, the family would presumably have to move again, to live in Sydney.

---

2   Blaikie, 'Who Is This Dr. Burton?' *Courier-Mail*, 19 June 1952, 2.

19. THE BEGINNING OF THE END OF A MARRIAGE

Cecily would reflect on Raju, who had seemed to understand her in a way that John was never able to. The relationship that developed between them affected Cecily in ways that she did not expect. Raju visited Canberra some years later, when his affair with Cecily was over and John was not yet aware of it. But by that time Cecily had undergone a radical change, partly provoked by her experience in Ceylon and her liaison with this man. She was by then on steady ground and more sure of herself. On seeing Raju again, Cecily decided that at least she had good taste. He was the charming, intelligent man who had infatuated her; although, recalling the unegalitarian way he treated his servants at home, helped her to distance herself from him. She and John never accepted the need for the unfair and hierarchical social systems that underpinned Ceylonese society and its economy.

Cecily was unfaithful to John; never before, and not for long. Nevertheless, when time, place and distance would put her Colombo affair into context, she believed she had been sinful and, consumed by guilt, in 1962 confessed to John. John would not forgive. Years later, Cecily would talk to us about 'guilt' as a destructive concept. '"Guilt" should be removed from the English language,' she would say, and 'instead, one should learn by mistakes, pledge to do better next time, and move on.' Guilt ate into her and John played on it. He was hurt by her revelation; she could see it in his eyes. She described him lying back in bed, as he did 'in his cogitating moments with the sheet pulled up over to his nose so you could hardly hear what he said and sat there in judgment on me, and told me absolutely nothing about his own life, nothing, and got me in this position of … the guilty one'.[3] Only later did she learn that he had been unfaithful to her on previous occasions. Yet, a decade or so later, John would use Cecily's infidelity against her, again and again.

We now know how unhappy Cecily was with her relationship with John, before we went to Ceylon. She loved him. Sexually they were compatible. But she saw his lovemaking as satisfying his sexual need and lacking in expression of love. She wanted more. Lovemaking, she believed, should develop out of an emotional intimacy, not something she felt she achieved with John. John could not understand what more he could do. How could she explain to him that she yearned for the tenderness and understanding that accompanied Raju's loving-making? It marked the beginning of the

---

3   Parker, interview by Meredith Edwards, 2004, 64.

end of his and Cecily's relationship – which lingered on tumultuously for the next decade or so. In the meantime, both Cecily and John had no option but to take farming as a way of life, seriously. However, this did not occur without each of their lives being forever changed by two separate events. Cecily's occurred towards the end of 1951. It was a psychological event and out of her control. John's occurred the following year, was very public and entirely of his own making.

20

Cecily's life-changing encounter

One September day in 1951, 35-year-old Cecily, mother of three, walked a few hundred metres uphill on a dirt drive to our mailbox at the entrance gate of Melrose on the Weetangera Road. It was something she did daily. From there she had a grand view of tree-covered hills and faraway mountains dark against the sky. Her knowledge that the Murrumbidgee River flowed through the countryside between her and the Brindabellas, though hidden by the hills, added to its magnificence. She found the vista completely beautiful and satisfying. An extraordinary thing happened on what had, until then, seemed like any other day. Cecily stood by the mailbox to take in the scene and it suddenly came alive. It breathed and glowed as everything did around her – the trees, the rocks, the road, the fence, the sticks and stones, even the earth itself. Everything shimmered and pulsated with vitality. At the same time an inward change took place in her – she felt blessed with a profound intuitive sense of the openness of everything, of everything she knew and did not know, of the oneness of the whole universe. She became aware 'in a mysterious and wonderful way, with intense meaning, that everything and everyone were connected, belonged together, were part of a great pattern'.[1] She was filled with awe.

---

1   Cecily wrote about this profound mystical experience in 1969 and again in 1996: Cecily family file; in an article 'Much Madness in Divinest Sense ...', *Canberra Jung Society Newsletter*, January–June 1997, 6. Where not otherwise referenced, we have drawn from these and other of her writings held on Cecily family file for this chapter.

Cecily might have been ecstatic, as so often people are with a beautiful though mystic experience, but she had no idea of what had happened to her. This cosmic episode related to nothing she had ever heard of and she found it terrifying. She did not know then that many people had had such an experience, and she did not then embrace the joy or the bliss that, she later learned, some people do with such a revelation; if she had, she would have felt comforted. Instead, she was overwhelmed and afraid – her feelings and sensations were so powerful, so foreign, so utterly incomprehensible. Looking back, it was as though she had seen the face of God, and felt his power, although at the time she had no thought of God. The experience taught her more about herself. She wrote:

> The attempt to express myself began after the mystical experience, which I did not feel at all as an ecstasy as I am supposed to have done, I rather suffered it as the profoundest possible disturbance. My feelings threatened to overwhelm me first in Ceylon and insanity was at hand – I fought like a tiger cat, because that wasn't where I wanted my feelings to go. Before Raju became important I was very moved indeed by the religious atmosphere which was completely new to me. I kept control sufficiently not to make a fool of myself, because the children had to be looked after and got home and because no one would understand, least of all John who would use it all against me for ever more. Having overcome this, I developed a kind of constant awful pain, the mystical experience followed. Once more I fought against the feelings overwhelming me.[2]

Her foundations shaken, her assumptions about reality shattered, what was she to do? Who should she talk to? For a time, the experience was too powerful to talk about and she kept it to herself, trying to appear normal, puzzling and wondering inwardly, then gradually she got used to living with her strange, changed self. Every day for a couple of weeks the world remained alive to her in the same vivid way; at night the stars came alive. Then the vision faded, though for months she could recall it at will. Was she going mad, she asked herself, but that did not make sense. It genuinely happened to her; it was real – subjectively real – and she was not going to deny it or push it away. She would search for the explanation. And until

---

2   R. S. Parker papers, NLA, MS 8200 Restricted, box 20, file 89, Cecily in a letter to Robert, 13 July 1965.

then she thought she could not feel fully sane; not until she understood it, found its meaning, put it in some kind of context, connected it to other things she knew or could find out about.

Cecily continued her life with us on the farm, working excessively hard physically, which she thought helped, and with determination she cared for John and us children and saw and entertained friends. At the same time, it was as if she were walking along the edge of a precipice, between madness and sanity – an abyss on her left, solid ground on her right. She could not choose between them, and did not want to; because both were real, both were valuable, and she could not abandon either. She intended to continue to walk carefully along this dangerous path, however shaky and in fear she was, until something would be made clear. Somewhere inside her there was a faith, a blind faith, that there was a way through her anguish. That kept her sane. Moreover, she had enough knowledge of psychology to realise that what had happened must have arisen from some kind of projection of her inner self. She did not believe the world had actually changed, and so she knew she was not suffering from delusions. It was something in herself, and herself in relation to the world, that had to be understood – though this was a dim realisation at the time.

After a while she talked to a few carefully chosen people, but was met with dismissive remarks, blank looks and awful warnings, and other discouraging responses; 'Forget it!', being the essence. This included John's father when he came to stay with us six months or so later. Though Jack was a religious man, he offered nothing. She talked to the Irish ambassador because he seemed to be a spiritual kind of man, their friend Russel Ward and other people she thought might understand, but they all reacted with words to the effect of, 'Rubbish, I used to feel like that when I was an adolescent and you get over it'. Cecily, however, could not get over it. It happened, and she could not go on pretending it did not happen. She took no notice of the advice, and was deeply disappointed that no one understood or took her seriously enough to try to help. She was alone in her distress, isolated in her search for understanding. She did everything possible to get John to understand how she felt about her experience. Had she not tried to hide the fact that she might simply have been cracking up, John might have taken practical action; he might have involved doctors if he thought she was having a 'nervous' breakdown, as mental illnesses were sometimes spoken about then. He reliably reacted quickly to a crisis that he had power to resolve. Instead, he was dismissive, saying she was talking 'mumbo jumbo' when she tried to discuss ideas that emerged from her reading that might explain her experience. He thought she had strange ideas and inappropriately said so to 10-year-old Meredith and, presumably, others in private, unwittingly putting Cecily down.

As well as throwing herself into farm work, Cecily studied mathematics, more to hold on to her sanity than to gain understanding. Physical work proved better for her sanity and she gave up maths. At the same time as she was trying to intellectualise her experience, she worked on John's manuscript, *The Alternative,* trying to win his approval. He needed her editorial help and benefited from her superior English writing skills, but he did not give her the approval she sought.

Cecily went often to the newly developing National Library of Australia, then in a small building on Kings Avenue in Canberra. There, she could browse books on the shelves and borrow what she wanted. But she had no idea what books might be of help. She began to read widely and avidly on a range of topics with little joy or reward, hoping that the right books would leap off the shelves and into her hands. Mysteriously, reading about the 'Third Eye' did this, which led to a book and then another and eventually she discovered Frieda Fordham's book on Jung, she told us. There, with tears and gratitude, Cecily found her answer. From reading about Jung and works by him, Cecily learned that her experience was not unusual and that what she had been through was understood and valued by others, that Jung himself had been through something like it and had an explanation for it. He called it getting in touch with the 'collective unconscious'. Her vision and her revelation had come from the depths of her own psyche, and those inner depths were to be treasured and explored. She knew then that, although she had glimpsed the psychotic's world, she was not insane. And so began her healing. Her fight against insanity would take a few more years, but reading Jung saved her from complete isolation, she reflected in 1965. Self-reliant and resilient, she pulled through. She did not see a doctor, take drugs, or receive any professional therapeutic help. She functioned well, physically and mentally, supported by her belief in Jung.

Cecily concluded that because she had repressed her feelings for so long, they were pushed down and down and down to the uttermost depths of her personality to what she called the psychotic level. Because she was never really neurotic, she seemed to skip becoming so by being practical and compassionate for all those things on the outside. She attributed her psychotic experience to the emotional strain she had been under for many years before the event, triggered by the extreme stress she had suffered in the preceding months and in Ceylon in particular. Encountering Buddhism and Hinduism in Ceylon was a 'culture shock' that required her to adjust to an entirely different way of life. It was these extreme circumstances, she believed, combined with the fact that she had constantly repressed personal emotions in order to cope with her life, that forced her back and back into herself further than she had ever retreated before. She experienced going back beyond her inner personal life, to the very depths of her psyche, down to the universal matrix from which all personal life, all individuality, emerges – to a point where she could go no further. When that happened, she had an equally strong reaction that allowed her to feel a part of the human collective unconscious as described by Jung. Even so, it took about five years before Cecily again felt fully sane, before the eruption of contents from her share of the collective underworld was comfortably assimilated into her full awareness, and she could understand why she, personally, had been precipitated into such a great psychic upheaval. It was for her an epiphany that fundamentally changed her world view and her life course. She maintained a lifelong personal and professional interest in Jungian analysis.

Nevertheless, Cecily remained in the woods for several years so far as her mental health was concerned. She continued to search for answers to questions she asked herself about her own needs and John's failure to understand her. She found in her friend Alec Hope, an Australian poet, a kindred spirit. She saw in Hope, as she did with Raju, something that she felt she desperately needed. Hope had a philosophical and poetic way of life. She approached him and engaged him in discussion about philosophy and the early Greeks. As with Raju, she became infatuated with him, and could not keep away. It was not a sexual or physical attraction that drew her to him as much as a love of his mind and his apparent understanding of hers. Cecily routinely made a trip to Canberra from the farm one day a week where she found she could not keep herself from wanting to drop in and see Hope. One day she decided. 'I can't beat this thing. I'm going to just give in.' From that day, having admitted her helplessness in the grip of her infatuation, she said, 'I was free'.³ She did not pursue a connection with Hope, who continued to visit the farm. He and Cecily remained friends without their relationship having gone any further.

Over her long, five-year struggle, Cecily made efforts to consciously and willingly make the experience her own and integrate it into her personality. At the same time, she struggled to recognise and accept the reality and validity of her own individuality and personal feelings. The universal and the personal – each was part of the whole. It was hard. She became much clearer about it later. When she succeeded sufficiently to feel normal, it still was not enough. She needed a more coherent mental picture of what had happened to her. She also wanted to let other people know, rationally and objectively, that there was a way through such difficult circumstances, that the disintegrative effect of psychosis need not be a hopeless condition, that the disruption could be understood and given meaning and that with much patience, great care and hard work, psychotherapy (perhaps with the help of medication) could be effective. 'If I could do it,' she thought, 'other people could do it.'

With hindsight, we believe Cecily had become a disciple of Jung's. She needed to have someone to believe in, to follow, other than John. She no longer saw her role in life as being to support John in his mission to make a difference in the world. John liked to lead and looked for disciples for his views. But from here on, Cecily was not going to be one of John's disciples. Cecily knew she could not change John's nature, only her own adaptation to him. She started to stand her ground when it mattered, let John know how his behaviour affected her, and left it up to him to assess the consequences of his not taking her or the children's feelings into account. She worked with him to overcome the challenges the family was presented with. Although at this stage Cecily was far from having reached self-assurance, she and her marriage appeared to be stronger. At the same time, she knew it was missing something. She still loved John but she felt he failed to make her happy.

The psychotic experience marked a turning point in Cecily's life. It had an immediate effect on her sense of being. She had crossed a line. She began to ask John to say 'please' and 'thank you', although he took no notice. But that was the beginning of her asserting herself. There was no going back. In the longer term, the experience informed her thinking and inspired

---

3   Parker, interview by Meredith Edwards, 2004, 45.

her thesis, 'Regression and Psychotherapy', for her master's degree written more than 20 years later, in 1973, and it shaped her career as a clinical psychologist. On finishing the thesis, she felt that not only had she put herself together, but that she had also succeeded in connecting strongly to a wide outside world as well as to the depths within her, as she explained it later to us.

It was as well that Cecily held on to her sanity, despite the grim deterioration in her mental health that she had suffered. John continued to be predictably unpredictable and Cecily could not guess what a new day might bring; she only hoped that with it might come some light and happiness at the end of the tunnel. But John was to cause more public controversy yet.

21

China: Neither 'dead nor red'

On 8 April 1952, in a tense Cold War political atmosphere, John caused shockwaves to ripple through the community by announcing his intention to attend a conference the following month convened by the Chinese Committee for Peace in the Pacific to be held in Peking (Beijing). The conference's object was to prepare for a full-scale conference in October 1952 to which representatives from every country in the Asia-Pacific region were invited. John led a delegation drawn from a self-titled group, the 'Australian Peace Partisans', who had also been invited to attend.[1] Its member delegates were the Rev. G. R. Van Eerde; Dr S. Macindoe, an agronomist from the NSW Department of Agriculture; Arthur Gietzelt, an ex-serviceman from Sydney; and Ada Bromham, secretary of the Women's Christian Temperance Union, from Melbourne. Major trouble loomed ahead for John and our family as a consequence.

Cecily supported John's peace initiatives but she resented his failure to engage in genuine consultation with her before he embarked on some or other dramatic course. And, on this occasion, so did the Labor Party. John was still an endorsed Labor candidate and he had not consulted his Labor Party masters before accepting the invitation. Arthur Calwell,

---

1   See Craig McLean, 'Fear of Peace? Australian Government Responses to the Peace Movement 1949–1959' (Master's diss., Victoria University, 2001), for an analysis of the government's efforts to restrict the movements of peace activists through the imposition of travel controls, most notably passport bans (ch. 3), and of ASIO's role in monitoring the efforts of the peace movement (ch. 4), accessed 9 April 2021, vuir.vu.edu.au/15299/1/McLean_2001_compressed.pdf; Phillip Deery and Craig McLean, 'Behind Enemy Lines: Menzies, Evatt and Passports for Peking', *The Round Table*, July 2003, 407–422, vuir.vu.edu.au/571/1/Behind_Enemy_Lines.pdf.

deputy Labor leader, demanded that John resign from the Labor Party. 'No man can serve two masters,' he said. 'No person can honestly belong to the Labor Party and attend what, after all, can only be a Communist-inspired – if not Communist-controlled – conference to weaken the Western democracies in their struggle with the Communist world.'[2] John had no intention of resigning and publicly criticised Calwell for his attack on him before ascertaining the facts and circumstances of the conference and what was hoped to be achieved. He said:

> The late Prime Minister (Mr Chifley) and Dr Evatt both advocated the recognition of China, meaning clearly that we should use our best endeavours to exercise our influence on Chinese policies in our own interests.[3]

John's view in 1949 was that it was in Australia's interest to give diplomatic recognition to the establishment of the People's Republic of China under Mao Zedong as it was an Asian Pacific nation. He warned that delay in recognising the new government in China could only help isolate the communist regime and 'serve to crystallise the beliefs of Peking in Australia's hostility to it'.[4] Evatt had distanced himself then from John's public stance on China. Now in 1952, after the outbreak of the Korean War and Australia having given its support for United Nations' intervention, Evatt, as leader of the Labor Opposition since Ben Chifley's death in June 1951, was angry that John was embarrassing the Labor Party.

Restrictions on the issue of passports for people to visit China had loosened in November 1951 and the delegates, travelling in their private capacity, were granted passports to travel to Peking. Had John not been included in the delegation the matter might not have reignited the fierce debate over passport control that followed. Richard Casey, then minister for External Affairs, condemned the conference as 'the usual Communist stunt', but made the point that, other than John, a 'distinguished ornament of the Labor party', the others in the delegation had no political importance.[5] Menzies even acknowledged that some of the delegation

---

2   'Calwell to Burton: "Resign if You Go to China"', *Sunday Herald* (Sydney), 18 May 1952, 3.
3   'Labor Party Stir. Calwell Requests Burton to Resign', *Morning Bulletin* (Rockhampton, Qld), 19 May 1952, 1.
4   Albinski, *Australian Policies and Attitudes toward China*, 27.
5   'Burton Trip Attacked', *Canberra Times*, 21 May 1952, 1; Australian House of Representatives (HoR), *Parliamentary Debates*, vol. 217, 20 May 1952, 508–10.

were well-intentioned.⁶ It was Evatt's extraordinary stand of opposing John's and the other delegates' right to be given a passport to go to the China that fuelled the fuss.⁷

Evatt was a passionate advocate for civil rights who, in the lead up to the September 1951 referendum to amend the Constitution to ban the Communist Party, had successfully led the 'no vote' campaign as a matter of civil rights, seeing the proposal as an infringement of freedom of speech and political association. He now challenged the government for its reluctance to take tough action against John's delegation going to Communist China. Casey said, 'He cannot have it both ways.'⁸ And Casey questioned how far Evatt was going. On 2 June 1952, in a statement to the press, Casey said that if Evatt was suggesting that the government should restrict overseas travel by individuals, it presumably would be to stop known communists from going abroad, 'but Dr Burton is not a member of the Communist Party – he is a member of the Labor Party'.⁹ Evatt's outcry played into the conservatives' hands and 14 members of the government voted with the Labor Opposition to enable Evatt to extend the bitter debate in parliament on John's attendance at the conference in China.¹⁰ It was a circus. Paul Hasluck, minister for territories, remarked to his cabinet colleagues, according to one source:

> This is a public relations problem – a contest between the Labor party and ourselves as to whether we can outdo Evatt by hammering the fact that an endorsed Labor man has gone to Peking …¹¹

While this debate was in progress, John seemed unconcerned at suggestions that he might be expelled from the Labor Party; he was carrying out the party platform in 'co-operating with South-East Asian countries for the purpose of peace'.¹² The Peace Partisan delegates explained to the press that they wanted to form their own views on what was happening in

---

6   HoR, *Parliamentary Debates*, vol. 218, 10 September 1952, 1187.
7   For a full account of the debate see McLean, *Fear of Peace?*, ch. 3, 79–83.
8   Evatt Collection, Flinders University Library, Evatt Files/Casey, R. G. 1943–1954, 'Reply to Dr. Evatt'.
9   Evatt Collection, Flinders University Library, Evatt Files/Casey, R. G. 1943–1954, 'Reply to Dr. Evatt'.
10 HoR, *Parliamentary Debates*, vol. 217, 20 May 1952, 508–10, reported in 'Burton Trip Attacked', *Canberra Times*, 21 May 1952, 1.
11 Phillip Deery and Craig McLean, 'Behind Enemy Lines: Menzies'.
12 'Dr J Burton Leaves for Peking talks', *Canberra Times*, 21 May 1952, 1.

Communist China and said that they would report publicly on their return on what they had seen and heard. Pemberton commented on the episode:

> How confusing would it have been for these partisans if they had known that the Communist Chinese regarded John as the enfant terrible of their conference in Beijing in 1952; or, had they realised how well John was regarded by the diplomats of newly independent Asian countries, notably India and Indonesia. Australian conservative historians, interested only in the British-American view of the world, have ignored this Asian perspective.[13]

On Tuesday 20 May 1952, the delegation left for China via Hong Kong. Adding emotion to the controversy, it was reported that 30 Australian servicemen, on their way from Sydney to the Korean battlefield, were on the same flight.[14] On 22 May, John boarded a Chinese train to Peking. The China experts at ANU whom John had consulted before he left had suggested that John would find conditions in China appalling. His initial impressions were to the contrary: the Peking train left on time, it was clean and comfortable with good food and his hotel room was clean and well equipped.[15] John had another reason to test the accuracy of the information he had been given about China. It had been suggested in Australia that some missionaries had been treated poorly in China and, like prisoners, were not able to get information out. Michael Lapwood, a Presbyterian minister from Melbourne, who had been a missionary in China, asked John to bring a letter back from his missionary brother in China who he had not heard from in a long time. On arriving in Peking, John asked the hotel receptionist if he could call two Australian missionaries. He was pointed to a phone and told he could 'ring them'.[16] John used the phone to make inquiries and was soon put through to Lapwood and they made arrangements to meet during the week of the conference, which was scheduled to commence on 28 May. Lapwood and his colleague came around from Yenching University in Peking and met

---

13 Pemberton, 'John Burton: The Heretic', 96.
14 'Labor Council Defends Right of Dr Burton', *Canberra Times*, 22 May 1952, 4.
15 R. S. Parker papers, NLA, MS 8200, box 46, file 189, letter John to Robert, 20 November 1952; and email from Burton to *Canberra Times*, 5 October 2006, Burton family file.
16 John's account of this is verified by a former member of the Communist Party of Australia who 'defected' and was recruited by ASIO as an agent: extract of interview of agent under cover of Minute to Royal Commission Section, 8 June 1954, NAA: A6199, 130, Burton vol. 4, 99. The name of the agent is suppressed, but from the content of his report it seems that he had known John quite well: he reported that Cecily was against John going to China, but that John's father had said: 'the only thing he did right in his life was to go to Peking'. The agent said that 'the rest of his family are up against it because his wife has to do all the work on the farm'.

John at his hotel. According to John, they told him that they had not been imprisoned, were happy to be working in China and they praised the new government for the progress it was making. Lapwood gave John a letter to take home to his brother, dated 1 June 1952, which set out his view of the conditions in China.[17]

The conference delegates were warmly welcomed; they attended gatherings and formal dinners without, according to John, being subjected to the Chinese propaganda they expected. However, they were presented with what, in John's view, was a 'provocative' conference agenda with items that prejudged issues for discussion. John later told the *Canberra Times* that, on arriving at the conference, he opposed the agenda and a new draft agenda was introduced. The Australians enjoyed full participation and John was elected to the Presidium of the conference as well as to the commission, which was set up to draft the Manifesto or Declaration of the Conference.[18]

From John's point of view the conference proceeded smoothly. That is not how it was viewed back home. On 1 June, John had cabled the Parliamentary Press Gallery with news of the opening day, including a report on accusations levelled against the USA that germ warfare was being used in North Korea.[19] The Melbourne dailies and other newspapers prominently headlined the claims as if John himself had made them. As to his belief in the veracity of the allegations, John had expressed no view other than it warranted investigation. John's reports of events did nothing to calm the controversy within the Labor Party about where his loyalties lay. The germ warfare allegations became a subject of international concern and the Red Cross made calls for an investigation. In recent times, more evidence has surfaced about the USA's biological warfare program during World War Two. According to Michael Pembroke in his book *Korea*, when the Korean conflict commenced, the US germ warfare program accelerated with greater funding and expanded facilities.[20]

---

17 A copy of the letter is in R. S. Parker papers, NLA, MS 8200, box 46, file 189.
18 NAA: A6119, 128, Burton vol. 2, 39. The final declaration is Appendix D, 77–79.
19 NAA: A6119, 128, Burton vol. 1, 101–2, report on three cables John sent to the Parliamentary Press Gallery; and see NAA: A6119, 128, Burton vol. 2, 39, Appendix E, 80–83 for full text of the cables. See also *Canberra Times*, 2 June 1952, 4.
20 Pembroke, *Korea*, see ch. 12, 'Secrets and Lies', 171. Pembroke details and references a Joint Chiefs' top-secret memorandum dated 25 February 1952 that approved the immediate acquisition of 'a strong offensive BW capability', with a final recommendation that the USA 'be prepared to employ BW whenever it is militarily advantageous'. He noted at p. 175: 'Uncannily, a day or two before it was issued, Mao Zedong informed Stalin, and Zhou Enlai informed the world, that the USA had carried out air drops in northeast China of several kinds of insects infected with plague, cholera and other diseases. And two weeks later, Zhou claimed that between 29 February and 5 March, American aircraft had conducted further sorties in northeast China, dropping germ-carrying insects.'

At home, Cecily had to deal with the press and confess ignorance as to where John was. She thought it strange that she had not heard from him since he passed through Hong Kong on 22 May. She expected to at least hear from him on his return through Hong Kong on 10 June. On Friday 13 June, concerned that he might not have reached Hong Kong at all, she asked the Department of External Affairs if they would help her find out where he was. 'My husband always lets me know when he is coming home, even if he has only taken a trip to Sydney or is to be half an hour late for dinner,' she told the press.[21] The press portrayed her quite differently from her normal resilient self. Headlined with 'Anxious Mrs Burton asks: "Find my husband!"', the Melbourne *Argus* reported: '"I am terribly worried about my husband," said the pretty wife of Dr John Burton in Canberra last night', and that he 'couldn't just vanish'.[22] It was a distressing time for her, and her concern about John's whereabouts only fuelled press sensationalism. 'Dead or Red', was the gist of speculative headlines about the group's mission and whereabouts in China.

In fact, John was never missing. The Parliamentary Press Gallery had received six cables from him about the conference proceedings and, given the small town community, he probably had expected they would keep Cecily informed. The full story later emerged. John had not planned to extend his stay after the conference as did the other delegates who went on a tour. He had a Chinese minder and, back at his hotel, John took the opportunity of raising his concern about three Australian airmen who had been in a Chinese gaol since December 1950 and were reportedly being mistreated. They had been employed by Cathay Pacific in Hong Kong, but were reported to have been taken prisoner when the Catalina they and a Chinese passenger had chartered from Chittagong in eastern Pakistan had landed, or drifted, into communist waters near the Portuguese colony of Macao.[23] John did not know what charges had been laid against them but understood that they had been accused of smuggling opium into the country, allegations they denied. John suggested to his minder that China was being given a bad name for treating Australian prisoners badly. The Hong Kong press had reported on the repressive new regime and its cruel treatment of the prisoners. Motivated by humanitarian concerns if the claims were correct, but concerned about the impact on Australia's relations with its Asian neighbours if the claims were mischievous, John

---

21 *Argus*, 13 June 1952, 1.
22 *Argus*, 13 June 1952, 1.
23 'Adelaide Man Held by Reds "Safe and Well"', *Advertiser* (Adelaide), 16 June 1952, 1, story from AAP Hong Kong, 15 June 1952.

saw his chance to pursue the matter. The smearing of new China was not in Australian interests and nor did he want Australian nationals to be roughly treated. In either event, he hoped to achieve the release of the airmen. John made inquiries through the minder, starting with Mao's office, as only John would.

In due course, a senior personal assistant to Mao came to see him and assured John that the men were being well-treated. John wanted more than an assurance and explained what Australia thought of China's role in this affair. The matter unresolved, the official declared he would find out. John waited for several days hoping to hear something. He missed his plane to Hong Kong, but he was determined not to leave until he had a satisfactory response. It was worth the wait. On 13 June, the official returned with news that the three airmen would soon be released. However, John was told that there was no train that day from Peking to get him to Hong Kong where he was to catch his plane home. He spent the day accompanied by his minder looking around the city. At an art gallery, he selected a traditional scroll painting of lotus flowers by Qi Baishi, a well-known and influential contemporary Chinese painter, or possibly it was a copy painted by one of Qi Baishi's pupils, the artist known to sometimes sign his best pupils' work. John's minder insisted the scroll be gifted to John and, over the next half-century, it hung proudly in the living rooms of each of John's homes. That night, he had dinner alone with Kuo Mo-Jo, a Chinese vice-premier and chairman of the Chinese Committee for Peace, who gave him information about the whereabouts of the airmen. The next day, his minder came to his room, wreathed in smiles, with news that a flight was going to Canton in time for him to catch his plane home. John forwarded a cable to the Press Gallery saying he was leaving Peking that day. He was driven to the airport to find that he was the only passenger. Whether the plane was especially arranged for him or not, John had the impression that he was being looked after rather than his movements being controlled. From Canton, he took a train to Hong Kong. When he arrived in Hong Kong, he found that a storm had caused flights to be cancelled. He sent cables through AAP Reuters that he had arrived in Hong Kong from Canton and a report on the airmen for distribution to the Australian press.

On 15 June, John saw a newspaper report of the day before: 'Today's cable to Mrs Burton has ended five days' anxiety for her'.[24] John cabled Cecily: 'Sorry anxiety. Movements as advised press gallery. Leaving

---

24 'Burton on Way Home', *Daily Telegraph*, 14 June 1952, 4.

tomorrow'. His cable to the press gallery said, as he told it, 'Weather bound, not Communist-bound'. When the weather cleared, he flew home. On 16 June 1952, John arrived home 'looking remarkably fit – pink-faced, alert, coatless in a chill wind, as though germs don't worry him at all', the 'Town Talk Columnist' sneered on the front page of the *Daily Telegraph* the following day. It reported that health officers got him through the formalities 'quicker than you can say "diplococcus intracellularis meningititis"'. The others in the group had no such luck. On their later return to Sydney, customs officials seized the papers, notes, literature and photos of the four delegates.[25] John was in Sydney at Mascot airport to meet them. They reported that none had been searched on entering China and questioned Australia's commitment to the democratic principle of free speech.

There was a great deal of interest in the story about John and the airmen but no belief that the men would be released.[26] John said that he understood the men were not in gaol and were being held in the same way as prisoners of war and he was confident they would be released. He criticised the government for its lack of action over the matter but, otherwise, he refused to comment further until he had spoken to the relatives to whom he had already written.

In late June, John embarked on a speaking tour with the Rev. Van Eerde to talk about the outcomes of the Pacific Peace Conference and to urge that Australian policy towards China should be reviewed.[27] ASIO still considered the peace movement to be a threat, presumably

---

25 Troy Bramston, 'Secret Agent's True Story Better than Memoir', *Weekend Australian*, 9–10 August 2014, 20, and *Age* (Melbourne), 25 June 1952, NAA: A6119, 127, Burton vol. 1, 30. Bramston raises the suspicion around whether Gietzelt was a 'secret member' of the Communist Party. Gietzelt denied it on ABC TV in 1976, and received damages for defamation after suing the ABC over the allegations. In a 2010 newspaper interview he said, 'I was never a member of the CPA … and I certainly didn't do their bidding.'
26 See 'Dr Burton Tells of Altered View on Red Chinese', and 'Dr Burton on Red Cross Visit', *Canberra Times* 19 June 1952, 1 and 4.
27 The first talk was at the Trades Hall in Canberra, 17 June 1952: *Canberra Times*, 18 June 1952, 1. ASIO records other places and audiences as follows: 26 June, Sydney University for students; 28 June, meeting of the Committee for Peace in the Pacific at 'Surreyville NSW' (possibly the Surreyville Dance Hall in Darlington, Sydney); 29 June, they talked to the Sydney Democratic Rights Council forum (noted as 'Communist influenced'); 30 June, Melbourne University for students; 15 July, Adelaide; 18 July, another in Melbourne; 16 July, Sydney again; 30 July, Brisbane; and one scheduled 5 July, in Newcastle – 'no details to date'. The records also contain copies of pamphlets issued, advertisements for the public talks, background information on the community groups who invited him to speak and the individuals who arranged for it and the organisations who paid his travel costs. NAA: A6119, 128, Burton vol. 2, 40, 41 and 85.

concerned about communist infiltration.[28] It compiled a list of his talks in a document in August 1952, classified as 'Top Secret', because 'some of the information contained therein originates from Top Secret sources which would become compromised if it were made public';[29] that is, ASIO agents infiltrating peace movements?

Helpful to our research is ASIO's confirmation of John's account that he brought home a letter to Michael Lapwood from his missionary brother in China. ASIO recorded that, at one of the meetings at which John spoke, Michael Lapwood was in attendance to present a roneoed copy of the letter. ASIO's surveillance provides other useful information; for example, that the talks attracted attention. There were 'more than 1,300 students' at a talk at Melbourne University, some interested in hearing what the speakers had to say and others who heckled; and 1,500 people attended a public meeting in Adelaide.[30]

John returned to Sydney to speak on 26 July only to find that the local council had taken out a court injunction and prevented the arranged use of the Double Bay Hall for the meeting, causing it to be moved to a private house. On 30 July in Brisbane, he and Van Eerde were confronted with a similar problem when, according to ASIO's records, the Communist Party of Australia had unsuccessfully attempted to book the city hall for them and the meeting had to be held 'elsewhere'.

Over this time, John made inquiries of the backgrounds of the airmen: Ross Bohm of Brisbane, John Richmond of Wollongong and William James of Adelaide. While in Adelaide, John visited James's unhappy mother to assure her of his belief that he had not been mistreated and was likely to be released soon – and they were. ASIO's records confirm the significant role John played in facilitating their release. On 5 August 1952, John used the telephone at Van Eerde's Redfern Methodist Mission to send a cable to a 'Liao Chenchih, President, Federation Democratic Youth, Peking', to assure him that from enquiries of the airmen's background, in John's 'personal judgement' none knowingly acted against China. It read in part:

---

28 See McLean *Fear of Peace?* 126: ASIO was quick to identify the World Peace Council and its offshoot the Australian Peace Council (APC) as being prime examples of the prototype communist front organisation.
29 NAA: A6119, 128, Burton vol. 2, 36.
30 'University Students "Grill" Dr. Burton', *Herald*, 1 July 1952, clipping in NAA: A6119, 127, Burton vol. 1, 51; 'Students Boo, Cat-Call Dr. Burton', *Telegraph*, 2 July 1952, clipping in John W. Burton papers, NLA, MS 8405, box 4, folder 18, News clippings 1947–91; ASIO report of 24 July 1952 on speech at Tivoli Theatre, Adelaide, 15 July 1952, NAA: A6119, 128, Burton vol. 2, 127–28.

> Urge soonest repatriation regret persistence matter important here stop September delegation going well
>
> Regards Burton.[31]

The airmen were released and reached Hong Kong on 12 August 1952, having been imprisoned by the Chinese for 20 months. Hong Kong newspapers reported their arrival in Hong Kong with claims that they had been cruelly treated and were in poor condition. James's mother, convinced by what she had read, complained in writing that John had wrongly assured her that her son had been well treated. John also wanted the truth. To satisfy her, he contacted newspaper proprietor Sir Keith Murdoch who, through News Limited, was the proprietor of the Adelaide *News*. Arrangements were made for a phone call so that Mrs James could talk with her son. John was able to listen in. 'Mum, we're all fit – no problem,' he recalled the gist of their words in his later years, and words to the effect that she should take no notice of the press reports: 'We're being well paid for it.'[32]

---

31   For full text see ASIO report 20 August 1952, NAA: A6119, 128, Burton vol. 2, 19.
32   Personal communication between John and his wife, Betty Nathan, Canberra, 10 January 2004. Sir Keith Murdoch, who had been ill with cancer, died in October the same year.

22

Paying the price for a mission of peace

John suffered both politically and financially from his trip to China and the fallout was long-lasting. He had hoped that at least one of the delegates to the preparatory conference would attend the substantive Asian and Pacific Rim Peace Conference to be held in Peking (Beijing) in early October 1952. People from other countries, including four members of the British Parliament, planned to attend the conference. However, at the height of the McCarthyism period in the USA and of its equivalent paranoia in Australia, the weight of political forces was against the Australians. The Australian Government decided to cancel the passports of any Australian proposing to attend. Van Eerde refused to hand in his passport and talked publicly of a High Court challenge of the decision. He explained that the sponsoring committee in China was not communist and included one delegate from each of the countries in Asia and the Pacific, and that he was the Australian representative. Other Australian delegates to the peace conference, he said, were chosen by the Australian unions and organisations that they were to represent and not chosen by Peking.

John received a letter from the acting head of the Department of Immigration that suggested a withdrawal of his passport could be avoided if he gave an assurance that he did not propose to travel to Peking. John promptly returned the letter endorsed with a handwritten note: 'I do not propose to travel to Peking in the near future; but cannot give any long-term assurances'.[1] He kept his passport. Some Australian delegates got around the passport problem by travelling to another conference via China, not having to declare whether they would first attend the Peking conference. Others were thwarted in their attempts, one travelling as far as Singapore before being sent home by authorities there because his Australian passport had been cancelled.[2]

ASIO's sources had reported extensively on the selection process of delegates of the Australian Committee for Peace in the Pacific, suspicious that the Communist Party would gain control of the delegation. Following and reporting on every move John made, it ultimately acknowledged that '[Burton] does not desire communist representatives to attend the Peking Conference'. In fact, it witnessed him actively working against communist influences.[3]

The original contingent, however, was intimidated out of attending the October conference. On 12 September 1952, the minister for External Affairs, Richard Casey, told parliament that he intended to seek the opinion of the attorney-general on whether sedition or treason charges could be laid against all five members of the previous delegation: 'Drs Burton and Macindoe, Rev Van Eerde, Gietzelt and Miss Bromham'.[4] Casey justified this sensationalism as following up on a report tabled that morning on the Peking conference by the Joint Parliamentary Committee on Foreign Affairs. The committee had concluded that the conference was not aimed at peace but was pursuing a communist agenda. It based this on the Declaration issued at the preparatory conference that stated in part that the Chinese guerrillas fighting against the Crown in Malaya were making a great contribution to the cause of peace fighting for national liberation. The Declaration, signed by the Australian delegates, had been read out by John at the conference. Without interviewing John or any other members of the delegation, the committee suggested that

---

1   John endorsed the letter dated 11 September 1952 that he had received. NAA: A6980, S200565, 21.
2   Denis Jacob representing the Tasmanian branch of the Builders Workers' Industrial Union. For more information see Laurence W. Maher, 'Dissent, Disloyalty and Disaffection: Australia's Last Cold War Sedition Case', *Adelaide Law Review* 16 (1994): 1–77; Australian House of Representatives, *Parliamentary Debates*, vol. 217, 1952, 872. See Pemberton, 'John Burton', *Union Issues*, November 1991, 12; and Deery and McLean, 'Behind Enemy Lines'.
3   NAA: A6119, 128, Burton vol. 2, 58.
4   'Sedition Opinion Requested', *Sydney Morning Herald*, 12 September 1952, 1. See also *Mercury* (Hobart), 12 September 1952, 1.

the attorney-general might examine the Declaration to ascertain whether there had been any infringement by the Australian signatories of our laws against sedition or treason.

An examination of the 1,000-word declaration showed that the conference did not condone guerrilla warfare. It spoke of peace in Korea being delayed while the use of ever more horrible weapons of war threatened to spread hostilities. It was consistent with John's view that the existing military conflicts, as were occurring in Vietnam and Malaya, were causing oppression of movements for national liberation and independence and would encourage the spread of communism; and that movements that sought to end national oppression and enslavement would contribute to the peaceful coexistence of nations. Nevertheless, there was press coverage of the fact that, if the attorney-general recommended the five be prosecuted under the *Crimes Act* for treason or sedition and the prosecution was successful, they could face the maximum penalty of the death sentence for treason and three years' imprisonment for sedition. The intimidatory threats were effective. None of the named people attended the main conference and the Australian media showed little interest in its proceedings – in all likelihood because the Australians there did not include John or any other prominent person.

John felt let down. The closest John got to confiding in anyone is likely to have been his long-time friend Parker. He wrote to Parker in New Zealand that the October peace conference 'could have led to mediation in Malay and Indo-China – at least as far as the Chinese were concerned', had someone from the original contingent been in attendance. 'Unfortunately, all these gentlemen backed out very quickly when the matter became political and I was left carrying the baby which died in my arms,' he said.[5] In the same letter, John told him that, 'The banks closed down on me the day after the sedition charge and I have had to set to without help.' He could understand that the government-owned Commonwealth Bank might have reacted nervously to the political talk about sedition charges being laid against one of its customers. In any event, a bank would be reluctant to extend further credit to a man in receipt of no wage and who, if gaoled, would have no ability to repay a loan.

---

5   R. S. Parker papers, NLA, MS 8200, box 46, file 189, 20 November 1952.

None of the group was prosecuted. But John's engagement with peace movements in China put his loyalty and integrity in question. His belief that freedom from colonial oppression in Asian Pacific nations would serve to quell unrest that might otherwise lead to the spread of communism was viewed with suspicion. In these McCarthy-like times, there was strong support for Australia to keep its colonial ties to the UK. You were either 'for or against' the Empire and, if you were against it, you were siding with the enemy: communists. The development of an anti-communist sentiment since World War Two fuelled this skewed logic. In this context, it is worth noting that John initiated the founding of *The Northern Territory News,* first published on 8 February 1952, as a counterbalance to the communist-led trade union that owned *The Northern Standard*. He wanted overseas visitors arriving in Darwin to have access to more balanced information.[6]

Taunts about John's trip to China would follow him for the rest of his life. Fifty-five years on, former prime minister John Howard dredged up John's name from the past to make public and derogatory comments about his views on China. The occasion was the 50th anniversary dinner for *Quadrant* magazine, held on 3 October 2006. Howard praised the magazine for taking up causes close to his heart to combat those of dangerous others. He exampled John, who he believed was dead, and historian Manning Clark who by then was dead.[7] He said:

> It's worth recalling just a few of the philo-communism [sic] that was once quite common in Australia in the 1950's and 60's. For example, Manning Clark's book *Meeting Soviet Man* where he likened the ideals of Vladimir Lenin to those of Jesus Christ. John Burton, the former head of the External Affairs Department, arguing that Mao's China provided a model for the 'transformation' of Australia.[8]

---

6   M. G. L. Dunn, 'The Royal Commission on Espionage, 1954–1955' (PhD diss., University of Adelaide, 1979), 53–54, with reference to D. Whitington, *Strive to be Fair: An Unfinished Biography* (Canberra: Australian National University Press, 1977), 108.
7   In 2008, John Kunkel, one of Howard's staffers, said in an article that he thought John was dead until he saw his 'angry' letter to the paper; 'Reflections on the "Howard Project"', *Institute of Public Affairs Review: A Quarterly Review of Politics and Public Affairs* 60, no. 2 (2008): 11. See also 'Howard and the Left', *Quadrant*, January 2010.
8   John Howard, 'Address to the *Quadrant* Magazine 50th Anniversary Dinner, Four Seasons Hotel, Sydney', transcript, released 3 October 2006, Australian Government PM transcript ID 22501.

'Transformation' was the single word Howard quoted as being John Burton's, but for which quote he offered no reference, no date, and provided no context. John was aged 92 and bedridden at the time, having had a fall and cracked some ribs. He read the *Canberra Times*'s report of the address the next day with front-page headlines: 'Reagan, Thatcher, are PM's heroes'.[9] His brain sprang to life and he endured pain to crawl out of bed to write a letter to Jack Waterford, then editor of the *Canberra Times*. His letter was published the next day as an opinion piece under the heading 'History wars: No, old China, I was there – you weren't'.[10] Howard probably saved John from lying in bed and dying from pneumonia.

Meredith and I observed that John seemed flattered to be remembered, albeit backhandedly, for his advocacy of a foreign policy that focused on Australia being part of Asia, rather than a province of the UK or the USA. John guessed that Howard's advisers had dredged up a comment John had made about his positive experience of the then fledgling republic of China in 1952. So, in his newspaper response, John contextualised his comment and explained that he was comparing Chifley's postwar reconstruction of a welfare state with the 'fascist-type capitalism that prevailed' after the Liberal Government came to power.

At the risk of indulging in a conspiracy theory, the controversy caused by John's father, Jack, over the indenture system of Indians in Fiji might explain former Howard's motivation for his vitriolic attack on John in the course of the dinner speech. Both the Howard and Burton families were part of Sydney's Methodist congregation. The Methodist Mission's division over CSR's use of indentured labour affected ordinary Methodist churchgoers in New South Wales. The Rev. John Burton's name was likely to be one bandied around in the household with disdain. Howard's father Lyall had worked as a mechanic for CSR and later benefited from a plantation owner's right to use slave labour in New Guinea. Both Lyall and his father Walter had been granted plantation tracts as returned servicemen. Journalist David Marr broke a story in 2006 entitled 'Howard's Hidden Past' in which he detailed that, when Lyall lost his job with CSR, he cashed in his status as a landowner to 'dummy' for trading house W. R. Carpenter & Co. Ltd. His father, Walter, did the same. Lyall later ran a Sydney service station for 30 years while, as Marr reported, 'he was also – on paper – a New Guinea planter with a string of estates where

---

9   Andrew Fraser, *Canberra Times*, 4 October 2006, 1.
10 *Canberra Times*, 6 October 2006, 11.

200 native labourers grew copra in his name'. 'The Howard case provoked secret, official investigations at the highest levels in Canberra, but they and their powerful backer got away with the scam,' wrote Marr.[11] Howard's interest in politics as he grew up would have brought the controversy over both John Burton senior and junior to his attention.

When Cecily talked to us about her life years later, she made little or no mention of the horror of John being spoken of as a traitor, or the serious charges over his head. In her writings, we find no mention of her concern for the angst John must have felt for himself and his family. But then, she had always dismissed the allegations against him as ridiculous. When talking about her life with John, she talked more about what had been wrong with their relationship than about external events that surrounded them. Nevertheless, it must have been a worrying time. Surely, the goings-on in John's life must have been the main topic of their day-to-day conversation. Knowing our mother as we did, she probably put his needs ahead of her own, listened attentively and responded appropriately to crises that put him under the public spotlight. Alternatively, he might not have wanted to talk about it or, possibly, she had no emotional energy left to offer him the comfort that he probably needed.

On John's return from China, having failed in his electoral bid and resigned from the public service, he had no financial security other than what income his farming might bring. From an outsider's standpoint, John was at a professional and personal low. His strength, however, was belief in himself. As well as his farm, he had matters on his mind about which he wanted to write.

---

11   *Age* (Melbourne), 10 June 2006; see also 'The Secret Howard Plantations', *Sydney Morning Herald*, 10 June 2006.

23

An interlude: Farming the Burton way

On their return from Ceylon, John and Cecily set about farming at 'Melrose', Weetangera, for a livelihood. They both enjoyed the healthy farm lifestyle and environment and, in Cecily's case, she thought it beneficial to her mental health. Our parents' positive attitude allowed us children to have a fulsome and happy time on the farm, unaffected by the drama that surrounded our father or by the inner turmoil our mother experienced. While John mucked around in the cattle yards, dug fence-post holes and constructed sheds and dams, he was either developing ideas on foreign policy matters and theories on how to attain world stability and peace, or he was thinking about innovative farming techniques. John ignored conventional advice on farming, as he did about most things, and followed his own. He surprised not only Cecily, but also his farming neighbours with his ingenuity. He read up on farming practices, thought up new ideas and experimented with new methods. He attended the Royal Easter Show in Sydney and purchased sophisticated machinery. His new hay roto-baler cut and scooped up hay and formed it into rolls, tied with rope rather than wire; these rolls could later be unravelled behind our tractor ready for stock to eat. It did away with manual labour and a pitchfork. Nearby farmers scratched their heads wondering how John would store round bales. His new winch elevator enabled him to stack the bales in a tall stand under a tin roof without farmhand help. Air circulated between the bales and reduced the risk of fire from internal combustion that plagued farmers in warm, moist weather. We climbed the haystack and made 'possies' there at weekends so we could sight visitors as they entered the gate at the top of the driveway.

The 'Melrose' farm wool clip off to the market, Weetangera, c. 1953.
Source: Family collection.

Within a few years of innovation and imaginative enterprise, John won the district's wheat prize. He led the way with modern shearing, wool-classing and milking methods. He built a two-storey, state-of-the-art woolshed. When urban Canberra commenced its sprawl, it became a venue for barn dances, country music and other entertainment. Shearing took place on the top storey where rotating circular wool-classing tables had been installed. Shorn sheep were released to the yards below via a narrow wooden chute. Underneath, our cows were milked by mechanised vacuum pumps; the pulling of teats and pushing of udders was not needed and bucket-kicking incidents were avoided. The cows were content, calmed by classical music broadcast through a transistor radio.

Wool and wheat sales provided our main income. We also produced milk, cream, butter, meat and eggs in sufficient quantities to feed us and our farm hands, Don and Puss Kelly. Our sheep, cows, pigs and chickens were healthy and John was comfortable with slaughtering, skinning and plucking, although sensitive to our feelings and the welfare of animals. Rabbits, a farm pest, he shot and we ate them too. Cecily mastered the cooking of a family favourite dish of baked rabbit and prunes. There was a well-established orchard when we arrived that produced quinces, loquats, figs, apples and walnuts and a variety of stoned fruit. We grew vegetables. I remember, in particular, an overgrown patch of tall green asparagus into which I threw myself and landed on a bed of soft feathery fern heads.

23. AN INTERLUDE

Cecily churned milk into butter in the small back veranda of our shack-like home, while John engaged in the fraught activity of brewing hops beer and ginger beer in the laundry. We complained that we only liked 'bought butter'. Cecily challenged us to tell the difference and tricked us more than once. As for John's beers, we entered the laundry with trepidation because bottles exploded at random from faulty capping. In my books, the ginger variety was a success. I must have had my fill of home-made hops beer as I have never drunk beer since. John thought it pretty good; he proudly opened bottles for the friends he persuaded to help him out on the farm as a worthy reward at the end of the day. The family ate well and we girls grew up to be sturdy, Clare taller and slimmer than solidly built Meredith and me. We hand-fed and patted our pigs, chickens and their offspring and poddy calves and lambs while they were being fattened. We made pets of our working dogs and rat-catching cats. It was a rich and textured life for us as children, but a worrying one for Cecily who had to make sure that we not only ate well, but had shoes to wear to school and other necessaries.

The Commonwealth Bank must have soon eased John's borrowing restrictions, because his bank account often went into the red. Its balance depended entirely on the size of the wool or wheat cheque. We excitedly awaited arrival of the twice-yearly David Jones mail-order catalogue. We pored over it, perhaps each of us choosing a woollen twin-set. Cecily would check with John to ask if it was safe to put in an order for winter clothes. Sometimes it was not and Cecily used her treadle Singer sewing machine to make dresses; one was an evening gown she made from old brocade curtains and their blue satin lining. At other times, the size of the seasonal income was a cause for celebration and floral summer cotton dresses were added to the mail order.

Cecily tried her best as a mother, not sure how to handle sometimes poorly behaved children and, as we came to learn, how to keep herself from having a complete mental breakdown. She held competitions with a reward of a sweet to be chosen by whoever of us behaved best that week. In the interests of good teeth, sweets were restricted and so it was a rare treat, generally for Meredith who won most weeks as the best strategist of the three of us. We listened religiously to the Australian Broadcasting Commission (ABC) radio's *Argonauts* program, submitted work to have read out and participated in certificate earnings and upgrades of our Argonaut status. We never missed an episode of the radio program *Blue Hills*, a long-running serialised Australian soapie.

Cecily rose early and worked hard to win John's approval. She dug out noxious weeds like scotch thistles, paspalum and Patterson's curse and, particularly when John was away, she rounded up sheep with the help of Bluey, our faithful cattle dog, although she felt hampered by never having been taught to ride a horse proficiently. Farm work and caring for us kept her busy, but she was alone in her mind and had no one she could confide in. Puss and Don provided cheerful company while they helped around the farm, but they were not people she would draw into her confused world. They were ready to start their own family and they looked to Cecily and John as parental and farming mentors.

One morning John asked Cecily what on earth she was doing sitting curled up on the living room floor outside the door to the bathroom. The small bathroom was an 'add-on' to the house that could be accessed from both the living room and from outside. The Kellys had moved into a shack at the back of the house, freeing up the caravan in which they first lived for our family's use. The couple shared the only bathroom in the house. They locked the internal door when they were using it and we each locked the external entrance when we occupied it. Don sang while he showered. He had a joyous unselfconscious voice, beautiful to Cecily's ear. She would sit outside the door and lose herself in his song. Only in retrospect do we now appreciate the importance of therapeutic moments like these to Cecily's state of mind.

The extremes of weather made farming life tough. In times of rain, always welcome, the nearby Ginninderra Creek tended to flood and sometimes prevented the school panel van from taking us to school. We did not mind. Drought was a worse enemy – with it came a threat of bushfires. Fires that flared in the west enjoyed a fast, wind-driven run from the Murrumbidgee River to the Weetangera district. Cecily was resolute and clear-headed. She packed belongings and essentials and drove them to the gate at the top of the drive ready for us to evacuate, if necessary, to the city to the east. In severe drought, the household's rainwater tanks dried up, providing no more than rusty red drips from the taps. John would load the truck with water tanks and take us with him along the Weetangera Road to fill the tanks from a communal bore water pump. Prolonged drought had a sunny side for our family, too. It provided John with a new income stream. When John excavated one of our dams with his small grey Ferguson tractor, a neighbour observed the machine's sharp turning circle and the ease with which it manoeuvred its attached earth scoop. Other farmers' superior and larger harvester-pulling, red Massey-Harris tractors

23. AN INTERLUDE

were no match for the job. Neighbouring farmers engaged John to dig dams with his tractor and some called on him to bale their hay with his roto-baler.

When grass was in short supply, John released the cattle to graze on the verge of the dirt Weetangera Road (now known as the 'Old Weetangera Road', which can today be traced via cycle paths) that adjoined our farm. We utilised the 'Long Paddock' so much that it formed part of our farm. The school panel van on its route home from Canberra travelled along that part of the road and, after it crossed the dry bed of Ginninderra Creek, Meredith watched out for the cattle. If they were out grazing, she would ask our compliant driver to stop and let her out, a mile or so before our farm gate. She would then round up the cows and walk them through the Long Paddock gate, cross country on the dry home paddock to the woolshed. Clare and I were charged with bringing home her school bag. The cows cooperated and headed for the yards where they would be milked and fed.

John's expectations of Meredith were high. He treated her like the first-born son he had not had. In hindsight she sees that he treated her like an adult; he discussed with her how he made his home-made beer, his farming innovations, and the mechanics of his roto hay-baler, for example. She learned to ask questions about things he was interested in to elicit a conversational response because John was anything but a chatterbox. He grunted directions and made comments from time to time. 'I was always pitching to him to appease him,' Meredith reflected, but, unlike Cecily, she was not looking to be understood. Meredith feels now that she was robbed of some of her childhood – the carefree fun times that Clare and I enjoyed playing around the farm yard. At the time, however, Meredith enjoyed the confidence John had in her and particularly the independence he gave her by allowing her to drive the tractor and ride horses bareback from the age of 11. On one occasion, Meredith, at 13, drove the tractor unlawfully, from a contracting job near the small township of Hall on the ACT–NSW border, along Weetangera Road across Ginninderra Creek and home. John drove the truck carrying his roto-baler. On another occasion, she drove the tractor to help him widen our house dam. This meant driving the tractor on an angle on the sloping dam wall with a harrow attached to the back, while John followed digging out the earth. Cecily was aghast when she saw the two at work, having come to the woolshed to talk with John. The risks John took shocked her – at least those she knew about – and she put her foot down.

Sometimes neither parent was aware of Meredith's misadventures. Once, when she was riding Sambo bareback – a squat, fairly docile, black pony – along the Weetangera Road, she saw visitors arrive in the distance. She decided to bring Sambo home via the cows' short-cut through the Long Paddock. On passing through the gate Sambo anticipated his direction and took off across the rough home paddock, with Meredith precariously hanging on to the reins, her long, thick plaits flying behind in the wind. Horse and rider made straight for the yard, Sambo not slowing to enter the narrow pass through the gate to his lodgings. Meredith missed having her leg shaved by centimetres. She was terrified, but aware of the visitors ambling down to the woolshed to greet John, with heart racing, she demounted, tended to Sambo and tried to look cool as if the stunt was a display of her normal proficiency. She greeted the visitors with a grin.

As at Tuggeranong, our family had an active social life and entertained many and varied visitors. At no time did John disconnect from political life; nor did Evatt disconnect from John. Evatt arrived, often unannounced, in his government, chauffeur-driven black car to demand John's counsel. Many of John's former colleagues and university friends visited. Cecily found most of them lively and interesting. Bob Hawke, then a university student and later Australian prime minister, found his way into the group to become a long-time family friend. Puss and Don Kelly joined in these occasions. ASIO's surveillance notes seemed to have captured the name of every visitor we had during this period, from listening in on phone calls in which visits were arranged and from follow-up clandestine observance. Browsing through them served to trigger our memories as to how much our visitors and their children filled our lives with stories. On one occasion, a young Rosalind Evatt, the Evatt's adopted daughter, came especially to tell John her exciting news that she had met the man she wanted to marry. Watching on, Meredith saw that John did not echo Rosalind's elation. Did he not care, or did he fear that she would be hurt? Cecily guessed the latter, believing that John was distrustful of young men, knowing what he had been like as a youth, she told us. He felt protective of Rosalind. Peter Carrodus was her new man and history tells that he and Rosalind lived 'happily ever after'.

We loved having other children visit the farm. Historian Don Baker sometimes brought his wife and children. Their youngest, aged about five, had straw-coloured hair – or at least Sambo saw it that way. He leaned through the wooden fence and chomped on it, trying to gulp a mouthful, recoiling on the child's squeal of pain. When Alec Hope visited with

23. AN INTERLUDE

his family, his daughter was taken aback on entering the woolshed after a sheep had been slaughtered. 'What's that red stuff on the floor,' she asked, pointing to a red sticky mess. 'Blood,' we told her, as if we saw it every day. She cried. John's colleague Peter (later Sir Peter) Heydon, a public servant and diplomat, arrived with his son Dyson, aged around eight at the time. Dyson was taken with one of our farm dogs and, pointing at it, said to his father, 'Look, horsey.' It dawned on Cecily that, assuming the boy was not backward – correctly, as he later became one of Australia's High Court justices – city children missed out on the broadening of minds and experiences that farm life gave us.

Cecily became president of the local tennis club where she, Meredith and, occasionally, John played. The local tennis courts were a couple of miles down the road and cared for by the family who operated the local telephone exchange – a convenience for ASIO we discovered when we read reports of John's and Cecily's phone conversations that had been listened into by ASIO agents.

Every January, the family packed up for a holiday at the south coast. On one occasion, John had Cecily drive a truck loaded with camping gear, to enable him to drive our car towing a caravan. The drive down the narrow, winding Clyde Valley road that was mainly unsealed and often treacherous then took five to six hours. At the base of the Clyde were long queues for the car ferries to cross both the Nelligen and Clyde rivers to Batemans Bay. By the time we were at Weetangera, our annual campsite shifted from Durras to what is now Rosedale Beach. John would set up the caravan, tents and a portable dunny (in the thicket of casuarina trees) on the grassy side of the sand dunes that lined the long white sandy beach. Sometimes he left stoic Cecily to look after us on her own and he returned to the farm to finish a harvest. At other times he unfolded a card table, placed his typewriter on it and pounded away at his book, taking breaks from time to time to try out a new fishing rod. While he wrote, we played and swam at the beach. At the end of the day one of us would wade across the lagoon to a friend's fridge to get him a bottle of beer.

In 1953, John and Cecily each lost a parent within weeks of each other. Cecily's father was 68 when he died in August that year at Katoomba Hospital from a coronary occlusion; John's mother had died in Sydney in July. Jack Burton, thereafter, often stayed with us to give his daughters a break from looking after him in Sydney. Jack was staying with us when we made plans to build our dream home on the property. It was to have a bedroom for each of us children, a study for John to give him the solitude to think and write and a spare room for grandfather Jack when he came to stay. Our parents engaged an architect to design the large house adjacent to the driveway protected by the pine break. Foundations were dug and large old cement bricks were sourced from an old house on a property nearby that was being demolished and which had belonged to the Zouch family. Load by load the bricks arrived at the farm. Jack spent several weeks painstakingly hand-scraping the cement from hundreds of the dismantled grey bricks. We pored over the plans, stepped out our bedrooms delineated by taut string attached to pegs and were excited about the prospect of a modern home. The house was never built. Events in 1954 caused a change of plans and the bricks that we had watched grandfather Jack Burton spend exhausting hours to scrape clean were left in columns abandoned near the pine trees alongside the Weetangera Road.

24

Holding it together

The year 1954 threw a spanner in our family's works. First, it was a record dry season in winter that continued into spring and summer. Undeterred, John kept 1,200 ewes in good condition in one paddock of 150 acres that had virtually no feed on it. He hand-fed them with wheaten and oaten hay he had grown, mowed and baled into stacks instead of harvested for the grain. His heavy capital outlay on machinery proved their worth by allowing him to cultivate crops with very little labour. Next, our production of milk for sale was obstructed. One of our income streams came from John's distribution of milk around the university and public servants' offices in Canberra. He skimmed cream from the milk and sold that too. This lucrative farming sideline ran into trouble when more highly regulated sterilisation requirements were introduced. John instigated a 'dry farming pilot experiment', the results of which indicated that the method potentially increased milk production in the ACT. For the short time that he was permitted to distribute milk in Canberra, it sold at a profitable 5 shillings a gallon. In his opinion, 'with new techniques, pasture knowledge, and mechanical equipment these areas in Canberra would produce economically adequate supplies of milk for Canberra consumers,' he told an inquiry in November 1955. However, the Health Department declared that the general environment of a sheep farm on which milk was being produced was unsuitable. John thought it unfortunate, 'because, the technique was one by which the milk was taken from the cow direct into the container which ultimately arrived at the home of the consumer'.[1]

---

1 *Canberra Times*, 26 November 1955, 2.

In March 1954, when John was well into completing his work, *The Alternative,* John Foster Dulles, US secretary of state, threatened China with atomic weapons. With a looming threat of war, John worked hard to finish writing his book for publication that year. He envisaged it would provide a blueprint to the foreign policy path Australia should follow as an alternative to blindly following the USA's power politics stance. On 3 April 1954, just as Queen Elizabeth II's momentous tour of Australia and the celebratory hype surrounding it came to a close, Russian diplomat Vladimir Petrov sought political asylum. The contrasting events were both 'interesting and consequential' in the nation's capital, Nicholas Brown noted in his history of Canberra. 'But such ornate fragments of politics and culture hung awkwardly off Canberra's spare frame.'[2] The Royal visit might have enhanced the prospect of the conservative Liberal Party winning the upcoming May federal election, but the Petrov defection would make it a certainty.

By May 1954, happenings within and around Cecily became too much. She came close to having a mental breakdown and had to get away. John, probably bewildered by his changing relationship with a more assertive Cecily than he was used to and distracted by domestic political events that followed the Petrov defection, had to cope with massive family disruption. He was up to his ears in farming, political controversy and trying to finish his book. Yet we had to be cared for. With the help of friends to care for us, Cecily retreated to the Brindabella mountains for a week's time-out. She arranged to stay at the historic Franklin's farm. There Cecily could rest, walk, enjoy the natural bush surrounds and listen to the birds and bubbling stream.

On Mother's Day, Sunday 9 May 1954, the day before Meredith's 13th birthday, John drove Cecily and the three of us children to Brindabella. It was a pretty drive on dirt roads that crossed mountain streams and wound through a bush full of wildlife, but no one in the car was happy, knowing we were to drive home without Cecily. I had found some chunks of coloured glass from old broken bottles and jars around our farmhouse and had strung them together with green string and presented Cecily with a necklace for Mother's Day. She wore it graciously. However, when we stopped on a bridge to look out over the Murrumbidgee River, another car approached and my mum put her hand up and over the necklace,

---

2   Nicholas Brown, *A History of Canberra* (Cambridge: Cambridge University Press, 2014), 143.

presumably embarrassed that people might think her decoration strange – which, of course, it was. When we arrived at the Franklin's farm, I recall that we were greeted by an elderly man with a limp who took Cecily by the arm. We left soon after, without Cecily. I cried all the way down the mountain with no mother to console me. Eleven-year-old Clare, tried to help her seven-year-old sister by reasoning that I should just pretend our mum was dead and was not there anymore. I cried all the more. John, driving, had no idea what to say or do and it was impossible to know what he was thinking or feeling either. Meredith was delivered to the Collings family in Forrest, the home of her school-friend Penny where she had stayed before. Somewhat traumatised, I was left with family friends in Turner whose children were kind and tried to engage me in the games they were playing in the garden with neighbourhood children. Clare stayed at the farm with John, entrusted to assist him with meals.

John's friend Parker, although he lived with his family and worked in New Zealand, was temporarily in Canberra working at the university. In letters, John had earlier suggested Parker should visit the farm when he was next in Canberra. Cecily had repeated the invitation before she went away when, on Saturday night 24 April, she and John ran into Parker during interval at a Canberra theatre. When Parker followed up and made contact, John invited him to dinner and also to accompany us on our drive to Brindabella to collect Cecily. Was John simply being practical when he suggested to Parker that he might enjoy the drive? Perhaps he welcomed company, to shield him from having to greet and engage with Cecily without any idea of how she was feeling or why she needed to go away at all. It is revealing to have Parker's perspective of Cecily at the time. After seeing her at the theatre that April night, he wrote a letter to his wife, Nancy, at home in New Zealand. He was honest about his attraction to Cecily. He told Nancy that when Cecily greeted him, she was 'looking extremely elegant, fit and pretty', and he wrote:

> How nice she is! I've always liked her and felt attracted by her, and I felt on this occasion that I had been right. She spoke very kindly to me, and insisted that I should (after this holiday week-end) go out to the farm any Sunday or every Sunday, and promised to arrange for transport for me to there (though I could go easily enough on the bike).[3]

---

3   R. S. Parker papers, NLA, MS 8200, box 23, file 114, letter 25 April 1954.

So, on 16 May, John, Clare, I and Parker drove to Brindabella to collect Cecily. It was, from Robert's account, a pleasant day. Cecily introduced us all to the Franklin family, the last of the Franklins, after whom Mount Franklin was originally named. Miles Franklin, the famous novelist, wrote about the country in some of her books. We had a picnic lunch and, according to Parker's description in a letter he wrote that night to Nancy, we picnicked 'in brilliant sunshine, but in a cool Wellingtonian air at the height of 2,200 feet, by the noisy little Goodradigbee River, which is just a mountain stream with rapids and little waterfalls here …'.[4] Meredith and I were amused to read, decades later, Parker's description of us to Nancy; we were, apparently, 'nice, natural, lively kids, healthy and bright but not unduly handsome'. On our return to Weetangera, Meredith had afternoon tea prepared to welcome Cecily home.

Cecily might have felt more rested on her homecoming had her return not coincided with the opening the next day of the Royal Commission into Espionage that Prime Minister Menzies had announced as a response to the Petrov defection. The long-running Petrov inquiry hearings caused anxiety, hurt and pain to the whole of our family. Parker, working in Canberra, wrote to his wife Nancy, telling her of the crowds of people who were nosing about the Russian Embassy 'to no great purpose'.[5] Some even came to Canberra from elsewhere to stickybeak, he reported, while locals, including he, were 'a bit blasé' about the sensational spy talk. It was a stressful time, not only for John, and Cecily on his behalf, but for Cecily personally. ASIO showed peculiar interest in her sister Pam Beasley, who was married to Harold John (known as Jack) Beasley, a communist. Pam, too, had been a party member and was a communist sympathiser. Walter Clayton, a person of interest to ASIO, had visited her casually some three to four years earlier and that was sufficient for ASIO to interview Pam about her husband's and her political views. She was called to give evidence before the commission on 5 November 1954, because she was 'the sister of the wife of B'. John was asked about his sister-in-law when he later gave evidence. Chief counsel assisting the commission, W. J. Windeyer QC, explained to him in private that this was done because he did not wish to call Pam. Yet, two days later she was called, having only a few hours' notice, and she, too, was asked about Clayton, presumably in an attempt to suggest that John might have known him through Pam, his sister-in-law. John and Cecily were angry at the attempt to smear Pam's reputation.

---

4   R. S. Parker papers, NLA, MS 8200, box 23, file 114, letter 16 May 1954.
5   R. S. Parker papers, NLA, MS 8200, box 23 file, 114, letter 25 April 1954.

24. HOLDING IT TOGETHER

Unbeknown then to Cecily, ASIO had been collecting information about Pam and Cecily and their family without checking its accuracy. A phone call to either of them would have clarified what they wanted to know. Instead, their 'agents' made wild and wrong guesses about simple facts like blood and marriage relationships. An ASIO field officer's report on Pam, dated 16 July 1952, linked Jack Beasley by his marriage to Pam to John Burton by his marriage to Cecily. While recording Pam's father as Robert Nixon, her mother was 'Name unknown' and 'believed to be living apart from her husband', despite the fact that it was on the public record that she had died in 1938. It also recorded Wilga Nixon, the wife of Cecily's brother Peter Nixon, as Peter and Cecily's sister; at face value, this would render Peter and his wife Wilga in an incestuous marriage as siblings. Peter and Wilga were, in fact, cousins. John and Cecily's marriage, it was 'thought', took place in Canberra, whereas it was on the public record as having taken place in London. The officer reached the profound conclusion that 'the lady in question [Pam] is said to be a sister of Mrs Burton, wife of Dr. J.W. Burton, Secretary of the Department of External Affairs', and it was noted that 'Dr Burton is a friend of the [Beasley] family'.[6] When, 30 years later, these records were made public, much of their content were redacted, purporting to be secret, but it is more likely that inaccuracies and untruths were too embarrassing to reveal. Cecily's associates were noted to have also included Mona Ravenscroft, described as a communist and the wife of Henry Tubman, the private secretary of R. G. Casey, who was at the time the minister for External Affairs, as well as 'Mr Ruddock, Mr Furth [sic], Mr Hood, and Finlay Crisp, of Canberra'.[7] Not surprisingly, it acknowledged that, apart from Ravenscroft, 'none of the above associates appears to be of particular interest to ASIO'. Fancy that!

Judith Wright was 'a person of interest' to ASIO too, in 1954. Talking of her life with her husband Jack McKinney, she wrote in her memoir:

> To be in favour of peace, as we were, seemed to be by the end of 1949 to declare oneself a red. We were accordingly regarded not only as oddities but as enemies of the establishment.[8]

---

6   NAA: A6119, 128, Vol 2, 146–47.
7   NAA: A6119, 128, Vol 2, 147.
8   Clarke, *Judith Wright*, 254.

Wright was living at Tamborine Mountain, then rural Queensland, looking after Jack, a war pensioner, and raising their daughter Meredith, then a small child. They had no telephone connection until late 1954. Her ability to spread a subversive word, had she wanted to, was limited.

Cecily had been in touch with Wright by letter and talked about her mental muddle and difficult relationship with John. In 1954, Wright made a visit to Canberra to give a lecture on 'an obscure poet' and to see Cecily. This visit interested ASIO. In 1996, in a letter to the *Canberra Times*, Wright told of the interest ASIO took in her seeing 'an old friend' in Canberra.[9] Cecily, on seeing Wright's letter, wrote a letter to the paper, identifying herself as the 'old friend' Wright had been visiting, and took the occasion to have a go at ASIO's ineptitude. Cecily referred to the much-blacked-out 1952 ASIO file on her sister Pam, which she had by then accessed under the *Freedom of Information Act 1982*, and said:

> The document gives details of our family, and is so inaccurate, under-researched, and at times even pointless, that it makes it impossible to have any respect for ASIO files of that time.

She detailed the absurd mistakes and went on:

> Before such a report was compiled, surely, any self-respecting spy would, at the very least, have checked the births, deaths and marriages register. But no! And why list 'associates' of no interest to ASIO? What a slap-dash job![10]

Wright wrote to Cecily the same day to thank her for her letter to the *Canberra Times*. She said, 'I of course am still under surveillance …'. By this, her 'sin' was to be an active conservationist and in close league with Coombs, who was concerned about similar issues. Wright wrote:

> Big business wants the Barrier Reef and all the rest of the goodies conservationists have temporarily rescued; it won't take long before we lose them now. Reports indicate that the Reef will be the next to go, in the interests of oil and minerals. Come out fighting, I decided.[11]

Famous last words.

---

9   'Writers Always in ASIO Files', *Canberra Times*, 25 October 1996.
10 'ASIO File Most Unimpressive', *Canberra Times*, 29 October 1996.
11 Letter from Judith to Cecily, 29 October 1996, Cecily family file.

Amid these politically charged and personally difficult times in 1954, John finished and published his first book. *The Alternative* proved as provocative as he intended. In presenting his outline of what Australia's postwar policy towards Asia should be, he was highly critical of America's Asian policies. He urged that Australia take a more neutralist stance in the region.[12] He attributed a cause of the growth of communism in South-East Asia to nationalist struggles against European colonialism and other forms of Western interference. He argued his long-held stance that it was in the interests of Australian security to understand, rather than to ignore or attempt to prevent, Asian desires for independence from colonial powers. Needless to say, his critical analysis of the assumptions guiding the Menzies Government's approach to security in the region was not popular with ardent anti-communists.[13] On a positive side, on 15 July 1954, Nehru wrote and thanked John for sending him a copy of the book – the day he received it – and that he anticipated that he would find it 'instructive'. Nehru added, 'It is evident that all of us have to make many adjustments in our thinking to fit in with the conditions of today. It is extraordinary how our minds lag behind events.' Spry, however, obsessed with the evils of communism and now responsible for the nation's security, had a different reaction to the book. He said, as the publisher noted on the dust cover, that 'it contains facts and episodes which are not normally available to the historian or the reader of international affairs', there could be some security risk if John had had access to 'secret' and 'top secret' official information.[14] He recommended to Menzies that John be prosecuted for its publication. Menzies was not so concerned but John was devastated by the suggestion.

ASIO's interest in John and his book's potential influence caused it to step up its surveillance of him and our friends. John made jokes about the clicking noises he heard each time he picked up our wind-up wall phone and waited for the local exchange operators to connect a caller. They, or any third party, could listen in to calls and John had no doubt that such exchanges were a well-used resource of ASIO after its establishment. Archived ASIO file entries on John confirm that the phone was bugged

---

12   Burton, *The Alternative*, 75.
13   Henry, 'Reflections on Dr. John Wear Burton', 69.
14   NAA: A6119, 130, Burton vol. 4, and A6119, 131, Dr John Wear Burton vol. 5. See also Gregory Pemberton, 'The Imperial Imagination: Explaining the Post-1945 Foreign Policy of Robert Gordon Menzies', in *Menzies in War and Peace*, ed. Frank Cain (St Leonards, NSW: Allen & Unwin, 1997), 170; and Pemberton, 'John Burton: The Heretic', 103.

(as it also was when we later moved house). In August 1954, agents noted 'intended' visits to the farm by 'Fran', the wife of Max Campion, 'an associate of suspected Communists'; Ron Heiser, a university lecturer in economics whom we knew, was or had been a communist sympathiser; and Don Baker. Listening in on Cecily's telephone conversations about Don must have confused ASIO agents at times. Later file notes suggest that the ASIO eavesdroppers mistook our friend and farmhand with the magnificent singing voice, Don Kelly, for historian Don Baker. If Cecily had known that her conversations were being listened to, she might have obliged ASIO by including the family names of our various friends.

Earlier in April, ASIO had already shown concern over John's continuing influence on Australia's relations in the Asia-Pacific region. It noted as significant a warning made to the press by Liberal Senator John Gorton (later, prime minister) 'to guard against propaganda', in which Gorton alleged that Burton was 'behind' the issuing of a statement on Indo-China published by three ANU professors and Bishop E. H. Burgmann.[15] As a consequence of an ASIO phone tap of a conversation between John and his young acquaintance Jim (later Justice) Staples, an agent approached Staples to try and discover if John planned soon to attend an 'All India Peace Conference' or something similar. Staples's noted response was that 'Burton is broke and he would not go to India if he had to find money for the trip'.[16] As events would have it, John would acquire some funds and travel not to India but to Indonesia the following year for such a peace conference.

One entry made in September 1954 on John's ASIO file is intriguing. An agent, having eavesdropped into a conversation of Cecily's, understood that John was about to fly to Sydney. ASIO had access to John's flight information so it could place him under surveillance at the airport. However, the agent found that John had made no flight booking and concluded that John 'may have made other arrangements'.[17] This gave cause for Meredith and me to wonder if, perhaps, an affair that we know John later had with Fran Campion, when she was doing some typing for John, had commenced at this earlier time.

---

15   NAA: A6119, 130, Burton vol. 4, 135.
16   NAA: A6119, 130, Burton vol. 4, 50, 30 October 1954.
17   NAA: A6119, 130, Burton vol. 4, 59.

24. HOLDING IT TOGETHER

In late 1954, for a mix of reasons including financial hardship, John and Cecily decided to sell the farm and move to Canberra. It was a blow that John could not get his dairy approved from which he might have been able to draw a steady source of income. However, we girls were growing up, Meredith was in her teens and the move would give us easier access to our friends, schools, sport and other activities. The Weetangera farm went on the market in October 1954 and, according to an ASIO 'source', it was sold in December for about £30,000 including plant and stock. ASIO noted that it was described as 'one of the best improved places in the A.C.T.', and that John would make a substantial profit from it.[18] It recorded that John had paid £16,000 for the property five years earlier and, from the proceeds, he repaid an overdraft of £6,000. From this, we conclude that the Commonwealth Bank was the 'source', for who else would hold such detailed financial information? John found a house in the suburb of Forrest to buy. We first moved into a rented house in Forbes Street, Turner, for some five weeks pending settlement of the purchase. John had no job or income stream, just ideas on how he might earn a living, and for the time he would draw on proceeds from the sale of the farm to support the family.

---

18   NAA: A6119, 131, Burton vol. 5, 240.

25

The Petrov inquiry

Petrov's defection on 3 April 1954 was a political gift for the Menzies Government. A general election had been set for 29 May 1954. Labor, led by Evatt as opposition leader, was expected to win the election.[1] The speculative furore over a Russian spy defecting would change that. On 10 February, Spry, as head of ASIO, had briefed Menzies about the likelihood of Vladimir Petrov defecting, although some believe that Menzies was made aware of the impending event well before this date and had planned a May election accordingly.[2] Menzies announced the defection on 13 April, the last practical day before the pre-election period when the government would be in 'caretaker' mode and have its political hands tied. The timing allowed Menzies, on Spry's advice, to establish a Royal Commission into Espionage that would commence taking evidence before the election, with a promise of sensational headlines leading up to it and of no findings until its report was completed and tabled after the election. Evatt was caught unawares. Neither Menzies nor Spry forewarned him, as opposition leader, that the announcement was to occur, nor that Petrov claimed to have brought with him documents that named three members of Evatt's staff. The announcement, planned for 2:30 pm, was delayed until the evening when Evatt was known to have left parliament.[3]

---

1   See Roy Morgan Research Centre Pty Ltd, *Election Predictions by the Australian Gallup Poll (1946–1972) and Morgan Gallup Poll (1973–1974)* (Sydney: The Research Centre, 1974).
2   See Robert Manne, *The Petrov Affair: Politics and Espionage* (Sydney: Pergamon Press, 1987), 63; Frank Cain, 'Australian Intelligence Organisations and the Law: A Brief History', *UNSW Law Journal* 27, no. 2 (July 2004), 154–56.
3   Manne, *The Petrov Affair*, 73–74. Evatt left to attend an old boys' function at Fort Street School and Calwell deputised for him. Manne suggests that Menzies delayed the announcement until Evatt was absent from the House. See also Wilhelm Agrell, *Mrs Petrova's Shoe* (London: I.B. Tauris, 2019) for Mrs Petrova's story and Manne's interview of her in her senior years.

Public interest in the defection was fuelled by drama surrounding Petrov's wife, Evdokia Petrova, also a Russian consular official. If there is one image children of the era recall from the Petrov affair, it was that depicted on the front page of newspapers across the country of Evdokia being dragged across Sydney's Mascot airport tarmac by Russian escorts on 19 April. She wore only one shoe, the other of her red shoes having fallen off and left on the tarmac.[4]

There was concern that the Russians might hold hostage Australian diplomats and attempt an exchange with the Petrovs. John did not believe that would happen. He used to tell us that Petrov was 'too stupid' to be of value to the Russians and, as third secretary at the Russian Embassy, he was not likely to have had access to any significant information for his defection to cause the Russians much concern. But it certainly caused concern in Australia. It was claimed that Petrov had documents that evidenced leaks by at least two people in the Department of External Affairs of which John had been in charge.

Menzies's decision to hold a royal commission – the Petrov inquiry as it came to be known – denied anyone the opportunity before the election of examining the facts surrounding Petrov's defection or the veracity or value of the information that he claimed he had. It was scheduled to open at Canberra's Albert Hall on Monday 17 May, but, after one day's hearing, was deferred until after the election.[5] The political climate was tense. As time elapsed, John suspected that old information relating to MI5's 1940s Venona investigation had been 'fed' to Petrov to offer in exchange for asylum and that ASIO orchestrated the defection in a timely manner to influence the election. The list of names Petrov claimed to hand over in April 1954 and who ASIO requested the royal commission to inquire into – Fergan O'Sullivan, Rupert Lockwood, Frances Bernie, Ian Milner, Jim Hill and Walter Clayton – was suspiciously similar to the list of people MI5 had investigated and cleared in the course of the Lapstone Experiment, in which John was involved.[6] John is supported in this view by many historians who have concluded from their research that Petrov's

---

4   For the story, see 'Officials Drag Mrs. Petrov into Aircraft', *Sydney Morning Herald*, 20 April 1954; for the image, *Herald*, 20 April 1954.

5   Burton, interview by John Clements, 1981, John said that enough information was 'leaked' to suggest that 'spies would be uncovered'; and see Robin Gollan, *Revolutionaries and Reformists: Communism and the Australian Labour Movement 1920–1955* (Canberra: Australian National University Press, 1975), 280.

6   Burton, interview by John Clements, 1981; *National Times*, 28 September – 4 October 1984, 11.

intelligence was not new.[7] The then External Affairs minister, Richard Casey, knew of the Australians' names in Venona at least by May 1952 when he asserted in parliament that there was a 'nest of traitors' in the public service.[8] Frank Cain noted that, 'Historians have long considered the Petrov papers to have had an element of fakery, especially as almost half the documents were written by Australians'.[9] Cain and Pemberton surmised that documents were planted with Petrov's material that he handed over and that documents were written by ASIO not Moscow.[10]

Evatt visited John at our Weetangera farm towards the end of his appearance at the commission because he felt disturbed by it. John asked Evatt why he did not raise in his evidence MI5's investigation carried out five years earlier of the Russian delegation when it visited Australia to attend the Lapstone conference. To John's astonishment, Evatt said that he knew nothing about it. John had assumed that Solicitor-General Kenneth Bailey would have given Evatt full reports on MI5's activities and the outcomes as it occurred. On learning that the information had been withheld from Evatt, John rang Bailey. They met on 22 July 1954 and John asked that he be called to give evidence about the earlier MI5 investigation into a similar list of suspected spies so that the commissioners were informed of its outcome.[11] He took this initiative because he suspected that Spry and Bailey, and others involved in the hearing who knew what John knew, were not giving the commissioners in their secret sessions all the facts.

On 2 November 1954, John was called to testify, but he was only allowed to answer questions asked of him. His fear that information was withheld from the commission proved correct. He was asked questions about some

---

7   Cain, 'Australian Intelligence Organisations and the Law', 302 on. See also, Norman Abjorensen, 'Origin of Petrov's Contacts Queried by Expert', *Canberra Times*, 6 October 1996, 3, and 'Petrov: History Rewritten', *Weekend Australian*, 6–7 November 1993, 19. Cain provides a full analysis of 'The Case' in *The Australian Security Intelligence Organization: An Unofficial History* (London: Frank Cass and Co., 1994).
8   R. G. Casey, Minister for External Affairs, House of Representatives, 27 May 1952. The debate was reported in '"Nest of Traitors" in Govt', *Sydney Morning Herald*, 28 May 1952, 1, in the course of which debate it was noted that John had left the department in mid-1950, whereas the document allegedly handed to the Communist Party was 'leaked' from the department in November 1951.
9   Frank Cain, 'The Petrov Affair and Fake Documents: Another Look', *Honest History*, accessed 9 April 2021, honesthistory.net.au/wp/cain-frank-the-petrov-affair-and-fake-documents-another-look-2/ drawn from his *Terrorism and Intelligence: A History of ASIO and National Surveillance* (North Melbourne, Vic.: Australian Scholarly Publishing, 2008).
10 Gregory Pemberton, 'Petrov: History Rewritten', *Weekend Australian*, 6–7 November 1993, 19. See also, Pemberton, 'Spy Mystery That Will Not Die', *Canberra Times*, 19 June 1991, Midweek Magazine; Cain, 'Australian Intelligence Organisations and the Law'.
11 Burton, interview by Michael J. Wilson, 1995, 37.

of the names in Petrov's document but he was not permitted to provide evidence about the MI5 list of supposed 'spies' given to John in 1948 or about his follow-up Lapstone investigation to prove that Petrov's list of names was not new to ASIO at all.[12]

Aspects of the commission hearing were sloppy. Reading the transcript of evidence, I was disconcerted to read that, at the outset, John's name was incorrectly spelled as John *Weir* Burton. It was also disconcerting for John at the time, to see Spry sitting behind Windeyer QC, counsel assisting the commission, throughout the whole inquiry as if instructing him. After preliminaries, the first question of substance Windeyer asked John was: did he know Walter Seddon Clayton? John replied that he did not. He was asked questions about his time in the public service and when he got to know people such as Hill and Milner who worked in his department. It was also put to him that Evatt had employed him to work as a staffer in his office after John had left the public service. The *Tribune* newspaper of 3 October 1951 suggested that John held a position in public relations in Evatt's office. John's denial was clear: 'a number of the Press rang me and informed me that I was to join the staff, but that was the first I heard of it, and the last'.[13]

Apart from these preliminaries, the rest of John's evidence was then heard *in camera*. It is important to understand how this came about and why his evidence remained secret until its public release 30 years later. In the course of questions put to John, he confirmed that he did suggest to Solicitor-General Bailey that his evidence should be given in private for 'specific reasons', but, critically, he was not permitted to elaborate as to what those reasons were at any time during the hearing. It being understood that the evidence he asked to give was of a highly secret nature, Windeyer asked the commission for the court reporter to leave and the hearing to be closed. The hearing was adjourned and an ASIO officer was engaged to record further proceedings. John recalled:

---

12   John details the reasons he wanted to give evidence, how the hearing room was cleared and the secrecy surrounding the proceedings in his oral interview: Burton, interview by John Clements, 1981.
13   ASIO investigated the *Tribune* report and were informed that Hazel Bell, Dr Evatt's personal secretary, performed those duties. It stated 'Dr. Burton, has not, to our knowledge, been observed in any official capacity at Parliament House since his return from Peking,' NAA: A6119, 128, Burton vol. 2, 94 and 96.

> Even the court stenographer was dismissed. A security official was designated to take notes in longhand. It was such an absurd situation, with counsel, briefed by the Solicitor-General who knew what I knew, trying to stop me giving information to the commission.[14]

When John realised that his efforts to give the confidential evidence he came to give were thwarted, he suggested to the commissioners that he might write a submission. He perceived the commissioners seemed to be relieved that this awkward hearing could then end and they agreed. Nevertheless, the questions asked of him, the answers he gave and his submission remained subject to a non-publication embargo for 30 years.

John handed a 47-page document consisting of nine written submissions to Bailey under cover of a letter dated 5 January 1955. Importantly, he submitted that the disclosures of Petrov added nothing fundamental to knowledge the Australian Government and Security had obtained from British sources more than five years ago, and that this fact should be published (Submission 6); and that Petrov's defection was at a time of great political moment and that there was no security reason for an investigation at that time (Submission 7).[15] Then John prepared a script for the press in which he explained that he had wanted to disclose the highly secret list of names of suspected spies that the department was given by MI5 in 1948 and to give evidence that would show that the substance of what was produced in the Petrov documents was already known to Security years previously. He said, Petrov and his documents 'gave an excuse to re-hash and add to, in a way valuable from a political point of view, material already on the files of Security'.[16]

---

14 *National Times,* 28 September – 4 October 1984, 11. See also Letters to the Editor, 'Hall Goes for a Burton', *Australian Financial Review,* 22 November 1984, in which John refutes the incorrect assertion in the same paper by journalist Richard Hall, 28 September 1984, that John had asked for the closed hearing. Hall subsequently published an acknowledgement that he had erred in attributing the remarks of Windeyer to John.
15 Extracts from the submission were published by Peter Smark and Bruce Stannard, 'The Birth of ASIO', *Australian,* 19 February 1972, Saturday Review 13. A copy of full submissions is held in 'Petrov Affair: Burton, John', 1955, Evatt Collection, Flinders University Library, and also held on the Burton family file.
16 'The Petrov Affair', 15 September 1955, NAA: A6199, 131, Burton vol. 5, 32, and see letter Burton to the Solicitor-General, 23 July 1954, NAA: A6119, 130, Burton vol. 4, 92, in which John discussed a closed hearing being relevant to 'circumstances bearing on the "old Case"'.

In relation to whether John's evidence should be published, Bailey's opinion was:

> I would not myself think there was any particular objection on Security grounds to the publication of this evidence, and that is also the view of the Director-General of Security. There may be other considerations of public policy, unknown to me, which motivated the Commission's decision.[17]

John received no acknowledgement of receipt of his submission by the commission. In hindsight, he realised that he had no evidence that his submission document was placed before the commission. Bailey attempted to justify the continuing 'secret' classification of his evidence and submission on the ground that only he and John knew about the earlier investigation of alleged leaks from the Department of External Affairs. More likely, the documents remained inaccessible to the public to protect the government from the political embarrassment John's evidence would have caused.

On 8 February 1955, before the commission completed it hearings, John wrote to its chair to express his concern about the 'inaccurate and alarmist reports' that appeared in relation to the evidence the commission had received about the Department of External Affairs while he was there.[18] He asked to examine the Petrov documents and to be given details of allegations about the department for which he was responsible, so that he could defend his and his colleagues' reputation. He incorporated a statement that he requested be immediately made public. His efforts to put the record right about the nature of Petrov's material were futile.

The political hysteria surrounding the Petrov story, despite the commission's failure in 1955 to produce anyone against whom the commission could recommend a charge of spying, poisoned Labor's relations with ASIO and ruined many innocent people's careers. John was not able to protect colleagues who he knew to be innocent. Lawyer Jim Staples, who had been expelled from the Communist Party because of his disagreement with the party over Stalin and Hungary, was dismissed from his position in the Attorney-General's Department as a result of having been a member of the party. Ric Throssell, though never a communist, was denied a security clearance that permanently affected his career

---

17 K. H. Bailey, 'Royal Commission on Espionage: Question of Publication of Evidence Given by Dr. J.W. Burton and Mr. Justice S.C. Taylor', 21 October 1955, 2, Burton family file.
18 NAA: A6119, 130, Burton vol. 4, 28.

25. THE PETROV INQUIRY

because ASIO continued to claim he had passed material to the Soviets.[19] Throssell always denied these claims. John and two permanent heads, Arthur Tange and Alan Renouf, doubted ASIO's advice on Throssell.[20] John said when interviewed in 1995:

> Well, I think what happened to Throssell was absolutely disgusting and tragic and I think ASIO should be sued for it … He just … he just felt destroyed. And Hill of course was destroyed in the same way. These were terribly dedicated Australians … Imagine a person like Throssell doing anything that would prejudice Australia in any sense. It's just absurd.[21]

Although John was not a subject of the Petrov inquiry – as early as September 1952, Spry had reported to Cabinet, consistent with MI5 documented statements, that John was not the source of any security leak – his public support of colleagues who suffered at the hands of the royal commission made his struggle to improve his public image difficult. Fallout from the royal commission was ongoing. Before it released its report in September 1955, journalist Alan Reid jumped the gun with a commentary on its findings in the *Sunday Telegraph*. He asserted that it blasted Evatt and that 'it criticises him for failure to stem Communist influence in the key External Affairs Department when he was External Affairs Minister'.[22] Reid wrote: 'The report links with Dr Evatt his former protege, Dr John Burton', and qualified this in adding that 'the blast' at both Evatt and Burton was 'indirect rather than blunt.' John sued Reid, the *Telegraph* and its publishers, Consolidated Press Ltd. He claimed it was libellous in that it implied that he was one of the 'reds in a key department'; it was as good at calling him a communist and a traitor. He won. On 1 May 1956, the court found that Reid did not have the protection of the defence of fair comment for the defamatory statements he made about John at the time he wrote the article because Reid could not have known the facts contained in the report since it had not been released. Reid had confirmed as much in his article, stating that, 'So far, the report has been kept a close secret with only Prime Minister Menzies and his closest political associates knowing the details.'[23]

---

19 Personal communications with Staples and Throssell.
20 Willheim, 'Is David Horner's Official History of ASIO "Honest History"?'.
21 Burton, interview by Michael J. Wilson, 1995, 39.
22 Alan Reid, 'Reds in Key Department: Spy Report Blasts Evatt', *Sunday Telegraph* (Sydney), 11 September 1955.
23 *Sydney Morning Herald*, 2 May 1956, 7.

Unfortunately for John, he was only awarded nominal damages of £100 – not quite the £25,000 he sought as an ambit claim – because the commission's report was published just a few days after Reid's article, when the defence of 'fair comment' would have applied, so resulting in a reduction of the damage John suffered at law. The award was enough, however, to buy each of us a party dress. Mine was pale lemon lace and my father's win was worth boasting about at school.

On 19 October 1955, Evatt gave his infamous speech in parliament that seemed to signal the beginning of his mental decline. While the thrust of his summary of the Petrov affair might be true, his emotions got in the way of a measured speech. Contrary to his intention, it did not serve him or the Labor Party well in the party's campaign to win a general election in December 1955. Evatt rightly noted that, after 18 months of inquiry, no spies had been discovered and not a single prosecution had been recommended. He accused Menzies of knowing at the time he appointed the commission that Petrov's defection had been deliberately organised by security officers under Menzies's ministerial control many months before 13 April 1954. Then, Evatt dropped his bombshell – a revelation of his naivety – that brought a stunned silence to the house and then an uproar of laughter from both sides of parliament. He revealed that in an effort to ascertain the truth of these grave matters he had written to the Foreign Minister of the Soviet Union, Vyacheslav Molotov, requesting that the Soviet Government reveal the truth about the genuineness of the Petrov documents. Trying to talk over the laughter, Evatt told that he had received a reply on behalf of Molotov stating that the documents could only be 'falsifications fabricated on the instructions of persons interested in the deterioration of the Soviet–Australian relations and in discrediting their political opponents'.[24] That is, not surprisingly, the Russian foreign minister denied there were any Russian spies in Australia. According to Calwell, the Molotov letter that Evatt thought would clinch his victory instead was his undoing. 'Evatt was so profoundly shaken by his sad experiences with the Petrov Commission that he became unnerved and dispirited. It all led to his physical breakdown,' Calwell wrote in his autobiography.[25]

---

24 House of Representatives, Evatt, 19 October 1955, Historic Hansard, .
25 Calwell, *Be Just and Fear Not*, 186.

Interestingly, Calwell said that he had seen John earlier that day taking roneoed copies of the speech to the parliamentary press gallery, although John had long since left the public service and did not again work for Evatt. Calwell had noticed that an extra page had been inserted in the copies of the speeches, because they were sticking out at an angle.[26] Calwell might have confused the timeline of when John had worked for Evatt and was in error in his recall of seeing him, given his senior years when writing his memoir. Evidence of his poor recall is seen in the error he made in his memoir of the age of his son when he tragically died.[27] Then again, John was still engaging with Evatt and assisting him in his spare time. If Calwell's memory of his sighting is correct, what did John think the impact of Evatt's speech would be? Would John have been equally blinded by anger to misjudge its effect, or would he have been unable to budge Evatt from his intent? In any event, Evatt was ridiculed by the press.

Spry almost matched Evatt's poor judgement when he jumped to his own and ASIO's defence. He accused Evatt and the ALP of communist techniques and of deliberately undermining ASIO. Then, he wrote a letter to Menzies's department head, Alan Brown, stating that he was incensed by Evatt's 'wickedly false' attack on him and ASIO.[28] On 22 October 1955, Spry wrote directly to Menzies himself, again provoked by Labor Party members' attacks in the course of parliamentary debate. According to political correspondent Alan Ramsey, this letter 'Reeks of Spry's cold war convictions, his obsession with communism and his hostility to the Labor party'.[29] Ramsey criticised Spry's non-partisan approach:

> Even by the Cold War standard of 30 years ago the letter from the head of the nation's security organisation was remarkably intrusive in a highly contentious area of political debate.[30]

If it was Spry's intention to manipulate a political outcome, he was successful. Evatt was lucky to hold his seat. In December 1955, John and Meredith left for Sydney to letterbox leaflets in the federal electorate of Barton to assist Evatt's campaign. They stayed on to hand out 'how to

---

26 Calwell, *Be Just and Fear Not*, 185–86.
27 The *Australian Dictionary of Biography* places the child's age at 11 at the time of his death in 1948, not at age 16, as Calwell wrote in his senior years in his memoir, *Be Just and Fear Not*, 142. See Graham Freudenberg, 'Calwell, Arthur Augustus (1896–1973)', *Australian Dictionary of Biography*, vol. 13 (Melbourne: Melbourne University Press, 1993).
28 Ramsey, 'The Spry Who Came in from the Cold War', 13.
29 Ramsey, 'The Spry Who Came in from the Cold War', 13.
30 Ramsey, 'The Spry Who Came in from the Cold War', 13.

vote' cards at the booths on election day. Their help was necessary. Evatt retained the seat by something like a margin of 200 votes. Afterwards he visited us, bringing Meredith a box of chocolates to thank her for her help.

The debate is ongoing as to whether the Petrov defection was engineered by the Menzies Government. Ramsey wrote:

> If Menzies did manipulate the Petrov Royal Commission brilliantly to win an election and cripple the Labor Party, Spry made it all possible with 'Operation Cabin 12', Spry's own creation, and the code-name given by ASIO to Petrov's defection in April 1954.[31]

John's view was: 'I think that Menzies was presented with a situation just prior to the election when the House was getting up and immediately saw and took advantage of the political possibilities.'[32] John maintained a belief that the Petrov affair was a tactical manoeuvre by a group of intelligence officers and some senior civil servants, assisted by MI5, and that Menzies was not party to the conspiracy. 'My hunch,' John told journalist John Stubbs, 'is that Menzies knew nothing until Petrov was handed to him on a plate. Then he responded readily.'[33]

Claims have also been made that ASIO, under Spry as its head, spied on Menzies's legitimate political opponents, so determined was he to keep the conservative government in power.[34] Ramsey wrote:

> It is one of the great ironies of Australian politics that the organisation Chifley had been so reluctant to establish in 1949 should, four years after his Government fell, became the instrument to destroy Chifley's successor, 'Doc' Evatt, and play so large a part in creating both the climate and the circumstance that would deny Labor's return to office for another 18 years.[35]

Menzies gave Spry unsupervised authority. John recalled that for years after he left the public service, and prior to the Petrov inquiry, his movements were tracked by ASIO and his phones bugged. He told journalist Mike Steketee, in 1972:

---

31 Ramsey, 'The Spry Who Came in from the Cold War', 13.
32 'Evatt "Right on Petrov"', *Canberra Times*, 15 February 1972, 1.
33 Burton, 'Petrov', *National Times,* 28 September–4 October 1984, 11.
34 NLA, Biographical cuttings on Charles Spry 1910–1994.
35 Ramsey, 'The Spry Who Came in from the Cold War', 13.

25. THE PETROV INQUIRY

> I could never send a message from my office to Dr Evatt's office without the American ambassador having the precise details within minutes. The ambassador used to drop little hints to let me know he knew what I knew.[36]

Political journalist Eric Walsh opined that Spry's very existence was almost a state secret.[37] Horner concluded that ASIO conducted 'covert entry with dubious legal cover'.[38] It is disappointing that Horner was not more scathing about Spry's blatant flagrance of the rule of law. For example, as late as 1959, he had a hidden microphone installed in lawyer Ted Hill's office. Hill's communication with his clients were by law protected by legal professional privilege. Spry, having been sprung, tried to defend himself in a letter to Menzies, saying that ASIO believed that Hill was working for the 'illegal apparatus' of the Communist Party. Yet the attempt to outlaw the Communist Party had failed years earlier. Horner's official history does not inform us whether anyone was ever called to account for ASIO's illegal activities.[39]

***

John's motivation to improve Australia's relations with its Asia-Pacific neighbours did not wane. In March 1955, after the close of the Petrov inquiry, he embraced the opportunity to exert his influence internationally in his private capacity: in the absence of an Australian official attending the Bandung Conference, John filled the void.

---

36 Mike Steketee, Obituary for John Burton, *Australian*, 10 July 2010, 8.
37 Eric Walsh, 'Top Spy', *Daily Mirror* (Sydney), 28 January 1969, 14–15.
38 Horner, *The Spy Catchers*, 418–22.
39 Willheim, 'Is David Horner's Official History of ASIO "Honest History"?', 12.

26

Indonesia with ASIO in tow

When we moved into our new home, 26 Hobart Avenue, in the south Canberra suburb of Forrest in early February 1955, Spry, as head of ASIO and concerned that John might have undue influence in the Labor Party, kept him under surveillance. In a letter of 1 March 1955, he wrote to the secretary of the Prime Minister's Department, A. S. Brown, stating his understanding that John 'was under consideration for appointment to the staff of the Leader of the Opposition'.[1] He went on to concede that ASIO had no evidence that 'Dr. Burton is or has been a member of the Communist Party of Australia', but he listed his concerns and in particular that John's book *The Alternative* 'suggests a serious degree of unreliability in the handling of classified official material'. As for the rumoured possibility of a job with Evatt, again, it was not something John knew about. Nevertheless, whatever he would decide to do for a living, John intended to continue to air his views on Australian foreign policy.

The first regional conference of nations emerging from colonial rule – to be held in Bandung, Indonesia – provided the opportunity. The 1955 conference was to oversee the establishment of what came to be called the 'Non-aligned Movement' in the context of the Cold War. The Australian Government received but did not accept an invitation to send official representatives. John thought it absurd for Australia not to be represented at such a significant conference held on Australia's doorstep. While Australia was not a member of the Non-aligned Movement – having not

---

1 NAA: A6119, 131, Burton vol. 5, 225. A copy of the letter of 1 March 1955 is also on NAA: S6717, A85, item 443020, it being the only document on the file that Meredith and I retrieved before it was sent out for 'sentencing' (destroying); we viewed it on 17 September 2019.

asserted its independence from Britain – 29 African and Asian nations, not all of which had achieved independence from their colonial rulers, sent official representatives. John believed that, whether the government wished to participate or not in a 'non-alignment' movement, the door should be left open in case the government adopted a different policy later.[2]

John approached sinologist Professor C. P. (Patrick) Fitzgerald who agreed to attend the Bandung Conference with him. They asked to be invited as private citizens. The Indonesians remembered John's diplomatic support during their struggles against the Dutch and duly sent invitations to them.[3] John self-funded his travel to Indonesia, while Fitzgerald received an invitation from the University of Indonesia to do some lecturing there, allowing him the opportunity to attend the conference. Cecily went with them. Prime Minister Menzies attempted to intervene. He asked ANU to refuse to grant Fitzgerald leave to attend, but to no avail. Menzies called Fitzgerald himself and suggested that Vice-Chancellor Douglas Copland go instead. Fitzgerald insisted that he and John would attend, having now received invitations to attend as independent guests.[4]

The Australian Government was concerned about what influence John and Fitzgerald might have at the Bandung Conference. John's criticisms of government policy had been outlined in *The Alternative*.[5] Its publication in 1954 had already influenced the ALP policy statement issued by its 1955 federal conference in Hobart. After Labor's defeat at the 1954 election, Evatt had abandoned his earlier attempts to win over the Catholic right and, according to Pemberton:

> This signalled the revival of Burton's influence over Evatt and the ALP. The foreign policy resolution accepted at the critical 1955 Hobart federal ALP conference was drafted by Evatt with the assistance of Burton. It helped precipitate the ALP 'Split'.[6]

---

2   Burton and C. P. Fitzgerald's report on the conference, 20 April 1955, 1.
3   Henry, 'Reflections on Dr. John Wear Burton', 79.
4   Personal communication with Mirabel Fitzgerald, daughter of Patrick Fitzgerald, 1 January 2014.
5   David Walker, 'Nervous Outsiders: Australia and the 1955 Asia-Africa Conference in Bandung', *Australian Historical Studies* 125 (April 2005), 40–59.
6   Greg Pemberton, 'The Challenge of Renewal: John Burton', *Union Issues* (Sydney), Spring 1991, 13. The Catholic action group's fear of communism had a conservative influence on the ALP and Evatt, with John, wanted in particular to include recognition of China in the party's policy platform.

John still had a valid passport for non-communist countries as well as China, having undertaken that he would not attend the Peking conference in China in September 1952. Nevertheless, he officially sought permission to go to Indonesia. The Department of Immigration had no cause to stop him. An officer noted in an internal memo that ASIO 'has never described Dr Burton to us as a Communist, though they have displayed interest in his movements'; before John left, the officer noted: 'As Dr Burton is no doubt aware, he could have left for Indonesia without coming near us'.[7] John, Cecily and Fitzgerald departed Canberra on 13 April 1955, via Sydney, to catch the plane to Jakarta. They were under ASIO surveillance at both airports, observed participating in press interviews and talking with colleagues. However, ASIO had received a report that a Commonwealth car driver had been seen to help Cecily and John with their suitcases. John's ASIO tail was tasked to find out if John had used a Commonwealth car, to which he was not entitled, to take him to the airport. Enquiries proved fruitless and it was concluded that a Commonwealth driver possibly saw John and helped him and Cecily with their luggage.

On arriving in Jakarta, John and Cecily were overwhelmed by the warm reception they received. Together with Fitzgerald, they stayed in Jakarta one night and then went to Bandung where they were provided with a cottage and servants to provide their meals and look after them.[8] They had a limousine and driver for easy access to the conference; they were also driven around Bandung on sightseeing tours and enjoyed drives into the countryside. Cecily was disappointed on being served a Dutch continental–style breakfast and other European food, so she asked for some Indonesian food, which was prepared for them for their next evening meal. The Australian ambassador, Walter Crocker, envying their VIP treatment, complained to Canberra that he had to observe the conference from the outside rather than as an invited official, and that he was funded to stay in a poor-quality hotel some miles out of town.[9] Moreover, John and Fitzgerald, although attending in a private capacity, were treated like conference delegates, free to speak, express views and engage with representatives of the various nations. It was grounds for concern by the Australian Government. John and Fitzgerald attended the

---

7   Memos of 14 January 1955 and 4 April 1955, NAA: A6980 18, 19.
8   Parker, Interview by Meredith Edwards, 2004.
9   Pemberton, 'John Burton: The Heretic', 104; 'Burton Is a V.I.P.', *Argus*, 19 April 1955, 2.

PERSONS OF INTEREST

conference daily, and Cecily attended most sessions and took notes. 'Back seats for officials while Burton honoured', Denis Warner headed a news article that we found in ASIO's file on John:

> One of the more remarkable sideshows of the Afro-Asian conference since Monday has been the spectacle of Dr. John Burton and his wife and Professor Patrick Fitzgerald, of Canberra National University, sitting in official seats while official Australian representatives are relegated to seats reserved for diplomats.[10]

"Excuse ignorance. Where is this country?"

George Molnar cartoon, which likely appeared in a Fairfax newspaper, 1955.
Source: Courtesy Katie Molnar; Burton family collection.

---

10   The Australian representatives referred to were diplomats who attended as observers. And see similar reports in the *Age* and *Canberra Times*, 19 April 1955.

On 18 April 1955, President Sukarno gave the opening address to 29 diverse participating nations. 'Yes, there is diversity among us. Who denies it?' he said.[11] The Afro-Asian region was populated by more than half the world's people, consisting of nine-tenths of the races, three-quarters of the languages and four-fifths of the religions of the world. Cecily wrote a full account of the proceedings that John thought 'captured the atmosphere very well'. She noted Sukarno continued with: 'But what harm is in diversity, when there is unity in desire? This Conference is not to oppose each other, it is a conference of brotherhood'.[12]

John also wrote full accounts. He summed up the importance of the conference in concluding that it represented the 'start of the end of the Cold War'. It was a conference about the right of self-determination, and the granting to all nations freedom and independence with the least possible delay. However, the aim of 'non-alignment' was inconsistent with colonialism and neo-colonialism and the theme of neutrality was viewed with alarm by ardent anti-communists in the USA, UK and Australia.

In Australia, it was noted that John and Fitzgerald were lunch guests of Indian Prime Minister Nehru during the conference. It was John's boldness that brought this about. On the day he arrived, he addressed a letter to the Indonesian prime minister, who was to chair the conference, to seek assistance in Australia's future participation and not be overlooked on any racial grounds. In providing some background on Australian opinion, he included some Labor Party decisions made at the Hobart conference. He sent copies of his letter to Nehru and to the prime minister of Ceylon. Mr Subimal Dutt, head of the Commonwealth Relations Division of the Indian Foreign Office (and who, in October, became foreign secretary under Nehru), assured John and Fitzgerald that previous exclusions of Australia had not been due to any racial or policy factor but because of geographic considerations. As a result of the letter and his conversation with Dutt, Nehru invited John and Fitzgerald to lunch. There, at lunch, Nehru took John aside and gave a similar assurance to that of Dutt. John had been keen to meet Nehru again and Cecily thought that John might be satisfied with the chat he had with Nehru and relax a bit. But no, after the meeting he said: 'Well, what's the next thing?'[13] He was his usual self, she said, getting the absolute utmost out of every opportunity and then moving quickly to the next.

11 Cecily's written account, 'Bandung, April 1955', 1, Cecily family file.
12 Cecily, 'Bandung, April 1955', 1. John's praise of it occurred in family conversations, March 1993.
13 Parker, interview by Meredith Edwards, 2004, 51.

A collection of papers on the conference was subsequently published, edited by Don Baker. It included Sukarno's opening speech, a final communiqué, a report by Fitzgerald and the statement both he and John wrote on their experience and reflections as observers. Evatt wrote its preface. John was wedded to the concept of non-alignment and, a decade later, edited a collection of essays with that theme.[14] The conference was historically important, sufficiently so for John's father to note in his autobiography:

> Probably historians in a hundred years' time will declare that the Afro-Asian Conference held in Indonesia in 1955 was the major turning point in modern history. Almost all the Asian and African leaders met at Bandung and represented more than half the world's population. Such a mass cannot be ignored. These leaders attacked colonialism in every form and solemnly vowed to take no mental or economic rest until every country on the globe was free from the domination of any other.
>
> We can be justly proud, as members of the British Commonwealth of Nations, that the Mother Country has already given full freedom to India and Pakistan, and is considering how best she can help peoples still under her flag to attain complete independence. This granting of self-rule to India will stand out through the centuries as one of the most-enlightened actions of any people.[15]

For Fitzgerald, accompanying John on the trip placed him firmly under ASIO's watch. The *Herald* reported: 'Professor maybe put "on mat"'.[16] Fitzgerald had been under ASIO's observation even before he attended the Bandung Conference, for associating with John during the Petrov inquiry proceedings. We know this because an ASIO report stated that Fitzgerald's motor vehicle was sighted at 8:50 pm on 21 January 1955 'parked outside the home of Dr John Wear Burton, a Communist sympathiser, 26 Hobart Avenue, at the same time as Ric Pritchard Throssell of 44 Ebden Street, Ainslie, who appeared before the Royal Commission on Espionage'.[17] There were subsequent ASIO records of Fitzgerald's vehicle being observed outside our home or at places in John's company, noting Fitzgerald as 'a Communist sympathiser'.[18]

---

14   Burton, *Nonalignment* (London: Andre Deutsch, 1966).
15   Burton, 'The Weaver's Shuttle', 202.
16   'Professor May Be Put "on Mat" Associating Himself with Dr John Burton in Proceedings', *Herald* (Melbourne), 28 April 1955.
17   Copies of ASIO reports of 4 October 1955 and 21 November 1955 were on display at the Chinese Exhibition, Australia Centre on China in the World, ANU, 26 July 2015.
18   NAA: A6119, 131, Burton vol. 5, 4 and 7.

Accompanying John on this trip was a high point in Cecily and John's relationship. Their time in Indonesia was a moment Cecily felt included in John's affairs and valued. By the time we left the farm, Cecily had gained personal strength. Her mental health improved as she became more her own person. This we perceived from a letter Judith Wright wrote to a friend on 30 September 1954 after she met up with Cecily and John in Canberra at a repertory play:

> The best thing about it [the play] was re-meeting Cecily Burton, which I had not expected to be such an experience. She has developed amazingly and is now a truly lovely person, perfectly inner-secure and radiant with affection for the world. (This I may say is not John's doing but is wholly her own). John on the other hand is thoroughly insecure and miserable, quite in contrast. I feel Cecily is a major acquisition, and I am very humbled before her.[19]

The memorable trip over, however, John and Cecily's relationship continued to decline. If Cecily was moving towards a more balanced relationship with John, it was at the expense of increased and more open conflict with him. Struggling to maintain her own self-assurance, she probably did not fully appreciate the insecurities from which he suffered. Living with him was never easy. After 're-meeting', Cecily corresponded with Wright, believing her to be a person who would understand and sympathise. Wright commented to a friend about Cecily's letters, describing them in a letter dated 8 April 1955 as 'such huge self-analytic letters, finds out just what is wrong, goes through enormous chastening and radical changes, ceases to be an intellectual and begins to learn to live, and next letter as bad as ever'. She went on to describe Cecily as being:

> like a snake half way out of its skin and stuck there, and probably always will stick. It's her relationship with John that is the trouble basically; … she cannot get him to accept her and will not accept him. In fact, of course they cannot possibly accept each other because if they did, it would mean giving up their precious egos. Cecily thinks she has shed hers already, but when she and John start their endless subterranean battles, back it comes of course, all the better for the change … It's a pity, but perhaps necessary for them both.[20]

---

19 Clarke and McKinney, *With Love and Fury*, 89.
20 Clarke and McKinney, *With Love and Fury*, 94.

John and Cecily did not have only domestic tensions to deal with. ASIO and the Petrov inquiry continued to plague them. Despite the comic side of its surveillance of us, being constantly under watch must often have made our parents feel uncomfortable. On their return from Indonesia, black cars pulled up outside our house. Two men, wearing stereotypical spy-like coats, hats and sunglasses, sat with notebooks on their knees and recorded visitors as they came and went, as later revealed by various ASIO records. Canberra was not an easy town for 'unobtrusive' surveillance, as historian Nicholas Brown observed, 'It was hard not to be seen in open spaces'.[21] It is hard to know what Cecily thought of this 'cloak and dagger' atmosphere, but she probably got used to it as being 'the norm' living with John. They shared political views and social values and, despite the difficulty of living with John, she was supportive of his ideals and was sympathetic about his unfair treatment by ASIO and the press during the Petrov inquiry debacle.

Once, Meredith cheekily approached a black car parked outside our place. She saw hats hurriedly come down over the two foreheads and opened newspapers being raised in front of their faces. Manning Clark's son, Andrew, confirmed that there was nothing subtle about their activities outside their house either. To Andrew's and our amusement, John, when telephoning Manning, would sometimes say 'Spry here'. John would do the same when phoning our local Methodist minister, George Wheen, who had reason to understand the satire. As an example of how pervasive ASIO's surveillance was, Wheen himself was under its constant watch. According to an ASIO report of 8 September 1955, Wheen publicly screened the 1952 Japanese film *Children of Hiroshima*, a docudrama that had been entered into the Cannes Film Festival in 1953. It had been introduced into Canberra by the Canberra Peace Group; any advocate of 'peace' was reason to attract ASIO's suspicion.[22] We had developed a close association with Wheen when we moved into our Forrest home in 1955. He was a son of a Christian leader, Harold Wheen, who had long-standing connections with our grandfather Jack; the Wheens and the Burtons having belonged to the same parish church when they lived in Roseville, Sydney. Wheen, like John, had also attended the University of

---

21 Brown, *History of Canberra*, 142.
22 Wheen apparently screened the film twice, once on a Sunday evening in lieu of a sermon and on the subsequent Monday evening to a public gathering, NAA: A6119, 131, Burton vol. 5, 22.

Sydney and, when there, had a reverse experience from that of John. He changed direction from his planned career in business to heed the calling of the ministry.[23]

Individually, or together, our family sometimes attended Wheen's sermons, particularly when grandfather Jack was staying with us. On one occasion, Wheen invited Jack to give a Sunday sermon, the event noted in the local press with Jack described as a 'distinguished New Testament scholar, and an authority on Pacific affairs'.[24] We all liked George. He was a regular visitor to our house, usually told a risqué joke and always had warmth to deliver. Cecily enjoyed the spiritualism the church offered. She saw spiritualism as something that came from within people and, in common with George, she loved people, loved discovering their core essence, being there with them and for them. Our parents did not discourage us girls from attending church if we wished in order that we might discover for ourselves what aspects of it suited us and what we might or might not believe in. John, however, often said to Meredith on her return from church, 'What mumbo jumbo did you hear today?'

As serious and nasty as it was living in a democratic society in which an unaccountable intelligence agency spied on its own innocent and hard-working citizens, we were brought up to believe in our liberal democratic society – that social change could be effected by exercising our right to vote. Spry's obsessive belief that all political left-wingers were suspected communists was treated as a household joke. It was the man, not the whole political system, that was flawed.[25]

---

23   'The Methodist', 9 July 1966, 7, NLA, Biographical cuttings on George Alfred Wheen, Reverend Dr.
24   *Canberra Times*, 18 September 1955.
25   Andrew Clark and I had the opportunity of defending our fathers' reputations by participating in a panel discussion, 'In the name of the father', facilitated by Dr Anne Summers, Sydney Writers' Festival, 2012.

27
A shift to the city: Enterprises and infidelity

When we left the farm for city life in 1955, John took initiatives in various directions to try and resolve his dilemma of how to earn a living. He felt that his resignation from the public service, the Petrov affair 'and probably other contributions to my reputation' left him with 'no option but to go it alone farming or doing something else equally private'.[1] He had stationery printed up, headed 'Policy Research' that named him as director. It seems that he hoped he would develop a private organisation to provide research, particularly on policy matters in the international and economic fields, to organisations that lacked resources. He applied to the minister for the interior and obtained the right to purchase an interest in the Perth building in Canberra's Civic Centre for the sum of £12,000, which gave him office space.[2] At the same time, he decided to invest in a nearby and established orchard farm, 'Linden', on Narrabundah Lane on the outskirts of Canberra. He suggested to our friends Max and Fran Campion that they join him in a joint farming venture. The policy research consulting business did not flourish and the farming venture had some tragic personal consequences.

Our family befriended the Campions while we were living at Weetangera when a friend introduced Fran to John as someone who could help type his manuscript for *The Alternative*. So that Cecily could accompany John to Indonesia, Fran and Max moved into our home in the suburb

---
1   Burton, 'Oral History Project notes', 6, Burton family file.
2   *Canberra Times*, 1 October 1955; and see ASIO's record, NAA: A6119, 131, Burton vol. 5, 25. Many years later, John gifted his interest in the building to the Transport Workers' Union.

of Forrest to care for us children and our dachshund-fox terrier puppy, Bimbo. The young couple wanted, but could not have, children so they loved looking after us and we loved them.

John later justified the ill-fated joint venture as doing the Campions a favour. He applied some of the proceeds of the sale of the Weetangera farm to the purchase. He thought the orchard would provide the Campions with an opportunity of earning a living; by entering into a mortgage arrangement with John, Max could amass equity in the property at the same time. Fran and Max moved into the farmhouse on the property to run the farm, albeit under John's direction. While John worked at the farm too, he had free time to research and write. According to ASIO records, John and Max transferred 'Linden' into the names of Cecily and Fran, presumably to minimise tax or perhaps to avoid the consequences of bankruptcy in the event the farm business failed.[3] The orchard was already producing apples, plums and seed fruits, and Max and John set about building chicken sheds to establish a poultry farm. John embraced a new method of egg production, one now described as 'battery hens'. The sheds were clean and modern, had artificial lighting, and the cages were equipped with automated feeding of pellets that dropped down to replenish what the chickens ate from the bowl. For water, the chickens pecked at a metal nipple that dripped water into their beaks. Droppings fell through the cage floor. As innovative as it was, we three children were not convinced that the chickens were happy; they were each housed in separate cages and had to endure isolated and restricted conditions for most of their lives. Meredith recalls that lighting was installed that turned on at 4 am to mimic daylight and extend the laying time of the hens. Time and research have proved the obvious; today the farming method is decried as unacceptable.

The joint farming venture meant that, as a family, we saw a lot of the Campions. While the families appeared to be enjoying friendship and happy times, John set off a train of events that caused havoc and harm to both families – not just to the four adults involved, but also to our sister, Clare. John was unhappy. Cecily would say that John could not be happy with an orchard 'because he couldn't round up the fruit trees as he was used to rounding up sheep'.[4] He had less control over running his farm

---

3   NAA: A6126, 420, Cecily Margaret Burton vol. 1, 25. According to ASIO's information, the purchase price was £7,200, NAA: A6119, 131, Burton vol. 5, 40, memorandum 14 September 1955.
4   Parker, interview by Meredith Edwards, 2004, 53.

than he was used to. He liked being in control and, as Cecily perceived it, he was losing control of us too. We were entering our teens and in town we could socialise more readily and be at home less. With hindsight, John's apparent unhappiness might have been a guilt-driven moodiness over his own infidelity and betrayal. It transpired that Fran had not been happy either. She had continued typing for John after we moved into town. John had kept in close touch with Evatt, who informally relied on John's political advice and ideas, and John sent him policy papers that Fran typed. No doubt John thought it good for Fran to be occupied.[5] However, the inevitable happened; either while we were living at Weetangera, or soon after we moved to Canberra, they commenced an affair. John and the much younger Fran were each restless in their marriages and John offered Fran comfort.

Perhaps Cecily was right when later, after becoming aware of the relationship and John's other illicit liaisons, she decided that John truly believed that he was addressing Fran's and other women's unhappiness by meeting their sexual needs. Had Cecily known at the time that John and Fran were lovers, she conceded, it would have been very hard to deal with. However, later in 2000, she wrote in a private journal: 'He was saving [Fran] from whatever, also from Max I suppose. So – I have never felt really threatened.'[6] No one might have found out about the affair had Fran not lapsed into severe depression and attempted to kill herself, causing her to confess to Max about her relationship with John. Cecily, aware only that Fran was ill and unhappy, offered her warm support. The farming partnership was dissolved within a few years of its start and the Campion's marriage eventually failed. That was not, however, the end of the unhappy saga, personally or financially. Max had mortgage debts he could not pay, and John tried to wind up his interest in the Linden property. A financial dispute between John and Max waged for years. It culminated with publicised debt enforcement proceedings, *Burton v. Campion*, and the forced public auction of the Campion's home.[7]

---

5   In a note to Evatt, 30 December 1956, in which John thanked Evatt for Christmas presents, he asked for something for 'Mrs Campion's' typing, stating that it was kind of her to do it 'but they need all they can earn', Evatt Collection/Burton, Flinders University Library.
6   Cecily's private journal, 'Free writing', 2000, Cecily family file.
7   'Legal Notices', *Canberra Times*, 21 January 1967, 17.

Max had recognised early that John and Cecily were having marriage difficulties. In 1955 he told Cecily that an atmosphere of tension was so thick 'you could cut it with a knife'.[8] Cecily found she could talk to Max. He was attractive, fun to be with and paid her attention, something she received little of from John. In relatively innocent circumstances, on occasion Cecily and Max went on outings together. Apart from indulging in 'a little canoodling now and again', according to Cecily, there was no more. Clare as teenager was infatuated with Max and, sensitive to her feelings, Cecily kept her relationship with Max platonic. However, Cecily did not reckon on the fallout from the dangerous games John and Max played. Max never forgave John for his affair with Fran and, while remaining a friend of the rest of the family, some four years later, in 1959, Max seduced Clare, exacting his revenge. Clare was 16 and impressionable. Cecily had had no idea that Max had engaged with Clare in an intimate way and it seems no one in our family knew about their relationship until Clare opened up about the affair in her adult years. She and Max developed a long-lasting friendship during which Max told Clare about the hurt John had caused him. It had a lasting deleterious effect on Clare's relationship with our father. She harboured a resentment against him and, at the same time, had a difficult and uneasy relationship with Cecily that neither Meredith nor I fully understood. Did she blame Cecily for allowing John to stray or for failing to protect her, or both?

In March 1957, before the collapse of the joint farm venture with the Campions, John accepted an offer to open and run a Canberra branch of Sydney's Morgan's bookshop. With the shop came Morgan's Sydney manager, Sabne Lewis, capable and knowledgeable, 'on loan' from the Sydney book store to assist John in setting up the new shop, show him how to order stock and help him understand the industry. John arranged for her to board with our elderly next-door neighbour. Sabne soon become a family friend. Partly Polynesian, Sabne had thick dark hair, brown eyes and was attractive in personality as well as looks. We were intrigued by her. Unfortunately, I was to learn a little later, John was particularly so.

John hosted a party on 22 March to celebrate the shop's opening in brand new and spacious premises fronting on to Green Square, a large square of manicured well-watered grass in the Kingston shopping centre. The event attracted ASIO's interest and it dispatched one of their agents

---

8   Parker, interview by Meredith Edwards, 2004, 60.

to mingle with the guests and report on it.⁹ At the outset, the shop attracted controversy. The *Sydney Morning Herald* reported that John had opened a bookshop in Canberra featuring 'left-wing literature'.¹⁰ John responded with a letter to the editor published the next day, stating that the description was completely false. Out of a stock of more than 6,000 books, there were not 20 that were 'left-wing' in attitude, he protested: 'I am prepared to back this claim by giving £50 to charity if you can show otherwise'. He went on to state that:

> As a matter of fact, although I am an experienced book-buyer I do not think I could find enough books to permit any shop to "feature" left-wing books. Our new shop has infinitely more books of a religious nature than of a political nature and this includes all religions.¹¹

John did, of course, stock copies of his own works in the bookshop. As a follow-up to Chifley's 1949 *The Light on the Hill,* in 1956 John had written a pamphlet, *The Light Glows Brighter,* published that year by Morgan's in Sydney. Evatt wrote its introduction and the pamphlet included a foreword by the federal president of the ALP, Joe Chamberlain. The document was distributed widely and caused a stir.¹² On the opening of the bookshop, Liberal Party member Jim Killen suggested John's pamphlet should be called 'the Light glows redder'.¹³ Much later, in 1960, John stocked and sold Manning Clark's *Meeting Soviet Man*, which fell into that 'left-wing' category. John hosted the launch of that book in a party atmosphere at the shop. By then, the shop was thriving.

One of John's friends told him that another of their friends, surprised to hear about John's new business venture, said behind John's back, 'How the mighty have fallen'. But if down, John was not out. He had many ventures on the go. In August 1957, John purchased the good will from Morgan's proprietor, A. H. Sheppard. Morgan's bookshop was renamed The Green Square Book & Record Shop. Some facetiously called it the 'Red Square' bookshop, reflecting the continuing controversy about John's political philosophy.

---

9   NAA: A6119, 337, Burton vol. 6, 149, 22 March 1957.
10 *Sydney Morning Herald*, 22 March 1957.
11 *Sydney Morning Herald*, 23 March 1957.
12 The pamphlet title has been incorrectly cited by Google books and elsewhere as 'The Light Grows Brighter'.
13 *Canberra Times*, 21 March 1957, 3.

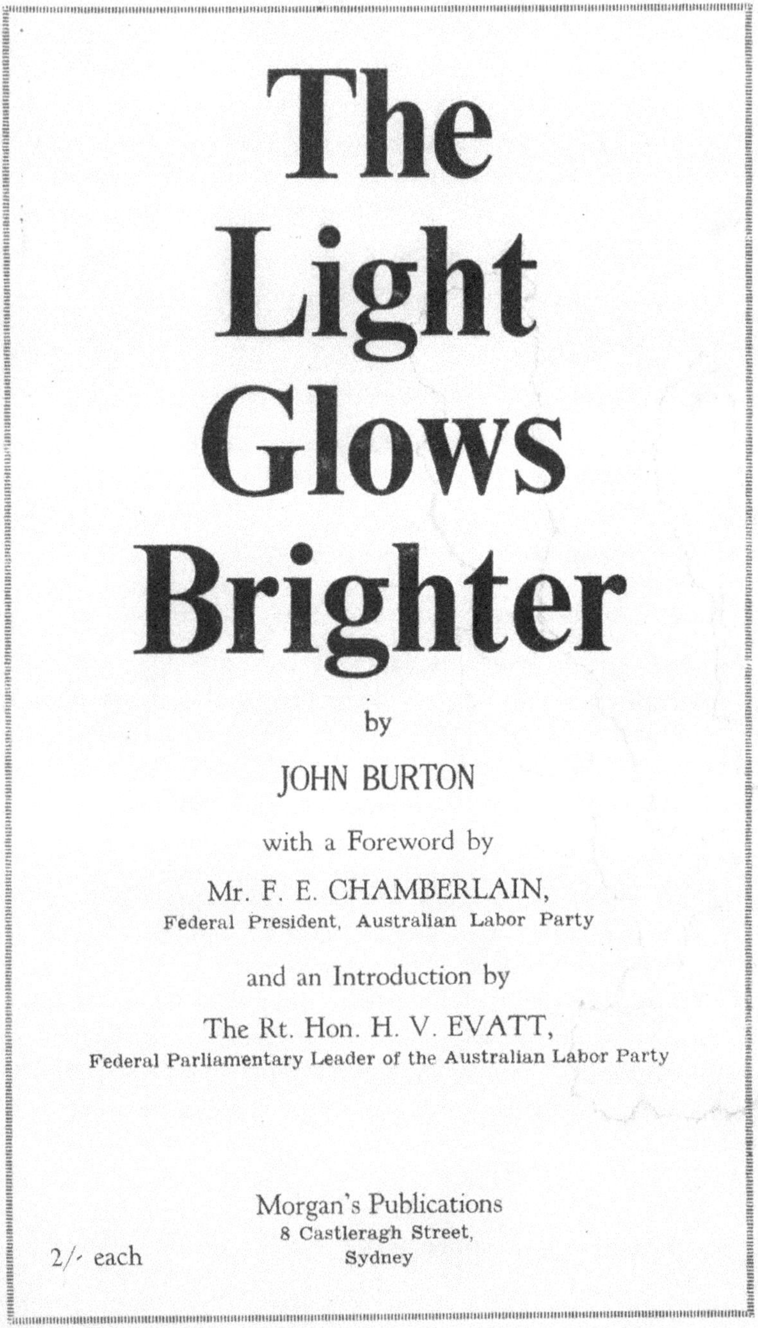

The Light Glows Brighter

by

JOHN BURTON

with a Foreword by

Mr. F. E. CHAMBERLAIN,
Federal President, Australian Labor Party

and an Introduction by

The Rt. Hon. H. V. EVATT,
Federal Parliamentary Leader of the Australian Labor Party

Morgan's Publications
8 Castlereagh Street,
Sydney

2/- each

John's controversial pamphlet, 1956.
Source: Family collection.

Sabne left her previous employer and Sydney life to work permanently for John as his store manager. She purchased and lived in her own flat in Canberra. We all, including Cecily, involved ourselves in the business, enjoying the array of books and records that passed through the shop. John imported a Gaggia espresso machine, the first in Canberra. Cecily took charge of serving cakes and coffee in the Espresso Coffee Lounge set up at the back of the shop. Perhaps informed by how easy it was to calm his milking cows with music piped through the barn, John piped music, particularly newly released recordings, throughout the store. Another initiative of his, novel at the time, was to install music booths equipped with headphones for customers to listen to tracks before they purchased their records. The Phillips record company lent John their 'Carnegie Hall equipment' to demonstrate the excellent acoustics of high-fidelity recordings.[14] John arranged a Sunday evening of music for invited guests using the equipment. He later introduced a record-lending library. It was a bookshop with a difference.

Cecily adjusted to the new, if frenetic, way of life. Under Sabne's guidance, she learned the trade. She selected and ordered books and became familiar with various record labels and their suppliers and what was in demand. John suggested to other Kingston shop owners that Friday night shopping should be reintroduced. It had proved popular in Canberra when introduced in 1926 but it was discontinued at some later date.[15] Meredith canvassed shop-owners' views and Canberra became accustomed to the Friday night shopping. The Green Square coffee shop became a popular meeting place at around 9 pm on Friday evenings when other shops closed. We knew most of the families who dropped by and we observed John generously offering coffee and cakes without opening the till. Then he complained that, rather than coming to purchase books, people came only for free coffee and a chat. The coffee shop was fun but a drain on the business, which initially was not proving very profitable. To change that, John's vision of the enterprise grew. He expanded the Kingston shop into leased premises next door and stocked electrical equipment and other goods.

---

14   NAA: A6126, 420, Cecily Margaret Burton vol. 1, 55, ASIO report on Cecily having invited a friend to the demonstration on 23 June 1957.
15   'Late Shopping: Increasing Popularity', *Canberra Times*, 10 February 1927, 9.

Canberra's upgrading of its public transport gave John the impetus for yet another idea. He bought an old Canberra bus no longer used for public passengers, painted it green to link it to the Green Square shop, stripped it of seats, had it fitted internally with shelves, and drove and operated it as a mobile school lending library. Then, he extended the mobile service to further afield. His idea that Green Square enterprises might deliver much wanted supplies to construction workers at camps in the Snowy Mountains, according to an ASIO report, became 'a very lucrative one'.[16] The little-known story of the Green Square bus's role in making more comfortable the lives of the mostly immigrant workers on the Snowy Mountains hydroelectric scheme warrants another chapter, which follows.

One business initiative John took on resulted in Cecily being somewhat sidelined from the main activity. In order to sell records, John had acquired franchises for Festival and some other less-known record labels, but he was unable to obtain licences to sell well-known labels such as EMI and HMV, already sold in Kingston at Bourchier's Music Store. In June 1958, to overcome the obstacle, John leased a small bookshop in Manuka, a nearby shopping centre, and together with paperbacks and other books, he was able to stock and sell those record labels. Cecily had the job of managing the new store, and for a time she was tied down to the counter in her small shop in Manuka Arcade with no relief staff. It was a lonely existence compared to the lively atmosphere and larger staff at the Kingston shop run by John and Sabne. John disposed of the Manuka shop in March 1959.

John was drawn to Sabne, probably not just to her beauty and fulsome figure, but in all likelihood to her troubled past. As with Fran, he seemed to see and justify himself as a knight to the rescue of vulnerable women. The development of his clandestine affair with Sabne was likely a symptom of John and Cecily's marital problems although, in turn, it clearly contributed to their marriage breakdown. As obvious as his relationship with Sabne was, given the time John spent with her at the bookshop and how late he came home, Cecily remained unaware of it, so far as we know. She welcomed Sabne as a family friend and included her in our family activities. Sabne was warm and friendly and respectful. However, an ASIO agent's watchful eyes detected strained relations between Cecily and Sabne at a dinner event. On 4 April 1960, an informal dinner was held at

---

16 NAA: A6119, 337, Burton vol. 6, 263.

the Lucky Chinese Restaurant, located next to our Green Square shop, in honour of the visit to Canberra of Rewi Alley, a New Zealand-born writer and political activist and a member of the Communist Party of China. ASIO's undercover agent was able to name all but one of the 12 guests there (possibly the agent himself!). John, it was reported, was to give an address to the Peace Congress later that evening to which the guests were invited but most were observed to go instead to the coffee shop at the back of our shop to continue socialising. From the highlighting on the report, it seems ASIO was interested more in an exchange between Cecily and Sabne than any political activity. Halfway through the dinner, Cecily apparently approached Sabne who had been seated at John's table, and suggested that she might move to the 'main table', to allow Cecily 'to be seated next to her husband'.[17]

John probably told Sabne that his relationship with Cecily was unhappy and she, needy herself, likely left it to him to manage his own disloyalty. Things got tricky, however, for all of us at home. In 1959, when the various Green Square enterprises were in full swing, John put himself in a ballot for eligibility to purchase land on the edge of Lake Eucumbene at the site of the old township of Adaminaby. As part of the Snowy Mountains hydroelectric scheme, the Eucumbene River had been dammed, flooding the old township site to create the enormous Lake Eucumbene. The town itself had been moved, brick by brick in the case of some buildings, to establish 'new' Adaminaby, some 6 miles away. To increase his chances of securing a block, John put another bid in under Sabne's name. Sabne and John each won an allotment on which there was either an established small fibro cottage, or on which John had them built. As to what financial arrangement he made with Sabne in doing this, I am unaware. Clear in my recall, however, is that old cups and plates and cutlery disappeared from our Hobart Avenue kitchen and reappeared in drawers and shelves of the two cottages. Cecily noticed some cutlery missing on one occasion and said absently, 'Where have these [whatever items they were] gone?' I knew I had seen them in Sabne's kitchen drawer when I visited her cottage once and realised then that Cecily did not know John had helped Sabne equip her weekender. I stood in our family kitchen, knowing the answer to Cecily's mystery and not knowing what, if anything, I should say. I probably said something weak, like, 'I think some things are in our cottage at Adaminaby.'

---

17   NAA: A6119, 337, Burton vol. 6, 1958–60, 278; NAA: A6126, 420, Cecily Margaret Burton vol. 1, 44–45.

John seemed not to consider that his affairs with Fran and Sabne might impact his marriage, at least, not if they were kept secret. He intended his marriage and family life to continue as normal. He did not know the extent of Cecily's unhappiness. He apparently did not see her as needy or vulnerable. Sabne's seductive looks and friendly personality were always evident. John's young friend Bob Hawke was enchanted by her. Meredith told me that on one occasion in the 1950s, when Sabne was babysitting us, Meredith came home from an outing after Clare and I had gone to bed and caught Bob and Sabne flirting in the kitchen; she saw Bob pinch Sabne's bottom. Family life at home was strained. John and Cecily were reasonably civil to each other without being warm or close. They were social with others during these difficult times and they hosted parties at the bookshop and at home. John complained about Cecily dancing with various 'chaps', many of whom admired her and showed it. He was jealous and cross with her and told her so.

Cecily's learned assertiveness, having recovered with the help of Jungian philosophy from what she regarded as a breakdown in the early 1950s, and started to quietly shift the power balance of hers and John's relationship. In search of fulfilment, she was moving out of John's shadow to explore her own identity. He had been used to having her as one of his admiring disciples; he wanted her to think he was wonderful, look after him and believe in everything he said and did. Perhaps Sabne did a bit of that for him.

John continued to write and have influence on Labor's foreign policy. His 1956 treatise, *The Light Glows Brighter,* had had traction. Some commentators suggested that Burton had as much influence out of the public service as he did in it; others acknowledged the pamphlet as having become the ALP's de facto policy platform. John followed up this publication in 1957 with *Labour in Transition,* seen as a guide for the ALP's policy on democratic socialism, which Labor Senator Bill Ashley alleged was aimed at nationalisation. Newspaper cartoons appeared illustrating that controversy over John's political influence even divided Labor Caucus in March 1957.

Cecily continued to support John in his enterprises and writing. But, at the same time, she started to look outwardly for acceptance and kindness from others, which was all too readily waiting to be bestowed on her from her male admirers.

27. A SHIFT TO THE CITY

LABOUR in TRANSITION

BY

JOHN BURTON

TWO SHILLINGS AND SIXPENCE

John's subsequent pamphlet, 1957.
Source: Family collection.

"Come away from that brat! D'you want to catch his spots?"

'Burtonville', Eyre Jr (Junior Harry Eyre) cartoon, undated (likely March 1957), depicting Senator Bill Ashley, minister and leader in the Senate in the Labor Government.

Source: Burton family papers.

"Arhh! Leave the kid alone! We're not catching any fish, anyhow!"

Burton rocking the ALP boat, Eyre Jr cartoon, undated (likely March 1957), depicting (from left to right) Senator Bill Ashley, Eddie Ward, Doc Evatt and Burton.

Source: Burton family papers.

Virgil Reilly cartoon, likely produced for the *Daily Mirror*, 1956–57, depicting Evatt and Burton, a commentary on the political flak created by John's pamphlets.
Source: Burton family papers.

George Molnar cartoon, likely produced for Fairfax newspapers in 1957 after the ALP Federal Conference in Brisbane, 1957.
Source: Courtesy Katie Molnar, George Molnar collection 1955–1991, National Library of Australia.

28

The Snowy Mountains bus, bubble cars and other ventures

In the early 1950s, thousands of workers from European countries were recruited to work alongside Australians on the ambitious construction of the Snowy Mountains hydroelectric scheme, the biggest civil engineering project ever undertaken in Australia. The winters were long and cold, the work gruelling, but the pay and accommodation were reasonable. John recognised the hardship these men endured – their loneliness away from their families – and saw a way of improving their lives. He approached Sir William Hudson, the commissioner of the Snowy Mountains Hydro-electric Authority, for permission for the Green Square bus to visit the construction camps to provide the workers with items beyond the essentials supplied to the camps. John had known Hudson, a civil engineer, since 1949 when Prime Minister Chifley appointed Hudson to manage the scheme. ASIO's version is that much of the success of Green Square enterprises came from this initiative because John had 'sole distribution rights' at the construction camps.[1] However, while the venture proved profitable, John did not require any 'sole' rights. There were no competitors who either thought of or were interested in finding a way to meet the needs of these workers. In any event, also noted by ASIO, John credited the success of his business overall to Sabne and her extensive retail trade experience.

---

1   NAA: A6119, 337, Burton vol. 6, 263.

Geographically isolated from large cities, the construction workers had little to spend their money on. A major problem was the roads. They were unsealed, steep and winding, some cut into mountain cliffs, and at times many were impassable in dangerous weather conditions. It was difficult to ensure reliable delivery of even basic consumer needs. A priority was to transport material for the construction of workers' huts, small churches and schools for the children in places like Island Bend, Guthega and Khancoban.[2] There was an unmet appetite for books and appliances, especially if they were delivered. John adjusted the fittings of the bus to accommodate a display of a variety of products including carefully selected books in various European languages, records and gramophones on which to play them and electrical items such as electric blankets and toasters. The bus was open for business until late at night to cater for shift workers. The advent of the Green Square bus warmed the hearts of many lonely men.

Demand for the goods John stocked was constant. The nights at the camps were long and cold and radio reception was poor. The workers relied on books and records for evening entertainment. Later John extended his stock to include stationery, magazines and foreign newspapers. Newspapers and small electric appliances sold well. Initially, John drove the bus himself to ensure the roadways could take the heavy vehicle but also to find out more about the workers' needs and their environment. In this action we see a glimpse of his father's Methodism and desire to improve the lives of those in need. It also demonstrates the belief he had in himself, like his father, that he knew best how this could be done. By mid-1958, he was running the bus up and down to the Snowy Mountains on a weekly basis. Sometimes he had to stop to hack trees and shrubs whose growth had encroached onto the muddy roads and obstructed the bus's progress to what was known as Thiess Village and, later, to Cabramurra where it was expected to be overnight each Thursday. Rain, hail or snow, the bus made it through. On one occasion when the roads were barricaded because they were too treacherous for vehicles, the men at the camps protested so strongly that an exception was made for the bus to pass.

John had left room at the back of the bus for bunk beds and essentials for a driver's overnight stays. It was an adventure for us to travel with him and sleep in a bunk bed on the bus overnight. Meredith marvelled at

---

2   See Ruth Arndt, 'A Bustling Business', *Canberra Times*, 19 October 2000, 11; and Arndt, 'Waiting for a Bus Have Snowy Workers Some Instant Relief', *Canberra Times*, 16 December 1999.

the high cultural tastes of the 'men on the Snowy' who were hungry for cultural material. Robert ('Bob') Armstrong, a civil engineer, while not an immigrant, wrote to me in 2011 about the life-changing effect the bus's visits had on him and others working on the Snowy project. He said:

> I soon discovered *Burton's Book and Record Bus* and it really did give me the incentive to buy and read and study good literature and appreciate all forms of music … It stopped me from heading to the bar after work and in the evenings after dinner. I think in a way your father kept me on the straight and narrow.[3]

He sent me a draft extract from a memoir he was writing of his description of the bus and its importance:

> Dr John Burton's bus was a lumbering large old ex-Canberra suburban bus in which he had removed all the seats and each side of the aisles he had put in jam-packed book shelves, record racks full of joy, a stationery department and a magazine stand for Australian and imported magazines and out-of-date foreign newspapers, the latter of which sold like hot cakes to the three thousand hardly English speaking workers from Europe. He drove the old bus from Canberra and did a weekly circuit of all major Snowy construction towns and camps. It was a priority that, irrespective of the weather, Burton's Book and Record Bus gets through, even if it had to be towed. It was really the only thing that kept a lot of us lonely single staff from becoming alcoholics, or losing our minds.[4]

Thanks to the bus, Bob built up an extensive eclectic library and record collection. He acquired books by Agatha Christie, Ernest Hemingway, F. Scott Fitzgerald, John Steinbeck, Norman Mailer, Truman Capote, Francoise Sagan and others, poetry including Keats and Dylan Thomas's *Under Milk Wood*, plays of Oscar Wilde and Noël Coward, the lyrics of Gilbert and Sullivan operettas and *The Complete Works of William Shakespeare*. His record collection included *Salad Days*, *Carmen*, the *Purple People Eater* and Irish folk songs.

Bob recalled the day in 1958 when he introduced his new girlfriend, Ruth, to the harsh conditions under which the Snowy scheme workers lived. The workers relied on pot-belly stoves and wood heaters for cooking and

---

3   Personal communication, 2011, Burton family file.
4   Robert Armstrong, draft chapter, 2011, Burton family file.

warmth, and power generators for refrigerators. Snow was thick on the ground. The couple arrived at his room in the Cabramurra staff barrack block and Ruth, intrigued with Bob's books, fingered the collection and said in jest, 'Can I move in?' Bob credited the bus's visits to his continued courtship of Ruth that led to a lifelong marriage. They lived at Thiess Village, where the bus also visited, for two years. The couple eventually settled in Sydney and lived a happy 51 years together until Ruth's death. The story Bob told me is that, one Thursday, when he was at work and Ruth was at the camp alone and bored, John and his bus arrived. Ruth asked John if he had any watercolour paints. He said he was sorry, he hadn't any. He was able only to sell her a Croxley sketch book. On John's next visit, he brought with him paints, pencils and artist paper for Ruth. The sketch book was treasured; it was filled with poetry the two copied into it and notes that Bob left Ruth each day before she woke. Without John, he said, Ruth would not have extended her stay and their relationship would have had no chance to flourish.[5]

As soon as John was sure of demand for what the bus stocked, he employed a skilled Canberra driver, a migrant born in Azerbaijan and who was fluent in several European languages, to trial the bus travelling regularly to selected Snowy Mountain camps. The workers welcomed the service and made personal requests for goods, electrical equipment, special song albums, writing paper and newspapers. The bus increased the frequency of its visits to twice a week. Word spread through the construction tunnels and men assembled at various points to wait for the bus. The driver had to rug up overnight to keep warm. Then, one night, he suffered a cerebral aneurism while sleeping on the bus. He was transported to Sydney as his condition was more than the Cooma or Canberra hospitals could manage. He recovered, but never resumed driving. John engaged various drivers, never any as reliable as the Azerbaijanian. At one time, John engaged his young friend Jim (later Justice) Staples to drive for him. Staples, having lost his job as a legal officer in the attorney-general's office apparently on discovery of his past membership of the Communist Party, welcomed the opportunity. The job helped him save sufficient money to help establish himself in, what became, a successful career as a barrister at the Sydney Bar. Staples told us many tales about his Snowy bus trips, including an encounter he had with police over 'sly grog' that Staples took into

---

5   Armstrong's story is drawn from his draft memoir and personal communication in 2011 after Ruth's death, Burton family file.

28. THE SNOWY MOUNTAINS BUS, BUBBLE CARS AND OTHER VENTURES

a camp to drink with the men. He was caught and had to talk his way out of an overnight stay in a police cell. Inevitably, the bus broke down, leaving Staples stranded and sometimes cold and wet while he attempted makeshift repairs. On 31 August 1960, according to my diary, worse, 'the bus engine went up in flames'. It was fixed, however, and by October 1960 its popularity was such that the road edges were carved by local authorities to ensure the bus could reach further afield such as Khancoban.

As if running a bookshop and mobile buses was not enough, in January 1959 John took up an agency to import and sell Messerschmitt three-wheeled 'bubble cars' from the shop. The cars had a 200 cc single cylinder engine. They were built in Germany in the 1940s and 1950s, initially developed to transport wounded soldiers. Two hundred and fifty of these tiny vehicles were imported into Australia. The vehicle was roadworthy and cornered well, but somewhat underpowered going up hills. The Perspex bubble roof opened to the side and closed down over the seated driver and passenger. The driver had a sense of being in a cockpit although the seat is only inches from the ground rather than high in the sky.

The Burton's Messerschmitt, Hobart Avenue, 1959.
Source: Burton family collection.

The component parts of the cars arrived in large wooden packing cases. John set up a workshop at the back of the shops where he assembled the vehicles. The process was not unlike the modern IKEA model. Boxes were opened and bits and pieces were fitted according to instructions. It required a smaller person, like me at age 13, to help with aspects of their assembly. On occasion, I would squeeze into a car to access the engine from inside and push through nuts and bolts to be screwed in the engine from the outside by John or his helper. The car was small enough to be displayed in the bookshop window. The first car sold on 10 January 1959. John gave Meredith a Messerschmitt to drive to university. She attracted more attention from male students than she wanted. Once, she emerged from a lecture to find her car missing. It had been hidden in bushes. Another time, boys took it to a campus theatre and lifted it onto the stage.

John kept juggling various balls, having too many in the air at any one time. He managed to control some, but others got away. In 1959, in partnership with Sir Mark Oliphant and Sir John Crawford, John applied for a licence to run a local television station. Their application caused a stir. The leader of the Democratic Labor Party, Senator George Cole, concerned about left-wing control over television when it was introduced in Canberra, asked questions in parliament about the three men's bid for their company to obtain a Canberra television licence.[6] The 'Burton team' was unsuccessful.

By 1960, however, John was finding it more and more difficult to cope. The licence hearings drew out to the middle of 1960 and John relied on Sabne and others to keep his business running. Sometimes he would have to drive a Messerschmitt to Sydney to deliver to a buyer. On many occasions, if a bus driver fell ill, John had to drive the Snowy bus and spend days at a time away from home. At one time, he had to run the bus on alternative weeks because of a driver's illness. At the same time, John continued to command media attention with his outspoken views. He made trips to Sydney and Melbourne to give talks or lectures. A television interview he had in Sydney on 8 May 1960 was headlined in a news article the next day, '"Party system outmoded" says Dr Burton'.[7] It reported John's view that the failure of the two-party system arose out of our democratic electoral system. His reasoning was that, in catering for a majority of voters, it often ignored the needs of minorities.

---

6   'Question Asked in Senate on Canberra TV', *Canberra Times*, 4 September 1959.
7   *Canberra Times*, 9 May 1960, 3.

Eventually, in June 1962, the owners of the large bookstore of Angus and Robertson Ltd took over the Green Square shop and Sabne as its store manager. For a time, it continued the services provided by the mobile unit to visit schools and libraries and communities in the Snowy region.[8] In the meantime, a lot had been happening in John's and Cecily's lives on both the shop and home fronts.

---

8   *Canberra Times*, 15 June 1962.

29

A family in crisis

On 17 January 1959, with temperatures hovering in the 90s (mid to high 30ºC), Cecily, John, Clare and I went to meet Meredith at the Queanbeyan railway station, across the ACT border. She was returning to Canberra from a week-long Student Christian Movement conference at Geelong in Victoria. For all the world, my 17-year-old sister in her pretty summer frock looked a million dollars and very happy. Meredith had obtained a teacher's scholarship to attend university. Following our father's footsteps, she had commenced an economics degree in 1958 at Canberra University College, later The Australian National University (ANU). Meredith was a year younger at school than those in her cohort because she had been progressed after a parent–teacher miscommunication. Being young for her grades as she progressed through school saw her commence university at age 16. Fearing failure, she studied hard in her first year and it took its toll. She worried about her exam results and felt certain she had failed. In early January 1959, when our family was holidaying at a friend's house in Seaforth, Sydney, anxious Meredith took up smoking. Then, her results arrived; she had done extraordinarily well. A relieved and happy Meredith left us in Seaforth to travel to Geelong to attend her conference.

On greeting her at the train station a week or so later, she was on a high – but too high as it transpired. She told us that she had had a wonderful time. She had met a young man, went late to bed, rose early, and had very little sleep. 'Max', her newly acquired boyfriend, was a history tutor and, she told us, he was coming to visit to meet the family. It was clear from her talk and demeanour that Meredith was not her usual self. Two days later Max arrived. He was pleasant and clearly fond of Meredith. However,

Meredith was manic and quite unwell. Max was asked to leave. Meredith later wrote to him and, perhaps because he had been frightened or hurt by the experience, he did not reply.

It seemed that Meredith was suffering bouts of psychosis that accompanied her manic behaviour. She needed medical attention. John was quick to act and contacted Cecily's sister Eleanor in Sydney. She and her husband, Frank Hughes, were general practitioners in Sydney and immediately arranged for Meredith to be admitted into Broughton Hall, a residential psychiatric hospital. By this time, Meredith believed she was Rita Hayworth. Accordingly, she acted and behaved impeccably when Cecily escorted her by plane to Sydney on 23 January. Meredith wore a blue-and-white polka dot cotton dress, which had a harem hem line that created a flounced skirt, and matching blue suede shoes. Her shiny brown hair was fashioned in pageboy style and she looked the part. Broughton Hall sat in large parkland grounds and offered a variety of recreational and therapeutic activities. The environment was calming and well resourced. We wonder now if Meredith's illness resonated with Cecily, she having endured a psychotic event some years earlier. While John had not appreciated that Cecily had been on the precipice of serious mental illness, he had quickly recognised that Meredith was ill. He wanted her to have the best attention available.

Cecily visited Meredith the following weekend, John visited the next and so it went on. They reported Meredith's ups and downs. If neither could make it one weekend, one of John's or Cecily's sisters visited Meredith. Fortunately, Clare and I were busy with school and other activities. I had swimming training most nights, I played netball, squash and tennis and attended art and music lessons. I also spent a lot of time with my school friends. We took ourselves to the movies and rode our bikes or caught buses to the Olympic swimming pool on the north side of town. At home, we had finches and canaries in a large outdoor birdcage to care for and goldfish in a tank inside. I also had Bimbo to confide in, my loyal doggie friend, his legs too long to allow him to be called a dachshund. He followed along behind my bike wherever I went and sometimes came to school. Helpful to me, during these troubled family times, was talking to myself by writing in my page-to-a-day diary.

John and Cecily, anxious about Meredith, paid attention to Clare and me as best they could. Each had different parenting styles and priorities. John was a good father in the sense of being the family provider. He placed high

29. A FAMILY IN CRISIS

priority on providing for our health care and education. Cecily was more concerned with our emotional wellbeing and security. They combined their strengths and worked together in Meredith's interest. At the end of February, the whole family travelled to Sydney to see Meredith and spend a few days with her at the Hughes's beach house. We came home without Meredith, however, who returned to her institutional care. A month later, Cecily brought Meredith home, ending her nine-week stay at Broughton Hall. She was happy to be home; appropriately happy, this time. The following Friday, Good Friday, the family and a friend of Meredith's and mine, drove to the Cotter for a picnic and a swim. The next day we had a drive to our old farm at Weetangera. Life returned to a semblance of normalcy. Unfortunately, the drug Meredith had been treated with to bring her mania down left her with an ongoing depression. For six months she was able only to resume her studies at University College on a part-time basis. It was then that Meredith's fellow students had their mischievous fun with the Messerschmitt she drove to and from the university. Despite her obstacles, Meredith's university results in 1958 and 1959 led to an offer of a place in the honours course at the University of Melbourne.

Meredith's crisis was over, but problems for the family generally were not. Cecily and John's marriage struggled to survive and Clare and I were not easy to manage at home. We were demanding teenagers concerned more with our own lives than that of our parents. There was constant discord at home. Clare had become 'too friendly', from John's point of view, with the young man next door. Had John known, then, what lay ahead for her in terms of having a relationship with Max Campion, he might have welcomed rather than opposed her taking an interest in someone younger. Arno was one of two young German men boarding next door in the same digs Sabne had stayed in. He was about 22, good looking, respectful and resourceful. John did not like his interest in Clare, however, and would not allow Arno in the house. Cecily stood up to John and confronted him. She saw it important that we brought our friends to the house.

I caused John concern by disappearing on summer evenings to attend swimming training at the Manuka Pool and, more often than not, I was not home in time to join the family for the evening meal. John knew a little about my swimming coach, a Hungarian refugee, but not enough to entrust his daughter to his care. As it transpired, there was good reason in this particular case, not that John could have known at the time. The coach was later investigated, convicted and gaoled for sexually abusing young girls. Despite John's support of many immigrants in their efforts to obtain work and settle in Australia and the advice he gave Arno and his friend about employment and investment opportunities, he displayed emotional irrationality when it came to these 'new Australians' getting close to his daughters.

We girls argued against his insistence on reviewing films we wanted to see. He assumed the right to 'veto' (his word, which we had first heard him use when discussing the 'power of veto' of members of the UN Security Council) any film he thought unsuitable. Meredith recalls that he 'vetoed' American films; anything American was suspect. He set curfews for when we must be home. He collected Meredith from dances or parties at 10 pm, when the function was in full swing. He waited up for her if she went out on a date and stood on the inside of the front door, she believes, to check up on whether her beau gave her a kiss goodnight. Perhaps it was his Methodist Protestant ethics that drove his need to restrict or control our activities or, more likely, it was knowing what he had been like as a young man. Cecily trusted our judgement implicitly and opposed John's restrictions. Family arguments broke out.

On the evening of 28 December 1959, John did not come home. The next morning, I rang him. He said, 'If you want to see me you will have to come to the shop.' I did not go there; instead, I cycled to the Manuka Pool with my best friend, swam, came home and made myself lunch and waited. John did not come home for dinner that evening either. We did not know why or what was happening. Cecily would later suggest that, with her becoming more self-assured and us fast growing up, John felt that he was losing control over the family; he had no sheep to round up and he could not keep control of his household. John stayed away. The arguments over Clare and me became 'the reasons' for him leaving home. Sabne was not mentioned. He slept at the bookshop, he said. If he spent nights with Sabne at her flat he did not say so. John's father, Jack, who had been staying with us, had left Canberra earlier that month, so explaining away John's absence was avoided.

New Year's Eve approached. A party at our place had been arranged. John delivered a note to Cecily to say that he would come home for it to avoid embarrassing her but that he would return to the shop afterwards. Cecily made the arrangements and allowed us to invite our friends. Arno came in from next door as part of the group of others in that household. Cecily's and John's university and family friends rolled in. We had loud music, there was dancing and kissing at midnight. We presented as a united family.

29. A FAMILY IN CRISIS

But for Cecily, putting on a brave show, it must have been a terrible strain. However, her resilience was calming for us and, while her mind must have been in turmoil, tensions in the house dissipated.

A day or so later, Cecily took us to visit John at the Green Square shop. He offered to take us to dinner at a Chinese restaurant in nearby Queanbeyan. If we expected a family discussion that would resolve everything, it did not happen. Nothing 'domestic' was discussed. Then, on the drive home, Clare, who could not stand the tension anymore, raised her issues with John: about him, Arno, everything, so far as my scrawled childish handwritten diary reveals. Emotional outbursts filled the car, tears and loud voices, but no resolutions nor constructive talks. It seemed that John was trying to establish 'the norm' that he and Cecily had separated. We girls did not understand that, believing that all would soon be resolved and John would come home. Clare followed up with a letter to John telling him just what she thought. He responded by noting comments on it and returning the annotated letter to her. It further fuelled her emotions, and the whole family was miserable.

Cecily kept the show on the road. In January 1960, she arranged a family holiday at the beach without John. He continued to live at the shop from where he travelled to the Snowy to keep the bus business running and to Sydney as his activities required. Cecily assured him that he was welcome to join the family at any time. He turned up at the beach for a day and, as a surprise for me, brought one of my school friends with him to stay with us for the week. John, however, returned to Canberra.

Another dispute was brewing. Clare had just completed her school leaving certificate and had done well in her matriculation. She had her heart set on being a preschool teacher. Both Cecily and John wanted her to go to university. Arguments broke out and she felt alienated as John and Cecily joined sides against her on this one. School was back for me; Meredith was preparing herself for her first university year in Melbourne; Clare's direction was in limbo. It was difficult for all of us, as rumours circulated about our parents' separation and neighbours and friends tried to intervene and attribute blame. My schoolfriends grilled me, one having seen John buying himself a new shirt from J.B. Youngs' clothing store in Kingston. Men did not do their own shopping in those days, and so, was he not living at home? Couples with children rarely divorced then either, and separation was only a step away. Canberra was a small town and our family had attracted a lot of publicity over the previous decade or so.

Gossip was to be expected. The parents of one of my friends shied away from allowing their daughter to spend time with us; yet this was a time when I needed my friends around me.

Marriage counselling was not then in vogue, although John was taken with the concept when he heard about it in New York some years later, and Cecily would train to become a counsellor in a later career move. However, in early 1960 when the family was struggling to deal with this domestic crisis, Cecily called on the family accountant, Bruce Owens, to try and fix things. She asked him, 'What do we do about this?'[1] On Wednesday 27 January 1960, Owens came to our home and talked at length to each of us and to John in particular. He tried to talk all of us into seeing sense; a mediation of a kind, but John was more or less hoping that we, not he, might be brought to order. We were up until 11 pm. I wrote in my diary, 'He helped us a lot'. Why the accountant? Poor Owens must have felt out of his depth. However, John by now had large debts from his capital investments and there were huge financial implications if a marital separation were to occur. Owens felt uncomfortable taking on this unofficial role, as I later learned from his son when we were both older. Taking John's concerns on board, Owens talked to Clare about her future and to me about my swimming activities and asked all of us to make compromises. We were three strong-minded children and John remained stubbornly uncommunicative. Cecily, always reasonable, firmly maintained her ground.

It was a confusing time for a 13-year-old. I wrote in my diary, 'I have been sad lately', listing 'Dad's upset' as the first reason, my girlfriend not talking to me, and boyfriend troubles as others. Then, with Owens's help, Clare, Cecily and John struck a deal. Clare was to complete one year at university and then, after that, if she wanted to leave and attend teachers' college, she could. Owens warned John that he could not carry on like this indefinitely and, if he did not go home, it would be the end of the marriage. Owens did his best to facilitate John's homecoming and family mattered to John. In any event, grandfather Jack was due to return in April; another reason for John to return home and be amicable.

On 9 February 1960, John came home – with conditions. Clare had to respect his wishes about Arno and I had to be at home for dinner! I wanted my dad to come home more than anything, but at the expense of

---

1   Parker, interview by Meredith Wilson, 2004, 58.

29. A FAMILY IN CRISIS

my swimming training? I wasn't happy about this demand. John slept the night at home. 'Damn him!' I wrote in my diary. 'So I will go to training after tea sometimes … I'm all in a muddle and not feeling very happy. The girls at school haven't been very nice (talking about me).'

Cecily managed to work out a roster for me around John's meal hour requirements so that I could attend training either before or after dinner – ('to suit dad'). On the first occasion that John became aware that I was off to training after dinner, he drove me to the pool. 'I don't know why,' I wrote in my diary. I now suspect he wanted to check out 'the Doctor', my Hungarian swimming coach. In general, he started to involve himself much more in my life and activities. On one occasion, he invited the coach home to our place with others in the squad for some food, singing and fun. It was his way of getting to know who I was mixing with and, important to him, regaining some control.

30

A love triangle

Cecily and John tried to keep up the appearance of a united marriage and family throughout 1960. Fortunately, our home was very much an open house. People called in unannounced and our friends freely came and went, which kept ASIO busy.[1] Sabne visited, as did other bookshop staff, neighbours, our parents' friends and their children. Nugget Coombs, who knew about our family troubles, visited too. He would sit cross-legged in a wide chair – his short legs making it possible – and, holding a glass of red wine, he would tell us stories in a strong deep voice that defied his small stature. An ongoing social trait of our family was that John and Cecily, having befriended people, did not abandon them. This would play out well in decades to come, as Cecily and John kept in touch with people with whom they had engaged in the past, including former boyfriends or husbands of us three children. Inwardly, our family was not always cohesive, but we seemed to provide a family haven for many others.

Cecily had obtained work in 1960 with ANU as a research assistant in the Department of Demography, working on a study of British migrants, which she enjoyed. Her path crossed with Robert Parker's at the university. They saw each other at collegiate morning teas and, it would seem, she started to talk with him in an open and personal way about John. In April 1960, Parker left with his wife Nancy for a period of study leave in the UK. Cecily reported on John in a letter to the Parkers: 'It is quite amazing – John has started getting breakfast and washing up, which he never did

---

[1] Meredith's former boyfriend, Barry, was a steady visitor, by reason of which both he and his family attracted ASIO's attention: NAA: A6119, 337, Burton vol. 6, 270, memo of 28 January 1960 with attached report on investigations into Barry's family background.

while I was working for him! Men are very hard to understand!' She told them that Clare and John were getting on better too and that 'altogether the household is pretty equable and relaxed'.²

Clare had been distraught because Arno had returned to Germany. She acquired a nervous 'jumping' habit, and it had become noticeably worse. Then, she received a letter from Arno and the spirits of the whole house lightened. She must have been home from Sydney during the university holidays as, by this time, she was enjoying university, finding that she was a natural student, excelling in English, history and psychology. Her 'jumps' though, developed into a nervous tic that refused to go away. Meredith's doctors supported her move out of Canberra and away from her parents to Melbourne where she might have 'a social' life. In 1960, Meredith transferred to the University of Melbourne and resided in University Women's College. John made a point of visiting her there from time to time. Coombs included Meredith in a meal with her college head, Myra Roper, in May 1960. In a letter in reply to Meredith's thank you note, he expressed his pleasure that Meredith's move to Melbourne provided an opportunity for her and her father to know one another better. He wrote, 'I can assure you it is worth while – he is a fine man'.³

Throughout 1960, I was throwing myself wholeheartedly into everything that came my way, having no more than an occasional quarrel with my father over my swimming. He smacked me on my leg with a ruler once, a rare action for him. I had grazed that leg earlier in the day having fallen down a stone wall at school and the ruler stung. We did not talk to each other for several days. Cecily did not intervene. She did not attempt to 'fix' everyone's relationships in the household. It was important that John worked out his own relationships with each of us and clearly, she believed, I could hold my own. She said of me in a letter to Parker: 'John doesn't stand a chance any more if she and I really want something – he does his best to talk her out of things, but doesn't succeed.'⁴ I managed to work out my relationship with John by working around him. When he was away on the Snowy bus run, I resumed my swimming. When he returned, I engaged with him. We played squash at the nearby courts, chess at home, and on one occasion he took me to what today we might call a 'chick flick'. 'He must be getting soft,' I wrote in my diary. He was

---

2   R. S. Parker papers, NLA, MS 8200, box 46, file 189, 6 April 1960.
3   Nugget to Meredith, 20 April 1960, Cecily family file.
4   R. S. Parker papers, NLA, MS 8200, box 46, file 189, 6 April 1960.

30. A LOVE TRIANGLE

trying harder to please us, and Cecily and I enjoyed him bringing each of us breakfast in bed on Sundays. Cecily told Parker that 'there really is a change in the place' and that John was 'much happier too'.[5]

My diary would suggest that family life more or less resumed. But, in truth, the household limped along. John must still have been seeing Sabne. He was frequently late home and away a lot, often at the Snowy for a week at a time because of the driver's illness. I wrote in my diary: 'he is never home'. Cecily must have sensed something was wrong because she told the Parkers in another letter to them in April 1960 that she wished she could take over in the Kingston shop for John: 'but it's all I can do to get Sabne to talk to me – so even if I were free it wouldn't work out'.[6]

In June 1960, she wrote to Parker telling him about her work and learning of the life histories and expectations of British migrants. She said, 'I wish you were here to have morning tea with.' She went on:

> I just thought I'd like you to know about Burton developments – because if you came back and found us the happiest couple in Canberra, or else separated and/or divorced you would wonder how it all came about.
>
> Well, not long ago I was all for up and going – I waited till all the kids were around and turned on a wonderful scene and meant every word of it for quite a few days. However, I quite simply couldn't. The facts of the matter are that John _believes_ he hasn't loved me for years and years, and not only that but he _believes_ he can only love me if I conform to his requirements. I say 'Here I stand, I can do no other', and until you think I am OK I am your wife in name only, or words to that effect, and I am staking my future on the fact that he has enough goodness and common sense to think I am worth having as I am – I hope I don't have to wait too long, because I don't like being celibate one bit. He is an idiot you know! Any way there is a good deal less reserve and more spontaneity around the house now, and the kids seem to think better of me rather than worse, all the dragons have now popped up their heads, so we don't need to expect any more! I have joined Meredith's gallery of family portraits (which formerly consisted of one – John) and I take this to be a very good sign. It's strange how things come about. Just because we think things are too awful to face they torture us – if we are prepared to put our heads on the block, fully expecting to be beheaded, nothing happens.

---

5   R. S. Parker papers, NLA, MS 8200, box 46, file 189, 6 April 1960.
6   R. S. Parker papers, NLA, MS 8200, box 46, file 189, 6 April 1960.

> I'd like you to show this letter to Nancy – mine to her is full of waffle, so I don't want you to read that if you don't mind – I write sometimes just to straighten myself out, and the letters probably deserve to be burnt immediately.
>
> Looking forward to your return,
> Cecily.[7]

My diary captured signs of a domestic breakdown three weeks earlier. On 25 May 1960, I wrote: 'Dad has told mum that for 10 years he hasn't really loved her, and he only lived with her because of us.' The following day, I wrote, 'Don't know what is going to happen about dad. Hope he won't leave the house, but it is torture for mum to have to live with him knowing this.' Then, my diary reveals, in the manner a 13-year-old might note such an event, that on Monday evening 30 May 1960:

> I got involved with a 'family discussion' about Mum and Dad. Mum says we might have to move. She can't bear living with someone who doesn't love her – dad.

John went to the Snowy the next day. Someone must have placated me, because my entry for 1 June read: 'We aren't going to move at all (hoorah!) Mum is feeling happier'.

John wanted to hold on to Cecily as his companion and wife. Cecily, deeply introspective, kept looking back, questioning what went wrong with their relationship in order to try and fix it. She knew she was unhappy living with John but did not understand what the problem was or what to do about it. How Cecily had felt about her marriage is gleaned from a fictional conversation she later wrote in 1964:

> 'This is not what I call a marriage', she articulated. She felt in despair, wondering how to make a marriage out of something that was not a marriage. 'Let us talk about it', she said to him.
>
> 'What is there to talk about?' he replied. 'I can't see anything wrong. You are a good wife to me, I have no complaints.'
>
> 'But I have,' she said. 'And that's just it; you never seem to feel there's anything to talk about, whether it's us, or anything else.'[8]

---

7   R. S. Parker papers, NLA, MS 8200, box 46, file 189, 18 June 1960, original emphasis.
8   Cecily's 'Free writing', 2000, Cecily family file.

Cecily tried to get John to understand her needs, but he did not. She wanted him to express his love for her, give her affection and understanding, as part of the lovemaking act. She knew it puzzled him that doing things for her, giving her things, was not demonstration enough that he loved her. She wanted him to take a real interest in her and to listen to her when she spoke about difficulties she perceived she had, but he did not seem interested. She felt let down. She asked rhetorically: was it only John, or were all men content with their relationships so long as they had wonderful sex?[9]

Looking back, doing it differently, she reflected that she would not marry anyone who was not interested in her as an individual. She believed that she was one of those people who simply wanted something different and she developed an interest in understanding more about human nature, knowing that she was not alone in how she felt. She considered there were men that she might get on with very well and even love, but whom she would not have married. It would have been 'too easy'. When a few years later she took an interest in relationship counselling, her desire to understand how others felt jogged her out of over-thinking her own situation to a degree. By then, however, she had fallen in love with John's best friend. Parker picked up on Cecily's concerns about her marriage and, in June 1960, he wrote an intimate letter to Cecily and John. Noting that the television licence inquiry – in which John, Crawford and Oliphant were involved – was dragging on, led him to talk about John's 'causes'. He started with the proposition to John that 'you are not an organisation man' and followed it with the barbed remark, 'You don't even like marital organisation – if it is democratic'. Parker asked John and Cecily if they had read Simone de Beauvoir's *The Second Sex*, 'the most elaborate attack on the institution of marriage I know of'. He elaborated:

> She's fighting to free women from the shackles of that man-made institution. Hence paradox: Cecily, for whom she's fighting, will dislike her for cutting the ground from under her feet; John, who is lampooned as the domineering male, may have a sneaking sympathy for the book. He may like it if only because it superbly insists on citing only one side of the evidence, and so makes out

---

9   The interpretations of how Cecily felt and thought arise from Cecily's private writings, journals and jottings, and conversations with us as adults. We have done our best to faithfully reflect her words and expressed feelings.

a formidable case by ignoring all qualifications and contrary indications to its thesis. Still, it does contain a devastating number of home-truths, deployed with a knife-edged intelligence.[10]

Parker was frank about his own situation. He thought there was truth in de Beauvoir's thesis that any kind of 'love' between the sexes cannot last for more than a few months or years, though he thought the timeline somewhat pessimistic. The breakdown of warmth or ease commonly occurs after 10 or 15 years; although, he suggested, children provide a very practical reason for preserving the institution. 'To be honest, that's the line I've acted on, and must probably now abide by, but if pressed I couldn't for the life of me say whether it's been worthwhile,' he confided.

Was there a subtext about his developing feelings for Cecily? Was this the beginning of a John, Cecily and Robert love triangle? Robert, as it is appropriate to refer to him from this point of our story, seemed to be displaying acceptance, if reluctantly, of people leaving a marriage relationship. Both Cecily's and Robert's letters seemed to reflect their own and each other's human need for sex, love, warmth and ease in a relationship. Robert expanded on his thoughts and concluded:

> This must sound incomprehensible. It shows I must have been thinking about you both (whom, God knows, I love) but probably has no particular relevance to the present time. I hope you are discovering what's best for each other because it's impossible to find what's best for oneself.[11]

John did not respond to Robert on an emotional level but, in a letter of 18 October 1960, he suggested Robert meet up with him in the USA in the course of his return travels from the Moscow Pugwash Conference in December. Was Robert interested in meeting up with him? Having in mind a book he had been working on, John wrote:

> Have finished a first draft of a great work, and plan to take copies with me so as to get comments … I have written a lot of bull; but when I read what others have written I think it is not so bad …

> Do you know what I would love most of all in life at the moment? To pick you up on way through – dump the family, (sorry Nancy). What are your plans? At least let me know where you will be about 7 December.[12]

---

10   R. S. Parker papers, NLA, MS 8200, box 46, file 189, 27 July 1960.
11   R. S. Parker papers, NLA, MS 8200, box 46, file 189, 27 July 1960.
12   R. S. Parker papers, NLA, MS 8200, box 46, file 189, 18 October 1960.

30. A LOVE TRIANGLE

Robert replied on 25 October 1960, that 'Nancy wants me to take desperate measures to comply with it …', but, he explained, 'finances did not permit'. John was palpably disappointed. 'A great pity,' he wrote on 9 November 1960, and, not leaving it there, suggested many ways that Robert might raise money to manage, or even accept a loan from John.[13] The plan did not eventuate.

The 'great work' that John referred to and the invitation he had received to attend the sixth Pugwash Conference, planned for 27 November until 5 December 1960, need to be elaborated on because, combined, they led him to find his place in academia. John had been searching for a job at a university where he could write and earn a living. As fate would have it, a month or so earlier, George Wheen had dared to invite John, his atheist friend, to give a talk at a church service. John accepted and it had proved fortuitous. Someone in the congregation approached him afterwards with an offer that John 'do a spell' at ANU. In September 1960, John joined the university's International Affairs Department on a six-month visiting fellowship to write a paper on 'Conditions for agreement by negotiating in current world politics'. John relished the idea of being paid to write about foreign policy. While at ANU, he was able to complete the work he had bragged to Robert about: *Peace Theory: Preconditions of Disarmament*, published in January 1962.[14] However, he did not enter academia without causing further controversy. It started within a month of him taking up the fellowship.

John's invitation to attend the Pugwash Conference came by way of a letter from Bertrand Russell, a noted British philosopher, logician, essayist and social critic. Russell's letter attached a draft program and explained:

> The subject of the conference will be 'Disarmament and World Security', and we hope to discuss the political, economic, technical and military aspects of these problems … From experience at previous Pugwash Conferences we know that these informal meetings of scientists can make a significant contribution towards solving the problems of the day. Recent events emphasize the instability of the present situation and the need for increased effort to improve goodwill between nations. It is clear that meetings of scientists, of the Pugwash type, have become more necessary than

---

13 R. S. Parker papers, NLA, MS 8200, box 46, file 189, 9 November 1960.
14 John's theory was that conditions of peace must be agreed before disarmament can be effected. Burton, interview by John Clements, 1981.

ever. We hope that the discussion at the Moscow Conference, on the various aspects of disarmament and the methods of setting up and implementing a world security system, will not only help to create a favourable climate of opinion, but will make some practical contributions.[15]

John sought leave from his department to attend. News of him going to the conference in Moscow while working at ANU caused alarm. He was granted leave, but without pay, to attend the conference. John was not impressed, as he indicated to his friend Robert, who by this time was a reader in public administration at ANU.[16] Writing to Robert, John said:

> This great institution cannot cope with people like me. A special meeting of heads of schools decided that I could not go to Pugwash while on the pay of the ANU in case I said something they did not like. Hence leave without pay! As I am paying my own fare in any event … you can imagine I do not love your colleagues. However, just to nark them I went out and bought a new car. I do not have the affection you have for this place. I hate [the] people. The tops are such weak non-selfless types (including the new Vice) who all play politics instead of doing a job. Maybe I expect too much. I like working with missionaries.[17]

The press enjoyed the story; 'Moscow trip for Burton' and 'Burton off to Moscow', headlined news that noted that the granting of leave from ANU caused 'a stir in Government circles'.[18]

Before John left Australia, he presumptuously sent Russell a work he had completed on 'Areas of Agreement' for the conference.[19] On 21 November, John travelled to Moscow where he met up with British, American and Russian intellects. Up to this time, the conference had been confined almost exclusively to scientists representing Western and Communist

---

15   Letter 7 October 1960, written from Merioneth, Wales, Burton family file.
16   Parker had from 1939 to 1945 been a lecturer in public administration at Victoria University College, Wellington, NZ, before returning to Canberra University College as a lecturer in political science (where he had worked in 1938). From 1947 he was a social science research fellow at ANU and from 1949, he headed the School of Political Science and Public Administration at Victoria University College. In 1954 he returned to ANU as reader in the Department of Political Science, Research School of Social Sciences. He later became professor of political science in 1963 and retired in 1978.
17   John to Robert, 9 November 1960, R. S. Parker papers, NLA, MS 8200, box 46, file 189, 'General correspondence Burton John W, 1938–88'.
18   *Telegraph*, 8 November 1960, and *Sun*, 9 November 1960, John W. Burton papers, NLA, MS 8405, box 4, folder 18, Newspaper clippings, 1947–91.
19   Letter 9 November 1960, acknowledged by Russell in letter 2 December 1960, Burton family file.

bloc countries. Sir Mark Oliphant, physicist and director of postgraduate research, School of Physical Sciences at ANU, had represented Australia at the first conference, which took place in 1957 in Pugwash, Nova Scotia, Canada. On this occasion, invitations had been extended to selected political and social scientists to discuss problems associated with disarmament, and Oliphant had recommended John to Russell.[20] In subsequent years, John would attend other Pugwash conferences in its series on Research on International Peace and Security, in his capacity as a UK social scientist.[21] This proved to be an opening for John to have ongoing influence in international peace initiatives.

John returned to Australia on 21 December 1960. He landed in Sydney, met up with his father, and the two flew back to Canberra for Christmas. He was away on our mother's birthday, 4 December, but browsing through my childhood diaries I was pleased to note that he took care to make an advance purchase of a gift of new sheets and towels. Soon after his return, John and Cecily entertained Oliphant, Manning Clark and Coombs for dinner at our house. They talked about the conference and other aspects of John's trip and also about a forthcoming event of an entirely different kind – as foreshadowed in his letter to the Parkers:

> When you come back you will both be dragged into the Sentimental Bloke being put on by Albert Arlen Productions at the Albert Hall. Lots of drop painting. Lots of exhibitionism.[22]

And, therein begins the story of our father, John Burton, becoming a patron of the arts.

---

20   Burton explained to the *Canberra Times*, 8 November 1960, 8.
21   Pugwash 9th Conference: Problems of Disarmament and World Security, Cambridge, UK, August 1962; 10th Conference: Scientists and World Affairs, London, UK, September 1962; and 11th Conference: Current Problems of Disarmament and World Security, Dubrovnik, Yugoslavia, September 1963. For a list of participants, see *Pugwash Newsletter* Special Edition, 44, no. 2 (October 2007), 39–155, accessed 10 April 2021, pugwashconferences.files.wordpress.com/2014/05/participants-and-meetings-1957-2007.pdf.
22   R. S. Parker papers, NLA, MS 8200, box 46, file 189, 9 November 1960.

31
Staging musicals: 'The Girl' and 'The Bloke'

John hired Nancy Brown to do the bookkeeping for his Green Square enterprises in 1957. Nancy was a singer, stage performer and playwright, and her husband Albert Arlen, a composer, songwriter, pianist and playwright. Both had enjoyed successful theatrical careers. John and Cecily were regular playgoers at the local repertory theatre where Albert and Nancy performed. There, John and Cecily befriended the happy and likeable couple.

Apart from two picture theatres, there was little to entertain Canberra's growing population in the 1950s. Formed in 1932, the Canberra Repertory Society helped fill a cultural gap in a new town of public servants and intellectuals. It initially staged amateur productions at local radio station 2CA's theatre in Civic and then moved to larger premises at Riverside Hut 18 in Barton. The society thrives today staging shows in its own, larger theatre on the ANU campus in the centre of Canberra. Local productions were enchanting in their camaraderie between audience and performers, many of the players likely to be a teacher, neighbour, colleague or friend of those in the audience. Parker took a lead part in the Repertory's production of Peter Ustinov's *The Love of Four Colonels* in 1957. We knew many of the amateur group of players, many of whom were public servants, academics and diplomats. Nancy and Albert were significant additions to the diverse troupe of keen would-be actors and writers of the 1950s who took part in the Repertory productions.

Albert was a stocky man who gazed at his musical score through thick black-framed glasses. In her memoir, *The Black Sheep of the Brown Family: A Magic Life!*, Nancy said: 'Melody poured out of him in such rich and exotic colours that the minute he sat at a piano to play his own works he became irresistible.'[1] Buxom Nancy piled her thick dark hair high on her head. She had a forceful stage presence and a magical voice that projected throughout any theatre. The couple, known as the Arlens, began a collaboration on a musical version of C. J. Dennis's poems, initially with writer George Johnston and later in 1955 with actor Lloyd Thomson. Excited by their work, they left their jobs in that year to take their first musical manuscript, *The Sentimental Bloke*, to London hoping to have it produced. Their hopes for a theatrical hit were dashed; the British public did not seem to get Australian larrikinism and humour. The pair returned to Australia in 1956 despairing and lacking financial and organisational backing for the show. Albert shelved the manuscript of 'The Bloke' for four years. He resumed a position in the public service and Nancy needed work.

With John's entrepreneurial flair behind Albert's passion and Nancy's fierce determination, *The Sentimental Bloke* was resurrected and eventually became an international stage hit. John proved to be their lucky charm as letters and memoirs boxed in the archival goldmine of the National Library of Australia reveal. 'Little did I know at the time that John Burton would be the shuttle that would launch our rocket!' Nancy wrote. 'He was to earn our undying gratitude and respect.'[2] 'The Bloke' was produced without professional backing on a shoestring budget and relied on loads of community good will and a cast of talented amateurs. It 'world premiered' in Canberra's Albert Hall, thanks largely to John's work and connections. It became Australia's longest running and one of its most successful musicals. How the Arlens' first home-grown musical, *The Girl from the Snowy*, and later 'The Bloke', got on the road and John's role as a patron of the arts is a 1960s Canberra story worth telling.

Nancy described working with John as 'a very salutary experience'.[3] In 1957, John learned from her that Albert's creative urge was resurging. Albert had started to outline a musical set in the Snowy Mountains,

---

1   Nancy Brown Arlen, *The Black Sheep of the Brown Family: A Magic Life!* (Mudjimba Beach, Qld: Pixstories, 2001).
2   Albert Arlen and Nancy Brown papers, NLA, MS Acc06.172. Information for this chapter unless otherwise referenced has been drawn from these papers and from the Albert Arlen and Nancy Brown papers, NLA, MS 6311, box 15, folders 71–73.
3   Brown Arlen, *The Black Sheep of the Brown Family*.

inspired by John's interest in the area from his bus exploits. Albert had decided that if there was a literary Man from the Snowy, there must be a Woman. He wrote a new script, *Girl from the Snowy River*. John saw potential in the work of these talented artists and acted on it. On 14 November 1959, Albert 'timidly' put a proposal to the Repertory Society to stage '*Girl from The Snowy River*, a musical romance'. The board, mostly academics, was somewhat scathing about musicals and took some persuading. Nancy was disappointed about the board's 'anti-musical' attitude and its suggestion that it 'would somehow lower the tone'. It was eventually agreed that the musical would be staged the following year. John came to rehearsals, 'intrigued to see how we worked' according to Nancy. Impressed with what he saw, he offered to act as Albert's manager without fee, with a view to using his connections and business nous to get Albert's shows beyond the Repertory and on the road. Through 1960 John put his heart and soul into the project and so, in assisting this creative couple to stage their musicals, he became a patron of the arts. He worked behind the scenes as 'Manager, Albert Arlen Australian Productions', to promote their work to possible backers who saw potential in extending audience reach beyond amateur local productions. He prepared back of the envelope figures on his 'Policy Research' stationery of which he had plenty, his policy consultation business plan having lapsed or been overtaken by his other enterprises.

John's initial aim was to make ends meet on a low-key staging of the show at the Repertory theatre at Riverside. Arlen's papers reveal John's simplistic figuring of the annual cash flow that was needed. Capital of £1,000 had to be borrowed. He calculated that £60 would be required to pay 6 per cent interest. Then there was £750 for the rent, plus electricity, phones and petty cash. The sum of £1,110 or £21 10s a week was needed. On his figuring he had a shortfall of £1 3s 9d. So, he scratched out a way to cover this: 'Biscuits?? – assume clear profit 6 pence per cup'. No. It would take the sale of 430 cups of coffee to pay the weekly expenses. He got rid of the 'coffee lounge approach to success' and wrote a *To Do* list on his Policy Research letterhead. It included registering a business name and having an appropriate letterhead on which to write letters to influential people who might attend the show and support the production. Ambitiously, he listed: 'Another go at *Sentimental Bloke*'. Last but not least on the list was 'etc. etc over a few grogs'.[4]

---

4   Arlen and Brown papers, NLA, MS 6311, box 15, file 72, undated, around December 1959.

The project got moving. John had connections and ideas and he was persuasive, presumably more so when discussions with others took place 'over a few grogs'. On 29 January 1960, the *Canberra Times* announced 'New Musical to Have Premiere at Repertory'. The cast for what became *The Girl from the Snowy* was to include Nancy Brown in the lead role with other local Canberran players. Albert, who produced the play and wrote the song lyrics and music, was to be at the piano.

In March 1960, John registered a business name, Albert Arlen Australia Productions, and new letterhead gave the place of the business as that of Green Square Enterprises, the bookshop's Kingston address. Albert was delighted. He wrote to John on the new letterhead:

> Dear Doc
>
> Can't thank you enough for your interest and enthusiasm about my work. I think the paper's 'beaut' and I feel as if I own 'M.G.M' already. Hope 'the Girl' lives up to all your anticipations. Nancy will give you all the latest on the Firm, coming up to have a 'Dekko'.
>
> Many thanks again
> Sincerely, Albert.[5]

It was time for John to invite special people to the opening of 'The Girl'. The first was Coombs. The Australian Elizabethan Theatre Trust had been set up in September 1954 under the guidance of Coombs as governor of the Commonwealth Bank. The trust's aim was to establish drama, opera and ballet companies nationally. Through Coombs, John had access to others, such as Sir Charles Moses, general manager of the Australian Broadcasting Commission (ABC), and John Pringle, editor of the *Sydney Morning Herald*. He also invited the chairman of the ABC's board, knowing that the board was looking to increase Australian content in television and radio programs. John wrote to stage actor and film star John McCallum and asked him to invite theatre company J. C. Williamson to send representatives to see first-hand the quality of the now renamed production *The Girl from the Snowy*.

Life at home was tense because of our parents' strained relationship, but they were civil and Cecily enjoyed John's new venture. She loved 'real people' like the Arlens and other performers in the troupe. The Arlens

---

5   Arlen and Brown papers, NLA, MS 6311, box 15, file 72, 'Correspondence relating to production of "The Girl from Snowy River" 1959–60', undated.

enriched the lives of all of us. They shared meals with us and on one occasion Cecily accompanied Albert to an art class conducted by Robert Parker's wife, Nancy, at which Albert had agreed to pose for students. Because of Albert, I took up private piano lessons with Bill Hoffman, Canberra's renowned music critic and conductor.

The show opened on 16 March 1960. It was Canberra Repertory's first full-scale musical play. Lady Hudson, wife of Sir William Hudson, was among the audience who expressed enthusiasm for the show. So did Harald Bowden, J. C. Williamson's Sydney representative – that is, of the dominant theatrical agency in Australia. On 18 March the *Canberra Times* declared it 'Top Entertainment', praising the music and strong individual performances. By this time, John had taken over negotiations for Albert. He already had engaged with Coronet Records, which had also sent a representative to see the show. On 18 March, he wrote to the Little Theatre and the Princess Theatre in Melbourne, enclosing copies of the review to pitch the show's success, and in one he declared: 'There is a very good chance of this hitting the Melbourne and Sydney stage, and at least getting to records.'

Ernest Lashmar, from Chappell & Co. Ltd Sydney sheet music company, had attended the show and entered an agreement to publish a selection of lyrics and sheet music of the songs from the musical. Coronet Records later agreed to release a record of the songs. John hoped to interest J. C. Williamson to take up production of the show and informed him of the audience's extraordinary reaction on opening night and that the music was to be published soon. For additional support, he wrote again to Coombs, this time enclosing a copy of the review of the first night of 'The Girl'. He told him of its success with Chappell and Coronet but that he was concerned that J. C. Williamson, although interested, generally only took on tried-and-tested overseas productions. He wrote: 'For these reasons I am very keen you should see it as soon as possible. It is Australian in theme and in authorship and something the Trust might like very much.' He went on to explain:

> J.C. Williamson want 'The Sentimental Bloke', also by Albert Arlen, but I feel they should not be able to pick on one thing and sit on others, and again it is something which the Trust might want to promote. It is ready for production, and while you are here Albert Arlen could tell you more about it.[6]

---

6   Arlen and Brown papers, NLA, MS 6311, box 15, file 72, letter 18 March 1960.

Coombs was about to leave for the USA. However, he had a staff member of the trust office attend the production, who reported on it favourably.[7]

The show ran for seven weeks, breaking previous box office records for the Canberra Repertory Society. The theatre was booked out. Grandfather Jack accompanied John and Cecily to a Sunday showing. People who could not get seats sat in their cars in the parking lot to hear the music. Radio 2CA broadcast it on the night of 21 May 1960. As successful as it was, Albert's royalties of 10 per cent of gross seat sales saw a cheque in his hand of only £112 19s 6d. At least John's calculations saw ends meet and the Repertory Society profited. But he wanted to do more for the Arlens' show. He had another idea. John made an informal approach to the Commonwealth Development Bank to borrow £2,000 to cover the costs of tendering for a Commonwealth bus and fitting it out, in order to take the show to the Snowy and country towns after its run had been completed in Canberra. John told his bank contact of the success of the show, the backing it had received and his vision. The response was encouraging and John formalised his request for a loan by letter of 23 March 1960:

> I have encouraged this idea and am acting as 'manager' to get it off the ground. I have done the same thing with books with an amazing success by taking a mobile through to the Snowy area – people are buying quantities of books and records who previously have never been in a book-shop. I think the reception of live shows if taken to the people would be the same.[8]

The same day he wrote to the manager, Commonwealth Bank Kingston, to seek £2,000 to finance his plan. He told of his proposal to tender for a Commonwealth bus for use as a travelling theatre to perform in country areas with a recruited team of about 10 permanent actors. His vision was to maintain a regular tour of a number of country centres with Canberra as its headquarters. He explained:

> Backing has been offered by publishers and others interested in stage productions; but the firm desires to retain its independence so that this new venture of taking productions to the people in non-metropolitan areas cannot be swamped by any organisation.[9]

---

7 Coombs let John know by letter 12 May 1960. By this time the Reserve Bank of Australia had been created to take over the Commonwealth Bank's central banking functions and Coombs was appointed its governor.
8 Arlen and Brown papers, NLA, MS 6311, box 15, file 72.
9 Arlen and Brown papers, NLA, MS 6311, box 15, file 72, letter 23 March 1960.

Then John got bold. On 11 April, he wrote to Festival Theatre in Pitlochry, Perthshire, Scotland, asking for a copy of the plan of the theatre because, he explained, 'we plan now our own theatre and are attracted by the design of the Festival Theatre'. Then, on 18 May 1960, he wrote to the Premier of New South Wales suggesting that Albert Arlen be asked to write and to produce a musical especially for the occasion of the opening of the Opera House on Sydney's harbour front. As to this, he received a reply on 27 May 1960 stating that his proposal would be given 'careful consideration', but nothing came of the initiative.

Next came the time for John to get 'The Bloke' on the stage. The Repertory Society board had previously procrastinated about staging it, debating the importance of box office takings for a lowbrow musical versus quality drama. When Albert's negotiations had broken down, he accepted another failure with 'The Bloke'. John took up the challenge. He would get the show on the road without the Repertory's support. Soon after the successful run of 'The Girl' ended, as Nancy told it:

> John Burton did an amazing thing. He came to my desk in his Green Square Book shop and placed before me a Commonwealth Bank book in the name of Albert Arlen Australian Productions with a credit of one hundred pounds saying 'I am now going to ring up Kent Hughes and book the Albert Hall for a year hence. … You have got to produce *The Sentimental Bloke*, and this will give it a start'.[10]

Nancy picked up the passbook, looked John in the eye and said she accepted it, 'but only as a loan'.[11]

On 16 June 1960, John wrote to the Commonwealth's ACT Services Branch and requested a booking of the Albert Hall in the new year. On 29 June he received a reply informing him that 7 to 11 March inclusive had been allocated for the production of *The Sentimental Bloke*. The Arlens' world changed. Albert resurrected his music and Nancy and Lloyd Thomson finalised the lyrics, written to C. J. Dennis's *The Songs of a Sentimental Bloke*. Nancy started to assemble an amateur cast, created and played the role of Rose, and produced the play. Albert was musical

---

10   Brown Arlen, *The Black Sheep of the Brown Family*.
11   Arlen and Brown papers, NLA, MS 6311, box 15, file 73, addition 6/12/99, 'The sentimental Bloke Musical Play', compiled from the diaries of Albert Arlen, by Nancy Brown. The memoir tells the history of getting the shows on stage. See also MS 6311, 'Draft of Arlen's contribution to "The world of the Sentimental Bloke"', 1976.

director and main pianist, and was accompanied by a drummer and percussionist. The Bloke's girl Doreen was played by Constance Vayne, a secretary in the Department of Defence with acting qualifications and experience. Hugh Brophy, also experienced, played Mr Smithers (the Stror-'at-Coot) and the Burton's friend and past farm-help Don Kelly, whose singing in the shower at Weetangera had entranced Cecily, played Charlie Skewes (Man of uncertain occupation). I loved the fact that my school geography teacher, Paul Kelly (no relation to our friend Don), was to play Fred, and to discover that he was a talented dancer. Dark, classically handsome Douglas Skinner played Ginger Mick, the 'Rabbitoh' man.[12] Ginger Mick's wheelbarrow prop was sourced from Queanbeyan, had 100-year-old wheels and was filled with real, stuffed rabbits. The last to be cast was Bill, 'the Bloke'. Blond and good looking, with just the right larrikin smile and experience to play the role was Edwin Ride, a young diplomat who worked in the Department of External Affairs, which John used to head.

The initial £100 John lent the Arlens paid for the printing of tickets and programs. The Arlens arranged a £400 credit through family connections for material from Georges, a Canberra fabric store, for costumes. A breakthrough came. The *Australian Women's Weekly* was persuaded to send a reporter to attend rehearsals, held in an old converted army hut, in the first week of March 1961, just before it opened. It produced a gushing two-page story written by Patricia Kent, 'I dips me Lid', with lavish photos. It gave the show cover-page publicity: '*The Sentimental Bloke... a new Australiana musical*', accompanied by a photograph captioned: 'In all their wedding finery Edwin Ride, our Bill, and Constance Vane, our Doreen!' Kent's article talked about the musical being based on C. J. Dennis's poem and how the 'coves and coots and sheilas who crowd the page of the poems sprang into vivid life'.[13]

Opening night, 7 March and grandfather Jack's birthday, saw a packed house. Our whole family attended. I was aged 14 then and I noted in my diary that I wore my new middy heels. Making the occasion more special was the attendance of the Commonwealth administrator and his wife, Sir Dallas and Lady Brookes, who I knew were intending to entertain a bus load of Telopea Park students including me and 'billets' visiting

---

12   The Rabbitoh was a hawker who captured and skinned rabbits and took them in a barrow to sell the meat at markets, shouting 'rabbit-oh' to attract buyers.
13   *Australian Women's Weekly*, 8 March 1961, cover page and story, 3.

from King Island, over a 'whacko arvo tea' at Government House the coming May. Harold and Zara Holt were also at the opening. Bowden, J. C. Williamson's representative, attended and sent a glowing report to the company's Melbourne directors, Sir Frank Tait and John McCallum, both of whom travelled to Canberra to see it on closing night.

Cover of 'The Bloke' music sheet.
Source: Pamela's piano piece collection.

Cover of 'The Girl' music sheet.
Source: Pamela's piano piece collection.

The box office was sold out on closing night, and Tait and McCallum had to sit in the aisle.[14] It was worth making room for them. McCallum was impressed. He decided that J. C. Williamson would present the musical for a six-week season at the Comedy Theatre in Melbourne.

---

14   Edwin Ride, *I Dips Me Lid: Diplomatic Memories* (Palmwoods, Qld: E. Ride, 1991), 72.

Lashmar also attended on the closing night and Chappells Australia took up the publishing rights of the music lyrics and scores for 'The Bloke', too. John's Green Square shop sold the sheet music, of course.

The success of the production was an occasion to celebrate. Box office takings covered all debts, including the costume fabric and hall hire, and John, in charge of distributing the profits, decided that there was enough left over for each of the players and others involved to receive a small bonus. On Thursday 16 March, John held a party for *The Sentimental Bloke* cast at our Hobart Avenue home. The troupe crowded into our living and dining rooms and danced and sang in a rowdy celebration. The show was on the road.

McCallum urged Edwin Ride to forsake his diplomatic career and take up professional acting. He agonised over the decision, but agreed to do the Melbourne season, with options for renewal if the show was a success.[15] *The Sentimental Bloke* opened on 4 November 1961 at the Comedy Theatre in Melbourne. John and I flew from Canberra to attend one of the performances and Meredith, studying at the time in Melbourne, joined us. It received brilliant reviews and ran for five months in Melbourne. It went on to run for three weeks in Adelaide, a scheduled two weeks in Brisbane was extended to nine weeks, and then it was staged at Sydney's Theatre Royal for four months – over a year in all in Australia. It went to New Zealand for a six-week tour. The play grossed over £250,000 at the box office. It became one of the most successful Australian musicals of the twentieth century.

A special recording of the music made by the ABC was played all over the world, and its 1976 television production won it new nationwide acclaim. The show was turned into a ballet by others and the Australian Ballet first staged it in Australia in 1985 and subsequently on tour in the Soviet Union. Arlen's success in Australia was recognised in 1991 when he was awarded an Order of Australia in recognition of his services to music and the performing arts.

---

15   Ride, *I Dips Me Lid*, 69–70.

32

Turmoil

By January 1961, John realised that he was in trouble; he felt he was losing Cecily. He told her that he really did love her. He tried hard to show it. Cecily was not convinced. She thought that his practical efforts lacked any renewed emotional connection.[1] Our household became tense and turbulent. John did not want to lose our affection, but in a household of teenage girls he found it hard to accept our interest in make-up, fashion and boys, and he made inept and sometimes offensive remarks. He continued to expect more of Meredith than he did of Clare and me. On seeing Meredith wearing a new lipstick once, he said, 'What have you got that scotch tape on for?' He had no sense of the impact of his reproof on her self-esteem.

John felt his loss of control over us. Cecily was more lenient and more trusting of Clare and me. John did not like me going on car trips to country towns for swimming carnivals. Clare had a festering resentment of John and rows broke out in the house with each of us and, when John did not get his way, he just stopped talking to us. At age 14 I wrote in my diary – and not for the first time – words to the effect of 'Dad not talking. Wish the whole family could get on together'.

Cecily was still supportive of John and his work. During the day she helped out at the shop. On occasion she would open up the Kingston shop, and I would go with her before school when I could. In her spare time, Cecily

---

[1] The sources for Cecily's thoughts and feelings in this chapter where not otherwise referenced are a compilation of Cecily's private journals, my diaries, personal communications with Cecily over the years and our own recollections.

worked diligently on John's 'peace theory' manuscript.[2] She stayed up late at night because John had said he had a deadline to meet, though in retrospect she believed it was self-imposed. She would burst her guts to get it done for him. Cecily was a skilled editor, and John's writing expression left a lot to be desired. He made generalisations that she questioned and, after understanding better what he was trying to say, she recast it to better express his ideas. John accepted and used most of the suggestions she made, but he failed to express his appreciation. Rather, he got annoyed at her questioning of the assumptions on which he based his theories, or pointing out leaps in logic and instances of poor expression. She was an excellent copyeditor but, because of her writing skills and her ability to grasp complex issues, she was not prepared to merely edit without critiquing the substance of his work. The published work benefited from her structural and other changes; however, while he formally credited Robert Parker in the book's Acknowledgements, he did not mention Cecily.

With happiness, I noted in my diary on Monday 24 April 1961 that flowers had arrived for Cecily from John to celebrate their wedding anniversary: 'Fabulous – a real big bouquet'. Then again, how disappointed I was on 9 November 1961, Sabne's birthday: 'Dad bought an 11/6 chocolate heart for Sabne, and said it was from me.' He had not yet let go of Sabne.

There was talk about moving to another house. The move was on and then off and then John fell into a no-talking mood – that is, until Cecily agreed to buy the house he had chosen. It was close to where we lived, modern and much larger than the one we had, with a self-contained flat. It had enough bedrooms to allow for John and Cecily to have their own, which ultimately occurred, and separate rooms for Meredith and Clare when they were home from university, one being large enough for them to share in the event that grandfather came to stay. John's choice of home was inexplicable to Cecily; it had more bedrooms and bathrooms than we needed. John wanted a fresh start or he was simply restless. He seemed to think that a new house would win back Cecily's heart. It also had a large undeveloped garden that he could cultivate and grow vegetables in, akin to the 'shovelling shit' on the farm that he found therapeutic for working on ideas in his head. Reverting to form, John bought Cecily a new car and a refrigerator without consulting her about either as to what she might like. He expected her to be overwhelmed and grateful. Instead, she said:

---

2   John's *Peace Theory: Preconditions of Disarmament* was published in 1962 (New York: Alfred A. Knopf).

32. TURMOIL

'Why didn't you ask me about it, what sort [of car or fridge] I would like?' John was hurt. He had not learned from her reaction 10 years earlier when he had presented us all with ponies without prior discussion.

When my parents told me that they had decided to buy a new house after all, I shrugged it off. I told my diary, 'I'm not going to bother to keep up – I don't know what will happen'. Then, on the morning of 12 August 1961, I was asked to clear out all my cupboards before I left for my basketball match because we were moving. Grandfather, who had been staying with us, returned to Sydney that day. I came home after basketball that afternoon to find the house empty; all the furniture had gone and no one was home. Clare was in Sydney and Meredith was in Melbourne, both at university. I found it an eerie experience as a young teen, until one or other of my parents returned to the house to complete the move. There had been so much talk of moving I had simply not wanted to know about it. By nightfall I was in my new room surrounded by my things in our new home at 5 Talbot Street, Forrest.

The new house did not 'fix things' between Cecily and John. Family arguments erupted. Within a few weeks, John, Cecily and I were all quarrelling. One morning Cecily was crying while driving me to school. Tears in front of us were rare, given Cecily's self-control and ability to always put our interests ahead of her own. But Cecily and John's arguments became constant and open. When Clare came home to an unhappy house for the holidays, she became very unhappy. She thought the family did not want her and that she was out of place. She and I argued and, together with Cecily, we were in tears for large parts of many days. Sometimes a family drive at the end of the day would help everyone 'feel better' for a while. Meredith returned home before Christmas too. She was doing well at university despite the interruption to her second year of studies when she had suffered a mental breakdown. It pleased John that she was following his lead, studying and excelling in economics. Accompanied by a flattering photograph two days before Christmas 1960, the *Canberra Times* wrote about '20 year old Meredith Burton' adding 'more lustre to the family record of academic distinction'. By the time she completed her first-class honours degree in 1962, she had been awarded four Exhibitions for first place in her subjects.

During this time, Robert and John maintained their relationship as colleagues. Throughout 1961, John was working on a paper on peace initiatives with Robert, John Crawford, Patrick Fitzgerald and Manning

Clark.[3] It involved him liaising closely with Parker, to whom John left its final drafting. They completed the document by the end of the year. On Christmas Day 1961, John wrote to the *New Statesman* newspaper editor, Norman MacKenzie, requesting it be published. 'It is Christmas Day – so greetings to you and Jeanne and family', he commenced before explaining the genesis of the paper and discussion it contained on the world situation and where it should be heading.[4]

Cecily and John should not have been together at this time. John did not break with Sabne as demonstrated by his gift to her of a chocolate heart, and what intimacies might have been occurring at this time between Cecily and Robert is a matter of speculation. John and Cecily attempted to keep their relationship alive, possibly because I still had another year of high school to complete. While John's father was in the house, everyone was circumspect – except Clare. On New Year's Day 1962, Clare declared that she would not come home until 'mum and dad solved their problems'. I thought that unfair of her. I had had to put up with it the whole time, so why should she not?

Meredith and I have now uncovered letters that tell us that, by June 1962, Robert and Cecily were in love and had become lovers. Robert's small motor vehicle played its part, as uncomfortable as it must have been, given that Robert was 6 feet 2 inches, a foot taller than Cecily! The lovers' letters were written in June and July 1962 when Robert was working in the Territory of Papua and New Guinea on administrative matters concerning the territory's independence. They openly discussed their love, the meaning of their relationship and, significantly, family commitments that prevented them from being together. They explored what they had in common. They were both interested in poetry, philosophy and the works of Goethe. While not poetically prolific like Cecily, she was heartened to learn that Robert had written a poem in 1950, 'Cool Change', to express his feelings. She told him how much she loved and missed him. Yet, it seems that Cecily was not sure whether she did or did not love Robert at this stage. In one letter, she wrote:

> it haunts me that I said to you before you left that I was not in love with you – or words to that effect. I am not even sure that it is true … Never in my life have I had such a beautiful satisfying

---

3 'East–West Conflict – What is the Fight About?', R. S. Parker papers, NLA, MS 8200, box 46, file 189.
4 Copy letter held Burton family file.

and profoundly moving relationship as with you – nor even approaching it. If this is not being in love in the *best* sense of the words, then nothing is.[5]

Robert Parker and Cecily, Canberra, 1966.
Source: Family collection.

---

5   R. S. Parker papers, NLA, MS 8200 Restricted, box 20, file 87, 'Family corr. Burton, Cecily Margaret, 1962'.

Cecily was not the outgoing extrovert as was Robert's creative artist wife, Nancy Parker. Cecily was quieter and appeared to be more acquiescent. However, from the beginning, it seems Cecily needed to analyse and articulate her feelings and have Robert engage in understanding her. She told him about her 'theme of oneness', believing, hoping, that Robert would understand it – and her – at a deep philosophical level:

> I have this passionate urge to save humanity and will not be satisfied until I do something beyond my personal life. I used to think my role was to serve the world through John, and my own work has come about by trying to understand why that did not succeed. Love, intelligence, reason, passionate ideals, self-sacrifice – all the virtues welded together are as nothing when there is a lack of understanding (comprehension not sympathy). It is like trying to work an atomic reactor without an elementary knowledge of physics. We just don't know the principles involved in human relationships.[6]

On a separate piece of paper she wrote a poem:

> You are a tall straight tree my beloved.
> The sun is your love for others,
> The earth is their love for you,
> Your work is the air about you,
> The rain is your rest and sleep.
> I am but the gentle breeze and violent storm.
> To tell you there is more than these.

What did Robert make of Cecily's letters containing her openly expressed doubt about whether she was in love with him accompanied by a mix of intimacy and heavy philosophic content? Wanting Robert to understand her childhood origins of troubled feelings, Cecily reverted to her lifelong fascination with the Hans Christian Andersen story of Kai and Gerda and the 'Ice Queen'. She might have been presumptuous in discussing at this stage how she and Robert might fulfil each other's needs, for Robert replied in practical terms. He aired his concern about putting their love ahead of his own family commitments:

> If you and I were free, or became so honourably (to the others we're now committed to) I would, with your consent, feel it very right to make a new start in any capacity which seemed best – including

---

6   R. S. Parker papers, NLA, MS 8200 Restricted, box 20, file 87, 'Burton, Cecily Margaret, 1962', reply dated 'Thursday' to Robert's letter of 15 June 1962.

taking a different or lower-paid job and living here ... In practice
things may not be quite like this. We have our other commitments
which may continue. I cannot jeopardise the support of my family.
I shall probably have to continue in Canberra.[7]

Only weeks later, in July 1962, Cecily wrote to Robert telling him that she had decided to give John's and her marriage another go – that is, she wanted an end to their affair for the time. Had Robert's response caused Cecily to feel insecure?

At home, I knew John was unhappy. I understood that he was suffering back pain, or so Cecily explained, and my diary notes record that he was having his 'neck stretched again' in mid-June. On 23 June 1962 I noted: 'Dad not good – also mum and he seem to be "discussing" quite a lot.' And discussing they were. Cecily told John about the development of her relationship with Robert. It was then that she confessed to him about her affair with Raju in Ceylon. It brought a strong reaction. He wanted her back, that is, to be with him, 'immediately, completely and unconditionally', he said. Her affair with Raju gave him the high moral ground. Cecily, perhaps now realising that she could not rely on Robert being there for her if she left John, felt that she had no choice but to give the marriage another go. Cecily told Robert: 'If at the end of twelve months or so I feel I can't live with him he will agree to let me go. He is immensely generous.'[8] Nevertheless, Cecily was torn. In the same letter, she told Robert that if he wanted to see her on his return, she would ask John to agree because 'I feel I cannot adjust myself to John's suggestion unless I know how you are'.

This was a lot for Robert to absorb in one letter, but Cecily, having broken off their affair, asked Robert to tell Nancy about them, if possible. 'Perhaps I am hoping it will give her as much understanding as it has given John,' she wrote. Then, she wrote about how wonderful a lover Robert was: 'with you I am at peace: your very urgency delights me'. Confiding further in Robert, Cecily told him that if she found she could live with John, it was because Robert had taught her to tell the truth; 'from you I know what a real relationship can be', she told him. 'I know what I have to do for the next sixteen months. Little by little I have to try to build up a

---

7   R. S. Parker papers, NLA, MS 8200 Restricted, box 20, file 87, 'Burton, Cecily Margaret, 1962', undated, June 'Saturday'.
8   R. S. Parker papers, NLA, MS 8200 Restricted, box 20, file 87, 'Burton, Cecily Margaret, 1962'.

truthful relationship with John.'⁹ Her letters to Robert did not cease. One of several more she wrote to Robert over the next few months was about the necessity of them leading separate lives. In another, she said:

> My relationship with John has become so much more real, though by no means always happy, that I understand I must put aside all thoughts of deciding anything at the end of next year. John is essentially a simple soul and a noble one and I cannot give him anything less than complete loyalty now …[10]

I was now 16 and, knowing nothing about Cecily's developing and then thwarted romance, I noticed that the household became somewhat frenetic. On 29 July, for example, Cecily returned from a trip to Melbourne, probably from visiting Meredith at university there, just as John left for a two-month trip to Indonesia undertaking research for work he was doing at ANU. 'What a household!' was how I summed it up. Cecily ceased her university job to take up a job offer to work as an administrative assistant at the newly formed Australian Institute of Aboriginal Studies. Robert returned to ANU at about the same time, which meant she and Robert would avoid seeing each other at faculty's morning tea gatherings in the building at ANU where John was also now working. Professor Bill Stanner, whom Cecily had known since her undergraduate days, had, she said later, been kind and foolish enough to offer her a job and she had foolishly accepted, which suggests her change of work may have been motivated by her commitment not to see Robert.

In September 1962, I came down with glandular fever and, being confined to bed for several weeks, it had a uniting effect on the family. John and Cecily cooperated in care arrangements and the house came alive with visitors, family friends, as well as my schoolfriends who streamed in and out of the house at any hour. Then, one evening that month, John and Cecily went to dinner at Robert and Nancy's house. John returned without Cecily at around 9:30 pm and I was still awake. He told me that Cecily wanted to stay on because 'she is enjoying herself'. Cecily came home just after midnight. I suppose I worked out, as John would have known, that Robert drove her home, presumably while Nancy did the dishes or had retired to bed. John was, again, on the back foot. We now know

---

9   R. S. Parker papers, NLA, MS 8200 Restricted, box 20, file 87, 'Burton, Cecily Margaret, 1962', undated.
10   R. S. Parker papers, NLA, MS 8200 Restricted, box 20, file 87, 'Burton, Cecily Margaret, 1962', undated.

from letters between Nancy and Robert written in mid-1962 that Nancy acknowledged her marriage to Robert was at an end.[11] Years later, in 1971, Nancy would marry Professor Geoffrey Sawer, whose wife Mamie had died two years earlier, and Nancy would move in to live with him in the Sawer family house, a few houses along in the same street as hers and Robert's family home. The Parkers' two youngest children, Trina and Quentin, attended my school, although they were younger than me and in lower grades. The Sawers' daughter, Elizabeth, was my friend and classmate. The three families knew each other well. Times 'were a changin'', and this form of 'wife and husband' musical chairs became a feature of Canberra's late 1960s and 1970s academic culture. We grew up accepting that the parents of friends of ours could become each other's step-parents!

11 R. S. Parker papers, NLA, MS 8200, file 112, 'Nancy Parker, Part 1'.

33

The breakup

In May 1962, in John's position as visiting fellow in the Research School of Pacific Studies, ANU, the Rockefeller Foundation of New York awarded him a grant to study Asian and African policies of neutralism and non-alignment.[1] The funding covered the cost of his travels in July of that year to Djakarta, Kuala Lumpur, Cairo, Belgrade and the UN headquarters in New York. It was a great opportunity. But *The Bulletin* mocked:

> Dr Burton, who thinks that Australia should not, for example, be aligned with the U. S. in Asia is now in the odd position of accepting American gold – provided by ultra capitalist sources like the Rockefellers – to prove, presumably, just that point.[2]

Others attempted to thwart the grant. Journalist Alan Reid tried again to cause harm to John's career and contacted the American Embassy to complain about John's grant. According to an ASIO report of 22 May 1962, embassy officials said they could do nothing, having no connection with the Rockefeller Foundation.[3] Professor Richard Walker of the University of South Carolina, who had visited Australia the previous year, tried to intervene. In a letter of 30 May 1962 to the Rockefeller Foundation (a copy of which we have obtained), Walker argued: 'Since [Burton] was thrown out of the Foreign Office his public statements hardly qualify him as a scholar, do they?' By letter of 3 August 1962,

---

1 *Canberra Times,* 19 May 1962, 2, and 14 November 1962, 3.
2 'Dr Burton's Neutralism', *Woroni* (ANU student newspaper), 1 June 1962, 1.
3 NAA: A6119, 834, Dr John Wear Burton vol. 7.

the foundation replied making short shrift of Walker's complaint assuring him that Burton's qualifications, references and academic standing had been thoroughly investigated.[4]

The atmosphere in the Research School at ANU was unpleasant. John felt his political and economic philosophy was misunderstood, that he had been unfairly treated in public life and, as a consequence, his work was not adequately acknowledged by his university colleagues. Particularly hostile to John's view was Professor J. D. B. Miller in the Department of International Relations. Richard Krygier, an anti-communist publisher, journalist and founder of *Quadrant* magazine with strong connections to the Committee for Cultural Freedom, wrote that one of Miller's first acts as head of department was 'to terminate the fellowship of Dr John Burton', because he had been head of External Affairs under Evatt. Krygier believed that Miller 'will want to have people who are both good scholars and who are committed to the free world'.[5] Krygier urged that every assistance be given to Miller in this endeavour.

John's work might not have been applauded by his peers at ANU, but what he might contribute to peace theories was not lost on international scholars. In June 1963, at the close of Cecily and John's trial reconciliation period, John was offered a permanent position at University College, London (UCL) as Reader of International Relations. He took up the offer and invited Cecily to come with him. He possibly knew she would not but naively hoped she would. After all, in taking up the appointment he was leaving Sabne too, it being Cecily he wanted to have beside him. Cecily declined. She had been prepared to give their relationship another go but moving overseas was not what she had in mind. John insisted thereafter that it was her decision to leave the marriage.

John seemed genuinely upset that Cecily would not come with him. He did not give up attempts to persuade her. He flew first to the USA and on arriving in New York City he discovered that marriage counselling services were offered there. In a letter to Cecily he said that he was impressed with 'developments in the science of marriage which is now not phoney-stuff'.[6]

---

4   Copies of the correspondence held on Burton family file. Letters sourced from university archives in Canberra and Melbourne indicate that a Rockefeller family member met John and Cecily over dinner at Manning Clark's home, and that archival material confirms that John's proposal – to work on peace in the Asian region and to undertake a study of neutralism in Africa – was successful on its merits.
5   Letter 28 February 1963, Humphrey McQueen, 'Quadrant and the CIA [1977]', chapter 17 in *Gallipoli to Petrov: Arguing with Australian History* (Sydney: Allen & Unwin, 1984), 190.
6   Undated, but received by Cecily on 21 June 1963, Cecily family file. The following correspondence unless otherwise indicated, took place in June 1963 and is held on the Cecily family file.

He talked about people who handle 'people like us' and suggested Cecily might join him seeking the help of professionals. If counselling between them was successful, he confidently said, 'it is not beyond belief' that Bob and Nancy, and Max and Fran could also benefit. In his view, if he and Cecily did not succeed, the others 'have no hope'. He pleaded with her that it was too important for her not to try. Cecily was certain in her reply. She appreciated his feelings but her answer was 'no'. She wrote, 'I have committed myself to you completely and utterly for 25 years, and as that did not work I do not believe anything else will. I have given everything, John, and simply have no more to give …'. John responded with: 'I am sorry to have to say it, but there is no one I love (and hate) but you.'

Changes to all of our lives were rapid. Cecily and I rattled around for a while in the large house. Meredith, living away from home, had difficulty understanding what was happening. In January 1963, she had married Clive Edwards, an economist she had met at university. In May that year, they travelled to Kuala Lumpur, Malaya, where Clive undertook field work for his PhD on Malaya's public finances. In June, Meredith was surprised to receive a letter from John just before he left 'on his great adventures'. In a letter, she asked him whether Cecily and Pam would follow him to London. His reply was unclear.

By July, John's exploration of the possibility of Cecily joining him came to an end, however. Cecily wrote: 'I cannot live with you, I do not want to, and I do not "want to want to." I find living with you painful and degrading and destructive of happiness all around us. So I intend to love you from a distance.'[7] The tone of the exchange deteriorated sharply as recriminations about the past crept in. John's letters took on a harsh, if not cruel, tone. He revisited Cecily's affair with Raju in Ceylon believing in hindsight that she had no longer loved him:

> since Ceylon you have not been a free person within yourself. The hand pats, the looks across the room were always an embarrassment because they were not affection but an inhibited attempt to display it. Your rejection of me, more than rejection but constant attack, after Ceylon was an attempt to lay at my door what you had done and hidden from me.[8]

---

7   Letter 6 July 1963, Cecily family file. The quoted extracts from letters between Cecily and John in this chapter where not referenced are from letters written in 1963 and are held on the Cecily family file.
8   Undated letter, written late July or early August 1963.

He indulged in a blame game. He suggested that, if Cecily had told him about the affair at the time, there would have been less tension between them and that 'Meredith would not have had a break-down; Clare would not be the person she is – and we would have lived a full life … It is you, you cannot live with'.

Cecily dutifully kept John informed of Clare's and my various activities, and John wrote often to each of us. Cecily started to work on bettering her own life. Without John, she had fewer people to feel responsible for. Grandfather Jack, whose primary residence was with us from the time we moved into Talbot Street, returned to John's oldest sister's home in Sydney. But there was Rosalie, a young friend of mine, still boarding with us until the end of the school year. Rosalie's family were farmers in country New South Wales. John invited her parents to send her to us in Canberra, so that she could better her education by going to my school, Telopea Park High. He believed that without good education her life would be relegated to being a farmer's wife, while her brothers would inherit property to farm. I feel sure he was also motivated by wanting to provide me with a young companion who would be a positive moral influence, at a time when my life was in turmoil. Cecily had also taken under her wing a young woman, Billie, who was a friend of Clare's who had some mental health issues. She stayed with us periodically. Then there was Sabne. Distressed at John's departure, Sabne stayed in touch. She had not been well and was hospitalised in August that year. Cecily visited her and cared about what might happen to her too, but, fortunately, had no responsibility for her.

Of importance was 'Doc' Evatt, who we all cared about. Just after John left Australia in mid-1963, Evatt and his wife Mary Alice moved into 10 Hobart Avenue, which had an adjoining back fence to our house. Evatt was ill and frail, and Cecily visited him in order to give John updates on his wellbeing. She braced herself for the pain she expected on her first visit, but she reported: 'His soul is gone but his face looks rather fine.'[9] Evatt had been appointed Chief Justice of the Supreme Court of New South Wales in February 1960 and had retired in 1962 because of ill health. He had visited us in Talbot Street on occasion the previous year.[10] According to Mary Alice, the Evatts' choice of a residence near ours was deliberate; he wanted to be near John for companionship. But John had gone.

---

9   Letter 20 July 1963, Cecily family file.
10 My diary entry of 10 February 1962, 'Dr Evatt came at lunch time (per usual)'.

33. THE BREAKUP

The Evatts' house has its own story. Dr Ralph Reader, founder of the National Heart Foundation of Australia among other achievements, lived there with his family until they moved into our family's much-loved former mansion and farm, 'Melrose Valley' at Tuggeranong. Years later, former deputy prime minister Tim Fischer moved into 10 Hobart Avenue and, in 2002, he told me that on realising it was a former home of Doc Evatt, he moved out again!

Cecily reported to John following a visit to Evatt and Mary Alice on 28 July 1963:

> Dr Evatt is practically locked in doors – perhaps he will be allowed out when the weather is better, but it may be he would wander off. It is pathetic and distressing to Mrs Evatt to lock and unlock the doors. The nurse follows him everywhere – what a terrible job! He talks inconsequentially as he often did, but now I suppose he can't talk otherwise. I'd like to have seen more of him, but he did not stay in the room. I don't know if the nurse is encouraged to remove him – it seems rather as though he is very restless – just potters around, and she follows. The first thing he said to me was that my eyes were a different colour. His back is bowed, and he is thin, but not nearly as frail as I had expected. Mrs E hasn't changed a scrap, but I find her much easier to talk to, though not easier to stop. I find everybody easier to talk to now.[11]

Cecily's last sentence reflects the relief she felt in a house without John. I hopped over the back fence too, to visit my father's old friend. As a child, I had found him gruff at times, but I knew him to be kindly and he had given me presents of books that I treasured. It was not easy to absorb how he looked now – sitting in a wheelchair, propped up by pillows, his legs covered by a thick rug. He could not lie down for fear of contracting pneumonia. He was about six-and-a-half stone and not aware of my presence. Evatt survived in this fragile state for another two years.

Cecily still had Clare and me to worry about. Meredith was no longer a concern. Within the first week or so of arriving in Kuala Lumpur in 1963, Tom Critchley, the Australian high commissioner, assisted Meredith in obtaining a teaching position at the University of Malaya. She needed a job to help support Clive while he was a research scholar, and her teaching position in the fields of monetary and development economics provided

---

11   Cecily family file.

her with the start to her acclaimed academic and public service career. Clare, having followed Cecily's footsteps and majored in anthropology and psychology, was completing her honours degree while I was still at school undertaking my leaving certificate. What I would do then, and where I would live, was the subject of correspondence between John and Cecily – and Meredith from Malaya trying to get them to sort something out.

Meredith questioned Cecily as to why she did not intend to join, or at least visit, John in London and take me with her after I finished school at the end of the year. 'You see, I cannot understand how you can accept to be parted for long – even these six months', she wrote on 12 July 1963, and:

> Are you waiting, mum, till dad makes up his mind and then would you definitely go? Why is it best that you stay behind? … Maybe I am still in the young married days and couldn't conceive of such a break. But do let me in on everything or reassure me that I have been told all – please.[12]

Receiving another letter from John, Meredith was not convinced that he was happy in London without Cecily. At the end of July, she wrote to Cecily again: 'It was the superficial happiness expressed in dad's letters that really began us thinking – believe it or not … He appears to us that [he] is not as happy as he makes out.' John reached out to Meredith to ask whether I might spend a few weeks with her and Clive in Malaya at the end of the year, it being his hope that I would travel on to the UK and attend university there. No one banked on my poor results, or at least in some subjects that had to be passed for matriculation purposes. A custody wrangle – of a sort – broke out between John and Cecily over where I should live. Their conflicting priorities came to the surface: Cecily was concerned with my emotional wellbeing, and John with my education and future in mind. John wanted me to join him, and Cecily knew that if I went to university in the UK, I might never return. Cecily thought it in my best interests that I remain in Australia with the rest of my family and my many friends. Meredith counselled that in the circumstances neither Cecily nor John should determine this for me. I was, after all, 17. It was an uncomfortable situation for Meredith to be in. Cecily wrote explaining what she could about her and John's relationship, but by this

---

12 The quoted letters between Meredith and her parents, unless otherwise indicated, are held on the Cecily family file.

time Meredith preferred to 'let the matter drop'. She told our mother that when she received letters from our father, 'I feel a little unstable, so I'd rather not go into the whys or hows of the matter'.[13]

By the end of September, plans had solidified. John offered to pay for me to fly to London on completion of my schooling in mid-December, the plan being that I would stay with Meredith and Clive in Malaya for a week on my way. Cecily agreed on condition John offered a return airfare so that I could decide for myself where I wanted to live. Clare, who Meredith and I regarded as the most brilliant of us, graduated in arts from the University of Sydney with first-class honours in anthropology and was awarded the University Medal. She applied for and won a research position at the Tavistock Institute in London and decided to travel by boat to join us in the UK early the following year to take up the position.

Cecily was free to start her new life; free of children and free to explore her relationship with Robert. She was ready to emerge from John's shadow and live, love and work on her own terms. In October 1963, she found a small two-bedroom house in the suburb of Ainslie that she thought she could afford despite the house in Forrest not having been sold. Meredith was concerned at her apparent impetuousness, believing Cecily was in a confused state of mind. She, like I, was unaware that Cecily's friendship with Robert had developed into a relationship of intense love. Cecily was resolute and moved into her new home in early 1964.

Cecily's decision not to join John was the right one for her, personally and professionally. However, they would both have difficulty untwining themselves from each other. Cecily's inner turmoil prevented her from transferring her affection wholeheartedly from John to Robert. She wanted Robert to be a part of her new life, but she was not ready to fully let go of John. In November 1963, she told John:

> One of the things I want out of life – perhaps it is what I want more than anything else – is to work out an honest relationship with you … it may lead to a final and respectful acceptance of differences, or it may not … But we are not finished with each other yet.[14]

---

13 Letter 21 August 1963, Cecily family file.
14 Letter 25 November 1963, Cecily family file.

She added that she was not suggesting that necessarily they should ever come together again, but that 'I don't know where it will lead'. John was confused by her mixed messages and protested that her statements were ambiguous. She replied that her position was quite clear. While parental concern for Clare and me gave Cecily and John reason to keep in touch, curiously, Cecily continued to air her thinking about their relationship. She told John that she had been reflecting over what she had said to him about their marriage and felt the need to clarify. 'I am distressed that I married you and find myself unable to keep my vows … I did not know myself well enough, or you either. But we have our wonderful children …' She went on to say that her worries would vanish if John found a woman who would love him. She did not consider the possibility that he might already have entered into another relationship about which Clare and I soon learned when we joined John in London.

In London, Clare and I observed for ourselves, not just the apparent success of John's academic career, but how quickly he had embraced and befriended his colleagues and their families in London – and a young Australian friend, Leone Gold. John was taken with Leone: her olive sun-freckled skin, dark short cropped hair, black eyes and infectious laugh. Leone doted on John, his charm, his looks, his politics and his brain; and she stood up to him and, in my observation, won any debate on any topic outside his field. Australian born, Leone had come to London to make a new life, having become disillusioned with Australian politics and her own family relations. She was a brilliant mathematician, fluent in French, and had a large circle of interesting friends and associates. Closer to my age than John's, he introduced her to me as a friend who might help me settle into London. I was easily won over because she had a piano in her flat that I could loudly and repeatedly bash out the few classical pieces I could play by heart, such as Grieg's Piano Concerto in A minor, and Tchaikovsky's Piano Concertos 1 and 2, without people slamming doors on me. Somehow, Leone found someone to take me into a touring basketball team, she enrolled me in French and typing lessons and had a travel agent friend provide me with all sorts of European bus tours. She also introduced me to avocados, which I had never seen in Australia, and the true baked Jewish cheesecake to be found only at a Sunday market stall in Petticoat Lane. Jewish by birth and looks, she was a rationalist and not religious in belief.

Leone Gold, Kent, UK, 1978.
Source: Family collection.

John's boat on the Thames, London, 1964.
Source: Family collection.

John had made an interesting new life for himself, and I benefited from Leone accompanying us on a trip to France and Spain where her fluent French and extraordinary cultural knowledge enhanced both John's and my appreciation of art, architecture and all things European. Back in London, we spent many long summer evenings on the boat he had bought, *Yo Yo*, exploring the Thames and its canals and enjoying a different perspective of the city, sunsets, swimming alongside the boat and watching with fascination the operation of the canal locks to allow us to pass through. John flew the UN flag on *Yo Yo* until the authorities confronted him, read the riot act and ordered him to fly the British flag.

The trauma for me, however, was the charade that John and Leone were not in a relationship. As if I could not see or hear that Leone was staying overnight with John in his double bed in our small flat! Why did John not simply tell Cecily so that they might agree on a divorce and spare me and Clare the futile hope that our parents would reunite? He and Leone attended to every aspect of my physical wellbeing but failed dismally in understanding causes and effects of emotional scarring. It would not be until Cecily told John in early 1965 that she wanted a divorce in order to marry Robert that John would admit his commitment to Leone. These were the days of 'fault-based' divorce, and whichever spouse first desired to remarry necessarily accepted 'blame' as an adulterer in order to be divorced.

34

Tugs of war of love and divorce

While Clare and I were in London throughout 1964, Cecily and Robert in Australia faced uncertainties about their relationship. Robert was conflicted; he wanted to be with Cecily, but he did not want to let Nancy and his children down, who were now all living in Canberra. Cecily, by letter in May 1964, suggested that Robert stand back, or 'stay away', until he found himself.[1] He had the opportunity to do so because he travelled a lot. Robert had headed the political science program in the Research School of Social Sciences, ANU, since 1962 and his work required him to spend quite a deal of time in New Guinea and elsewhere. But Cecily missed Robert and could not 'stand back' from Robert herself, despite her best intentions. When Robert had periods in Canberra that year, he visited and stayed over with Cecily when he could, officially residing at University House. When he was away, they corresponded. Cecily kept Robert informed of her activities, helped him with his writing and, in turn, he encouraged her interest in writing. A piece she wrote in March 1964 for a creative writing exercise illustrates her continuing introspection:

> I saw a picture in my mind last night … I saw something like an amoeba or jellyfish floating expanded and relaxed with its edges loose, its inside parts aimless and at rest. The creature was not entirely unaware, but the environment was congenial, and it seemed to be taking time off. Then suddenly, from somewhere, there was a threat. Immediately the animal was still, its boundaries took shape, its internal parts became ready to take action; it was

---

1   R. S. Parker papers, NLA, MS 8200 Restricted, box 20, file 88, 'Burton, Cecily Margaret 1964'.

> potentially, if not immediately, hostile. It was an organized creature then, a distinct individual ready to act as such; not just easy-going, floating, nondescript and apparently lifeless. Its preparation to defend itself made it more definite and meaningful; it was distinct from its environment. I thought as I saw this, that some people must have such a threat in order to recognize themselves – that they need it constantly, or they do not know who they are. They do not know where their boundaries are, or what their internal organization is unless they feel they are under attack; they must be on the defensive to know themselves.[2]

Cecily re-engaged with some former friends and admirers. Gerald Firth helped her with the garden of her new home and he joined her on some outings and they ate several times together. She hosted dinners and extended party invitations to Frank Chamberlain (Radio 2CA's 'Canberra on the line') and Manning Clark, who 'appeared from nowhere on the other end of the telephone last night' prompting her to invite him, she explained by letter to Robert. She had dinner with Coombs, about whom she wrote to Robert, 'he is down and unhappy – caught in a trap from which he can't escape', referring to his failing marriage and his unhappiness at home.[3] In a loving letter to Robert in August 1964, she wrote:

> I am really awfully dependent on you – I wish you were here. It is wonderful to feel dependent, and wonderful to feel I can trust you to turn to. I don't suppose I ever really trusted anyone before.[4]

Then followed more letters, heavy in content as Cecily pursued her need to be understood. Robert, unlike John, listened and really tried hard to understand, but his responses did not fully satisfy her.

Cecily's year of freedom and personal privacy came to an end when first Clare returned from the UK and then I came home before Christmas, to prepare myself for university.[5] On our return from abroad, both Clare and I assumed our right to move back 'home' – that is, into Cecily's tiny house that she had bought to start, what she hoped would be, a new life with Robert. The house was bursting at the seams with the two of us sharing a room and constantly arguing. Robert stayed overnight sometimes, but it was a miserable time for him and Cecily.

---

2   Cecily family file.
3   R. S. Parker papers, NLA, MS 8200 Restricted, box 20, file 88, letter 30 July 1964.
4   R. S. Parker papers, NLA, MS 8200 Restricted, box 20, file 88, undated, July or August 1964.
5   From the UK John managed to cajole the Vice Chancellor of the ANU into providing me with provisional admission to enrol in a combined arts/law degree.

34. TUGS OF WAR OF LOVE AND DIVORCE

Over the Christmas holidays, Robert joined his wife and family at their holiday home to spend time with his children. Cecily looked forward to the New Year rolling in when troublesome Clare and I would move out and leave her in peace and, she hoped, Robert would make the break with Nancy and move in with her. Unfortunately, the New Year saw little improvement in Cecily's enjoyment of life. Clare and I, still living at home, were at each other's throats. Robert was again away, on study leave, and Cecily told him in a letter that Clare and I made her and each other 'very miserable'.[6] She later wrote a cheerier note to Robert in which she mentioned that I had gone off to Sydney and Clare had decided to look for a flat to live in. Cecily had managed to secure a room for me at Bruce Hall, a residential college for out-of-town ANU students, from the commencement of the 1965 first semester. I had, after all, just returned from my father's care in the UK. John agreed to pay for it. Clare secured research work and moved into shared rented accommodation. Cecily and Robert must have sighed with relief once we left her house.

By early 1965, Robert's domestic situation had crystallised and he and Nancy dealt with their situation amicably and efficiently. They decided that 'enough is enough'. Nancy filed for divorce citing her husband's adultery with Cecily, and Cecily signed the necessary 'confession' document as the 'Co-Respondent'. The divorce was finalised in May that year. The only legal barrier to Robert and Cecily marrying now was John. On 2 January 1965, Cecily wrote to John to tell him that she wanted to marry Robert. To divorce him, she would have to provide details of his adultery with Fran and name her the 'Co-Respondent'. He had never owned up to his affair with Sabne, although Meredith believes that Cecily had become aware of it. The alternative was for John to agree to initiate divorce proceedings, in which case Robert would be the named 'Co-Respondent'. It did not sit well with Cecily that, even though she had decided in 1963 that 'enough was enough' when John left for the UK, in order to marry the man she now loved she would have to take the 'blame'. She thought it particularly unfair if, as she suspected, John had had affairs throughout their marriage about which he had said nothing.

Robert considered that John possibly rationalised himself as the injured party because 'it is too difficult for him to be magnanimous to the person who has rejected him: it was an offence against your marital duty and also a blow to his pride', he told Cecily.[7] Robert shared other insights

---

6   R. S. Parker papers, NLA, MS 8200 Restricted, box 20, file 88, 2 January 1965.
7   R. S. Parker papers, NLA, MS 8200 Restricted, box 20, file 89, 28 April 1965.

into John with Cecily. To a comment Cecily made to the effect that John would do better as a politician than a writer of books, Robert said, 'he's too uncompromising and too incapable of working with other people in the way politics requires; he doesn't trouble to understand other people – I doubt if he's really interested in them as individual human beings; what he wants is to save Humanity'.[8] John procrastinated and Cecily issued a petition for divorce. Subpoenas were served on him and Fran to obtain the information Cecily needed to support her petition, which resulted in a flow of unhappy letters.

To complicate family relationships further, John visited Canberra in April 1965. Meredith prepared lunch for us all at her place. She and Clive had returned from Malaya to live in Canberra in early 1964 where Meredith was engaged in tutoring in economics at ANU. The following day we all, including Cecily, at whose house we first had drinks, went to dinner as a family. Cecily and John 'behaved well' according to my diary note, although unsurprisingly John displayed no warmth to Cecily. Cecily's account to Robert, who, by this time had taken a year's study leave from ANU and was in the USA before travelling on to the UK, was that John behaved towards her as he always had, 'cold and dead and just as though he would really prefer I didn't exist'. Cecily wrote of John, 'He is just the same as he was. It is quite extraordinary. Silent and rather sulky, and quite charming at times to the others in my presence.'[9]

John left for London on 17 April and, on 29 April, he informed Meredith by letter that he intended to marry Leone, his Australian girlfriend. Since she was not much older than Meredith, and that while Clare and I had met her Meredith had not, it came as a shock. Then again, John had shown us the luscious nightdress that he brought for Leone on his trip. I had two parents proposing marriages to their new loves, and a sister, Clare, who announced in May that she was to marry too. I was involved in student anti–Vietnam War protests while trying to study in my first year of law and so, apart from noting the various family antics in my diary, I dwelt almost entirely on my own life. Two more divorce proceedings were afoot in 1965 that were a fallout from our parents' problems: *Parker v. Parker* and *Campion v. Campion*. Robert, Nancy, Max and Fran ended their marriages. Cecily and John were to follow – although at this stage John was still not cooperating.

8   R. S. Parker papers, NLA, MS 8200 Restricted, box 20, file 89, 23 August 1965.
9   R. S. Parker papers, NLA, MS 8200 Restricted, box 20, file 89, letter to Robert, 8 April 1965, original emphasis.

34. TUGS OF WAR OF LOVE AND DIVORCE

After John's departure, Cecily aired doubts to Robert about marrying him. Her expressed reason was that she was concerned about past relationships of Robert's, referring to friendships that he had forged while he was on an extensive trip to Africa and elsewhere some time before. She talked of shadows between them of which he seemed unaware, and she wanted him to acknowledge these issues before they married. She wrote:

> I can never be the same person to you as I was to John … the sadness and the pain will never go and I do not want them to. What sort of person would I be if I did? John probably has the bottom place in my heart and can never be moved from it … I suspect it is much more like this with you and Nancy than you are able to realise … and that is why it is haunting you …[10]

She told him that she was not sure she could marry him, unless she could be herself. Then, in a letter two days later, coincidentally hers and John's wedding anniversary, she told Robert that she was sorry she had expressed doubts about marrying him.

Cecily's indecision about marrying Robert was a repeat of her indecision about marrying John. Before both marriages, she expressed her love for her man as well as her uncertainties and worried about them not accepting her for who she was. With Robert, she seemed to want to know more about his past relationships and whether he had the ability to understand her at a reasonably deep psychological level. She kept pressing Robert, telling him, 'I am not at all certain that I am getting through to you at all. Through to your imagination. Robert darling, that is where I want to get. One glimmering of this and I will be very happy.'[11] Robert responded in return, best as he could, by drawing comparisons between his feelings towards Nancy, and Cecily's towards John. He wrote:

> Reading these letters of yours again, I think I can see you having very much the same feelings about him as I have been about Nancy: simply the difficulty of seeming to abandon them to loneliness or unhappiness, and at the same time the memory of how impossible it was, and unhappy they were, when we were together with them. Damn human nature.[12]

---

10 R. S. Parker papers, NLA, MS 8200 Restricted, box 20, file 89.
11 R. S. Parker papers, NLA, MS 8200 Restricted, box 20, file 89, 27 April 1965.
12 R. S. Parker papers, NLA, MS 8200 Restricted, box 20, file 89.

Cecily continued her introspection in her letters to Robert. She talked about her now long-past mystical experience and about how her reading Jung's works saved her from complete isolation. She told Robert that even so, for a few more years after, she felt she was fighting against insanity; that while trying to intellectualise her experience, she was also trying to win John's approval by working on his first book. The intensity of the exchange and their philosophical content deepened. Cecily told Robert that when she is with him, she gets caught up in his 'aura' – his niceness – and then, she stated, that she knows from her association with others that she can react too sensitively to their 'auras' and that she could see that this was due to 'a lack of firm knowledge of what I am myself'.[13] Some of her letters were almost preaching in tone with regard to her relationship with Robert. She anticipated future problems, and debated whether she would marry him unless he accepted all sorts of things she perceived about herself. In the same letters, the tone changed when she discussed ideas she was attempting to formulate in the thesis she was writing for the master's degree in psychology she had embarked upon.

Robert responded with intimate detail to her searching questions. He conveyed the 'deep and mystic sense of unity' that he felt for her beyond anything he had experienced before. In one letter, which Robert wrote from Washington on 18 May 1965, he said: 'Every now and then I am forcibly struck by the realisation that you are quite the most interesting woman I have known.' Then, he addressed some of her concerns on an intellectual level:

> The questions you ask of the world, and of me, are so searching that sometimes I have to fend them off by saying I knew their basic answer even without asking the questions. Well, in a way, that's true. The conviction of the oneness and interdependence of all reality simply grew in me as part of the evolution of my own adolescence. As you know, I must struggle to screw down my 'niceness' in order to let you have what I really think, and I did this the night I wrote [that] your Work did not touch me because I had always taken its essence for granted.[14]

To illustrate his attempt to grapple with Cecily's ideas, he acknowledged his 'arrogance' in reacting to her work: 'For in a number of things you had gone distinctly beyond what I had ever thought. You were groping for

---

13   R. S. Parker papers, NLA, MS 8200 Restricted, box 20, file 89, 3 May 1965.
14   R. S. Parker papers, NLA, MS 8200 Restricted, box 20, file 89, 18 May 1965.

34. TUGS OF WAR OF LOVE AND DIVORCE

a wider range of unity than I had bothered about.' Cecily's letter writing was no doubt therapeutic for her; perhaps it was for Robert too. She told Robert that writing to him led her to make a connection with 'that strange creature, myself as a child, with whom I have felt so long a stranger …'. She explained:

> My aggressiveness, strong individuality, rebelliousness, desire for my own way, determination, standing up for my rights – all these things which have been foreign to me for years, have come to consciousness, and made me recognise myself as that child, Cecily Nixon, who caused everyone so much trouble …[15]

The most puzzling content of the letters Meredith and I pored over in 2016 in the National Library of Australia archives was where Cecily actually wrote to Robert about the possibility of having children! She said, 'I know you want to have children', and 'If we have children (are we brave enough) should we have a flat?' This letter was written in 1965 when she was 48 years old.[16] What could she have been thinking, we asked each other.

Despite the tension between John and Robert over Robert's intention to marry his best friend's wife – Cecily – or perhaps because of it, John and Robert exchanged letters about John's work. John still valued Robert's friendship and intellect. On 28 June, Robert and John met up for lunch in London. It is likely they discussed the divorce proceedings but, it seems, the purpose of the lunch was because John wanted Robert's views on his upcoming book, *International Relations: A General Theory*, published that year.

Cecily kept writing to John too. His infidelity preyed on her mind. In June 1965, she wrote to him about all the women with whom he possibly had relationships even before her indiscretion with Raju in Ceylon. 'It would explain a great deal,' she suggested. 'Why you could never look me in the eye, why you were unkind, your insecurity, why you always made yourself out to be horrible, why you made me do the choosing of you (or did your best to put me in that position) …' John admitted it – or some part of it – conceding that he had several affairs when he was overseas at conferences during wartime.[17] He did not mention any subsequent illicit relationships.

---

15 R. S. Parker papers, NLA, MS 8200 Restricted, box 20, file 89, 30 May 1965.
16 R. S. Parker papers, NLA, MS 8200 Restricted, box 22, file 99, 10 May 1965.
17 R. S. Parker papers, NLA, MS 8200 Restricted, box 20, file 89, Cecily reported this to Robert, letter 6 July 1965.

John's confession about his infidelity did nothing for Cecily's self-esteem, as we see from a self-deprecating extract of a letter she wrote to Robert:

> There are times when I wonder how you ever put up with me at all. I am nothing but a nothing, I'm not a thing at all. I can't even cook and sew really well, I disturb and upset you, I'm only a reasonable mother, I've been a hopeless wife. I'm saying all this quite cheerfully really, because I can't really help being so mediocre.[18]

In the midst of Cecily's introspection, she included some thoughts in a letter to Robert about what she should wear for their wedding. Robert responded by designing some outfits for her. Then she revisited the concern she had about John engaging in the sexual act without emotional expression. She discussed the difference between feelings and emotions. Yet again, she recalled Hans Christian Andersen's 'Snow Queen', and her belief that the story continued to fascinate her because there was something about that 'Ice Queen' that was so like her; in the end, her heart of ice was melted.

In another letter to Robert, she referred to what Aldous Huxley had to say about sex and she took Robert through her thoughts about sex sublimation. She reflected on being precocious from her time at Montessori, her fight to keep her sanity, her infatuation with Raju in Ceylon and with poet Alec Hope. Do we glean from these letters that Cecily, finding that Robert was no different from John (or any other man, perhaps?) in terms of displaying inadequate emotional expression in the course of having sex, is questioning her own understanding of love? Confusion in her thinking reigned. From Cecily's perspective, she felt she was 'slowly becoming a different sort of person'.[19] She told Robert that she realised she knew very little about herself, how meaningless her life had been (except for having children), and how 'I have lived through nearly 50 years of utter nonsense thinking it was all real living'. She related those feelings to the healthy effect of menopause, but later stated: 'I feel as though I have built on a rubbish heap instead of on good clean earth and the stink of residue won't leave me alone.'[20]

---

18 R. S. Parker papers, NLA, MS 8200 Restricted, box 20, file 89, '1965', 28 July 1965.
19 R. S. Parker papers, NLA, MS 8200 Restricted, box 20, file 89, '1965', 9–13 July 1965.
20 R. S. Parker papers, NLA, MS 8200 Restricted, box 20, file 89, '1965', 1 September 1965.

34. TUGS OF WAR OF LOVE AND DIVORCE

Three months later, in September 1965, Cecily again expressed doubts about marrying Robert. She told him that she felt that she could not marry him until she got 'rid of the terrible pain of the past, until I sort myself out and know who and what I am'. She mentioned a meeting she had with some notable men they both knew, and that one of them, John Kerr (before he became a notorious governor-general), had said to Cecily: 'So, you have decided to marry some other guy, and not one of your old admirers like Nugget or me.' Kerr's wife, Peg, was present when he made the comment. In Cecily's next letter to Robert, she describes her relationship with him as 'devoted', but followed it with: 'I am not in love with you. I do not love you in the way that people usually do love …'. This, she explained, by telling him that she is 'not like other people'.[21]

Reading her letters, Meredith and I could not help wondering how Robert managed her emotional complexity. His and Cecily's relationship had potential for one of great love and understanding, but Cecily was still searching for something that was missing in Robert, as she did with her mother and with John. But Robert found a way through. His letters were openly loving and offered Cecily the world. She came to believe that at last she loved and was loved by someone who understood her. Nevertheless, the passage would not be plain sailing. Both were scarred by a fault-based divorce process and the resolution of disputes over the division of marital assets that left them with financial worries and concerns about their respective children's futures. 'It was never going to be a seamless exit and entry,' Cecily wrote, when considering the moods and feelings she experienced when moving out of an old relationship and into a new one.[22]

In October 1965, Cecily and Robert went to New Guinea for a month for Robert's work. If Cecily believed that by shedding John, ASIO would go away too, she was wrong. Cecily's arrival with Robert in Port Moresby in October 1965, her departure and the people she associated with in between were recorded.[23] Robert was of interest to ASIO, not because he was suspected of anything, but because of ASIO's interest in the research work he was doing on the Territory of Papua New Guinea's constitutional and administrative arrangements as the country moved towards inevitable independence. Independence was granted a decade later.

---

21   R. S. Parker papers, NLA, MS 8200 Restricted, box 20, file 89, '1965', 11 September 1965.
22   Cecily's 'Free writing', 2000, Cecily family file.
23   NAA: A6126, 420, Cecily Margaret Burton vol. 1, 14, report 4 January 1966.

In 1966, I became an unwitting 'source' of information on Robert's and Cecily's activities and whereabouts. Through Robert's contacts he had secured holiday work for me in Port Moresby, first as a typist in the Australian Government's administration section in 1965–66 and on a later trip to assist with the Magistrates Training Courses at the university in Port Moresby. The pay was good and taxes levied by the Australian Government were low (to provide incentives for Australians to work there), and I could afford to fund my travel and living expenses for the two months or so each year that I worked there. It satisfied my travel lust too. On my return to university in Canberra for the 1966 academic year, I was befriended by a former patrol officer who had been repatriated to Australia and who had commenced an arts degree at the university by way of retraining. We had Papua New Guinea in common. It was years later that he admitted to me that he had been 'assigned' by ASIO to befriend me (I assume, in exchange for his university fees being paid when he resettled in Australia) to gain what information he could about my 'stepfather' Robert Parker. Student informants were known as 'sparrows'; they are everywhere but none are noticed. My friend's name was also Robert, and to avoid confusion I will call him Bob. On one of Robert's trips to Papua New Guinea, his briefcase went missing for several hours after his arrival in Moresby. It turned up, but Robert found that his papers had been played with; they were out of order. I had no idea then that my idle chat with Bob allowed ASIO to monitor Robert's movements and activities. On 24 June 1966, Robert wrote a letter to the *Canberra Times* on the theme of ASIO and the threat it posed to civil liberties – and democratic politics. He wrote another on 19 March 1973, perhaps after another similar experience. He knew about how its activities had affected John and John's colleagues, and now he was experiencing some of its work himself.

Bob did, I believe, form a genuine friendship with me, or he would not have owned up later that he was told to befriend me as part of his ASIO spying activities. He initially won me over by his generosity in lending me his Volkswagen car for a period he was away from Canberra. I asked why he would entrust it to me when I had, in fact, rolled another friend's VW only a few months earlier during the holidays in the hills just outside Moresby. 'If you have rolled a VW,' Bob said, 'you will now have learned from the experience, so I trust you.' Trust went both ways, and in the course of our friendship I naively spoke freely about my family and my stepfather's visits to Moresby. I learned later that Des Ball became a 'sparrow' in his honours year at ANU to report on 'student unrest' on campus.[24]

In March 1966, Robert and Cecily moved into a more spacious and prestigious home in Grey Street, Deakin. Robert was uncomfortable living with Cecily without being married to her. He urged John to hurry up and sign the divorce papers. He understood from John that the divorce hearing had been set for 24 January, and that the 'decree absolute' would be granted after a period of three months. In June 1966, Robert wrote to Gerald Firth, who was then in London, to ask him to try and find out from John what the status of the Burton divorce was. He wanted to marry Cecily as soon as he could. 'This delay is getting irksome … we are anxious not to live in this social twilight world any longer than we can help …'[25] A message came back that the divorce had been granted at the end of May. John had reason to push ahead with the divorce; he wanted to marry Leone.

Robert and Cecily planned to marry 'very quietly' on 21 June. John and Leone married in London on 7 June 1966, beating Robert and Cecily to the post. Robert and Cecily's proposed wedding date came and went. Cecily did not receive the papers from London until 25 June. They married on 25 July 1966. In October they travelled as Professor and Mrs Parker to Lord Howe Island for a delayed two-week honeymoon. According to Robert, they needed it, 'for a rest and to enable Cecily to get used to a change of name'. John sent a Christmas card to Cecily and Robert in an envelope addressed to 'Mrs C. Parker'. Cecily reproached him pointing out that he should have addressed her as Mrs R. Parker, as she was a married, not a widowed, woman. John's barbed reply was: 'Sorry about the identity problem. Some of us don't have a problem and therefore do not think about it! Cause and effect.'[26]

---

24 Ball, drinking with a friend (name withheld) in Civic, Canberra, in early 1969, told the friend that during his 1968 honours year he had been paid a research assistant's salary to provide reports to ASIO. Ball had studied economics, in which Meredith tutored him, before he switched to focus on political science and security studies.
25 R. S. Parker papers, NLA, MS 8200, box 13, file 22, 9 June 1966.
26 Correspondence, December 1966, Cecily family file.

35
Looking to Jung

In 1965, Cecily was tiring of her administrative job at the Australian Institute of Aboriginal Studies. She was expected to more or less 'run the show' because the anthropologist in charge worked and lived in Sydney. She was persuaded to stay and, in 1967, she was given the position of research officer, which involved documenting fragmentary knowledge on Aboriginal sites, informants and other materials. With an increase in salary and less administrative responsibility, she felt happier at work and in herself. She told Robert that this was the first time in her life that she could remember not being under great strain: 'No John, no terrible job'.

Eventually, this mostly 'pencil and paper work' palled. Having discovered Jung and drawn on his philosophy to help her personal growth and better handle her relationship with John, Cecily wanted to help other people with relationship difficulties. She rang Margaret Evans, a leading marriage guidance counsellor, and asked her advice on how she might pursue a career change. Evans suggested she do some marriage guidance training. 'You don't have to stick with it, but it's good training.'[1] Cecily took up the suggestion and, in addition to counselling training, she went to courses on interpersonal relations and group leadership and realised that this vocation would be right for her. In January 1969, as a qualified counsellor, she commenced part-time work with the Canberra Marriage Guidance Counselling service.

---

1   Parker, interview by Meredith Edwards, 2004, 83.

In early August 1969, she had to take a year's break from her work, however, to accompany Robert on his study leave, during which he would work in Hove in Sussex in the UK. Cecily thought that, as Robert's wife, it was expected of her. She was not a traveller, nor did she take well to upheaval and leaving a job she loved, her family and friends and the gracious split-level home in O'Connor with a leafy garden they had just moved into and which she had had little time to enjoy. Robert loved new places, meeting new people and being in new worlds. Cecily was jealous of how easily he engaged with others as soon as they relocated – so different from how she felt she was. Apart from enjoying a fortnight's holiday in the vicinity of Venice and Verona, Cecily decided not to travel everywhere with Robert while they were away. Instead, they explored Sussex together at weekends. When they were apart, Robert wrote to her about everything he did, saw and observed. He wanted to assure her that he could be with and enjoy other people and love her at the same time. Cecily found it hard to adjust to a new environment but made the best out of the trip. She embarked on a year-long course at the Institute of Group Analysis and took a term's course in student counselling. Between October 1969 and June 1970, she worked as a part-time counsellor with Brighton and Hove marriage guidance counselling service.

They returned to Australia in July 1970, in time for Robert to return to New Guinea for a fortnight for a constitutional development seminar.[2] Cecily resumed her marriage guidance work and was kept busy with clients referred to her by friends and acquaintances as well as from the counselling service. In addition, she did some student counselling at ANU and was engaged by the ANU Education Research Unit to undertake interviews in Canberra and interstate. She also commenced a master's degree in counselling psychology at ANU that included practical experience as well as a written thesis. Influenced by Jungian philosophy, she completed her thesis in 1972, titled 'Regression and Psychotherapy', and was awarded her degree in 1974. Robert engaged with her over her thesis, although she thought that he did so 'without ever probably understanding' what drove her to write it, or its importance to her.[3] He, on the other hand, proudly wrote to his son about her work, noting that she had some fresh things to say on the subject about 'Regression' and talked with pride about the

---

2   R. S. Parker papers, NLA, MS 8200, box 10, file 85.
3   Cecily's 'Free writing', 2000.

quality of Cecily's work in a letter to his daughter mentioning that Cecily had also turned to writing poetry and had several small pieces published in the *Canberra Times*.

While enjoying her work, at the end of 1973 Cecily left the marriage guidance counselling service because she became unconvinced that conventional marriage guidance methods were appropriate. She did not believe counselling should only be about how couples can get back together and make a marriage work. She had no illusions about her own marital relationships. While she was in a reasonably satisfying marriage with Robert, she still did not feel completely fulfilled and so, being emmeshed in a marriage she did not find totally fulfilling, she was not going to preach to others that it was the 'right' thing to do. She came to see that sometimes marriage partners as well as their children might benefit from a separation, if the parties could find happiness in themselves.

A dilemma of the times faced women like Cecily. Most were financially dependent on their husbands. It was unlikely that Cecily could have become the successful counsellor she became without Robert. Men, too, depended on their spouses for love, support and a steady companionable presence in their lives, but generally they were financially independent and they did not have to give up their family name for the sake of having a mate. In addition, Cecily lived in and conformed to a culture in which many women perceived themselves as incomplete without a man. Jung's works guided Cecily into understanding that 'wholeness' came from within oneself, not from joining up with another. Later she read, and urged her daughters to read, Penelope Russianoff's *Why Do I Think I Am Nothing without a Man*, to help us achieve 'wholeness'. However, Cecily continued to believe that marriage partnerships were the basis of personal fulfilment. Searching for the right partner was the challenge, she believed; and to help people better choose a partner, they first had to find their own identity.

From 1974, Cecily used her training to lead many and varied groups in sensitivity and group dynamics: university students, marriage guidance trainees, schools, churches, the Family Planning Association and the Abortion Counselling service. She conducted an encounter group for Presbyterian missionaries. She also tutored various groups in aspects of psychology and attended Gestalt and psychodrama workshops, among others. She participated in a series of talks and case demonstrations given by Canberra doctors and psychiatrists at the Woden Valley Hospital.

Between 1974 and 1981, Cecily became a group leader at St Marks Theological Institute. While she imparted knowledge and skills to others, she kept learning herself.

Cecily was also employed at the School Without Walls in 1974 as a 'non-counsellor' and community relations coordinator. It was a new experimental secondary school, which emphasised choice, voluntary effort and maximum communication between pupils and teachers and parents. Cecily enjoyed the warm and friendly atmosphere but disliked the school's indifference to all ideas of excellence and effort. She was uncomfortable in the unstructured environment and the social pressure that was placed on everyone to conform to the school's philosophy. The answer for Cecily was to work on her own. She left the school in the first half of 1975 to commence a private practice in clinical psychology – the beginning of her 'real' career.

According to a colleague of Cecily's who Meredith interviewed, Cecily appeared not to be a team player. Cecily's non-conformist approach smacks of John's individualism. As a public servant, he was not seen to be a team player either. Both Cecily in her counselling of individuals and John in his resolution of problems between disputants focused on the source and cause of discontent before applying preset rules to the situation they were dealing with. Cecily understood that there could be a variety of deep-seated underlying causes for individual relationship problems, and she wanted to help people find themselves as individuals.

Having stumbled upon Carl Jung, Cecily felt that she was well-placed to help others suffering in complex relationships as she had suffered. Jung's philosophy was to guide the rest of Cecily's life. She understood him. His life and writings brought her to understand herself better, she felt better understood by others and understood others better too. Meredith and I found clues as to how Jung resonated with Cecily in her heavy underlining of sentences in his written works. For example, she highlighted the oft quoted paragraph:

> As a child, I felt myself to be alone, and I am still, because I know things and must hint at things which others apparently know nothing of, and for the most part do not want to know. Loneliness does not come from having no people about one, but from being unable to communicate the things that seem important to oneself, or from holding certain views which others find inadmissible ... But loneliness is not necessarily inimical to companionship, for no

one is more sensitive to companionship than the lonely man, and companionship thrives only when each individual remembers his individuality and does not identify himself with others.[4]

Cecily embraced Jung's use of the concept of the Mandala, 'magic circle', as the symbol of the centre goal, or of the self as psychic totality. He wrote: 'We must ask questions which challenge the whole personality.' He said: 'I knew that in finding the mandala as an expression of the Self I had attained what was for me the ultimate.'[5]

It was through Jung that Cecily came to understand what had happened to her at the top of the driveway that day in September 1951 when the trees and mountains shimmered, and her world was never again the same. She embraced his technique and dug deep down into her soul to discover her whole. She called it 'mid-life enlightenment'. Finding Jung told her that in feeling different, which she always believed she was, she was not alone. Cecily found and read books by others who had personal experiences beyond explanation that for all the world appeared to be activated by an external force, but which was not so. In her copy of Morag Coate's *Beyond all Reason: A Personal Experience of Madness* (1964), Cecily marked a paragraph in a chapter, 'The Tide of Unreason', in which the author discussed a short period when she felt she had lost her reason and become insane:

> Months earlier when I was alarmed in case I might be losing my sanity, the fact that I could feel this fear showed that I was not more than partly submerged in my own inner mind. I was like a swimmer who has gone out of his depth and fears drowning; sometimes my head was above water, sometimes under the surface ...

The author went on to describe what had happened to her as she got into deeper and deeper water and lost rational view of life. She was taken away by ambulance, and when she awoke as her normal self, she realised she had recently been mad. Cecily might have been saved from that fate because, through studying psychology, she understood the power of the mind. She had clung and hung on to her precipice and avoided suffering madness before she found Jung.

---

4 C. G. Jung, *Memories, Dreams, Reflections*, recorded and ed. Aniela Jaffé, trans. Richard and Clara Winston (London: Collins, 1963).
5 Jung, *Memories, Dreams, Reflections*, 117, 197.

When Cecily was 83 years old, she wrote:

> During my struggle for mid-life enlightenment, which thrust itself upon me in 1952, I discovered the psychology of Jung. This explained much about human nature, including my own, which had been puzzling me. Jung's work is still the source of my deepest and broadest understanding, though I value highly the work of many other psychologists. I continue to learn, but expect to stop practising this year.[6]

Jung grew up in a more religious household than that of Cecily; his parents' disputes led to their separation, and he lost his father when he was in his teens. But there are similarities in what troubled both Jung and Cecily in their childhood. Jung, in *Memories, Dreams, Reflections*, told of being 'deeply troubled' by his mother's being away in hospital when he was cared for by a maid. He became distrustful when the word 'love' was spoken. He saw his mother as the strong parent and his father, although reliable, as suffering 'powerlessness' – very similar to Cecily's perception of her own parents. Jung's young world-view also changed with the sudden appearance of his new-born sister, leaving him with 'a vague sense of distrust which sharpened my curiosity and observation', although the event did not trouble him as Eleanor's arrival did for Cecily. Like Cecily, he did not like competitiveness. Interestingly, Jung wrote about discovering that he was 'actually two different persons' – the schoolboy lacking in confidence and another, more powerful. He had an awareness that he compensated his inner insecurity by an outward show of security, acknowledging that the schoolboy did what was expected of him while the other was 'more grown up, sceptical, mistrustful, remote from the world but close to nature, earth and the sun …'.[7]

Cecily appears to have been less aware of her two different selves. She had always felt that she was different from others and that people generally did not understand who she really was on the inside. She lacked confidence and spoke and wrote about her perceived incompetence and inadequacies. Yet, she presented a different self to others: as confident, strong and capable. She proved in her life with John, and thereafter, to be extremely competent, able to adapt to John's constant change in career direction and to assist him physically on the farm and intellectually with his writing. It took her time to realise her own power; the time would come when John could not hide from others his awe of her.

---

6 Journal, 1999, Cecily family file.
7 Jung, *Memories, Dreams, Reflections*, 50–51, 61–62.

36

Coming into her own: Counselling Cecily style

In July 1975, Cecily commenced private practice as a counsellor and psychotherapist at her home in O'Connor, running groups as well as seeing individuals and couples. One thing led to another and Cecily eventually embarked on a career as a well-regarded and respected psychotherapist. Over a period of three years, Cecily's practice grew as word-by-mouth recommendations provided her with a solid client base. In May 1978, Cecily and Robert moved into a two-storey, dignified home that backed onto a reserve on the hillside of Curtin. Its downstairs area of two rooms, a bathroom and its own entrance made an ideal studio for Cecily in which to run her counselling practice. Here Cecily could talk with her clients in a lounge room atmosphere. Shelves of books, paintings on the walls, pot plants and casual furniture created a peaceful ambience with a comfortable balance between the professional and the personal. One of Cecily's clients recalled a plant cutting in a pot protected from the frost by plastic wrapping sitting outside Cecily's door and saw it as a nurturing symbol.

Meredith interviewed many of Cecily's former clients from which, collectively, we try to convey a picture of how Cecily came across to them and an idea of her counselling style. According to those interviewed, Cecily greeted clients with an open, unpretentious smile and she exuded warmth. She offered them a couch to sit on and settled herself in a chair opposite with a coffee table between them. She would sit with her legs crossed, her hands in her lap, waiting for her client to speak. There were often moments of silence in her sessions, but not uneasy ones. She did not try and fill silences with chatter. She did not indulge in small talk. This accords with our own recollections of Cecily; in her social interactions, if Cecily asked someone how they were, she expected an honest, rather than a merely polite, reply. If she talked about the weather, it was because there was something different or wonderful about it that was worth commenting on.

In developing her own style, Cecily heeded Jung's approach that, for the purpose of therapy, the problem is always the whole person, never the symptom alone; and true to Jung's teachings that each person is different, Cecily individualised her approach to her clients rather than using any special techniques. She sent one client away with children's books to read. She often encouraged her clients to write down their feelings or thoughts, and sometimes she would ask the client to draw what she or he had just said or felt. She had felt pens and paper on hand. She asked questions that often took her clients out of their frame, to somewhere else, in order to give them a different perspective of where they were at in their lives. She would answer questions by asking more, rather than providing answers.

Her former clients talked about Cecily as warm, supportive and non-judgemental. She was perceived as encouraging, always calm, empathetic and an 'active' listener. A former client – I will call her Mary, not her real name – described the power of Cecily's understated style. Cecily did not say much to her at all on their first meeting; she just listened and asked her some gentle questions about her earlier life that, at the time, seemed unrelated to the issues of concern that Mary had raised. Mary started to cry at her first meeting with Cecily in the course of her response; crying was something she rarely did. Later, Mary became self-aware of the links between matters that occurred during her childhood and the relationship issues that had brought her to see a counsellor. By getting her to deal with some buried emotions, Cecily had provided Mary with a glimpse of someone different from whom Mary thought she was. Mary found it an uncomfortable experience but it helped her to make a decision about a relationship she was in. In effect, Cecily had given Mary a 'tiny nudge' in the right direction – like a 'tiny mirror' reflecting back what she had felt.

Another client – I will call her Kim – saw Cecily after Kim's father had died and she had then separated from her boyfriend. She felt she could not 'move on' after these events. She had never been to a counsellor before. She found Cecily in the phone book, later deciding it was a fortunate choice. One of the first questions Cecily put to Kim was: 'Tell me about your childhood.' It seemed an unusual question, unrelated to why she had come to see Cecily, so Kim gave her a brief and sanitised version. Over the next two years, Cecily 'peeled [Kim] back like an onion', gently, but with persistence. She sent Kim home with library books that Kim read in case Cecily questioned her on them. Over time it became clear to Kim that the reason she had such difficulty getting over her father's death had roots in her childhood. There were times during the therapy and after that she would become angry because 'once the layers are peeled off, you cannot go back'. Overall, Kim described the time she had with Cecily as 'like entering another universe'. Reflecting back on her life decades later, Kim regarded her time with Cecily as a turning point; it changed how she saw her life and herself. Over the next 30 years, although Kim did not see Cecily again, she always remembered her and, in her words, 'You don't need to be with a therapist for therapy to go on'.

There were times when Cecily broke from being non-judgemental in order to be firm or directive. On one occasion, a client – I will call her Sandra – showed Cecily a letter from her mother that had distressed her. Cecily said, 'I can hold onto that letter for you', and did. Later, Sandra surmised that Cecily did this because she saw, but did not say, that Sandra's mother had been emotionally manipulating her daughter. Mostly playing a passive role, at times, Cecily would see a need to strongly interact at several levels. On another occasion, according to Sandra, Cecily said, 'You must not do that', in response to something Sandra talked to Cecily about. Even so, Cecily appeared to be on a journey with her, not directing her. Sandra was another client who said Cecily had changed her life.

One of Cecily's clients who she saw in 1972 for many years had been sexually abused as a child, long before child sexual abuse and incest were truly understood. Lucy – not her real name – having gained insight from her sessions with Cecily on how the trauma had affected her, re-entered the workforce to discover that she was not a lone survivor of sexual abuse. From talking about it, she was able to encourage others to do so.

Cecily had a client who, in the late 1980s, had suffered stress at work. She told her colleagues at work that Cecily helped her, and two of them went to see Cecily too. They went because they were suffering from stress at work, but all three had very different personal lives and problems. Cecily built up the self-worth of each, made them feel okay so that they could cope with the stressors in their lives. She made helpful suggestions and observations, sometimes 'giving permission' to limit contact with a relative, even a mother, who might be causing them distress; she drew out what, given their emotional morass, they could not work out for themselves. She helped people reflect rather than react.

Cecily was careful about what she revealed about herself to her clients. Sometimes she talked about something personal to help illustrate a point. On one occasion, Cecily told a client, I will call her Jane, that when Cecily had had an operation on her eye – probably a cataract removal – the anaesthetic had had an adverse effect on her. She explained that she managed to counter the side effects by managing her diet. Jane took this as an illustration of how Cecily took some control of her own life by being an equal participant in the medical process rather than placing herself entirely in her doctor's hands. The message Jane received was that Cecily encouraged her clients to participate in their counselling relationship with her. Jane had been completing a psychology degree at ANU at the time. But it was Cecily, more than the course, that Jane said had enabled her to see herself through her own eyes rather than through the eyes of others. When Jane's counselling sessions finished, Cecily gave her a book of poems by Kahlil Gibran. In a moment of self-revelation, she also gave Jane a Haiku poem she wrote herself, beautiful in its simplicity:

> Through open windows enters
> Silent dawn bringing
> A hundred bird songs.

Jung believed that dreams inform us and Cecily embraced this idea. A regular question she would ask was: 'What have you been dreaming about?' When a client described a dream, Cecily would ask: 'What do you think that might mean?' An exploration of the interpretation that often as not opened up a path to assist that person's self-awareness.

Cecily expanded her practice to include therapy groups. She held evening 'self-knowledge' groups of six to eight people who were free to attend individual sessions without being asked to make a commitment for a set number of sessions. Participants reported that Cecily managed the group dynamics well and appeared unfazed by outbursts of anger from someone in a group. She did not become too close to them as she did not want to be seen as a surrogate mother. Former clients reported that Cecily believed in them; this was important to those who felt that no other close adult did.

Throughout the 1980s, in addition to private clients and some referrals from a local general practitioner, Cecily was retained by solicitors or individuals to provide expert reports to present to courts to support a party's position. Her forensic services covered civil, criminal and family law matters. She also attended professional conferences and seminars and participated in weekend retreats.

In February 1984, Cecily became a member of the Australian Psychological Society and the Institute of Clinical Psychologists, the two relevant professional bodies in Australia. She became a founding and life member of the Canberra chapter of the Australian Clinical Psychology Association. Not that she had any enthusiasm for institutional activities, as such; what she enjoyed most was the actual work of counselling and reading in the field. She was also instrumental in establishing the ACT Jungian Society, which held its inaugural meeting in 1984. In June that year, Cecily gave the first public lecture of the new society, speaking on 'The Essence of Jung's Psychology'.

In 1985, in pursuit of the benefits of dream analysis, Cecily established a weekly Dream Group that she led free of charge. By 1987, places in her weekly lunchtime group were filled with a core group of about five regular attendees and others who came and went. They brought their own lunch and Cecily provided tea and coffee. People put in $2 or other small change with the proceeds to be given to the Jungian Society. In private, Cecily affectionately called the group participants her 'dream boats'. Her role as group leader was to get the group to engage with each other, gain insights and become more reflective of their own lives. She encouraged the participants to keep a dream diary so that they could discuss each other's dreams and reflect on them. From her own understanding of the literature, she also told her dream boats what symbols in dreams might mean. She sometimes shared her own dreams with the group for their analysis. One woman, I will call her Sue, recalls one where Cecily was near a murky pool with unpleasant things in it, and she was nervous about going into it. Sue believed there must be something troubling Cecily. She suggested that Cecily privately visualise 'getting into the water'. Cecily did that and reported back to Sue that it had helped her deal with a troubling issue. Cecily gave a little of herself in this way and, while she did befriend some of her dream boats, she maintained a professional distance.

In 1986, Cecily obtained a certificate in Myers–Briggs Personality Types, to help with her understanding of people and how best to relate to them. She gained 'great sustenance' from the local Jungian Society, giving lectures, and arranging or running one-day workshops. On one workshop on 'active imagination', for example, she asked participants to bring crayons and drawing paper to help them better understand the work and principles of Jung. She reviewed Jung's *Answer to Job* for the society newsletter in which she explained that the gist of the work was concerned with the inadequacy of traditional Christianity to cope with the problems of today; a message with which, surely, John would have agreed.[1]

In 1987, Cecily was made the first life member of the local Jungian Society, in recognition of her contribution to the founding and running of the society. At the end of the year, Cecily and Robert hosted the Jungian Society Christmas Party. It was 'a soiree filled with such excellence, that its reputation deserves to be spread to the four corners', psychologist Caroline Rolls reported in the chapter's next newsletter. Each of the 20 or so members brought a plate of food to share that became a 'feast of tastes'. Between courses, a soprano member of the group sang songs accompanied by Robert at the piano and another person on the flute. Skits of Jung and Pooh Bear portrayed a 'mystical encounter' that dealt with the inner journey of life, and there was a presentation of a 'chance meeting' between the four functions: thinking, feeling, intuition and sensation. The audience's task was to guess at the identities.

Cecily became known in Canberra for her interest in the psychology of Jung in her private practice work and became so busy that she considered not advertising her service and rationing the time she spent with each client. She became a role model for young psychologists. Retired clinical psychologist and director of the Canberra Marriage Counselling Service from 1981 to 1988 – now Relationships Australia – Dr Malise Arnstein attests to this. Arnstein regarded Cecily's peers, Margaret Evans and Leila Bailey, as the 'Grandes Dames' of clinical psychology in Canberra, and Cecily, specialising in Jungian psychotherapy, was the third 'Grande Dame' in this respect.[2]

Absorbed in her work, Cecily became less inclined to accompany Robert on trips overseas that he so enjoyed. He had friends and relatives he liked to visit and lamented that they might not meet Cecily. 'The chance of Cecily travelling gets increasingly remote – she feels the need so little and is so absorbed in her practice … So, you'll have to come here to meet

---

1 C. G. Jung, *Answer to Job* (London: Routledge, 1955).
2 Personal communication, 10 September 2018.

her …', he wrote to Canadian friends.³ Cecily had found her purpose in life – to work with people to try and improve their lives – and she rarely travelled with Robert from that time on.

Cecily's purpose in life included us – improving her own family's lives and relationships – although she felt she was failing to improve her own. While John was mostly absent through our adult lives, Cecily was always there to give us, and her grandchildren, wise counselling. Our mother was the silver thread that bound our family together through our adventures and adversities, the family's emotional hub; the family matriarch.

There were always issues on which we sought her help. She was quiet and reserved and, at the same time, confident and self-contained. Because she appeared to be complete, wise, self-aware and accepting and non-judgemental of others, we had little understanding of her inner turmoil, which she shared with few others. We 'dumped' our issues on her and nothing we told her seemed to surprise her. One of her clients described her as 'unflappable'. It is clear to us, now, that we drew on Cecily excessively to support us in our self-focused lives. We clearly overwhelmed Cecily – or I at least did – with our outpouring of goings-on in our lives. If only we daughters had understood her needs and loaded on her fewer of ours!

Three sisters, Meredith, Clare and Pam, Canberra, 1995.
Source: Family collection.

---

3   R. S. Parker papers, NLA, MS 8200, box 40, file 184, 'General Correspondence, letters to Percy and Virginia Black', 7 June 1984 and 29 November 1985.

Meredith, Clare and I were all intense about our various fields of work. We bewildered our children by our overly busy and ambitious lives. We all worked in areas in which we believed we could achieve social change to benefit the disadvantaged and women in particular. John's philosophy was that 'you shouldn't have to work; you should only want to work', and want to work we did. Clare declared that we were born with a Methodist work ethic and Meredith and I agreed with her – it came from both parents.

Cecily's love of people and interest in them for whoever they were did not prevent her from having views, as did John, on who might make suitable partners for us. By way of background, John had frowned on Meredith dating 'cordies' (Duntroon military cadets) and was angry about Clare seeing her young German 'boy-next-door' friend, while Cecily discouraged me from wanting to marry a carpenter and, before I married my first husband Dan, questioned whether I would be happy living with someone who was 'just a teacher'.[4] As it happened, all three of us married men from working-class backgrounds who were intent on completing higher education. All three of us saw our husbands through their doctorates. Meredith and Clare, in time, went on to complete their own PhDs and my then husband Dan supported me through my master's studies in law. John, having always stressed the importance of us having the education to be self-reliant, proved right in that regard, as we all achieved careers that allowed us to be financially independent. We three needed them, as none of our marriages survived the test of time.

Our marriage breakups, understandably but sadly, impacted on our children. Cecily developed especially close relationships with her grandchildren, connecting with them through books, outings to galleries and concerts, intimate conversations and letters. She encouraged them to talk openly with her, about our parenting or any other issues. All our children developed into sensitive and insightful adults because of, or despite, our parenting and hopefully not our neglect. A good deal of credit for that outcome goes to Cecily.

---

4   Dan Coward and I married in 1968. He obtained a doctorate in history. He is now Dan Huon and living in Tasmania.

37

Revisiting relationship difficulties

Finding a profession of her own and becoming a leader of others in the field of clinical psychology provided Cecily with the tools to make a difference to the lives of others in her own right. But what Cecily aimed to achieve for her clients she had not yet managed to achieve for herself.[1] Her search for answers as to what went wrong with her relationship with John continued in her correspondence with him throughout her marriage to Robert. On one occasion, John responded that she should 'wake up to herself'. She at first thought this ridiculous, but, on reflection, she conceded in a letter to him in October 1969 that it now made sense. She said that watching Meredith and Clare with their children, she thought that they were better mothers than she ever was, 'in a quite essential way'. She attributed their problems to her bad mothering, stating that she was 'quite inadequate and really unfit to be a mother'. We felt sad reading this, as it seemed that her introspection and over-analysis must have disturbed her. She wrote:

> In some ways something must have gone so wrong with my own early life that I grew up to repress my proper healthy feelings and to live by strange, almost inhuman standards, of detachment and objectivity, though being in my inner most nature far removed from such behaviour. My real feelings broke through of course, from time to time, but in a distorted and harmful way, and quite

---

1   Cecily's expression of her feelings, where otherwise not referenced, are derived from a study of her writings, journals and letters held in Cecily family file, personal communications with us, and her letters to Robert Parker in R. S. Parker papers, NLA, MS 8200.

> unrecognizably. Although I had the best intentions in the world, I must have been unwittingly a cruel and wicked person in many ways to those close to me, and this includes you ... It is only now that I have changed, slowly I suppose really, over the last few years, that I can see my past self more clearly.[2]

She went on to try and appease John by saying that he had borne too much of the burden and hoped her letter would relieve him a little of that.

On marrying Robert, Cecily had moved out of John's shadow and had resisted falling into Robert's, standing beside him rather than behind. She adapted to the role of wife while maintaining her sense of self and independence. However, she had a developing feeling her life with Robert had to be something more. She still suffered from feelings of not being understood by Robert and therefore not loved by him for who she was. Robert did not understand Cecily's discontent, or even that she felt it. He was a kind and caring gentleman, but, like John, he found it hard to express his love or his feelings in ways that satisfied Cecily. Robert loved her, thought she was beautiful and constantly told her so. But Cecily thought Robert could do better in understanding her psyche, in understanding her. She did not stop questioning her relationship openly with Robert and looked to him to give something more than he could.

One of the things Cecily impressed on us as her daughters was that one cannot change people's behaviours, only your own reaction to them. But, on reading her letters, it appears that she had difficulty applying this in her own relationships. She seemed to want Robert to act differently towards her, although she expected him to not try and change her. Part of Cecily's attraction to Robert was the gentleness of her father that she saw in him. He was softly spoken and measured in thinking, as was Cecily's father. With John, she experienced the unpredictability and selfishness of her mother. 'I married my mother first,' she told us when we, all three children, experienced marriage relationship difficulties, 'and then I married my father.' She believed that people generally married someone in whom they saw a parent, and if the relationship went wrong, moved on to a relationship with a person in the image of the other parent. She would smile and say, 'I think people only get it right third time round when they marry someone who suits them.' While Cecily never had the chance to test her theory, ironically, John later did and proved her right.

---

2   Cecily to John, letter 16 October 1969, written from Hove, UK, Cecily family file.

Cecily was finding that, like her father, Robert avoided conflict by shying away from robust discussion. If Cecily were unhappy about something, he would console her, rather than dig too deeply to find its cause. Unlike John, Robert would at least listen and smile when Cecily expressed a complex thought about people and their feelings, but he would never quite 'get it', Cecily would say. If Cecily had a complaint, he took it as a criticism and felt hurt, when she hoped he would listen and consider whether he might make adjustments to his responses or behaviour to satisfy her. The very sensitivity Robert displayed as part of the gentle person Cecily loved caused him to feel deep hurt when she told him how a behaviour of his affected her. It left him feeling that he had failed her in some way. Once she pleaded to him, 'Put yourself in my shoes', in an effort to have him understand how she felt after he had said or done something that upset her. He considered this, and replied, 'But dear, no one can put themselves in other people's shoes'.[3] That helped her understand how people's psyches differ. From Cecily's point of view, he was a compassionate and emotional man, but did not venture down the empathetic track to help improve his understanding of her.

Cecily indulged in keeping Robert informed of her feelings, because she wanted him to understand her. In 1975, Cecily and Robert corresponded for almost the whole year while Robert was overseas, the main topic of which was about sexuality and relationships, and theirs in particular. Their relationship reached a precarious point. By mid-1975, it appeared that Robert and Cecily's might not survive. Cecily felt unloved; Robert felt she lacked interest in making love to him – a vicious cycle couples often confront. In one of Robert's letters to Cecily when he was away, he spoke openly about a female friend of his who, he told Cecily, understood him although she was not his lover. Cecily told Robert how strongly she felt about a male friend of hers, which Robert concluded was more so than he felt about his friend. 'I didn't know that that longing was continuing in you so strongly', he sympathised in his letter by return. Nevertheless, Cecily felt hurt by Robert's closeness to his female friend. She told him that she wanted to 'sleep downstairs' when he came home, because she did not want to suffer pain from someone she cares about.[4] Robert responded in horror:

---

3   Cecily recalled this in a personal communication to the author.
4   R. S. Parker papers, NLA, MS 8200 Restricted, box 22, file 99, 27 May 1975.

> For me to stay in another unknown period of celibacy after the hell of this six months [period of it] would be cutting myself off from the only thing without which I find life really not worth living. It is the thing of which I've felt most bitterly deprived throughout my life.[5]

He said he already had 'substantial slabs of celibacy' while being with Cecily:

> 18 months or 2 years (was it?) when I yielded you up to John (there was no sexual life in my home then, nor had been for 3 years before I took up with you); six months on study leave in 1965 before we married; periods of months (quite a few months) in the last few years when, on some occasions, we were trying for just the same adjustments as you are proposing now.[6]

The response was not what Cecily had expected. She was attracted to Robert sexually, as she had been to John; there was 'chemistry' between them. Sexual intimacy was important to her for a fulfilling relationship, but her expectation was that it should always be an expression of emotional love. Disappointment flowed when the reality of her husbands' sexual needs dawned. John had been neglectful in failing to express his love during the physical act of lovemaking; Robert was simply frank about his needs.

Robert went on to express a deep dissatisfaction with the way in which his and Cecily's relationship had developed. He explained that he did not want his female friend instead of Cecily; that was a 'preposterous idea', but that he would be more content with someone who had a better spontaneous rapport with him than Cecily had – 'provided that there was also the deep attraction that you have for me'. But then, he didn't think such bliss was attainable in a real world. He said:

> And then I even moved to thinking that being alone might be preferable to staying with you if things went on as they have been doing – and that once alone, even something blissful might still happen one day – ... I have been deeply torn, and teetering on the edge of giving us up as a hopeless job.[7]

---

5 R. S. Parker papers, NLA, MS 8200 Restricted, box 22, file 99, 1 June 1975.
6 R. S. Parker papers, NLA, MS 8200 Restricted, box 22, file 99, 1 June 1975.
7 R. S. Parker papers, NLA, MS 8200 Restricted, box 22, file 99, 7 June 1975.

Perhaps Robert's exasperation was a wake-up call for Cecily. For things got better between them. He told Cecily that he was mystified by her repetitive expressions of her feelings and what he perceived to be criticisms of him. Cecily wanted them to be direct with each other, but he found it difficult to express his feelings as she asked him to, only to find her telling him that she did not want him to feel hurt by her directness. He told her that he was in a bind. He wrote: 'Too many words this year. Too much hurt, emphasis on negatives – what about the positives?'[8] They kept writing and a point came when Cecily told him that he seems 'to be beginning to understand how I feel, and I am tremendously grateful for that'. It was a breakthrough from her point of view.[9]

There were still times when Cecily perplexed Robert. Sometime in 1977, in the course of one of their discussions, Cecily told Robert that all his feeling seemed to go into his piano playing. Even so, having observed that Robert expressed emotion through his music, playing it and listening to it, she thought he kept even those emotions under control and mentioned to him that he even bottled up feelings when he played the piano. Nevertheless, by then, Robert felt he was doing better in Cecily's eyes, and noticed Cecily's growing confidence. Robert told his son, Rod, in a letter that year about his and Cecily's discussion on how each of them expressed their feelings. He said, 'I guess it's true that most of my life I haven't had good access to my feelings, whatever they are …'.[10] He confided about his not being whole without a woman close and yet that he had 'not been at all successful at *being* close to the quite outstanding women who've consented to live with me – and this has been a problem with Cecily as much as with Nancy'. He also told Rod that, encouraged by Cecily, he had embarked on a process of introspection, and had tried to loosen up and open up.

It is clear that Cecily regarded a partner as necessary for wholeness – rather than wholeness being a prerequisite for a strong relationship. Despite all her self-analysis, Jungian learning, and the importance to her of family and friends, Cecily continued to see a satisfactory long-term relationship with a man as necessary for her personal fulfilment. A cultural shift in thinking might have assisted both Cecily and Robert, but, at the time, it is difficult to imagine that either of them would have believed it was possible to find happiness and fulfilment on their own.

---

8   R. S. Parker papers, NLA, MS 8200 Restricted, box 22, file 99, dated '31 June' [sic] 1975.
9   R. S. Parker papers, NLA, MS 8200 Restricted, box 22, file 99.
10 R. S. Parker papers, NLA, MS 8200 Restricted, box 24, file 117, Family correspondence, Roderick Bolton, 10 September 1977.

Cecily and Robert in later years.
Source: Family collection.

They worked on to achieve what appeared to be a successful marriage. By 1980, Cecily had started to expand her interests and share more with Robert. Robert, an accomplished pianist, practised daily on his grand piano and accompanied other musicians who attended their house. Cecily started daily piano practice of her own. She had piano lessons for a time as a child, but after years of lessons, she still felt hopeless and did not continue. Now, she was interested in having lessons again from Robert's piano coach. Robert and Cecily were impressed with his teacher's basic approach. She initiated beginners by mingling the fundamentals of scale, structure and harmony. This helped Cecily understand what music was about with a few elementary lessons and Cecily scheduled in a practice period every day on Robert's piano. It gave them something more in common. Some 18 months later, Robert wrote to his sister with pride about Cecily's achievement.

Cecily started to exercise regularly, too, daily skipping with a rope and swimming in a nearby public pool and, by 1982, she swam several mornings a week before breakfast. Between her professional counselling, she scheduled time for other hobbies that included her garden, ballroom dance classes at which she became proficient, and catching up with her reading in the fields of psychology and counselling. She always made time for us children and her grandchildren.

37. REVISITING RELATIONSHIP DIFFICULTIES

However, Cecily never found complete satisfaction in her marriage relationships. When she was in her 80s, she confided to Meredith that 'if I found the right man now, even now, I would leave Robert'. Would there ever have been 'the right man' for Cecily, we wondered, in circumstances where she did not, could not, see herself as 'whole' without one? The need for financial security might have played a part as it did with many other married women at the time. Intellectually, she maintained her view that a healthy relationship between two people could only be enduring if each were whole, and remained whole on marrying, rather than merging two into one. But then, Cecily never experienced such wholeness before entering into either of her marriages. She sought it on entering those marriages. Was she still searching for the idyllic happiness she perceived she had before she turned two?

Robert and Cecily stayed married; Leone and John ultimately did not. In 1978, John left UCL and, as he was nearing retirement, he and Leone moved to Kent. The Conflict Analysis Research Centre that John by this time had established at UCL in 1966 was transferred to the University of Kent at Canterbury. John headed the centre there but, in effect, handed his work over to Professor John Groom, who took up his baton.

John and Leone bought a smallholding at Biddenden and later moved to Oxley Farm in Smarden in Kent where they lived with their son Mark, then 10. John continued to work at the centre while he ran his farm. John's 'playing' at being a farmer, according to Mark's adult reminiscences, gave John a huge amount of pleasure, 'never more so than when it involved "old Fergie" tractors'. Leone designed the farmhouse and John developed the garden, determined by the 'turning circle of the tractor and the gang-mower'.

Leone seized the chance of John being in semi-retirement to concentrate on her career. She was by then a highly regarded Professor of Mathematics and the main breadwinner. She was dependent on John only to keep the home fires burning and care for young Mark after school while she commuted to London for work. John seemed to be uncomfortable with the role reversal, although he enjoyed having time with Mark, time to make home-brewed beer and to prepare meals, his specialty being roast leg of lamb and baked vegetables. He also had time to think, read and write. His mind was occupied with a developing vision of a problem-solving framework and system that could be applied generically to resolution of conflict. He looked for opportunities to get back into academia.

PERSONS OF INTEREST

John and Mark, Kent, UK, 1969.
Source: Family collection.

John with his home brew, Kent, UK, 1969.
Source: Family collection.

Leone and Mark, Kent, UK, 1969.
Source: Family collection.

Tensions started to appear in their household. Meredith visited them when she was in the UK in the late 1970s and spent a weekend counselling each of them at their request. She was uncomfortable in the role and feared that it might strain her relationship with John. She felt that her efforts had been futile.

At the same time, Cecily and John's 'love–hate' relationship lay unresolved. In August 1980, John surprised Cecily by writing: 'I would love to live out the remainder of my life with you. This may be more romance than reality – but comradery would not be platonic.'[11] Cecily knew by then, however, that while she still loved John, she could never live with him.

It became apparent that, by 1980, when Cecily and Robert were resolving their relationship difficulties because they wanted to remain a couple, John and Leone's marriage was fast failing. John wrote to Cecily and talked about his and Leone's unhappiness. He saw the problem as being with Leone not him, again blaming his partner for his relationship failures. He told Cecily, 'Leone is a sick girl: her diabetes is far from under control and in addition she has security or inadequacy problems'.[12] John wrote to Robert too, but it was less personal. He invited Robert to comment on a book he published the previous year, *Deviance, Terrorism and War: The Process of Solving Unsolved Social and Political Problems*.[13] Robert set it for his 'bed time reading' along with other books that had been written by his 'friends'.[14]

In November 1980, ahead of a planned trip to Australia, Leone sent a letter to Meredith about her continuing unhappiness with John: his negative attitudes and unwillingness to take her needs and feelings into account. These were a repeat of some of Cecily's complaints about living with John. Leone was feistier than Cecily, and John and Leone argued loudly and often. In the course of John and Leone's deteriorating relationship, we observed that Mark suffered from parental discord and tension in the house, just as I had as a teen living with Cecily and John.

---

11   Written between 6 and 29 August 1980, Cecily family file.
12   Letter 16 June 1980, Cecily family file.
13   John Burton, *Deviance, Terrorism & War: The Process of Solving Unsolved Social and Political Problems* (Canberra: Australian National University Press, 1979).
14   R. S. Parker Papers, NLA, MS 8200, box 46, file 189. Robert reviewed it nevertheless, and replied at length 9 July 1980.

John's past visits to Australia had been rare, and he chose mostly not to venture to Canberra, the place of memories of unhappy professional and personal relationships. After his father Jack died at age 95 in Sydney in May 1970, he had even less reason to visit Australia. However, in December 1980, John, Leone and Mark made a Christmas visit to Canberra. The family, including Cecily and Robert and some of Robert's family, gathered to exchange presents on Christmas Eve. We all spent Christmas Day at the home of John's nephew and his wife, Ian and Susie Hendry. They ran the Affleck winery across the border to the north of Canberra and provided us with an ice-breaking reunion, although probably a little uncomfortable for Leone.

Leone and John's breakup was drawn out and painful. Unlike Robert and Cecily, who were unlikely to part unless one or other of them had another soul mate to go to, John and Leone separated without either of them having another potential lifetime mate on the horizon. Both found solace in their careers. John moved to the USA in 1983 as a visiting scholar at the University of South Carolina. Across the Atlantic Ocean the divorce proceedings were a nightmare. Lawyers exchanged letters and drained monies from both parties' accounts as a War of the Roses saga developed. I had the horror of thinking that if I did not reconnect in some meaningful way with my father at this time, I might find myself at his funeral one day in the USA. When my father told me he was flying from the USA to London to see his lawyers, I decided to join him in London and try to help him and Leone see sense and resolve their differences in the interests of young Mark.

It did the trick. During the week that John and I spent together in the UK, he and Leone agreed on a final division of their property and assets. Each complained that I was biased in favour of the other. The deal was struck late at night at their old farm home in Kent where Leone was living with Mark, now in his teens. It was strange having a brother a few months younger than my youngest daughter. We went out to dinner as a family and, as we drove home, Mark and I held hands in the back of the car while the two 'adults' continued to exchange barbed remarks. We arrived home close to midnight, and I oversaw both John and Leone place their signatures on the agreement we had reached over dinner. Then, John and I got into his car to travel back to London. 'You did a good job,' I said. 'You acted like it really hurt when Leone demanded a last piece of furniture from you, because none of this is really about money for her, it's all about emotions and love lost.' 'What do you mean, I acted like it hurt? I have been stripped of everything,' John protested. 'Well,' I said, 'it's a good settlement if no one feels like they won.'

Before I left London, John owned up to having met another woman, Betty, of whom he was very fond. I taunted him: 'I am not travelling to America to sort you out when that breaks up.' He told me this was different and that it was 'a mature relationship'. I remember my loving daughterly response: 'I am sure that the only thing mature about it is Betty.' I was probably right. Betty was the best person ever for John, and they made each other very happy.

38

John's 'real career'

John's decision to start a new academic career on the other side of the world turned out to be the right one for him. In August 1963, he had been offered tenure at UCL. John had started to make his mark early in the field of international relations with the help of Quakers. He had enjoyed their support when he became involved in the peace movement in Australia in the 1950s. He later connected with the Quakers through the Rowntree Trust. The family foundation was a philanthropical donor of the Pugwash initiative.

In August 1963, John attended a conference convened on the initiative of British and American Quakers in Clarens, Switzerland. Eastern bloc countries were represented among the 27 or so attendees. All were interested in forming an organisation that might bring the East and West together in their research efforts concerning social and political matters in a scientific environment. John had ideas and expressed them. He was influential in the conference's resolve to establish international Conferences on Research on International Peace and Security (COROIPAS). These conferences would be similar to the Pugwash conferences, but with an international social and political focus, rather than Pugwash's natural sciences focus. The Continuing Committee met in London in early December 1964, out of which the International Peace Research Association (IPRA) was founded with John as its secretary general. The association would, in John's view, take the pressure from Pugwash to expand its work into those fields, which was causing division among scientists. The two organisations were to work together, with representatives from each taking part on the other's standing committees. Pugwash agreed to this. It was John's job to get the new association going and establish behind-the-scenes communications that he hoped might achieve quiet results. Pugwash had established a precedent when, without publicity, it intervened in discussions between the superpowers over test bans.¹ It was influential in enabling the 1963 Limited Test Ban Treaty, allowing the UK to take the credit for the peace initiative, a game plan that John supported.²

In a 1964 article, John discussed power politics in the Cold War, and the circumstances that were forcing nations to reverse their policy of breaking off communications with hostile countries, and to talk more instead. He wrote:

> Quakers have their own methods of dealing with disputes, they know that in situations of tension one should seek increased and not decreased communications. But nations have been known to decrease communications as soon as tensions occurred, thus making tensions worse. To break off diplomatic relations is a nonsensical action. Circumstances are forcing the nations to reverse this policy.
>
> If Quakers could translate into international terms the processes by which they operate, the 'steering' model to which political scientists are referring would mean more to ordinary people.³

John's embracing the support of Quakers is interesting because he had never held himself out as having a faith, once he decided against studying theology. It was Cecily who regarded herself as a religious person but of no denomination. She felt close to the Quakers and identified with their philosophy of peace and their practice of communing in silence unless and until there was something someone was moved to share. Notably, John's father understood the value of the Quakers' and others' spiritual religiosity. He wrote in his autobiography:

> It is this 'inner Light' of the Quakers, this *intuitus mentis* of Descartes, and this 'bhakti marg' of the Hindus that seem to me of the essence of true religion. It is along this path of meditation and devotion that the saints in all ages and in many faiths have trod.⁴

---

1 For more on this, see Paul Rubinson, 'Pugwash Literature Review', Urban Institute, April 2019, accessed 10 April 2021, www.urban.org/research/publication/pugwash-literature-review.
2 Letters from John to family members, 10 and 29 August 1963, Burton family file.
3 Burton, 'The Evolving International System', *Frontier* 7, no. 3 (Autumn 1964), 209, copy held in John W. Burton papers, NLA, MS 8405, box 1, file 1, published papers 1956–64.
4 Burton, 'The Weaver's Shuttle', 208.

Perhaps his father's and Cecily's appreciation of Quaker philosophy helped John to realise its value to international peace movements. The Quakers later became a most important source of support for John in his pursuit of peace through the theory and practice of conflict resolution.

When John first arrived in the UK to teach international relations at UCL, it was at a time when students interested in governance at the international level were given, as their main text, H. J. Morgenthau's *Politics Among Nations* (as was I when I studied the subject at ANU in Canberra shortly after this time). The students also relied on *Power Politics*, the work of the head of department, Georg Schwarzenberger, which, like Morgenthau's works, argued that a balance of power exercised by superpowers was the means to peace. John had been relieved to find a 'tolerance' of ideas – his ideas, which were so different – and Schwarzenberger welcomed and befriended him. They could not have had more diverse philosophies to impart to students of international relations, but it worked well at the outset. Dunn, in his book on John's philosophy and work, pondered how the two related as colleagues.[5] Dunn notes that the two were sure to differ and, in time, they did.

I had arrived in London only days before Christmas 1963. John and I were invited to Georg's country home on Christmas Day. My Australian winter coat was inadequate protection from the icy-cold weather, but the warmth of the welcome we received was more than compensation and we thawed out in front of a roaring log fire. While indulging in rich food and Christmas cheer, I listened to John and Georg jest about their poles-apart views. At 17, I was curious and bold enough to ask naive questions about power politics and diplomacy. I had already been influenced by John's denouncement of deterrence – 'deterrence did not deter' – and his belief that the dominant power politics theories were false.

Although John welcomed 'tolerance' of his views after his ANU experience, as time passed, he wanted more than to be listened to; he wanted his teachings embraced and applied. He questioned whether any of the prevailing theories or methodologies had actually made a difference to the amount or intensity of conflict in the world and, if not, why maintain them.[6] However, difficulties arose from the different approaches of UCL and the London School of Economics (LSE) that manifested particularly

---

5   Dunn, *From Power Politics to Conflict Resolution*, 51.
6   Gregory Tillett, 'Booknotes', *Australasian Dispute Resolution Journal* 16, no. 2 (May 2005), 145.

when students from each sat for exams together. John was not able to win the acceptance of the LSE to his less conventional approach to the teaching of international relations.

Over time though, at UCL and later in the USA, John worked on developing a more complex model of dispute resolution, distinct from conventional negotiation, arbitration and mediation. Dunn observed that, within a few years of taking up his UCL appointment, John 'incrementally' left international relations behind as he travelled down the related path of conflict analysis and resolution in pursuit of a general theory for world peace.[7] This would become John's 'real career' – the one he wanted to be remembered for – his role in furthering the theory and practice of analysis and resolution of conflict. He pursued it for the rest of his long life. Adam Hughes Henry wrote: 'In his second career Burton was viewed internationally as a former high-ranking Australian diplomat who became a cutting-edge scholar of new thinking.'[8]

The destructive border dispute that led to hostilities between Malaysia, Singapore and Indonesia – and the Borneo confrontation – in the mid-1960s provided John with an opportunity of putting his thinking into practice. He had been pivotal in establishing a Conflict Analysis Research Centre in the UK.[9] The British prime minister, Harold Wilson, had tried to get the disputing parties together. With his encouragement, the centre, then at UCL, intervened with some success. It invited each head of government to send to London three representatives to discuss the problem *in camera* to get to the heart of the problem.[10] The framework the centre used in its impartial third-party facilitation process came to serve as a problem-solving model of what retrospectively became regarded as 'track two' diplomacy.[11]

---

7   See Dunn, *From Power Politics to Conflict Resolution*, 79. The centre's home has remained at the University of Kent since its transfer from UCL in 1978, and John's work is honoured by a continuing lecture series in his name.
8   Henry, 'Reflections on Dr. John Wear Burton', 74.
9   'John Burton Lectures', Conflict Analysis Research Centre, University of Kent, undated, accessed 10 April 2021, research.kent.ac.uk/conflict-analysis/events/john-burton-lectures/.
10 John. W. Burton, 'Peace Begins at Home' and 'International Conflict: A Domestic Responsibility', *The International Journal of Peace Studies* 6, no. 1 (Spring 2001).
11 Robin Fraser, 'Track Two Diplomacy – A Distinct Conflict Intervention Category' (Master's diss., University of Victoria, 2012); and see Ron Fisher, *Interactive Conflict Resolution* (Syracuse, NY: Syracuse University Press, 1997).

With the permission of the United Nations, the centre participated in processes to help resolve conflicts in Northern Ireland and Moldova, among others. Measuring success of the method was difficult because, necessarily, outcomes of such facilitated confidential dialogue between disputants could not be publicised.[12] Communication, open and frank and *in camera*, was the key.

Initially, John was driven by the search for an alternative to the use of force as a means of resolving international disputes. However, the struggle he had in the UK to articulate his model and how it differed from peace talks and other methods of dispute resolution led him to expand his thinking. He drew on research of industrial conflict literature, social psychology and existing dispute resolution systems and frameworks in an effort to work towards a generic approach to resolving conflict. He would eventually find an accepting home for a multidisciplinary approach in the USA.

It took some time for John to establish himself in the USA after he left the UK in 1983. I met up with him in April that year at a conference in Mexico. We returned to his bachelor flat in South Carolina. The dogwoods and azaleas were in full bloom but not so colourful is my memory of John, a sad and lonely man wanting to change the world. My diary note reads: 'Discussed the conference and his proposals and how we can appeal to [Prime Minister] Hawke's vanity and get him interested in an international facilitation centre'. The Quakers were still his benefactors. My then partner, journalist Alan Ramsey, and I had the pleasure of staying with one of his Quaker colleagues, in Boulder, Colorado, from whom I learned how revered my father was for his peace work.

After completion of his fellowship in South Carolina, John obtained a teaching position for two years at the University of Maryland. In 1984, I visited him there and found a much happier man. He was now living with Betty Nathan who he had told me about in London. Betty became the true love of John's life. Like Cecily and Leone, she was intellectually bright and university educated. She was 13 years his junior, not such an obvious gap at their senior ages and, having a Jewish heritage, she was very similar in looks and stature as Leone: dark eyes, short, dark hair and physically fit. Like Cecily, she was a very able editor and turned John's writing into accessible prose. Betty was a caring, sensitive and a very

---

12   J. C. R. Bayley and J. W. Burton, *Northern Ireland Interim Report* (London: Centre for the Analysis of Conflict, UCL, January 1971); and see Michael Hall in collaboration with Joe Camplisson, *From Conflict Containment to Resolution: The Experiences of a Moldovan-Northern Ireland Self-help Initiative* (Newtownabbey: Island Publications, 2002).

sensible partner for John. He adored her from the moment he met her until he died. She dealt with, rather than dwelt upon, his difficultness. With Betty around, John was energised; he looked younger, smiled more and became academically very productive.

In 1985, John obtained a research and teaching position at George Mason University (GMU). Helpful to John's academic standing in the USA was his existing reputation in his field. In particular, acclaim for him appeared in an article by Andrew Wilson in *The Bulletin* in 1982 in the context of a Bill being considered by both houses of the US Congress for a Peace Academy. The Bill proposed to allocate government resources and set up machinery for conflict resolution. In detailing its history and purpose, Wilson wrote:

> The pioneer of these developments, which have resulted in US Administration backing for the Peace Academy Bill, is an Australian. A former head of the Commonwealth External Affairs Department in the Evatt period, John Burton started work in the field in the 1960s …
>
> With the knowledge and approval of the British Government, his team has involved itself in quite a number of crises in the past 15 years. Its operations, called 'workshops', have included setting up meetings between nominees of the governments of Malaysia, Singapore and Indonesia in the Borneo confrontation; meetings between nominees of both sides in the Cyprus dispute; meetings, in both Britain and the US, between parties to the Palestine dispute; and more recently meeting on East-West tension in London and Moscow.[13]

John's thinking, when he had left the UK, was that basic human needs were central to the cause of disputes and identifying them was essential to understanding the root source and cause of any conflict. Around this core he eventually developed his peace theory to the point of articulating a problem-solving framework and system that could guide the practice of conflict resolution at all levels of society to promote sustainable resolutions to conflict in domestic and industrial disputes as well as disputes between nation states.[14]

---

13 Andrew Wilson, 'A Psychiatrist for Nations in Conflict', *Bulletin*, 27 July 1982, 81–82. The Bill was before both Houses of Congress but seems to have died before the next session.
14 See in particular John's work, *Resolving Deep-rooted Conflict: A Handbook* (Lanham, MD: University Press of America, 1987) and *Conflict Resolution: Its Language and Processes* (Lanham, MD: Scarecrow Press, 1996).

38. JOHN'S 'REAL CAREER'

John the academic, USA, mid-1980s.
Source: Family collection.

His theory was founded on the assumption that individuals, families and communities have basic needs that extend beyond physical needs of food, clothing and shelter. They include, for example, the need for identity and respect. Hostilities, confrontations and wars, triggered by seemingly obvious events, usually arose out of perceived failures to have certain of these needs met and, John came to believe, that conflict resolution should be directed towards analysis of the behavioural and systemic sources of the conflict.

The GMU's Center for Conflict Analysis and Resolution (CCAR) gave John the opportunity to further develop thinking and to teach and train others in the field. Unlike the time he headed a government department as a young man, here he was seen as 'an elder' – 'Mother Burton', one of his colleagues called him – a better position from which to lead new thinking. According to Dunn, it was at GMU that John saw that basic human needs were central to conflict and its resolution: 'He went beyond Maslow in articulating the framework from which he developed a research agenda that would allow him to look at conflict as a whole and the need to delve into its sources and causes for its resolution.'[15] John further developed his belief that disputing nations were more likely to express their real concerns behind closed doors where there was no need for rhetoric for public ears.

My daughter Amanda and I spent time with John and Betty in Washington DC in 1986. I recall John telling us about his participation in the facilitation of peace talks under the auspices of CCAR between members of the British Parliament and the Argentine Congress to discuss the Falkland/Malvinas dispute. A study of the dispute revealed that the real goal of Argentina was the country's acceptance as a 'Western' state and not recognition of its claim to sovereignty of the islands as such. Disputes such as this and that of the Greek and Turkish Cypriots demonstrated to him the benefits of an analytical problem-solving approach as against power negotiation.[16]

These 'track two' initiatives concerned with informal, unofficial efforts to resolve or mitigate violent, intractable conflicts were also utilised in Northern Ireland, Sudan, Liberia and elsewhere. Records of them are contained in the conflict and peace research archive at 'Point of View', the CCAR institute's retreat, research and conference centre, Masons Neck, Virginia. From offering postgraduate studies in the field, CCAR developed a prestigious university teaching program to become what it is today, the Jimmy and Rosalynn Carter School for Peace and Conflict Resolution (the Carter School).

Much has been written about his work. The John Burton Library and Resource Center at the Carter School, with its dedicated focus on conflict analysis and resolution, attests to this. I found an example of John's international influence in the field in Karin Utas Carlsson's work *Violence Prevention and Conflict Resolution*. The report covers Maslow's human needs theory and an alternative paradigm for peace and was distributed by the Department of Educational and Psychological Research at the Malmö School of Education, Sweden, in 1999. In including an analysis of John's theory, the author states that she is very much influenced by Burton's thinking. Her dedication, 'To Markus and his generation', highlights the work of Einstein and Burton. It reads:

---

15   Personal communication, 18 April 2019.
16   Burton, 'Conflict Analysis', unpublished paper, 1994, 41, Burton family file.

> 'Our world is threatened by a crisis whose extent seems to escape those within whose power it is to make major decisions for good or evil. The unleashed power of the atom has changed everything except our ways of thinking. Thus we are drifting toward a catastrophe beyond comparison. We shall require a substantially new manner of thinking if man-kind is to survive.' (A. Einstein, 1946.)

> 'It would be a shift in thinking of a profound kind – like finding the earth is round and not flat – if we were to discover that conflicts have generally a win-win potential and not a win-lose one.' (J. W. Burton, 1986.)[17]

In 1988, John became a 'Distinguished Jennings Randolph Fellow' of the US Institute of Peace. On 26 April that year, he delivered the second Annual Vernon M. and Minnie I. Lynch Lecture, entitled, 'On the Need for Conflict Prevention'. Over time, John authored more than 20 books on world peace and the theory and practice of conflict resolution, starting with *The Alternative* in 1954 and finishing with *Violence Explained* in 1997.[18]

Throughout the time John lived in the UK and the USA, he wrote fortnightly air letters addressed to 'Dear all' and, using carbon copies, he sent them to each of Meredith, Clare and me, and some to Cecily and Robert. They kept coming, whether we answered or not. They were mostly undated other than the note 'Monday' or 'Sunday' – John had little feel for history – and written for the moment to check in on us and keep us informed of his doings. Today these letters are a rich source of archival material on his work, the international disputes in which he was involved, on world affairs and how he viewed them at the time. I kept them, partly because of my interest and studies in international relations and because I was impressed with his persistence in working to find solutions to war and violence. I am grateful to David Dunn who, when undertaking research for *From Power Politics to Conflict Resolution*, painstakingly put the letters into chronological order with reference to postmarks where available and events and conferences mentioned in the letters.

---

17 Karin Utas Carlsson, *Violence Prevention and Conflict Resolution: A Study of Peace Education in Grades 4–6*, Studia Psychologica Et Paedagogica Series Altera CXIV (Malmö: Department of Educational and Psychological Research, Malmö School of Education, 1999), accessed 10 April 2021, tradet.org/filer/avh_peaceed.pdf.
18 John Burton, *Violence Explained: The Sources of Conflict, Violence and Crime and Their Prevention* (Manchester: Manchester University Press, 1997).

The most notable aspect of John's personal philosophy, which I believe drove his thinking, was the consistency of his belief that the path to world peace was through global economic stability and – putting it boldly at its highest – prosperity. From a young age he saw self-determination and freedom from exploitation as important to achieving this. In his senior years, John saw those as important in satisfying the basic human need of belonging – that is, identity. The influence of his father and his Methodist teachings was strong during his childhood and provided the basis for the philosophy that drove the development of his political and economic ideals. His thinking was reinforced from his public service experience that, in turn, informed his later intellectual and practical work in the fields of international and domestic conflict resolution. Because so much has been written about John's work in the field of analysis of conflict and resolution that supports the view that his philosophy and political agenda were driven by these idealistic notions, there is no need for me to attempt to cover John's 'real career' in detail. Others qualified in the field are more able to do it justice.

What is left for me to do, having attempted to paint a full picture of John's earlier life in Australia, is to continue his story from the time he returned to Australia in 1989 to live out the rest of his life. However, because John's influence as a public servant in postwar Australia has remained a subject of historical controversy, it is worth mentioning here that, after John's death in 2010, Dennis Richardson, then secretary of the Department of Foreign Affairs and previously head of ASIO and therefore well-placed to know who John was and what he stood for, described John as 'a distinguished and highly respected member of the Department of External Affairs'.[19] He said, 'Many years on he still has a place of honour in the Department, which he headed up.' Important to me, too, is the Australian War Memorial's recent recognition of John as an important 'peacemaker' in Australia's foreign policy history.[20]

---

19 Letter Dennis Richardson to Betty Nathan, 30 June 2010, Burton family file.
20 Peter Londey, 'Brave New Australia', *Wartime* (Australian War Memorial) magazine, no. 88 (Spring 2019). Londey drew on his research on John Burton's role in the development of Australia's postwar foreign policies and strategic allegiances for a forthcoming volume of the Official History of Australian Peacekeeping, Humanitarian and Post–Cold War Operations series.

39

Coming full circle: Cecily, Robert, John and all

I do not recall that John visited us again in Canberra between his and Leone's visit to Australia in 1980 and mid-1986 when I played an unintended role in the advent of the return of the prodigal father. I was diagnosed with second-stage breast cancer – a scary illness in those days – and feeling powerless from a distance, John wrote to Cecily asking to be kept informed. Cecily was by then the undoubted resolute head of our Australian family. She kept John informed of my progress without questioning or judging him. The family pulled together to consider what treatment options might be most effective. John buried his hurt with what Canberra and ANU had dished out to him many years earlier and came to Australia with Betty to share Christmas with us that year. We welcomed them warmly and, to our surprise, on their next visit they purchased a holiday house on the NSW south coast, with an intention of visiting more often. John enjoyed having his family again. The treatment I had lasted for several years before I was finally out of the woods, the ordeal benefiting the whole family: large family gatherings became a custom. Our half-brother Mark visited us too and became a 'real' brother to his Australian sisters.

In 1989, on an occasion when John and Betty were travelling home from the south coast, they stopped to inspect a farmhouse with large acreage for sale, 'Witwood'. It was near Braidwood and just a 20-minute drive from my Bungendore rural home where I had been living with a menagerie of animals for some years. Well into his 70s, John decided to become a farmer again! He and I had now had rural lives in common, although John became a real farmer while I commuted to Canberra daily to run my law practice.

John and Cecily, the matriarch, mid-1980s.
Source: Family collection.

Betty had family of her own in the USA whom she did not want to leave. She and John came to a deal. They would spend half the year in Australia and half in the States with a manager in charge of the farm. In the short time they lived there, before John's health failed him, he planted hundreds of trees down the 1-kilometre driveway to act as a wind and fire break, installed irrigation for them and acquired 50 head of Aberdeen Angus and Hereford cattle. He ran his cattle, shot foxes and kept up his writing at their Braidwood home. The improvements he made to the property and his farming methods once more attracted interest of neighbours and others.

In 1993, the day before a guest interested in John's farming techniques came to visit, John noticed strangers stomping over his property and was momentarily alarmed, believing he was under surveillance again. The guest was would-be farmer Bill Hayden, then governor-general of Australia. His term was coming to an end and he wanted to return to Queensland and run cattle, too, and presumably, his security guards wanted to first check out Witwood. Hayden, who I had met through Ramsey when Hayden was opposition leader of the Labor Party, was younger than my father and the two had never met, although they knew of each other. I had told my father of Hayden's wish to visit his farm to obtain some farming tips, so

39. COMING FULL CIRCLE

John and Betty opened their home to him. John usually rode around the paddocks on his four-wheel rider with his dog sitting behind him. On this occasion John showed the governor-general around in his car.

Coombs visited John at his farm too. It was not far from Judith Wright's property 'The Edge' within the Half Moon wildlife reserve near Braidwood. Neither Cecily nor John, as close as they had been to Coombs and Wright over the decades, were aware of the love connection that had developed between the two by the 1970s, only that they had worked together on some Indigenous and environmental issues they both felt passionate about. With my lawyer's hat on, I engaged with Wright to discuss some legalities surrounding some of her social activism.[1] Cecily kept in touch with both of them individually. After Wright's husband Jack died in 1966, she had moved to Braidwood and, from that time on, she and Coombs saw more of each other and corresponded regularly. They enjoyed a deep but secret love attachment for the rest of their lives. Their love story was revealed by letters made available after their deaths.[2] Their romance is reflected in Canberra's heritage; two of Canberra's new western suburbs that lie snugly side by side in Molonglo Valley are named Wright and Coombs.[3] After his visit to John's Braidwood farm, Coombs attended more of our family events in Canberra but we never saw him and Wright socially together.[4]

---

1   Judith Wright had two missions to benefit others, about which she consulted me in the late 1970s at my legal practice, Pamela Coward & Associates. She wanted to bequeath her 41-hectare Braidwood property 'The Edge', which she regarded as a wildlife refuge, to ANU, and she wanted to draft and execute an Aboriginal Treaty with the Australian Government. The latter was in her capacity as secretary of the Aboriginal Treaty Committee (1979–83) and history tells us of the fate of that mission. As to the former, I had no success because the university protested that it had no budget to upkeep the property. In 1984, Judith bequeathed the property to the Australian people for ecological research through ANU. Judith died from a heart attack in Canberra on 25 June 2000 and was not to know the property would eventually be sold on the open market to a private buyer.
2   Miyuki Jokiranta, prod., *Love and Fury: Judith Wright & 'Nugget' Coombs*, ABC Program, 23 April 2013, and broadcast on ABC Radio, 19 April 2013. Judith lived alone at The Edge in her later years.
3   The story of Judith and Nugget's relationship is told in Fiona Capp, 'In the Garden: Judith Wright and Nugget Coombs', *The Monthly*, June 2009, accessed 6 April 2021, www.themonthly.com.au/issue/2009/june/1274320360/fiona-capp/garden.
4   For correspondence regarding ANU management of The Edge, see Papers of Judith Wright, NLA, MS 5781, box 81, file 583. Under the terms of Wright's bequest, the property was to be used for ecological research. In 1999, the university told Wright it had no further use for it. The university gave it to the Duke of Edinburgh's Award for just $1. It was sold on the open market for almost half a million dollars in 2014.

Nugget Coombs and John, Canberra, 1993, at Meredith's home.
Source: Family collection.

For New York–raised Betty, her new lifestyle could not have been more different. She adapted graciously and embraced her Australian family, including Cecily and Robert. She wrote a delightful novel set in the arty country town of Braidwood and the surrounding Australian farmland, *Top Paddock* (1993). Its protagonist is, of course, an Australian academic farmer, and the good and evil characters are a delightful (sometimes not so well-disguised) mix of family members, friends and townsfolk she had met.

Betty and John gardening at 'Witwood', near Braidwood, NSW, early 1990s.
Source: Family collection.

Clare and Cecily, family Christmas 1992, at Pam's farm, 'Yarrandale'.
Source: Family collection.

My father and I both prepared well for bushfires, a real threat for both our properties. We relied on tank water and our own devices to protect our homes. But, in 1994, Robert and Cecily, living in suburban Canberra were the ones affected. The fire came over the hill from Mount Stromlo and into their garden. It burnt some of their grounds but spared their Curtin home.

From 1986 onwards, our family continued our Christmas gatherings: John, Betty, Cecily and Robert, Meredith, Clare and me, and sometimes various of our former partners with whom Cecily as the family glue had always kept in touch. Cecily made it easier for us all to negotiate our way through our lives and relationships and, thanks to her uniting skills and the generous natures of Robert and Betty, we became a warm and inclusive extended family.

In the meantime, a cloud had formed on the horizon for Robert. While I was still receiving chemotherapy, Robert's eldest, Rod, was diagnosed with lymphoma. Robert suffered the agony of watching his son undergo gruelling treatment for the disease to which he ultimately succumbed. Rod died in 1988. Robert and Cecily had supported each other through Rod's and my illnesses and, while each was desperate that their own offspring would survive, they each cared deeply for their stepchildren. Robert played a father role to me in my late teen years, and Cecily was an important figure in Rod's and his young daughter's life. John's return and the resultant close relationships that grew between our extended family and the respect each of our parents and step-parents had for each other was a joy and comfort to us three girls and our half-brother Mark. We gathered often for family celebrations at my rural property equidistant to John's farm and Canberra. As I recovered from surgery and the effects of radiation and chemotherapy, the family 'healed'.

John and Betty's two-country living arrangements worked for a time until John suffered a massive heart attack in 1993. He was ambulanced to Canberra for hospital but was too weak and ill to undergo an operation. He was transferred to Sydney and was confined to bed at his sister's Wahroonga home until he made a shaky recovery sufficient to undergo a triple bypass. It was touch and go, but he survived. From his St Vincent's Hospital recovery bed, John made phone calls to real estate agents. Ahead of a slump in rural property prices, he achieved a sale of his well-kept property and cattle as a going concern. Betty and John moved into a house in a leafy street of Bruce in Canberra, a stone's throw from Calvary Hospital. John did make a trip back to the USA with Betty, but had another heart attack alighting from a plane and, after getting themselves home, he could not travel so far afield again. Clare, who had lived in Sydney and Brisbane, but not Canberra since she was young, moved back to Canberra and bought a house in O'Connor where Meredith already lived. We were a complete Canberra-based family again.

39. COMING FULL CIRCLE

'Open Day', Melrose Valley, Tuggeranong, 1995.
Left to right: Robert, Cecily, John, Betty, (Pam not in view), Meredith.
Source: Family collection.

Clare, Cecily and John, Cecily's 80th birthday party at Clare's house, O'Connor, Canberra.
Source: Family collection.

John and Betty, Canberra, mid-1990s.
Source: Family collection.

Betty made short trips alone to the USA where her children and grandchildren lived. John defied the medical odds. He survived several ambulance emergencies for TIAs (mini-strokes) and, according to his cardiologist, he lived some 20 years beyond what the state of his progressive heart failure indicated he might. If patient control over their body is an indicator of prospects of survival, no wonder John did so well. He wrote a four-page closely typed letter to his specialist in November 1998 attaching handwritten charts of his fluid intake and blood pressure, detailing his clinical history and how he felt and what he did about it over a period of two days. He explained that he had, in his area of work, been 'advocating getting at the roots of problems, explanations, before remedies'.[5] He conceded that this might not be relevant in this case and that maybe his suffering was just typical old-age and that he should 'let time take its course'. He signed off, 'Over to you'. Because of the care provided by his bemused and conscientious medical team and Betty's loving dedication to John's care, he survived another 12 years. Betty had reasonably expected John to die sooner and had planned to return to the USA where her grandchildren were fast growing up, but she stayed to be with John.

---

5   Collection of letters, Burton family file.

39. COMING FULL CIRCLE

John at his desk, Canberra, c. 2007.
Source: Family collection.

Inactive in body, John was not inactive in his mind. He spent time writing, and from his armchair, he thought and talked about his developing ideas. He also listened to, and talked with, the myriad of carers who came to the house to provide respite for Betty. He liked hearing their stories as they prepared lunch for him and assisted with chores. Many of them opened up to him about family difficulties or their career aspirations. Some brought their wives or partners to one of his Friday night soirees to meet him. John and Betty's Friday night open house soirees at their home in Bruce became legendary. Family, ex-spouses, friends, some foes, former colleagues, PhD students, academics and journalists dropped in. Planet John was a drawcard, despite his failing hearing, being virtually chair ridden and reliant on a portable oxygen cylinder and a walker to move about. Betty set out glasses, cheese and biscuits and other bites to eat, not knowing if 5 or 15 people would arrive on any particular Friday evening. They were noisy, informative and happy events, the conversation usually current political issues and always lively. Children who came with their parents would drop into the pool adjacent to the living room that, solar heated and enclosed, John swam in regularly for gentle exercise while he was able.

Cecily and Robert came often while they could. John and Robert had a more formal relationship than they enjoyed when they were young. Cecily, however, now spoke her mind, expressed her thoughts and was critical of John's sweeping assertions when she thought fit, and John listened to her. She responded to one of the draft articles he gave her in March 2006 with: 'I think your ideas for the future are wonderful, very much to be wished for. But your way of expressing them is something else again!' She provided constructive comments and concluded with 'I am glad you gave me the chance to comment. Thanks! I am reminded of the early, early days of working on *The Alternative* et al.'[6] John remained a thinker and kept reading and writing, attempting to persuade those family, friends and colleagues around him to pursue his work. He wanted to establish a Peace Institute, and in a vain effort to fund it by winning the *Reader's Digest* 'jackpot' he became a subscriber. He drafted a paper, 'The Mess We Are In', apologising to the younger generations for the state of the world left for them to live in. He died before it was completed.[7]

From our perspective, John learned a lot from Cecily and her ability to listen to people. This occurred too late from Cecily's perspective, but at least others benefited. With regard to her relationship with John, they had come full circle. She no longer required nor sought his approval. Cecily and John still cared for each other. John admired her legs, which were still shapely at age 80. Cecily still loved him, though, as she often told us, 'I could never live with him'. She was her own person and it was John who now looked up to and admired her.

Betty, intelligent and interesting, with a love of culture and Australian Aboriginal art in particular, was accepting of the family dynamics, and engaged fully with us all; she knew that John truly loved her. The one happy and successful marriage in the five that took place in which Cecily or John were involved was that of Betty and John. They married in October 2006 when John was age 91, after they had been living together in blissful unity for 20 years. John was almost confined to a chair and went nowhere without oxygen. Why did they marry at that time? John told Meredith that it was about 'public commitment'.

---

6   Burton family file.
7   The draft paper is held on the Burton family file.

Betty's story is different. In 2019, having just turned 90, she told me by email that the reason for their marriage arose from the fall John had when he cracked a few of his ribs, before he made the effort to get out of bed to respond to Prime Minister Howard's vicious *Quadrant* dinner speech. His immobility required more physical help than he liked to admit. He kept urging her to return to the USA to be near her children. They had never discussed marriage; at their age it had not seemed important. She sensed that John's Methodist upbringing was causing him, perhaps, to worry about the situation he had placed her in and so, she asked him: 'Would you want me to stay with you if we were married?' His face lit up and he replied, 'Yes.'

They intended to have a private ceremony without involving the family. However, they could not contain their excitement and, when they told us, we insisted on 'crashing' the event – or at least be allowed to stand in a corner of the room and witness the occasion. It was a romantic ceremony conducted by a celebrant in their living room and John stood up to take his vows. They looked radiant; Betty in a flowing summer dress and John wearing an embroidered silk waistcoat that Mark, his son, had given him some years earlier. John's mind was sharp, his dry sense of humour intact and his love for Betty patent. Sadly, Clare was no longer with us to celebrate the occasion.

John and Betty, wedding day, October 2006.

Source: Family collection.

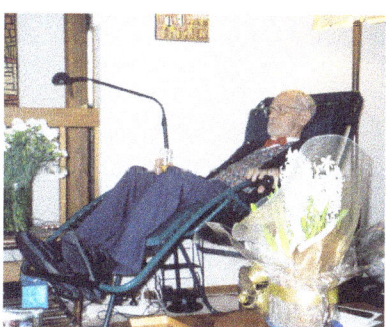

John relaxing on his wedding day, October 2006.

Source: Family collection.

40

A family shattered: Loss of Clare

On 1 August 1998, family tragedy struck; John's and Cecily's lives were never the same again. Clare suffered acute abdominal pain and was hospitalised. On 10 August she was diagnosed with widespread cancer; it was possible that it was ovarian cancer in origin, but we will never know. It was too late to treat her. She declined rapidly, stoically staying alert to arrange her affairs and to say goodbye to her three children and other relatives and friends. She died in hospital 12 days after being admitted, on 23 August 1998. Her sudden illness and death shattered us. The tragedy had a uniting effect on the family, but the loss of a child is one that no parent should have to go through. We watched this brave being, our sister, adjust rapidly to her unexpected fate. She made a list of friends and past loves to whom she particularly wanted to say goodbye. They came from near and far. The hospital waiting room had no less than three or more bodies sleeping overnight those 12 days, to keep a watch over her and be there.

It affected Cecily badly. Her relationship with Clare was complex. Clare did not spare Cecily her conviction that Cecily's nurturing of her as a baby contributed to Clare's emotional difficulties into her adulthood. She unwittingly hurt Cecily by 'dumping' this on her over many years. In hindsight, Clare's illness might have contributed to her anger and to some irrational behaviour we observed. Cecily, forever the counsellor, had responded as a counsellor would – at arms' length – allowing Clare to believe that Cecily could take criticism in her stride. But Cecily found

Clare's intensity of feeling confronting. Cecily talked with Clare when and whenever Clare wanted to talk, pushing down her own hurt, in order to help Clare, but Cecily felt that she had failed as Clare's mother.

Clare and I often argued and we had a troubled sisterly relationship. For me, the love and appreciation she exuded when I had time alone with her at the hospital warmed my heart. I knew we had always loved each other and, in a way, our emotional closeness as siblings got in the way of a friendship as adults. As children, despite the age differences, Clare and I were closer playmates and confidantes than were Clare and Meredith or Meredith and me. When it mattered, we were close again, for which I am grateful.

In April that year, Clare had ended her relationship with her partner Geoff, who she had been living with in Canberra, and he returned to his home state of Queensland before Clare fell acutely ill. Clare worked very hard in the months May to August as an employment equity consultant and undertook major gender equity projects with various organisations as required by them. Her most significant was Women in the Australian Defence Force. She held interviews with senior managers, staff and women with grievances, and collated massive amounts of material for the reports she wrote in order to examine the cultural, social and institutional barriers to the merit-based progression of women in their careers.

She was about to board a flight to New Zealand to embark on work for its defence forces when the onset of severe pain caused her to cancel her arrangements. After she was first admitted to hospital, her pain eased and she was discharged with a misdiagnosis of twisted colon. Our close family friend Doug Cocks lived nearby and visited her twice daily. Late one night, she telephoned him, in pain and frightened. He drove straight around to see her and she told him she thought she was going to die. The next morning Meredith joined them to discuss what should be done. I came in from my farm to talk with her. Having recovered from my poor cancer prognosis, I had become expert in navigating the medical maze. I will never forget the gist of our conversation. Clare was convinced that she had cancer. I assured her, with words to the effect of, 'No, Clare, your pain is too acute. Pain of that severity would only happen at the very last stages of cancer, not at this time, before any diagnosis.' How right *and* wrong I was. She was readmitted to hospital thin, in pain and unhappy. By 13 August it was realised that the cancer was well-advanced and she

40. A FAMILY SHATTERED

had possibly only months to live. Doug rang Meredith from the hospital too distressed to be coherent. Meredith went to the hospital and was greeted by Clare with, 'We never did know who would be the first to go.'

Before Meredith could adjust to the news or telephone us, Clare discussed with her how she could recover money owed to her for her consulting work that she wanted her children to have. Meredith phoned us and, later that day, we all, including Cecily, John and Betty and one of Clare's children, Kate (Charlie) who then lived in Canberra, gathered at the hospital.

Clare's spirits lifted to a degree; she finally had a diagnosis and was under competent medical care. She had insufficient time to face the reality of death – or had she done this in the days gone by when she was in so much suffering at home? Was it just us, suffering from having so little time to come to grips with her certain pending death? Clare kept up our spirits – in a literal sense too. We brought in gin and tonic one evening and poured drinks for everyone. Clare sipped too, while we drew up rosters to ensure that Clare had company round the clock. A day or so later, we urged that she be transferred to the public ward and abandon her private insurance so that she would have 24-hour access to doctors for pain relief as required. Reliance on a specialist medical practitioner in a private hospital might work well for a broken leg, but I knew that only the public system had medical teams to deal adequately with serious and complex medical conditions. It was the right move.

Within another day or two, Clare was skin and bones; her stomach had filled up with fluid and new pains developed every day. She required increased doses of morphine. Doug stayed overnight at the hospital, every night except once when an ex-boyfriend of Clare's flew in from interstate and stayed overnight instead. Her children, Rachael, Steve and Charlie, did the same, bedding down in the waiting room. They suffered badly. Their father and his wife came from Sydney to see Clare and support their distraught children. Clare was joyous that she lived to see Steve's firstborn, Ben, her first grandchild.

Too many people wanted to see Clare and the stimulation was too much for her. She tried to engage with them through a cloud of morphine. We all wanted to be needed. I tried too hard to be practical, offering advice about treatment options, and it was altogether too much for her and she said so. Cecily struggled to cope. She missed visiting only one day when it became too much for her. However, Cecily played the valuable role as postbox, communicating with everyone and looking after their needs, despite her own immense suffering. Our father just sat around, wanting to be there, saying little.

Meredith and I managed our work commitments as best we could. Meredith was deputy vice-chancellor of the University of Canberra at the time. She travelled between the university and Calvary Hospital to fit in two to three visits a day. I drove between my farm, my barristers' chambers in the city and the hospital, and tried to meet commitments to hear cases scheduled to come before me on an administrative appeals tribunal. The family worked well as a team, powerless and deeply distressed at the prospect of the loss of Clare.

My children suffered from afar, keeping in touch with us by phone. They both then lived in Tasmania. Cassandra and her older sister, Amanda, were orphaned when they were just six and seven respectively when my then husband Dan and I took over their care. Clare had known their natural parents and the plight they faced in the knowledge that the father had a short life-expectancy. When, unexpectedly, the children's mother died, leaving the two little girls in the care of their unwell father, he had urged Clare to find foster parents for them after his death. Amanda and Cassandra had a special bond with Clare.

Lying in her hospital bed, Clare kept her sense of humour and encouraged us to engage with it. She laughed recalling past memories. She made amusing, sometimes caustic, observations about the medical team and others around her. Each of us, after spending time with her, shared her priceless words with others when we returned to the waiting room. As sick as Clare was, one or other of us was there to accompany her and her drains and morphine drip to the balcony several times a day and during the night for her much-needed cigarette. On these occasions, she was at her most amusing. It was not the time to urge her to give up her smokes.

Treatment options were limited. No one knew what sort of cancer she had, only that she was now suffering from extreme irritation to her stomach lining. She received conflicting advice from two specialists, an oncologist brought in when her dire condition was apparent and the other a palliative care doctor. She asked that both be present together and air the opinions in front of her so that she could assess the pros and cons. The two male medicos stood at the end of her bed and exchanged their points of view. Clare listened and when they appeared to find common ground, she rolled her hands in a 'wrapping up' motion and asked: 'Have we reached

40. A FAMILY SHATTERED

a consensus?' They had. Chemotherapy could be tried in an effort to stall the spread of cancer. However, within days, it became apparent that palliative care was the only realistic option. Then, a decision was made that, for her comfort, fluid from her stomach should be tapped. The entry of a drain was likely to cause infection and lead to a quicker death. She accepted the drain knowing she might not make it to a palliative care facility. Her stomach was drained regularly and by 22 August it was clear that Clare was fading fast. She retained her amazing spirit. She asked that I work with her with pen and pad in hand, to take notes, fill in forms and not leave anything about her estate to chance after she died. She delegated to others too, ensuring that all her affairs were in order and that her consultative work was handed on to appropriate experts. Meredith and Doug had set off to inspect Clare Holland House hospice for Clare. They returned to hospital to find Clare vomiting.

Clare died the next day. She was 55. Cecily was suffering beyond what she could cope with. Robert had a minor operation scheduled for the day following Clare's death. Cecily had to be there for him. A week on, Meredith's journal records the state of dysfunction most of us were in. She wrote of Clare's death, of her own daughter and one of Clare's not being well, of Cecily being 'a wreck' and of John 'soldiering through'. At the same time, when she needed him most, Meredith's man had let her down by returning to be with his former partner.

Clare had a huge intellect, a forceful personality, sometimes difficult to converse with if your views did not exactly coincide, and had become well-known and much loved by feminists and others for her internationally acclaimed work on gender equity in the workforce. Her doctoral thesis was published in 1995 as *Subordination: Feminism and Social Theory – a History of Ideas* and was, according to (Dame) Quentin Bryce, later governor-general, an 'acclaimed' text. Bryce said:

> Clare wanted to change the world, and she did.
>
> She did so through her extraordinary contribution to the Women's Movement and in particular to women's employment opportunities and experiences.
>
> Clare was digging deeper and deeper into where gender bias is located.[1]

---

1   Quentin Bryce, 'Burton, Clare (1942–1998)', *Obituaries Australia*, accessed 10 April 2021, oa.anu.edu.au/obituary/burton-clare-1373.

Clare as we remember her.
Source: Family collection.

40. A FAMILY SHATTERED

Clare's contribution to gender equity and a better world has lived on through her work. She co-authored *Women's Worth: Pay Equity and Job Evaluation* (1987) and wrote *The Promise and the Price* (1991). Annual lectures on gender equity take place in her name, ANU has a scholastic award in her name, and a street in the Canberra suburb of Franklin is named Clare Burton Crescent.

Clare asked that her memorial service take place at the Methodist National Memorial Church in Forrest. Her request surprised us. We had all attended that church from time to time, and Meredith and Clive were married there. However, we were atheists so we were not into church-based worshipping. We planned a service for family and friends and chose those to speak and reminisce about Clare, including Quentin Bryce. On arriving at the church, we were overwhelmed to find a crowded quadrangle of people: women and men, from all over, who came to farewell Clare. On entering the church, there was a large feminist banner at the front behind which people were to speak.

It was wonderful to see the esteem in which Clare was held by so many, but sad at the time – particularly for her children – to have the quiet service turn into a large public event with many unscheduled speakers wanting to participate. Perhaps even more sad for me and Meredith and probably our parents is how little we knew about the changes she made to so many lives. We were inundated with letters and emails, and we read obituaries, from all of which we learned more about Clare and her work. We owned copies of her books, and knew about the consultancies she undertook in Australia and New Zealand to rid the defence forces, universities and elsewhere of gender inequality, but we did not engage enough with Clare about her work and achievements. Why? Partly because she had lived away for so long until her move to Canberra a few years before her death, but often because emotional baggage from our family life caused us to fear that robust discussion of political or feminist issues might turn into emotional brawls that would end in tears – hers and mine, in particular.

There is no doubt that Clare experienced a deal of unhappiness in the last year or so of her life. None of us had an inkling of her relationship breakdown before she separated from Geoff, except for Cecily who Clare had being seeing for months about it. Geoff, who had left his Queensland home and job to live with Clare, was devastated at her change of heart. He felt that he had been given no warning that she was unhappy living with him, other than an awareness that her outbursts of anger had increased. We now know that Clare was ill, very ill, and that she had received inappropriate medication from her doctor for pain relief for various inadequately diagnosed symptoms. It is enough to account for her unhappiness and apparent erratic behaviour.

When Clare died, Cecily told us that she felt they had never 'reconciled'. That puzzled me. I had seen the genuine warmth with which Clare spoke to Cecily of her love and gratitude in those last days as she lay dying in hospital. It was hard to get Cecily to articulate why she felt this way, other than to say that she believed they had not come to any true understanding. Just as Cecily felt that she and her own mother had never reconciled before her mother died, she felt with Clare that a rift that had developed between them had never closed. That disturbed Cecily deeply. Cecily did not want a photo of Clare to have in her home. She said that having a photo of smiling faces reflected nothing of the real person. 'They don't speak to me, as people present do.' It seemed the pain and hurt was far too great. Then, Cecily's spiritualism, in all likelihood, allowed her to carry Clare in her heart and to remember her as a daughter she truly loved.

John's relationship with Clare was fraught. A love–hate one? Love, yes, and of course not hate in the real sense, but close at times. I can see now that Clare was unhappy at home as a teen. She and John's past issues never resolved. As an adult, Clare challenged and argued with him about feminist issues about which he had limited understanding given the culture in which he grew up and worked. This, despite the fact that we grew up with no suggestion that women were restricted in their career choices, or enjoyment of lifestyle, by reason of gender.

Clare's death affected John deeply. He appeared to cope at age 83 with Betty by his side. However, a view I caught of him as I passed by their bedroom in the hallway of their house distressed me. He was alone, doubled over, head in his hands, kneeling on the floor, weeping. I had never seen him cry before, and never since. The loss of Clare let loose feelings that I had never experienced before either. It caused me to look back at how Cecily might have felt in December 1982, when her younger sister died of cancer – Pam, who Cecily loved very much. To lose a sister is heart-rending, but being her younger sister and one she was close to must have come as a terrible shock and affected Cecily profoundly. Did Robert, or any of us children, fully appreciate the ongoing grief and sense of loss that must have accompanied that event? Then, she suffered the death of her daughter. It left her, as it did the whole family, in the depths of sadness and despair.

41

Blue autumn: Cecily passes

The glorious Canberra autumn sees leafy green trees and shrubs turn to yellow, then gold and red. I could see them through Cecily's hospital window, although she could not see out from her bed. It was the autumn of 2007. 'You've got to be out of here before the leaves drop,' I said. 'The prunus deep reds are in glorious contrast to the golden poplars.' 'My favourite season,' she replied. She saw none of that autumn. Cecily missed what she loved most – second to people – the beauty of her natural surroundings.

Cecily and Robert had, until the mid-1990s, remained physically fit for their ages. However, in 1994, Cecily had had a serious fall down her stairs at home. Shocked, sore, bruised and suffering a neck injury, she rested in bed for several days. She met her client commitments, counselling while lying in bed. When she felt well enough to walk, she attended a physiotherapist who insisted on an X-ray before touching her. It revealed broken neck vertebrae. A single wrong movement might have caused quadriplegia. Cecily was ambulanced to hospital and strapped onto a board to keep her flat until a surgeon was available to operate. She recovered reasonably well but her neck injury permanently limited her activities.

At that time, Robert still played tennis and his piano and both he and Cecily enjoyed walking, but their garden had become too much for them. By the time Cecily turned 80 in 1996, they agreed they needed more support. They purchased two independent living units attached to an aged-care facility in Deakin with a model of care of graduated living. They lived in one unit and Cecily saw her clients for counselling in the other, situated across the hall. They could sit on their terrace among potted plants and walk in the well-developed community gardens that they did not have to look after. The move was not too soon. In August 1999, Robert had an operative procedure to remove his prostate gland, but bladder problems caused him to be incontinent and he had to wear pads day and night. His mobility was compromised from symptoms of Parkinson's disease. He required more and more of Cecily's assistance as his disease developed.

Caring for Robert took its toll on Cecily. A community nurse helped out with showering Robert two or three times a week, but Cecily had to carry the load of the rest of his care and care for herself. She changed his soiled sheets each morning, guided his tall body into a shower when a nurse was not available and to a chair during the day. Robert's carers took no notice of Cecily's needs. On one occasion, Cecily had a cold and felt wretched. She tried to keep up her counselling work, going from one apartment to the other, talking with clients, and checking in on Robert, until she could manage no longer and she ceased her counselling work.

At this time, in 2000, Cecily, physically and emotionally drained, started a journal. She wrote something each day. Often, she struggled to know what to write. She commenced with 'I don't feel like writing. Feel tired and ill, and a bit depressed'.[1] The next day she opened with, 'Don't feel like it much, but no doubt something will come'. And it did. Words poured out and her thoughts flowed. She reflected again on her childhood. One reflection was on how different she felt from others at school; that she was always questioning or disagreeing at least inwardly. She felt that other people were not interested in what she was interested in or thought. She wrote what seemed to be a constant feeling: 'I think I just felt hardly done by and misunderstood, and alone, lonely inside. Yet that would have been only a part of me. I wasn't a loner, just felt different.'

In a letter to my daughter Cassandra, Cecily also spoke frankly of her struggle coping with Robert's frailties:

> I have to admit, I suffer from quite a lot of resentment about the situation I am in and the enormous dependence Robert has on me. At times it seems too much to bear. I don't mean that he is clinging or demanding or anything like that, but the fact remains that I just have to be there almost all the time to attend to his various needs,

---

[1] Cecily's 'Free writing', 2000, Cecily family file.

physical and mental. Without me he couldn't manage at all. Even the nurses and so on need help and guidance. It's quite frightening to think that I just have to keep well and strong enough to carry on indefinitely and I don't feel strong or well. However, I seem to keep going and I don't look like succumbing for a while. I can take a few hours off too, and I rest a lot, walk almost every day, read a lot and have lots of friends and relatives visiting. So, I don't dwell on difficulties which don't bear thinking about. I just wanted to let you know that I am from time to time a very resentful human being. However, I take loving care of Robert and we both do the best we can. So, we have more happiness than pain, I think.[2]

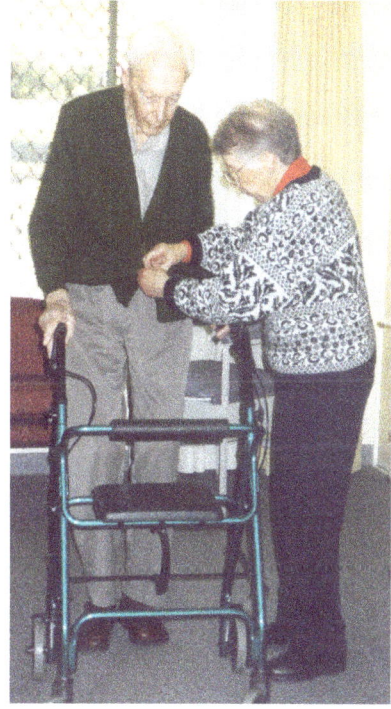

Cecily caring for Robert, Brindabella Gardens Nursing Home, May 2002.

Source: Family collection.

Soon, the situation became untenable. Once, in the presence of a nurse Cecily simply burst into tears, and the nurses realised that Cecily required respite. Robert spent periods of time at the Brindabella Gardens Nursing Home, which gave her a break. In 2002, Robert's illness had progressed beyond what Cecily could cope with, and he moved into permanent care at Brindabella Gardens' high care unit, Shakespeare Cottage. Meredith and I visited him regularly. Cecily took a taxi to visit him daily. Robert died at age 87 on 31 July 2002.

After Robert died, Cecily stopped writing, declaring in August 2002 that 'The mood has passed now'. She started again a few months later, in October 2002, heading her journal, 'The other side'. She opened with:

---

2   Undated letter, courtesy Cassandra.

> I feel very hesitant about writing this, yet I feel I need to, and I want to. The task sits over me and in me like a grey cloud. But why should it? I'm not writing in anger, I want to write only what is true, and I want to complete, or to try to complete the picture Rob has left of himself.[3]

She took the opportunity of analysing their relationship in extraordinary detail, sorting out in her mind how she felt about Robert and the reasons for it as she wrote. It included Robert's 'niceness' to all appearances and the cruelty and unfairness she felt from his behaviour towards her. He was, she believed, 'not at all interested in me as a person, except perhaps in a detached, observing kind of way, and in a shallow way'. She went on to note both John's and Robert's failure to excuse or apologise for mistakes and never to do anything in the way she asked. She felt she had been treated with contempt by both of them. As I read this, I was surprised at the strength of Cecily's feelings about the behaviours of both of her husbands. Robert did have a distance from others in the way he related to them. Robert's former wife, Nancy, probably overcame this by her sheer outgoing exuberance. Surely Cecily, in counselling other married women, learned that even the most loving of male partners could find it humiliating to admit to being wrong, or demeaning to apologise for something or to take directions from them? Maybe no man could have understood and satisfied Cecily emotionally. I must ask, too, why Cecily felt she needed a sexual or marital partner to fulfil her need to be understood.

Cecily's health started to deteriorate seriously in August 2004 when she had the first of many more falls and was hospitalised. From the hospital bed she decided the time had come for her to move into a high care facility. She 'downsized' and moved from her apartment to a studio apartment in the main block of her Deakin facility where she could access more care. It had a kitchenette and was in easy access to a communal dining room. She had at least one meal a day in the dining room and someone would check on her if she did not show for it. She did well there for a while, but complained to us that she found the company of the older people there 'boring', and preferred to have her meals in her room. Nevertheless, she was polite and charming to her fellow residents and chatted to them when she did join in. Otherwise, she was happy in herself with television, videos and her radio for news, current affairs programs and classical music. She had plenty of books to read and many visitors.

---

3   Journal, 6 October 2002, Cecily family file.

41. BLUE AUTUMN

In March 2006, a stroke led Cecily to an agonising six-week stay in hospital until she was well enough in May to be transferred to a pleasant and roomy residential rehabilitation facility near the hospital. The grandchildren visited her in hospital, some travelling from interstate. They loved her deeply and energised her to keep engaged with their lives, and from her bed she continued to offer them advice. By June, when she was discharged home, it was clear that Cecily was in need of more intensive care. She already had her name on the waiting list for Brindabella Gardens where Robert had experienced good care, and she activated her request to move. In September, after an anxious wait, she was given a room in Brindabella Gardens. It was small with an ensuite bathroom and a tiny veranda from which she could see birds and the gardens. Other than mealtimes when Cecily went to the dining room, she preferred to stay in her room and listen to the radio, read, and talk with her many visitors. She told us she did not want to sit around in the lounge area with a lot of old people, most of whom had lost acuity of mind. Many were non-verbal; others she thought, had verbal diarrhoea. We discussed her future with her. It was at this time that she wrote a living will in which she requested that she have no active treatment should she have another stroke or succumb to pneumonia. However, life does not work to a plan.

In March 2007, she had another fall. She was helped up and into bed and the following day had another fall. She was found on the floor, in pain, unable to be moved. Her carers did what had to be done and called an ambulance. She was taken to emergency to be checked out and have her pain relieved. Meredith's journal entry of 25 March 2007 captures aspects of the episode. Cecily had suffered crushed vertebrae in her lower back, she had fluid on her lung and infection, and had very low sodium levels. She was in need of oxygen. She was in a lot of pain and could hardly move, even to eat. Meredith and I listened to a myriad of questions doctors asked of Cecily in an effort to find the cause of her fall. She was lucid, knew who she was, where she was, and when asked who the current prime minister was, she answered: 'John Howard, unfortunately.' She was quite clear in instructing us, however, that having endured an ambulance ride to the hospital and the horror of waiting overnight in a crowded and noisy emergency unit, she would like to be treated for the cause of the fall. She hoped that her medication would be adjusted and that she would be discharged to the nursing home in a more comfortable state. She was admitted to a ward for treatment for a stroke and stayed in hospital for the whole of the 2007 autumn – the autumn she missed.

Frail Night

I sit and watch
through slatted blinds
a frail picture of the night
go past -
thin grey tissue paper
pretending to be the world:
where flat - the air,
where creased - illusion
of a nearby landscape,
crumples, darker
are trees and bushes;
little holes make do for stars.

Now and then
the paper burns in station lights
then reappears -
as the train speeds on.

Cecily Parker.

Cecily's poem 'Frail Night', published in the *Canberra Times*, October 1995.
Source: Cecily family file.

41. BLUE AUTUMN

I found a poem of Cecily's on an old cutting from an undated *Canberra Times* newspaper that is reflective of a sad soul, and apt to reproduce here. Cecily suffered depression in hospital. She expressed no wish to live. She could think of no reason to live and it was difficult for us to disagree with her. The injections of warfarin into her stomach to thin her blood caused her pain and bruising. However, the treating team saw it important that she be treated for depression before her true wishes about her future, and any will she might have to live, could be determined. It took time for anti-depressant medication to be effective. At times in hospital, Cecily refused to eat; she wanted to die. Then, when Meredith turned up with an Anzac (oatmeal) biscuit, Cecily smiled and could not resist it. When her anti-depressant medication took effect, the language she used about her life coming to an end changed. She said that she had lived a good life and that there was nothing more ahead of her to enjoy – other than her children, grandchildren, great-grandchildren and friends.

John was concerned for Cecily. Not that he expressed his concern by a show of emotions. He asked after her on each occasion we returned from visiting her, absorbed the details of her treatment and asked what she wanted out of it. Although he, too, often expressed a wish that his life would end, when we told him that Cecily wanted that too, he was appalled. In principle, the concept of assisted dying appealed to them both. In practice, the mind and the body resisted the notion. In both John's and Cecily's cases, their brains seemed to keep their bodies ticking along, despite both having advanced heart disease. Each hoped that they might simply never wake from a sleep at some stage, but that just was not going to happen to either of them before enduring a good deal of misery, discomfort, hospital attention and a mishmash of medications. At this time, Meredith asked John what he considered the best things that had happened to him in his life. 'Not winning the seat of Lowe and buying a farm,' he said, and added, 'having kids.' He listed both Betty and Cecily. He told her that the marriage with Cecily had been good at the start, but that, given the times, she was not able to 'express her identity' through her work. Amused, Cecily thought that a rationalisation because it was John who stopped her from expressing her identity.[4]

---

4   Meredith's journal.

The stroke Cecily had suffered, while not leaving her with any significant paralysis, did release some of her inhibitions. Meredith and I spent a lot of time listening to her reflect on her life. She was frank about how she had felt over the years about significant people in it; she expressed her feelings in more detail than she had done before. She expressed deep guilt about being 'horrible' to her mother who had died so young. She also talked frankly about Robert and how her love for him had faded, mainly because of his inability to empathise with her. It was the same complaint she had about John, although he had never been as kind, nor polite, or gentle in demeanour, as had Robert. Nevertheless, Cecily told us that she was happy with what she had done with her life and hoped she had improved the lives of others through her counselling and her dream groups.

Meredith and I rostered our attendances around hospital meal times as, too often, meals would be left on Cecily's tray out of her reach. Her call buzzer was often out of reach too. When it was in reach, often when she pressed the button for a nurse to help her to the toilet, no one came. It was infuriating. Her medications often changed without reference to her previous regime and sometimes she was given drugs to which she was allergic. Meredith and I each spent five or so hours with her some days to monitor her care, convey her instructions and ensure she was awake when her treating team and her specialists in particular did their rounds; otherwise, she had to wait another day or two to see them. We were vocal and demanding and the nursing staff probably regarded us as 'sisters from hell'. We knew by this time that Cecily could not be discharged to her hostel room because she could no longer dress herself or walk to a dining room. On Sunday 8 April, Meredith wrote of Cecily:

> Right now, it sounds like she could die very soon – back on diuretics and so her sodium level will fall. She is very, very weak. For her sake, it won't be early enough. Again, this week has been hell for her. She was moved to geriatrics on Tuesday and we thought that would be better. For her, the attitude of nurses that she needs to be told what she wants really annoys her. ... Pam went to meet the doctor 9.00 Thursday mainly to talk them into putting mum on oxygen when she left the hospital. She had to wait hours ... and blew her top in frustration. Then doctors and nurses came from everywhere and at last focussed on extent of mum's multiple problems. Pam was at last relieved about the outcome. She is due

> home – to nursing home – Wednesday. Greatest news was getting a place for Mum in Shakespeare cottages where Robert had been: a room of her own. Very lucky as they come available so rarely.[5]

We and Cecily were indeed lucky. Cecily was discharged from hospital the following day direct to Brindabella Gardens' Shakespeare Cottage high care unit. Her new room looked out on to an oval where children spilled out after school. Cecily had to leave behind more of her personal belongings other than some special mementos. She had to say goodbye to so much in her life, her books, music tapes, clothes, gifts and personal papers. The sad process of ageing was softened only by her being placed in the best of hands for palliative management. Meredith captured the emotions in her journal entry of 15 April 2007:

> [Mum] thought it would be a miracle to be out of hospital by Wednesday but that was achieved. What a relief for everyone. So much less stress in the [nursing] home's quiet atmosphere and good staff. A day or two later she passes urine – another relief as otherwise back to hospital to get permanent catheter. Still not eating much but food much better. We are still visiting 2 times a day and around meal times. She likes seeing the kids playing in the oval out of the window, peewees there and autumn colours in the trees. Now she is comfortable. She says she is weaker every day and 'that is a good thing'! She worries Pam is not ready for her to go and wants me to keep telling Pam she is. Pam says she is ready.

Cecily kept her intellect to the end. She told me that some of the nurses at Shakespeare Cottage were angels. I was with her when one of her 'angels' came into her room. Cecily lay peacefully in bed with a tummy full of painkillers when I heard her ask the nurse her name. The conversation went like this:

> 'What is your name?'
>
> 'Hilary,' the angel said.
>
> 'How am I to remember that?'
>
> 'Easy. Sir Edmund Hillary,' said the nurse.
>
> 'What?'
>
> 'You know mum, the fella that climbed the mountain,' I said, trying to help out.
>
> 'No,' said Cecily. 'He has two Ls in his name.'

---

5 Meredith's journal.

Meredith and I were still vigilant about Cecily's care. We visited during the day and again before her bedtime to make sure her dentures were removed and cleaned, and that she was comfortable. Meredith recorded Cecily's last days:

> Sunday 22 April
>
> Mum is so weak. Eating nothing but a teaspoon or two of yoghurt and some milk. We gave her the bad news that the nurses don't think her death is imminent but we can't see how she can go on for much longer …
>
> Saturday 28 April
>
> Mum died just before noon, Thursday 26th. I was there but Pam was not which upset her greatly, especially because she was with her for hours the night before and was convinced that death was imminent and the nurses talked her out of that – no need to be there next day. She died relatively peacefully – a few grunts at the end, and then peace.

Cecily was no longer with us. John survived her by three years and died on 23 June 2010. They both left their separate legacies – cherished by those who knew them.

Select bibliography

Primary sources

Burton, John W. Paper presented to a conference on 'New Directions in Australian Foreign Policy: Australia and Indonesia 1945–50'. *Indonesia: Unfinished Diplomacy*, 4: Monash University, Melbourne, 31 May–1 June 1996. John Burton Papers #C0006, Box 18, Folder 12. Accessed 21 August 2021. wizwah.gmu.edu/johnwburton/items/show/1048878.

Burton, John W. and Cecily Burton. Family files of private papers, journals, writings, and letters.

Burton. John W. Snr. Family files of papers, writings and letters.

Burton, John W. Snr. 'The Weaver's Shuttle: Memories and Reflections of an Octogenarian'. Unpublished autobiography, c. 1956. Copy at John Wear Burton further papers, 1900–1970, MLMSS 2899 Add On 990. Mitchell Library, Sydney.

Burton, Pamela. *Cecily*. Canberra: Privately published, 1994.

Burton, Pamela. Childhood diary.

Edwards, Meredith. Journals.

National Library of Australia

Memoir of Colin Moodie, between approximately 1990 and 2000, MS Acc13.173.

Papers of Albert Arlen and Nancy Brown, 1924–2001, MS 6311, MS Acc06.172.

Papers of John W. Burton, 1956–1998, MS 8405.

Papers of Gerald Firth, circa 1935–1993, MS Acc01.273.

385

Papers of Robert Stewart Parker, 1908–2002, MS 8200.
Papers of D.C.S. Sissons, 1950–2006, MS 3092, MS Acc09.106.
Papers of Judith Wright, 1944–2000, MS 5781.

Secondary sources

Abse, Joan, ed. *My LSE*. London: Robson, 1977.

Agrell, Wilhelm. *Mrs Petrova's Shoe*. London: I.B. Tauris, 2019. doi.org/10.5040/ 9781838600914.

Albinski, Henry S. *Australian Policies and Attitudes toward China*. Princeton, NJ: Princeton University Press, 1965. doi.org/10.1515/9781400874545.

Andre, Pamela and Sue Langford, eds. *Australia and the Postwar World: The Commonwealth, Asia and the Pacific: Documents 1948–49*. Canberra: Department of Foreign Affairs and Trade, 1998.

Andrews, C. F. and W. W. Pearson. *Report on Indentured Labour in Fiji: An Independent Enquiry*. Calcutta: Star Printing Works, 1916.

Arnett, Georgina. *The Unknown Judith Wright*. Crawley, WA: UWA Publishing, 2016.

Ball, Desmond. 'From External Affairs to Academia: Coral's Encounter with the KGB's Spy Ring'. In *Power and International Relations: Essays in Honour of Coral Bell*, edited by Desmond Ball and Sheryl Lee. Canberra: ANU Press, 2014. doi.org/10.22459/PIR.11.2014.02.

Ball, Desmond and David Horner. *Breaking the Codes: Australia's KGB Network, 1944–1950*. St Leonards, NSW: Allen & Unwin, 1998.

Ball, Desmond and Sheryl Lee, eds. *Power and International Relations: Essays in Honour of Coral Bell*. Canberra: ANU Press, 2014. doi.org/10.22459/ PIR.11.2014.

Bayley, J. C. R. and J. W. Burton. *Northern Ireland Interim Report*. London: Centre for the Analysis of Conflict, University College of London, January 1971.

Beaumont, Joan and Matthew Jordan, eds. *Australia and the World: A Festschrift for Neville Meaney*. Sydney: Sydney University Press, 2013.

Black, David, ed. *In His Own Words: John Curtin's Speeches and Writings*. Bentley, WA: Paradigm Books, Curtin University of Technology, 1995.

Brown Arlen, Nancy. *The Black Sheep of the Brown Family: A Magic Life!* Mudjimba Beach, Qld: Pixstories, 2001.

Brown, Nicholas. *A History of Canberra.* Cambridge: Cambridge University Press, 2014. doi.org/10.1017/CBO9781139196260.

Burton, John W. *The Alternative: A Dynamic Approach to our Relations with Asia.* Sydney: Morgan's Publishing, 1954.

Burton, John W. *Conflict Resolution: Its Language and Processes.* Lanham, MD: Scarecrow Press, 1996.

Burton, John W. 'Conflict Resolution: The Human Dimension'. *International Journal of Peace Studies* 3, no. 1 (January 1998). George Mason University. Accessed 2 April 2021. www3.gmu.edu/programs/icar/ijps/vol3_1/burton.htm?gmuw-rd=sm&gmuw-rdm=ht.

Burton, John W. *Deviance, Terrorism & War: The Process of Solving Unsolved Social and Political Problems.* Canberra: Australian National University Press, 1979.

Burton, John W. 'The Evolving International System'. *Frontier* 7, no. 3 (Autumn 1964), 207–10.

Burton, John W. Interview in *Resolution* (Centre for Conflict Resolution, George Mason University) 1, no. 5 (November 1985): 1, 4.

Burton, John W. *The Light Glows Brighter.* Sydney: Morgan's Publishing, 1956.

Burton, John W. 'Looking to the Future: An International Relations for the New Millennium'. *Evatt Papers* 3, no. 2 (1995).

Burton, John W. *Nonalignment.* London: Andre Deutsch, 1966.

Burton, John W. 'Peace Begins at Home' and 'International Conflict: A Domestic Responsibility'. *International Journal of Peace Studies* 6, no. 1 (Spring 2001).

Burton, John W. *Peace Theory: Preconditions of Disarmament.* New York: Alfred A. Knopf, 1962.

Burton, John W. *Resolving Deep-rooted Conflict: A Handbook.* Lanham, MD: University Press of America, 1987.

Burton, John W. *Violence Explained: The Sources of Conflict, Violence and Crime and their Provention.* Manchester and New York: Manchester University Press, 1997.

Burton, John W. Snr. 'India in Fiji'. *Missionary Review* (Sydney), 4 September 1916.

Burton, John W. Snr. *Papua for Christ* (also entitled *Our Task in Papua*). London: Epworth Press, 1926.

Burton, John W. Snr. *The Fiji of Today*. London: Charles H. Kelly, 1910.

Burton, Pamela. 'John Burton: Undermined by Dishonest History'. *Honest History*, 1 September 2014. Talk delivered at Manning Clark House, Canberra, 18 August 2014 in the Honest History lecture series. honesthistory.net.au/wp/wp-content/uploads/385A-John-Burton-Undermined-by-dishonest-history.pdf.

Cain, Frank. 'Australian Intelligence Organisations and the Law: A Brief History'. *UNSW Law Journal* 27, no. 2 (July 2004): 154–56.

Cain, Frank. *The Australian Security Intelligence Organization: An Unofficial History*. London: Frank Cass and Co., 1994.

Cain, Frank, ed. *Menzies in War and Peace*. St Leonards, NSW: Allen & Unwin, 1997.

Cain, Frank. 'The Petrov Affair and Fake Documents: Another Look'. *Honest History*, 15 March 2017. Accessed 9 April 2021. honesthistory.net.au/wp/cain-frank-the-petrov-affair-and-fake-documents-another-look-2/.

Cain, Frank. *Terrorism and Intelligence: A History of ASIO and National Surveillance*. North Melbourne, Vic.: Australian Scholarly Publishing, 2008.

Calwell, A. A. *Calwell: Be Just and Fear Not*. Hawthorn, Vic.: Lloyd O'Neil, 1972.

Clarke, Patricia, ed. *Judith Wright: Half a Life-time*. Melbourne: Text Publishing, 1999.

Clarke, Patricia and Meredith McKinney, eds. *With Love and Fury: Selected Letters of Judith Wright*. Canberra: National Library of Australia, 2006.

Coombs, H. C. *Trial Balance: Issues of My Working Life*. Melbourne: Sun Books, 1981.

Crisp, L. F. *Ben Chifley: A Biography*. London: Longmans, 1961.

Day, David, ed. *Brave New World: Dr H. V. Evatt and Australian Foreign Policy 1941–1949*. St Lucia, Qld: University of Queensland Press, 1966.

Day, David, 'John Joseph Curtin'. In *Australian Prime Ministers*, edited by Michelle Grattan. Sydney: New Holland Publishers, 2000.

Deery, Phillip and McLean Craig. 'Behind Enemy Lines: Menzies, Evatt and Passports for Peking'. *Round Table* 92, no. 370 (July 2003): 407–22. doi.org/10.1080/0035853032000111125.

Dunn, David J. 'Engaging Provention: A Pressing Question of Need'. Occasional Paper 28. George Mason University School of Conflict Analysis and Resolution. 2013. Accessed 2 April 2021. activity.scar.gmu.edu/sites/default/files/Dunn%20Working%20Paper.pdf.

Dunn, David. *From Power Politics to Conflict Resolution: The Work of John W. Burton.* New York: Palgrave Macmillan, 2004. doi.org/10.1057/9780230536708.

Dunn, M. G. L. 'The Royal Commission on Espionage, 1954–1955'. PhD diss., University of Adelaide, 1979.

Edwards, P. G. *Prime Ministers and Diplomats: The Making of Australian Foreign Policy 1901–1949.* Oxford: Oxford University Press, 1983.

Fahey, John. *Traitors and Spies: Espionage and Corruption in High Places in Australia, 1901–1950.* St Leonards, NSW: Allen & Unwin, 2020.

Fettling, David. 'An Australian Response to Asian Decolonisation: Jawaharlal Nehru, John Burton and New Delhi Conference of Non-Western Nations'. *Australian Historical Studies* 45, no. 2 (2014): 202–21. doi.org/10.1080/1031461X.2014.911758.

Fettling, David. *Encounters with Asian Decolonisation.* North Melbourne, Vic.: Australian Scholarly Publishing, 2017.

Fettling, David. 'J. B. Chifley and the Indonesian Revolution, 1945–1949'. *Australian Journal of Politics and History* 59, no. 4 (2013): 517–31. doi.org/10.1111/ajph.12030.

Finnane, Mark. *JV Barry: A Life.* Sydney: University of New South Wales Press, 2007.

Fisher, Ron. *Interactive Conflict Resolution.* Syracuse, NY: Syracuse University Press, 1997.

Fitzpatrick, Sheila. *My Father's Daughter: Memories of an Australian Childhood.* Clayton, Vic.: Melbourne University Publishing, 2019.

Foot, Rob. 'The Curious Case of Dr John Burton'. *Quadrant*, November 2013, 44–53.

Foot, Rob. 'Dr Burton at the Royal Commission on Espionage'. *Quadrant*, October 2015, 53–60.

Foot, Rob. 'Was John Burton Australia's Alger Hiss?' *Quadrant*, June 2016, 52.

Fraser, Robin. 'Track Two Diplomacy – A Distinct Conflict Intervention Category'. Master's diss., University of Victoria, 2012.

Furphy, Samuel, ed. *The Seven Dwarfs and the Age of the Mandarins: Australian Government Administration in the Post-War Reconstruction Era*. Canberra: ANU Press, 2015. doi.org/10.22459/SDAM.07.2015.

Garrett, John. *Footsteps in the Sea: Christianity in Oceania to World War II*. Suva and Geneva: WCC Publications, Institute of the South Pacific in association with World Council of Churches, 1992.

Gollan, Robin. *Revolutionaries and Reformists: Communism and the Australian Labour Movement 1920–1955*. Canberra: Australian National University Press, 1975.

Grattan, Michelle, ed. *Australian Prime Ministers*. Sydney: New Holland Publishers, 2000.

Haigh, Gideon. *The Brilliant Boy: Doc Evatt and the Great Australian Dissent*. Cammeray, NSW: Simon & Schuster (Australia), 2021.

Hall, Michael, in collaboration with Joe Camplisson. *From Conflict Containment to Resolution: The Experiences of a Moldovan-Northern Ireland Self-help Initiative*. Newtownabbey: Island Publications, 2002.

Hall, Richard. *The Secret State: Australia's Spy Industry*. Sydney: Cassell Australia, 1978.

Hasluck, Paul. *Diplomatic Witness: Australian Foreign Affairs, 1941–1947*. Carlton, Vic.: Melbourne University Press, 1980.

Hellier, J. E. *The Missionary Brothers: Memoirs of the Rev. John Wear Bell and the Rev. Joseph Bell*. Leeds: Walker and Laycock, 1889.

Henry, Adam Hughes. *The Gatekeepers of Australian Foreign Policy 1950–1966*. Melbourne: Australian Scholarly Publishing, 2015.

Henry, Adam Hughes. 'Reflections on Dr John Wear Burton: The Forgotten Mandarin?' *ISAA Review* 12, no. 1 (2013): 67–84.

Hickey, Des and Gus Smith. *The Star of Shame: The Secret Voyage of the Arandora Star*. Kenthurst, NSW: Rosenberg Publishing, 2006.

Hodge, Errol. *Radio Wars: Truth, Propaganda and the Struggle for Radio Australia*. Cambridge: Cambridge University Press, 1995.

Horner, David. *The Spy Catchers: The Official History of ASIO, 1949–1963*. Sydney: Allen & Unwin, 2014.

Jung, C. G. *Answer to Job*. London: Routledge, 1955.

Jung, C. G. *Memories, Dreams, Reflections*, recorded and edited by Aniela Jaffé and translated from the German by Richard and Clara Winston. London: Collins, 1963.

Kadiba, John. 'The Methodist Mission and the Emerging Aboriginal Church in Arnhem Land 1916–1977'. PhD diss., Northern Territory University, 1998.

Lal, Brij. V. and Vicki Luker, eds. *Telling Pacific Lives: Prisms of Process*. Canberra: ANU E Press, 2008. doi.org/10.22459/TPL.06.2008.

Lee, David, ed. *Australia & Indonesia's Independence: The Transfer of Sovereignty: Documents 1949*. Canberra: Department of Foreign Affairs and Trade, 1998.

Lee, David. *Stanley Melbourne Bruce: Australian Internationalist*. London: Continuum International Publishing Group, 2010.

Londey, Peter. 'Brave New Australia'. *Wartime* (Australian War Memorial) magazine, no. 88 (Spring 2019).

Macintyre, Stuart. *Australia's Boldest Experiment: War and Reconstruction in the 1940s*. Sydney: NewSouth Publishing, 2015.

Maher, Laurence W. 'Dissent, Disloyalty and Disaffection: Australia's Last Cold War Sedition Case'. *Adelaide Law Review* 16 (1994): 1–77.

Maher, Laurence W. 'The Lapstone Experiment and the Beginnings of ASIO'. *Labour History*, no. 64 (May 1993): 103–8. doi.org/10.2307/27509168.

Manne, Robert. *The Petrov Affair: Politics and Espionage*. Sydney: Pergamon Press, 1987.

Maywald, Bonita. 'Is It Possible to Re-imagine an Australian IR through John W. Burton's Experience and Seeing Other-wise to Develop Alternative Approaches in our International Relations?' Master's diss., The Australian National University, 1999.

McLean, Craig. 'Fear of Peace? Australian Government Responses to the Peace Movement 1949–1959'. Master's diss., Victoria University, 2001. Accessed 9 April 2021. vuir.vu.edu.au/15299/1/McLean_2001_compressed.pdf.

McNair, John. 'Mary Poppins and the Soviet Pilgrimage: P. L. Travers's Moscow Excursion (1934)'. *Journal of Multidisciplinary International Studies* 10, no. 1 (2013): 1–12. doi.org/10.5130/portal.v10i1.2343.

McQueen, Humphrey. 'Quadrant and the CIA [1977]'. Chapter 17 in *Gallipoli to Petrov: Arguing with Australian History*. Sydney: Allen & Unwin, 1984.

Meadows, Eric. '"He No Doubt Felt Insulted": The White Australia Policy and Australia's Relations with India, 1944–1964'. Chapter 5 in *Australia and the World: A Festschrift for Neville Meaney*, edited by Joan Beaumont and Matthew Jordan. Sydney: Sydney University Press, 2013. doi.org/10.2307/j.ctv1rm259b.9.

Miller, Rachel. *Wife and Baggage to Follow*. Canberra: Halstead Press, 2013.

Nicolson, Nigel. *Portrait of a Marriage: Vita Sackville-West and Harold Nicolson*. London: Weidenfeld and Nicolson, 1973.

Oakman, Daniel. *Facing Asia: A History of the Colombo Plan*. Canberra: ANU E Press, 2010. doi.org/10.22459/FA.10.2010.

Parker, Cecily. 'Much Madness in Divinest Sense…'. *Canberra Jung Society Newsletter*, January–June 1997.

Pemberton, Gregory. 'John Burton: The Heretic'. *Evatt Papers* 3, no. 2 (1995): 93–105.

Pemberton, Gregory. 'John Burton'. *Union Issues*, November 1991, 12–14.

Pemberton, Gregory. 'The Imperial Imagination: Explaining the Post-1945 Foreign Policy of Robert Gordon Menzies'. Chapter 9 in *Menzies in War and Peace*, edited by Frank Cain. St Leonards, NSW: Allen & Unwin, 1997.

Pembroke, Michael. *Korea: Where the American Century Began*. Richmond, Vic.: Hardie Grant Publishing, 2018.

Plowman, Peter. *The Chandris Liners and Celebrity Cruises*. Kenthurst, NSW: Rosenberg Publishing, 2006.

Rickard, John. *An Imperial Affair: Portrait of an Australian Marriage*. Clayton, Vic.: Monash University Publishing, 2013.

Ride Edwin. *I Dips Me Lid: Diplomatic Memories*. Palmwoods, Qld: E. Ride, 1991.

Rowse, Tim. *Nugget Coombs: A Reforming Life*. Port Melbourne, Vic.: Cambridge University Press, 2005.

Sawer, Nancy. *Telling It to Abi*. Broulee, NSW: Nancy Sawer, 2000.

Sissons, D. C. S. 'The Australian War Crimes Trials and Investigations (1942–51)'. In *Bridging Australia and Japan: The Writings of David Sissons, Historian and Political Scientist*. Volume 2, edited by Keiko Tamura and Arthur Stockwin. Canberra: ANU Press, 2020. doi.org/10.22459/BAJ.2020.04.

Spratt, Elwyn. *Eddie Ward: Firebrand of East Sydney*. Adelaide: Rigby, 1965.

Stone, I. F. *The Hidden History of the Korean War: 1950–1951: A Nonconformist History of Our Times*. 2nd ed. UK: Little Brown, 1988; original edition, 1952.

Suares, Julie. 'Engaging with Asia: The Chifley Government and the New Delhi Conferences of 1947 and 1949'. *Australian Journal of Politics and History* 57, no. 4 (2011): 495–510. doi.org/10.1111/j.1467-8497.2011.01610.x.

Tange, Sir Arthur. *Defence Policy-Making: A Close-Up View, 1950–1980 – A Personal Memoir*, edited by Peter Edwards. Canberra: ANU E Press, 2008. doi.org/10.22459/DPM.07.2008.

Throssell, Karen. *The Crime of Not Knowing Your Crime: Ric Throssell against ASIO*. Melbourne: Interventions Inc., 2021.

Tillett, Gregory. 'Booknotes'. *Australasian Dispute Resolution Journal* 16, no. 2 (May 2005).

Toohey, Brian. *Secret: The Making of Australia's Security State*. Carlton, Vic.: Melbourne University Press, 2019.

Tubbs, Michael. *ASIO: The Enemy Within*. Croydon Park, NSW: Michael Tubbs, c. 2008.

Walker, David. 'Nervous Outsiders: Australia and the 1955 Asia-Africa Conference in Bandung'. *Australian Historical Studies* 125 (April 2005): 40–59. doi.org/10.1080/10314610508682910.

Walker, David. *Stranded Nation: White Australia in an Asian Region*. Crawley, WA: UWA Publishing, 2019.

Weir, Christine. 'An Accidental Biographer? On Encountering, Yet Again, the Ideas and Actions of J.W. Burton'. In *Telling Pacific Lives: Prisms and Process*, edited by Brij V. Lal and Vicki Luker. Canberra: ANU E Press, 2008. doi.org/10.22459/TPL.06.2008.16.

Whitington, Don. *Strive to be Fair: An Unfinished Biography*. Canberra: Australian National University Press, 1977.

Willheim, Ernst. 'Is David Horner's Official History of ASIO "Honest History"? Was Colonel Spry a Traitor?' *Honest History*, 14 April 2015. Accessed 9 April 2021. honesthistory.net.au/wp/is-david-horners-official-history-of-asio-honest-history/.

Woodard, Gary. 'Cold War Downunder: Foreign Policy and Defence in Australia 1945–50'. In *Australasian Political Studies 1997: Proceedings of the 1997 Australasian Political Studies Association Conference 29 September–1 October 1997*, vol. 3, edited by George Crowder. Adelaide: Dept of Politics, Flinders University of South Australia, 1997.

Recorded oral history interviews

Burton, John. Interview by John Clements, London, UK, 25 February 1981. John Clements Oral History Collection. Special Collections, Murdoch University.

Burton, John. Interview by Ronald Fisher, Fairfax Virginia, USA, 6 April 1990. Audio tape. GMU Oral History Project. Special Collections, George Mason University libraries.

Burton, John. Interview by Michael J. Wilson, Canberra, 23 August 1995. Australian Diplomacy 1950–1990 Oral History Project. NLA Oral History Collection, ORAL TRC 2981/23.

Burton, John. Interview by Edgar Waters, Canberra, 19 January 2000. NLA Oral History Section, ORAL TRC 3958.

Parker, Cecily. Interview by Meredith Edwards, Canberra, 2004. Transcript. NLA Oral History Section, ORAL TRC 5094.

www.ingramcontent.com/pod-product-compliance
Lightning Source LLC
Chambersburg PA
CBHW061255230426
43664CB00033B/2918